HIC JACET

Sir Walter Raleigh Militis, Domini et Gubernatoria Virginiae, 1578

HIC JACET

The Life and Downfall of
The Elizabethan 'Twelfth' Knight
Knighted at the Feast of the Epiphany
in the year 1585

by
Barbara O'Sullivan

Caesar Publishing
Paperback Edition: ISBN: 978-0-9559912-0-2
This book is also available in Hardback:
ISBN 978-0-9559912-4-0

Copyright 2010 – Second Edition
Paperback
ISBN – 978-1-4457-9054-1
Miss Barbara O'Sullivan
Caesar Publishing and Media Limited

The British Library, in a letter dated 30th November 1998, has given the author permission to quote from Sloane MS 1133, 'New Atlantis' and the author also has a letter from The British Library dated 5th February, 1997 concerning (New Atlantis), which states, [… You may rest assured that you need have no concern at all about copyright of the manuscripts mentioned in your letter, unless you wish to reproduce them photographically. In a letter from The British Library dated 22nd July, 2003, the author is granted permission to quote from Sloane MS 1133 (and Harley 7368 (the Play Sir Thomas More). Similarly, in a letter dated 6th November 1996, the author is given permission to quote from 169M84W/9 Hampshire Record Office.

A Note about Elizabethan Spellings

The Elizabethan spellings in the contemporary documents contained within this book have been left unaltered for the sake of historical authenticity, and clarity of meaning, although some readers and librarians may not concord with this opinion.

Acknowledgements

The author Barbara O'Sullivan is indebted to and would like to thank the following, for their assistance to the author during the years 1989 to 2009 when this book was being written and compiled.

Dr Glen Black, Oriel College, Oxford University, Oxford
Ben Webster, Oriel College, Oxford University, Oxford, (my Tutor at David Game School of English in Kensington, London during my A' level literature studies concerning certain texts of William Shakespeare and other contemporary and modern texts.)
The British Library, Mr. Hilton Kelliher, Curator of Manuscripts, the British Library
Dr. Andrea Clarke, Department of Manuscripts, the British Library
J. Conway, Reading Room Manager, The British Library
His Grace, The Duke of Northumberland, Alnwick Castle
Mrs Anne Telfer, Secretary to Duke of Northumberland, Syon House, London
Colin Shrimpton, The Northumberland Estates, Alnwick Castle
Sarah Darling, Alnwick Castle
A.C.L. Hall, The Archive, Dulwich College, London
Miss C Marchant, Assistant Manager, Westminster Abbey Bookshop
Mr. Wingfield Digby, Sherborne Castle, Dorset
Miss Ann Smith, Curator and Archivist, Sherborne Castle Estates
The Late Mr. Walter Sparrow, Actor
The Reverend Canon Woods, Sherborne Abbey, Dorset
The University of North Carolina, Raleigh,USA, Mr. Bevan and Robert G. Anthony, Jr. Curator at North Carolina University, USA
Brian A. Harrison, Supernumerary Yeoman Warder and Honorary Archivist, Tower of London (Retired)
Dr. L R Atherton, Reader Services Department, Public Record Office
Dr. A. S. Bevan, Reader Services Department, Public Record Office
A H Lawes, Reader Services Department, Public Record Office
Alasdair D.K. Hawkyard M.A. F.R.Hist.S – translator of Elizabethan handwriting.
David Bevan Chief of Information Services Section State Library of North Carolina and John Welch, Assistant State Librarian, North Carolina Department of Cultural Resources
Pat Dyer, (P/S Padre G B McAvoy), Resident Chaplain of the Central Church of the Royal Air Force, St. Clement Danes, Strand, London
The Mayor of Winchester: Councillor Ray Pearce and I.M. Curtis, Mayor's Secretary
Hampshire Record Office: Miss G A Rushton, Miss A E Allen and

Acknowledgements continued …

Mrs M Cooke, Archivists at Hampshire County Council
Sherborne Abbey, Dorset - The Reverend Canon E J Woods
Colonel M J Woodcock, OBE, Chapter Clerk & Administrator, The
Cathedral Church of Saint Peter in Exeter
Alasdair Hawkyard, London, Elizabethan historian and translator of
Elizabethan handwriting.

Also thanks to Publish America, publishers, for initially giving me the
opportunity to publish a shorter version of Sir Walter Raleigh's history
in 2004, (The King's Quinto the Life and Times of Sir Walter Raleigh
(1552-1618), which is no longer available through them, due to the
author's choice of publishing through Caesar Publishing, (see a full list
of author's published works at the back of this book).

The book, Hic Jacet Sir Walter Raleigh

This book takes into account many of the contributing factors which led to Raleigh's downfall upon the death of Queen Elizabeth I in March, 1603. Raleigh's downfall was swift and merciless under King James I from May,1603, when Lord Cobham drew Raleigh into a snare and implicated him in the Spanish Bye and Main Plot, 1603, for which Raleigh and other conspirators were tried at Winchester Castle in November,1603, and imprisoned in the Tower of London, (briefly being permitted to voyage to Guiana in 1617), and upon his return was finally executed on 29th October,1618.

The book also considers the lives of Raleigh's closest friends, Henry Percy, the Ninth Earl of Northumberland ("The Wizard Earl"), (who was implicated in the Gunpowder Plot in 1605, and imprisoned in the Tower of London with Raleigh, Thomas Harriot who was also implicated in the Gunpowder Plot in 1605 and imprisoned in the Tower of London (although briefly).

The book also considers some of the history of Raleigh's friends, Christopher Marlowe, Elizabethan dramatist who was murdered in 1593, and Thomas Kyd Marlowe's co-writer, who was arrested and tortured just days before Marlowe's murder which leads to Kyd's early demise, and his gravestone [at St. Mary Woolnorth], London, was destroyed in the Great Fire of London in 1666, and no trace of it remains.

A Note about the Play Sir Thomas More - William Shakespeare

There is evidence that at least part of the reason for Kyd's arrest was concerning the play Sir Thomas More, (Harley MS 7368 The British Library), signed by Anthony Munday and at least five dramatists including Dekker, Chettle, and perhaps Heywood; (hand D wrote the insurrection scenes), (Kyd), which led to Kyd's arrest. The play Sir Thomas More was later attributed to William Shakespeare. Kyd's entire literary works were confiscated by the Star Chamber during his arrest and imprisonment (F.S. Boas Thomas Kyd), and very few of his literary works have survived.

Acknowledgement is made to the British Library by Barbara O'Sullivan for permission to include the text of the play Sir Thomas More within this book), which permission is set out in a letter dated 22nd July, 2003, from The British Library, 96 Euston Road, London, NW1 2DB, from Dr. Andrea Clarke, Department of Manuscripts.

Also, in a letter from Mr. W.H. Kelliher, curator of manuscripts at The British Library, dated 3 March, 1998, addressed to the author of this book, and the text of that letter is quoted below:

"The 'Booke of Sir Thomas Moore' is a collaborative effort by several playwrights. Late last century three of its pages were proposed as Shakespeare's own autograph contribution, and subsequently the matter was examined in detail by the palaeographer Sir Edward Maunde Thompson in his *Shakespeare's Handwriting, 1916.* Thompson's work, along with that of later scholars, tended to confirm the attribution. More recently, the question of authorship has been subjected to scrutiny of various kinds in *Sir Thomas More: Essays on the play and its Shakespearian interest, ed. by T.H. Howard-Hil, 1989.*

The play has been in print since 1842, and texts are included in several collections of Shakespeare's works and apocrypha. Some of these are noted in the enclosed photocopies of the relevant entries from our Catalogue of Printed Books and the *Index of English Literary Manuscripts,* vol. I, ed. Peter Beal, 1980. Among the many reproductions of the Shakespeare leaves that are available I should mention that given with discussion, by Samuel Schoenbaum in *William Shakespeare: records and images,* Oxford, 1975, pp. 109-115.

As one of the Library's greatest treasures the original (Harley 7368), which has suffered rather badly from physical deterioration over the years, is not normally made available in our Students' Room. However, a leaf from it, now temporarily withdrawn from display at the British Museum, is to be transferred to a Shakespeare case in the new exhibition area at St. Pancras in the late spring or early summer. I enclose a draft of the label written to accompany it.

Yours sincerely,
[signed by]
W.H. Kelliher
Curator of Manuscripts.

In Dr. Andrea Clarke's letter (British Library, dated 22nd July, 2003), Ms. Clarke informed me that Mr. Kelliher has now retired from the British Library, and therefore The British Library were unable to grant permission for me to include the text of the exhibition label that Mr. Kelliher wrote himself. In the absence of this permission, I will include the label concerning the play Sir Thomas More, (Harley MS 7368), because I believe it is important for the sake of clarity, for the reader(s) of Hic Jacet, to be allowed to see it, and it appears directly below.

Label for Shakespeare case at The British Library, St. Pancras, [London] compiled and written by Mr. W.H. Hilton Kelliher, The British Library, London

"William Shakespeare (1564-1616)
Harley 7368, f.9
[Shakespeare the artist]

'The Booke of Sir Thomas Moore', about 1593-1595.

This document is generally accepted as the only literary manuscript to survive from the pen of the greatest English playwright. The playhouse copy, or 'Booke', of which it forms part is a collaborative revision of an earlier drama tracing the career and downfall of Henry VIII's staunchly Catholic lord chancellor. It is copied mostly in the hand of Anthony Munday, with additions and revisions made by five other dramatists, including Dekker, Chettle and perhaps Heywood. Another hand, commonly labeled 'hand D', wrote the insurrection or 'Ill May Day' scene that runs to three pages, the first of which is shown here. The nature of the revisions proves it to be an authorial rather than merely a scribal addition, and its attribution to Shakespeare is based mainly on features of treatment, style, imagery and spelling that can all be paralleled in his known work. The evidence of handwriting, however, which depends on comparison with the six surviving signatures, is rather more ambiguous. [161]

This incomplete transcript, written as early as 1593 or as late as 1601, was submitted for a licence to Edmund Tillney, Master of the Revels, who noted down cuts required to be made in politically sensitive material before performance. These specifically mention the May Day scene, of which he wrote 'Leaue out ye insurrection wholly & ye cause thereof & begin wt sr Tho: Moore att ye mayors sessions wt a report afterwards off his good seruic don being Shrive off London vppon a mutiny against ye Lumbards. Only by a short report & nott otherwise att your own perilles. E. Tyllney'. [102]"

The text of 'The Ill May Day Scenes' from the play Sir Thomas More, which led to Thomas Kyd's arrest and possibly Christopher Marlowe's murder, based on the assumption that these possibly concern the King Henry plays, (which theory is dealt with later in this book, in the Thomas Kyd and Christopher Marlowe chapters), appear in the full text of the play.

The full text of the play Sir Thomas More, as far as it has been made available, (Harley MS 7368) appears within this book, see Table of Contents.

The Rhyme which led to Thomas Kyd's Arrest

Appears below, and was located by the author in a book written by
A.W. Pollard, 1925, "Christopher Marlowe"

[("A Rhyme set up against the Wall of the Dutch churchyard, on
Thursday May the 5th, between Eleven and Twelve at night. And
there found by some of the Inhabitants of that Place; and brought to
the Constable, and the rest of the Watch, beginning,

[1]
"You, Strangers, that inhabit in this Land,
Note this same Writing, do it understand.
Conceive it well, for Safe-guard of your Lives,
Your Goods, your Children and your dearest Wives.")].

The Privy Council decided that immediate action must be taken in
order to prevent riot or insurrection, and appointed Sir Julius Caesar,
Sir Henry Killgrew and Sir Thomas Wilkes to seek out and examine
by secret means, all persons suspected as being responsible and they
were given leave to search the premises of any writers thought to be
involved in the above plots. It was directed that a search be made for
any papers or writings which may lead to the guilty persons being
identified, after which they should be put to torture until they
confessed and revealed all they knew of the matter.

Some of the rioters were apprehended and found to be apprentices to
trades. They were put into the stocks or carted and whipped and this
was done in order to serve as a warning to other apprentices.

[("The Court, upon these seditious Motions, took the most prudent
Measures to protect the poor Strangers and to prevent any Riot or
Insurrection: Sending for the Lord Mayor and Aldermen; resolving
that no open Notification should be given, but a private Admonition

---

[1] This is the rhyme which appears in the play Sir Thomas More and led to the arrest and
torture at Newgate Prison of Thomas Kyd (Christopher Marlowe's co-writer) on the 12th May
1593. Christopher Marlowe was arrested on the 18th May 1593 and murdered on the 30th May
1593. William Shakespeare had appended three pages to this play and claimed it as his own
play, although those three pages are now in the British Museum.

only, to the Mayor and discreetest Aldermen. And they not to know the Cause of their sending for. Orders to be given to them to appoint a strong Watch of Merchants and others, and like handicrafted Masters, to answer for their Apprentices and Servants Misdoing. The Subsidy-Books for London and the Suburbs, to be seen: how many Masters, and how may Men, and to what Trades, and if they use double Trades. The Preachers of their Churches to forewarn them of double Trades. And such as be of no Church to be avoided hence. And a Proclamation of these Things to be made publickly in Guild-Hall.

After these Orders from the Council Boards, several young Men were taken up, and examined about the Confederacy to rise, and drive out the Strangers - Some of these Rioters were put in to the Stock, carted and whipt; for a Terro to other Apprentices and Servants. Mss. Car. D. Hallifax").].

One of the first victims to be arrested upon suspicion of the above offences was Thomas Kyd, when on the 12th May 1593 his writing chamber had been searched and papers were found which were considered to be written from a heretical viewpoint and were found to be blasphemous.2

Poor Thomas Kyd who had always lived such a peaceful life and was only ever concerned with his books and his love of learning, was immediately seized and carried off to Newgate Prison, where he was to spend eight terrible months and his health deteriorated rapidly. He was not allowed to know any of the evidence held against him until he came to trial when he would hear it at Court. He was allowed no Counsel to defend him. He had no chance of cross-examination of the witnesses, and all this was commonplace during Elizabethan trials. All

2

his literary work was confiscated by the Star Chamber. [Please see Thomas Kyd chapter for a full treatment of Kyd's life].

HIC JACET

**Sir Walter Raleigh
1552-1618**

**Captain of Queen Elizabeth I's Guard
from 1585 to 1603 (d.1618[3])**

---

[3] Lady Ralegh was presented with Sir Walter Ralegh's head in a red leather bag after his execution, to be later embalmed. She carried it about with her almost to the day of her death. Her Grace the Duchess of Roxburgh explained to me that Carew Ralegh purchased West Horsley Place in 1656. According to tradition, Lady Ralegh, who lived with her son in the place, kept the head for a number of years until it was buried in the local parish church at West Horsley; the burial place is now concealed below the organ; but plans for the renovation of the church include moving the organ and, hopefully, exposing the burial place to public view." The resting place of Sir Walter Raleigh's body is beneath the chancel at St. Margaret's Church, Westminster." I am indebted to (see acknowledgments) Brian A. Harrison, Supernumerary Yeoman Warder, Tower of London – Author of Prisoner's of The Tower of London available on Amazon.co.uk

13

HIC JACET 1

HIC JACET
SIR WALTER RALEIGH

"Caeser will raise me up I trust" ... Sir Walter Raleigh 1618

Historie of the World. Preface ~ Hic Jacet

"O eloquent, just, and mightie Death! Whom none could advise, thou hast perswaded; what none hath dared, thou hast done; and whom all the world hath flattered, thou only hast cast out of the world and despised. Thou hast drawne together all the farre stretchèd greatnesse, all the pride, crueltie, and ambition of man, and covered it all over with these two narrow words, Hic jacet!" ~ Sir Walter Raleigh

Prologue

The Death of Queen Elizabeth I
2am March 24 1603

Queen Elizabeth I of England was born on September 7th 1533 at Greenwich. The second daughter of King Henry Viii. She succeeded to the throne of England and her Coronation was held on the 2nd April, 1559.

The 70 year old Queen had been unable for sleep for 20 days being from the 1st March 1603, and since she could endure her illness no longer, her life ebbed from her body and she passed slowly out of this life and into the next world at 2 a.m. on the 24th March 1603. Sir Walter had described her as "a Lady that time hath surprised" but as we learn more we find that not only was the great Queen surprised, but Sir Walter, upon her death was also to meet with surprise and upon her death his downfall was to be so sudden and swift that he hardly had time to gather his wits about him before he was ensnared and then arrested.

The death of the virgin Queen of England had brought about the union of crowns, uniting England with Scotland and bringing an end to the terrible religious struggles between Protestants and Catholics. The son of [4]Mary Queen of Scots, King James VI of Scotland came to London amidst great ceremony to lay claim the throne of England and now we see that he becomes James I of England. That the King wanted peace throughout his Kingdom was well known to all men but more importantly, he wanted to make peace with Spain and that is why he did not trust Sir Walter Raleigh.

---

[4]Mary Queen of Scots - her English relatives King Henry Viii and Margaret Tudor James v of Scotland her father and Mary of Guise her mother. A prisoner of Queen Elizabeth I for 20 years after her return from France (her first husband Le Dauphin Francois).

*****
THE KING'S QUINTO
******

"I shall prove under the Proprietors hands, by the Custom-Book, and the 'King's Quinto', of which I recovered an Ingot or two:

I shall also make it appear to any Prince, or State, that will undertake it, how easily those Mines, and five or six more of them, may be possessed, and the most of them in those Parts, which have never as yet been attempted by any, nor by any Passage to them, nor ever discovered by the English, French, or Dutch. But at Kemish's return from Orinoque, when I rejected his counsel and his course, and told him he had undone me, and wounded my credit with the King past recovery, he slew himself: For I told him, seeing my Son was slain, I cared not if I had lost 100 more in opening the Mine, so my credit had been saved."

Sir Walter Raleigh – 1617
Guiana upon arrival, in his letter to
Sir Ralph Winwood
(Secretary to King James I of England)

Dedication to the Late Walter Sparrow, Actor
1927-2000

This book is dedicated to my friend the late Walter Sparrow, actor, who passed away on May 31, 2000. He is sadly missed. I have lost a great and generous friend. The World has lost a great actor.

Walter Sparrow was born on January 22 1927, in London, England. Walter appeared as the blind man, Duncan in the 1991 movie, "Robin Hood: Prince of Thieves" with Kevin Costner and he told me that he had been honoured to work with Kevin Costner. In 1993 Walter appeared as Weatherstaff, in the movie, "The Secret Garden". In 1995 Walter was cast in the movie, "Now and Then", starring Demi Moore and was thrilled at the prospect of working with her. During our friendship, Walter flew off to America when filming was about to commence and took the role of "Crazy Pete." Walter appeared on British television in numerous programmes over the years, but began his acting career with the Royal Shakespeare Company when he was a young man.

Through my friendship with Walter Sparrow in 1995 and 1996, I was inspired to write this book, and Walter took a great interest in the history of Sir Walter Raleigh (1552-1618), when I met him in a Chiswick restaurant, and he was instrumental in locating through the Mayor of Winchester in England, the English translation of the verbatim account of the trial of Sir Walter Raleigh, which took place in 1603 and was located in a book written by Richard Tonson in 1677, which was in turn, located by the archivists at the Hampshire Record Office. I had been searching for a translation of Raleigh's trial since I was a young child of 11, after a visit to the Tower of London with a school party, and although I had located the original manuscripts of the trial at the Public Record Office in London, known as KB8/58, I could not afford to have them translated from the Elizabethan Secretary's hand. Walter Sparrow and I, spent many happy hours together, discussing the prospective film script of Raleigh's Trial, over numerous dinners in posh London restaurants. Walter bought me my first word processor in 1995 and I began work on this book. We both agreed that when I had finished researching and writing this history book, Walter Sparrow was going to turn it into a film script. My character, John Talbot who presents Sir Walter Raleigh's history to the reader, was written with Walter Sparrow in mind and I had hoped that one day he would take the role of John Talbot, if a film was ever made of "The King's Quinto". Walter Sparrow and I, even discussed film directors, and we decided that Roman Polanski would be the director we would approach because of his particularly sensitive portrayal of Thomas Hardy's "Tess" (of the Durbervilles).

Sadly, that film script will never be written by Walter Sparrow now, because this book took me 7 years to research and write, and Walter Sparrow died before I could show him the finished manuscript, just as an artist keeps his painting hidden until it is finished. Walter was unaware that I had found a publisher for this work.

Rest in peace, Mr. Sparrow. I miss you.

Barbara O'Sullivan

Raleigh's Letter to Charles Howard, Knight of the Garter, Baron and Councellor, and of the Admirals of England

"TO THE RIGHT HONORABLE MY
Singuler good lord and kinsman,
Charles Howard, knight of the Garter,
Barron, and Counceller, and of the
Admirals of England the most renowned:
And to the Right Honorable Sr. Robert Cecyll Knight,
Counceller in his Highness privie Councels.

For your Honors many Honorable and friendlie parts, I have hitherto onely returned promises, and now for answeare of both your adventures, I have sent you a bundle of papers which I have devided between your Lo. & Sr. Robert Cecyl in these two respects chiefly: First for that it is reason, that wastful factors, when they have consumed such stockes as they had in trust, doe yeeld some cullor for the same in their account, secondly for that I am assured. The triall that I had of both your loues, when I was left of all, but of malice and revenge, makes me still presume that you will be pleased (knowing what little power I had to performe ought, and the great advantage of forewarned enemies) to answeare that out of knowledge, which others shall but object out of malice. In my more happy times as I did especially honour you both, so I found that your loves sought me out in the darkest shadow of adversitie, and that the same affection which accompanied my better fortune, sored not away from me in my manie miseries: all which though I cannot requite, yet I shall ever acknowledge: and the great debt which I have no power to pay, I can doe no more for a time but confesse to be due. It is true that as my errors were great, so they have yeelded very grievous effects, and if ought might have beene deserved in former times to have counterpoysed anie part of offences, [5]. I did therefore even in the winter of my life, undertake these travels, fitter for bodies lesse blasted with misfortunes, for men to great abilitie, and for mindes of better incouragement, that thereby if it were possible I might recover but the moderation of excess, and the least taste of the greatest plentie formerly possessed. If I had knowen other way to win, If I had imagined how grater adventures might have regained, if I could conceive what father meanes I might yet use, but even to appease so powerful a displeasure, I would not doubt but for one yeare more to hold fast my soule in my teeth, till it were performed. Of that little remaine I had, I have wasted in effect all herein, I have undergone many constructions, I have beene accompanied with many sorrows, with labor, hunger, heat, sickness, & peril: It appeareth notwithstanding that I made no other bravado of going to the sea, then was meant, and that I was neither hidden in Cornewall, or elsewhere, as was supposed. They have grossly belied me, that forejudged that I would rather become a servant to the Spanish king, then return, & the rest were much mistaken, who would have perswaded, that I was too easeful and sensuall to undertake a journey of so great travel. But, if what I have done, receive the gracious construction of a painefull pilgrimage, and purchase the least remission, I shall thinke all too little, and that there were wanting to the rest, many miseries: But if both the times past, the present, and what may be in the future, doe all by one graine of gall continue in an eternal distate, I doe not then knowe whether I should bewaile my selfe either for my too much travel and expence, or condemne my selfe for doing lesse then that, which can deserve nothing. From my selfe I have deserved no thankes, for I am returned a begger, and withered, but that I might have betted my poore estate, it shall appeare by the following discourse, if I had not onely respected her Majesties future Honor, and riches. It became not the former fortune in which I once lived, to goe journeys of picorie, and it had sorted ill with the office of Honor, which by her Majesties grace, I hold this day in England, to run from Cape to Cape, & from place to place, for the pillage of ordinarie prizes. Many yeares since, I had knowledge by relation, of that mighty, rich, and beawtifull Empire of Guiana, and of that great and Golden City, which the spanyards call El Dorado, and the naturals

Manoa, which Citie was conquered, re-edified, and inlarged by a
yonger sonne of Guainacapa Emperor of Peru, at such time as
Francisco Pazaro and others conquered the saide Émpire, from his two
elder brethren Guascar, and Atabalipa, both then contending for the
same, the one being favoured by the Oreiones of Cuzco, the other by
the people of Caximalca. I sent my servant Jacob Whiddon the yeare
before, to get knowledge of the passages, and I had some light from
Captaine Parker sometime my servant, and nowe attending on your Lo.
that such a place there was to the southward of the great bay of
Charuas, or Guanipa: but I found that it was 600. miles father off, then
they supposed, and manie other impediments to them unknowen and
unheard. After I had displanted Don Anthony de Bearer, who was
upon the same enterprise, leaving my ships at Trinidad, at the port
called Curiapan, I wandred 400. miles, into the said country by land
and river: the particulers I will leave to the following discourse. The
countrey hath more quantity of Gold by manifolde, then the best
partes of the Indies, or Peru: All the most of the kings of the borders
are already become her Majesties vassals: & seeme to desire nothing
more than her Majesties protection, and the returne of the English
nation. It hath another grounde and assurance of riches and glory, then
the voyages of the west Indies, & an easier way to invade the best
parts thereof, then by the common course. The king of spaine is not so
impovrished by taking 3 or 4 port townes in America as we suppose,
neyther are the riches of Peru, or Neuva Espania so left by the sea side,
as it can be easily whasht away, with a great flood, or spring tide, or
left drie upon the sandes on a lowe ebbe. the port townes are few and
poore in respect of the rest within the land, and are of little defence,
and are onely rich when the streets are to receive the treasure for
Spaine: And we might thinke the Spanyards verie simple, having so
many horses and slaves, that if they could not upon two daies warning,
carrie all the Golde they have into the land, and farre enough from the
reach of our footmen, especiallie the Indies beeing (as it is for the most
part) so mounteynous, so full of woods, rivers, and marshes. In the
port townes of the province of Vensuello, as Cumana, Coro, and S.
Iago (whereof Coro and S. Iago were taken by Captaine Preston and
Cumana and S. Josephus by us) we found not the value of one riall of
plate in either: but the Cities of Barquasimeta, Valentia, S. Sebastian,

Cororo, S. Lucia, Allenguna, Marecabo, and Truxillo, are not so easilie invaded: neither doth the burning of those on the coast impoverished the king of Spayne anie one Ducket, and if we sacke the river of Hache, S. Marta, and Cartagena, which are the portes of Nuevo reyno and Popayan. There are besides within the land which are indeed rich and populous, the townes and Cities of Merida, Lagrita, S. Christopheruso, the great Cities of Pampelone, S. Fede Bogota, Tunia and Mozo where the Emeralds are founde, the townes and Cities of Morequito, velis, la vill a de Leua, Palma, unda, Angustura, the greate Citie of Timana, Tocaima, S. Aguila, Pasto, Iuago, the greate citie of Popaian it selfe, Los Remedios, and the rest. If we take the ports and villages within the bay of Urab in the kingdom or rivers of Dariena, and Caribana, the cities and townes of S. Juan de Royda, of Cassis, of Antiocha, Caramanta, Cali, and Auserma have gold enough to pay the King part, and are not easily invaded by the way of the Ocean, or if Nombre de Dios and Panama be taken in the province of Castillo de oro, and the villages upon the rivers of Cenu and Chagre. Peru hath besides those and besides the magnificent cities of Quito and Lima so many Ilands, portes, Cities, and mines, as if I should name the with the rest, it would seeme incredible to the reader: of all which because I have written a particuler treatise of the west Indies, I will omit their repetition at this time, seeing that in the saide treatise I have anatomized the rest of the sea townes as well of Nicaragna, Iucata, Nueva Espanna, and the Isands, as those of the Inland, and by what meanes they may be beste invaded, as farre as any meane Judgement can comprehend* (his book The Great Rich and Beautiful Empire of Guiana1596) But I hope it shall appeare that there is a way found to answere every mans longing, a better Indies for her majestie then the King of Spaine hath any, which if it shall please her highnes to undertake, I shall most willingly end the rest of my daies in following the same: If it be left to the spoyle and sackage of common persons, if the love and service of so many nations be despised, so great riches, and so mightie an Empyre refused, I hope her Majestry will yet take my humble desire and my labour therein in gracious part, which if it had not beene in respect of her highnes future honer & riches, I could have laid hands and ransomed many of the kings & Cassiqui of the Country, & have had a reasonable proportion of gold for their redemption: But I have chosen rather to beare the burthen of poverty, then reproch, & rather to endure a second travel & the chaunces therof, then to have defaced an enterprise of so great assurance, untill I knew whether it pleased God to put a disposition in her princely and royall heart eyther to follow or foreflow the same: I will therefore leave it to his ordinance that hath onely power in al things, and do humbly pray that your honors will excuse such errors, as without the defence of art, overrunne in every part, the following discourse, in which I have neither studied phrase, forme, nor fashion, and that you will be pleased to essteeme me as your owne (though over dearly bought) and I shall ever remaine ready to doe you all honour and service.

Walter Raleigh, 1617[?]

[refers to first voyage to Guiana, 1596 - Raleigh brought back to England the only son of King Topiawarri]

"Because there have been divers opinions conceived of the golde oare brought from Guiana, and for that an Alderman of London and an officer of +her majesties minte, hath given out that the same is of no price, I have thought good by the addition of these lines to give answers as well to the said malicious slaunder, as to the other objections. It was is true that while we abode at the Island of Trinedado, I was informed by an Indian, that not farre from the Port, where we ancored, there were founde certain minerall stones which they estimeed to be gold, and were thereunto perswaded the rather for that they had been both English, and French men gather, and imbarqued for quantities thereof: Uppon this liklyhood I sent 40 men and gave order that each one should bring a stone of that myne, to make triall of the goodnesse, which being performed, I assured them at their returne that the same was Marcasite, and of no riches or value: Notwithstanding divers trusting more to their owne sense, then to my opinion, kept of the said Marcasite, and have tried thereof, since my returne, in divers places. In Guiana itselfe I never sawe Marcasite, but all the rocks, mountaines, all stones in the plaines, in woodes, and by the rivers sides are in effect thorow shining, and appeare marveylous rich, which being tried to be no Marcasite, are the trew signes of rich mineralles, but are no other than El madre del oro (as the Spanyards terme them which is the mother of golde, or as it is saide by other the scum of gold: of divers sortes of these manie of my companie brought also into England, everie one taking the sayfest for the best, which is not generall for mine owne parte, I did not countermand any mans desire, or opinion, and I could have afforded them little if I shoulde have denied them the pleasing of their owne fancies therein: But I was resolved that golde must be found either in graines separate from the stone (as it is in most of al the rivers of Guiana) or else in a kinde of hard stone, which we call the white Sparre, of which I saw divers hills, and in sundrie places, but had neither tyme, nor men, nor instruments fitte to labour. Neere unto one of the rivers I found of the said white Sparre or flint a very great ledge, or banke, which I endeavored to breake by al the meanes I coulde, because there appeared on the out side some small graines of gold, but finding no meane to worke the same uppon the upper part, seeking the sides and circuite of the sayd rock, I founde a clift in the same, from whence the daggers, and with the heade of an ax, we gotte out some small quantitie thereof, of which kinde of white stone (wherein golde is engendred) we sawe silver hills and rocks in everie part of Guiana, wherein we travelled. Of this there hath beene made mainie trialls, and in London it was first assaide by Master Westwood a refiner dwelling in wood street, and it helde after the rate of 120000 or 13000 pounds a tunne. Another sort was afterward tried by Master Bulmar and Master Dimoke assay master, and it held after the rate of 23000 pounds a tunne. There was some of it againe tried by Master Palmer comptroller of the minte, and Master Dimoke in Golde Smiths hall, and it helde after 26900 pounds a tunne. There was also at the same time, and by the same persons a triall made of the dust of the said myne which held 8.pound 6.ounces weight of gold, in the hundred: there was likewise at the same time a triall made of an Image of Copper made in Guiana, which helde a third part gold, besides divers trialls made in the countrey, and by others in London. But because there came of ill with the good, and belike the said

Alderman was not presented with the best, it hath pleased him therefore to scandall all the rest, and to deface the enterprize as much as in him lyeth. It hath also been concluded by divers, that if there had been anie such oare in Guiana, the same discovered, that I would have brought home a greater quantitie thereof: first I was not bounde to satisfie anie man of the quantitie, but such onely as adventured, if any store had been returned thereof: but it is verie true that had all their mountaynes beene of massive gold, it was impossible for us to have made anie longer staye to have wrought the same: and whosoever hath seene with what strength of stone, the best golde oare is invironned, he will not thinke it easie to be had out in heaps, and especiallie by us who had neither men, instrumentes, nor time (as it is saide before) to performe the same: There were on this discoverie, no lesse than 100 personnes, who can all witnesse, that when we past any braunch of the river to vewe the land within, and staid from our boats but six houres, wee were driven to wade to the eyes, at our returne: and if we attempted the same the day following, it was impossible either to forde it, or to swim it, both by reason of the swiftnesse, and also for that the borders were so pestred with fast woods, as neither bote nor man could finde place, either to land, or to imbarque: for in June, July, August, and September, it is imposible to navigate any of those rivers, for such is the furie of the current, and there are so many trees and woods overflowne, as if anie boate but touch uppon anie tree or stake, it is impossible to save any one person therein: and were we departed the land, it ran with that swiftnesse, as we drawe downe most commonly against the winde, little lesse than one hundred miles a day: Besides our vessels were no other than wherries, one little barge, a small cockboate, and a bad Galiota, which wee framed in hast for that purpose at Trinedado, and those little boates had nyne or ten men apeece, with all their victuals, and armes. It is further true, that we were about 400. miles from our shippes, and had been a moneth from them, which also we left weakely mande in an open roade, and had promised our return in 15 dayes. Others have devised that the same oare was had from Barbery, and that we carried it with us into Guiana: surely the singularitie of that device, I do not well comprehend, for mine owne parte, I am not so much in love with these long voiages, as to devise, thereby to cozen my selfe, to lie hard, to fare worse, to be subjected to perils, to diseases, to ill favours, to be parched and withered, and withall to sustaine the care and labour of such an enterprize, excepte the same had more comfort, than the fetching of Marcasite in Guiana, or bying of gold oare in Barbery. But I hope the better sort will judge me by themselves, and that the way of deceipt is not the way of nor or good opinion; I have herein consumed much time, and many crowns, and I had no other respecte or desire then to serve her majesty and my Country thereby. If the Spanishe nation had beene of likle beleefe to these detractors, we should little have feared or doubted their attempts, wherewith we now are daily threned. but if we now consider of the actions both of Charles the fiste, who had the Maydenhead of Peru, and the aboundant treasures of Atabalipa, together with the affaires of the spanish king now living, what territories he hath purchased, what he hath added to the actes of his predecessors, how many kingdomes he hath indangered, how m any armies, garrisons, and navies, he hath and doth maintaine, the greate losses which he hath repayred, as in 88 above 100 sayle of greate shippes with their artillery, and that no yere is lesse unfortunate but that many vessels, treasures, and people are devored, and yet notwithstanding he beginneth againe like a storme to threaten shipwracke to us all, we shall finde that these abilities rise not from the trades of sackes, and Civil Orenges, nor from ought else that either Spaine, Portugal, or any of his other provinces produce: It is his Indian Golde that indaungereth and disturbeth all the nations of Europe, it purchaseth intelligence, creepeth into Councels, and setteth bound loyalty at libertie, in the greatest Monarchies of Europe. If the Spanish king can keepe us from forraine enterprizes, and from the impreachment of his trades, eyther by offer of invasion, or by beseiging us in Britayne, Ireland, or elsewhere, he had then brought the worke of our perill in greate forwardness. Those princes which abound in treasure have greate advantages over the rest, if they once constraine them to a defensive warre, where they are driven once a yeare or oftner to cast [compare to Bacons Essays 'Of Princes'] lots for their own garments, and from such shall all trades, and entercouse, be taken away, to the general losse and impoverishment of the kingdom and common weale so reduced: besides when men are constrained to fight, it hath not the same hope as when they are prest and incouraged by the desire of spoyle and riches. Father it is to be doubted how those that in time of victorie seeme to affect their neighbour nations, will remaine after the first view of misfortunes, or ill success; to trust also to the doubfulness of a battel, is but a fearefull and uncertaine adventure, seeing therein fortune is as likely to prevaile as, vertue. It shall not be necessary to alleage all that might be said, and therefore I will thus conclude, that whatsoever kingdome shall be inforced to defend it selfe, may be compared to a body daungerouslie diseased, which for a season may be preserved with vulgar medicines, but in a short time, and by little and little, the same must needs fall to the ground, and be dissolved. I have therefore laboured all my life, both according to my small power, and perswasion, to advance all those attempts,, that might eyther promise return of profit to our selves, or at last be a lett and impreachment to the quiet source, and plentiful trades of the Spanish nation, who in my weake judgement by such a warre were as easily indaungered and brought from his powerfulnes, as any prince in Europe, if it be considered from how many kingdomes and nationes his revenewes are gathered, and those so weake in their owne beings, and so farre severed from mutuall succor. But because such a preparation and resolution is not to be hoped for in hast, and that the time which our enemies embrace, can not be had againe to advantage, I will hope that these provinces, and that Empyre now by me discovered shall suffice to inable her Majesty, and the whole kingdome, with no lesse quantities of treasure, then the king of Spayne hath in all the Indies, east and west, which he possesseth, which if the same be considered and followed, ere the Spayards, reinforce the same, and if her Majesty will undertake it, I will be contented to lose her highnes favour and good opinion for ever, and my life withall, if the same be no found rather to exceed, then to equall whatsoever is in this discourse promised or declared. I will nowe refer the reader to the following discourse with the hope that the perilous and chargeable labors and indevours of such as thereby seeke the profit and honor of her Majesty, and the English nation, shall by mean of qualitie and vertue receive such construction, and good acceptance, as them selves would looke to be rewarded withall in the like."

HIC JACET: SIR WALTER RALEIGH

Walter Raleigh

Winter 1626
at 5 Bell Yard, London

As I now make haste to step forward in so humble a manner, I will say to my reader that I carry with me some embarrassment in the presentation of Sir Walter Raleigh's history, because I am an uneducated servant and he was a skilled orator and writer during his own lifetime.

I find that I cannot bear to look further than my own mind for a criticism of my work. To criticise it would be to damn my attempt to prove him no traitor to his King, nor his country. I declare that if I find criticism from any quarter, then my work has been halted before I begin. In that event I say that no eyes will meet with my words and that they will be buried amongst his truth. To seek out the truth over many long years only to find it condemned, is to face malice and betrayal a second time, heaped upon the first. That is too much for an old man to bear for the sake of Sir Walter's innocence.

If my soul could induce me to work so hard that I might urge others to learn of Sir Walter Raleigh's downfall and the reasons for his execution, then I would rest peacefully in the hereafter in the cold, dark clay that is waiting to claim me.

I wish that I could draw you into a story of happiness and gaiety - since I know it would please you, but that story has already been told, and I find that I cannot offer it again.

If you seek a true account of Sir Walter Raleigh's trial at Winchester Castle in 1603 then you will find it faithfully recorded here. As we progress, it is my promise that I will reveal important documents to you, concerning his downfall

I now suffer extreme anguish as I sit alone at my old wooden table, placed so near the window and yet so far into a darkened room overlooking a narrow alleyway, known only to Londoners, as 5 Bell Yard, that sometimes I can barely view the words I have written. My mistake is to show this work to others and I trust to God that it will not bring about my downfall.

How many long and miserable years I have endured in gathering up this history, and as to the bleak and lonely path it has led me down, I cannot say within these pages, because this is not the place to reveal it.

I find myself well prepared and have before me ink, parchment and several new feather quills which I brought with me from Lombard Street, as you will learn. I take little account of the hourglass as it spills its fine grains of sand with each passing moment, because darkness turns to light readily enough as I work and I need never cause myself to count time in that way.

As the words of the Scrivener's Apprentice unfold from my mind and are recorded within these pages, then I will be guided by the hushed voices of ancient men. They in their turn will kindly raise their lanterns for us so that we may look into their anxious faces, made bright by the burning of tallow candles, with the glow that fills our minds. Then our way is already lit and will lead on our journey for the truth about Sir Walter Raleigh's downfall.

It is necessary that at times our journey will lead us down narrow streets as we pass the cramped rows of gabled houses with their leaded, misty glass window panes, not daring to peer into them. We will experience a feeling of being watched by these ghosts of ancient times, but as we are only viewing them through our own minds, they will not be disturbed by us so very much. We will see the inhabitants of London dashing out of their houses and into our path because they are anxious to stop and speak to us as we slowly make our way forward. Some will merely seek to beg an old penny from us to buy their bread, since they are poor and trapped within their own memories of poverty. Then we must be kind and humble to them, as we can do little to assist them. They are left only with the will to lead or follow us as they choose.

When we meet with these spirits as they walk ahead of us, over the egg shaped cobbles of ancient London, we will view it through their eyes, so that they might come alive in the mind of the reader who attention they wish to capture. They will be dressed in their long black cloaks as they lead us forward in search truth, and they will speak, but sometimes it will barely be a whisper, and yet what they utter we must hear, for it is history to us and their misery must never be forgotten. If they fear to tell us their story then it is because their memories are awakened to the true horror of their times and they may hesitate to step forward. They will walk among the rats in the narrow streets of the plague infested City of London of 1603, where the rats will scurry for their lives because the ghosts of these men disturb them as they walk among us once more.

The Tower of London in 1603 conjures up terrible reflections in the human mind, working through the sensations best by the eye where they will feed upon the imagination of my reader. What else may we rely upon, except our senses, to bring forward a picture to show us the reality of this horror?

*Those who find themselves afraid, will stand back and wonder, never knowing the truth behind Traitor's Gate.

The cause of my anguish is not that I am incapable of writing this history, since I have been a servant to Sir Walter Raleigh for many years, and therefore I am able to recount his history to you without looking into any history book to prove me right or wrong. I would willingly do so, but for the fact that I am what is considered to be an uneducated man, and for this reason I have tried to abandon all my dreams of completing this work before my death, or of my deepest desire to find a willing publisher.

I hope that I do not sound unkind when I say to any man, well educated in this history, that the great glory of this man cannot be summed up accurately or presented to any reader, within one book. No author can lay claim to all that is this history, without omitting some small but important detail, or some otherwise unheard of fact, that might offend or please the reader.

If I have given cause to please or offend my reader, then I beg his forgiveness.

If his memory has been savaged by a fate so long ago that memories are dimmed, then I claim all I have and shine it upon his memory. From that dim and fading light I will bring his dead to life once more and his memory will be brought alive.

If a great man has been so savaged by fate that he has been ignored in his own lifetime, and dammed into the history books, so that only his several admirers believe in him, then a book must be created on his history and life must be breathed into it so heavily that not only his admirers feel he is alive, but the whole World must believe in him.

For his former servant to create a book about him, omitting no keen detail and recording every fact, is to send him down an unkind path where none could follow.

By this I mean that he must first listen to the memories of his hero and understand him when he was a young man, full of the ambition that would lead him into a position at Court. A man conscious of his own keen intellect and yet thwarted by his background as the son of a Devon Yeoman, with an accent that would be recognised at Court as that of an uneducated man who rose so high in Queen Elizabeth's favour and who guarded her honour unto his death. The last of her Knights - so that his end came about when she died. And yet he suffered for more than twenty days as she had by her sleepless nights.

The history of Sir Walter Raleigh must fill his author with a breath that is his own; leading his keen ears to listen to his hero breathing into his ear, when he is all alone, and in darkness, where he knows no fear and to acknowledge that he is near-by. Further, he must be content to awake alone, and to feel the spirit of his chosen subject all around him and to feel his spirit cry out to him in a dream in the depths of the unknown emotion he once felt, or to watch him walk across the room, and to let him speak of his own desire to he heard, but most of all to be able to hear him speak.

To do so would be to feel the security of him standing beside you, so that you might feel his praise for your work. Only then can you write about a man you never knew.

If such a man wakes in terror of offending his subject, he might understand that no sleep touches a great hero so deep, that he is unaware of what is written after his death.

You might possess the wit to create the history of a man who has gone before you and yet you must first live and breathe him, until his very soul stands beside you and speaks of itself.

If my tears are shed as I sit alone and weep for them, then it is out of a love that cannot be repaid and I seek no reward. I cannot pity those men who died in innocence because their spirits are still among us, and if the thought of them causes a man to wake from his sleep through fear of his own conscience then it is just.

As I stare into the glowing embers of the fire, I am aware that the room is warm and yet I shiver. The walls lighted by the bright glow of the burning wood, reveal to my eyes, the otherwise darkened room, and all about me I see the dark shadows of the past rising up from the depths of my mind as I am cast back into the year 1603. The shadows are horrible as they dance across the walls, waiting to speak. There are eight of these lonely spirits and yet I cannot say whether others will join us. First I see the ghosts of Watson and Clarke, the Priests who suffered their fate at Winchester Castle on the 4th December 1603, when they were pronounced traitors to King James I of England and were hung drawn and quartered. Their severed heads being carried around Winchester Castle and up into the battlements, where they were displayed, so that no other men might take it into his head to rise up against his King. On the 6th December Lord Cobham's brother, Brook, was tried and executed. On the 10th December Lord Cobham and Lord *[Grey] were to be executed. On the 13th December, Sir Walter Raleigh was to die.

John Talbot
at 5 Bell Yard, London - Winter, 1626

Here a Man's Soul is to be found, washed in anguish
over Sir Walter Raleigh's Chest of Hidden Parchments

I draw my thoughts inward as I near the end of my life just as all men must do if they are well prepared to die. Now I find myself able to establish my early thought as ambition, when others accused me of being born with a lack of it. I know and describe my ambition to be like a fire that has lit my mind, where it has etched itself so deeply in my soul, that nothing will cause it to be extinguished, until my work as a Scrivener, is accomplished.

For my purpose, I call myself a master of Sir Walter's history - but let no man say that I have caused myself to be surrounded by the deepest misery that any living soul could endure, as I reveal the history of Sir Walter Raleigh's swift and miserable downfall at the hands of King James I of England, after the death of Queen Elizabeth I, in March, 1603.

Those who wish to be heard are becoming anxious and if time itself would fall backwards, then they will through their own words come alive once more, if only for a few short hours upon the stage of life, where we might hear and judge those were denied justice and went unheard and unpraised in their own lifetime.

I would not wish to delay you unduly, excepting that I must introduce myself, so that you may see here no hidden motive. Nor would I allow you any thought which might cause you to believe this work a dalliance, with which I sought, through a calm mind, to amuse myself to profit from the misery of others as these spirits step forward to speak, in order to record their words on these pages.

I have already confessed that I am an old man, and my years will betray me as such to any who dare to look upon me. I take the trouble to describe myself to you here, because I fear that you would never recognise me if you saw me, when I would have you do so, not least for the sake of this history, which I am proud to record for you. Although many are familiar with the portrait of Sir Walter Raleigh, very few would claim my acquaintance.

Let me say that time has caught me out as I find I am too old to please myself by my own reflection, through my faded blue eyes, so that I could never hope to please another. I might turn away and blame it upon the calendar and never injure my own pride. No! It is better that I do not look into my own face again, when all I could hope to find is an unwelcome reflection. I will dwell here, in ignorance of my own appearance, so that in future, any who have cause to seek me out, might blame themselves instead, for looking into such a book as this.

I am not so very tall as to be called remarkable, and when I attempt to stand upright I tend to stoop, when once I was proud of my strong shoulders. When I walk through the London streets in the cold air, I find that my bones ache, when once I could have said that I was proud of the tilt of my head, and that I was handsome enough with my golden locks of hair and clear blue eyes. Then I could have called myself vain, as I took myself around London with great pride, and the young ladies danced into my path to seek out my company. Now my hair is grey and thin, and if my face bears the marks of my years of misery, then I can only ask that you let me reveal my story, for surely I have earned the right to do so. My fingers are gnarled with age, and my palms are no longer smooth, since great maps of wisdom may be found upon them, if I hold them against the candlelight in order to observe them. I would have no pity from you at all, since my hands and my mind have served me well in my role as a servant to Sir Walter Raleigh, and after his execution in 1618, I sought a position as a Scrivener's Apprentice, where I continued to serve him through this work, which I have planned for many years. Surely one man may serve another and no longer carry the title of servant?

As the words of the Scrivener's Apprentice unfold from my mind and are recorded within these pages, then I will be guided by the hushed voices of ancient men. They in their turn will kindly raise their lanterns for us so that we may look into their anxious faces, made bright by the burning of tallow candles. Then our way is already lit and will lead on our journey for the truth about Sir Walter Raleigh's downfall.

It is necessary that at times our journey will lead us down narrow streets as we pass the cramped rows of gabled houses with their leaded, misty glass window panes, never daring to peer into them. We will experience a feeling of being watched by these ghosts of ancient times, but as we are only viewing them through our own minds, they will not be disturbed by us so very much. If will see the inhabitants of London dashing out of their houses and into our path, it is because they are anxious to stop and speak to us, as we slowly make our way forward. Some will merely seek to beg an old penny from us to buy their bread, since they are poor, and trapped within their own memories of poverty. Then we must be kind and humble to them, and can do little to assist them, when they are left only with the will to lead or follow us as they choose.

When we meet with these spirits as they walk ahead of us, over the egg shaped cobbles of ancient London, we will view it through their eyes, so that they might come alive in minds of their readers, whose attention they wish to capture. They will be dressed in their long black cloaks as they lead us forward in search truth, and they will speak, but sometimes it will barely be a whisper, and yet what they utter we must hear, for it is history to us, and their history must never be forgotten.

If they fear to reveal themselves to us, then it is because their memories are awakened to the true horror of their times, causing them to hesitate to step forward. They will walk among the rats in the narrow streets of the plague infested City of London of 1603, and the rats will scurry for their lives because the ghosts of these men disturb them as they walk among us once more.

HIC JACET: SIR WALTER RALEIGH

I now suffer extreme anguish as I sit alone at my old wooden desk, placed near the window in a room overlooking a narrow alleyway, known only to Londoners as 5 Bell Yard, and if you had a mind to seek out that place, then you would find me there. How many long and miserable years I have endured in gathering up this history and as to the bleak and lonely path it has led me down, I cannot say within these pages, because this is not the place to reveal it.

I find myself well prepared, and have before me ink, parchment and several new feather quills which I brought with me from Lombard Street. I take little account of the hourglass, as it spills its fine grains of sand with each passing moment, because darkness turns to light readily enough as I work, and I need never cause myself to count time in that way.

As I stare into the glowing embers of the fire, I am aware that the room is warm and yet I shiver. The walls are lighted by the bright glow of the burning wood, revealing to my eyes the otherwise darkened room, and all about me I see the dark shadows of the past rising up from the depths of my mind as I am cast back into the year 1603. The shadows are horrible as they dance across the walls, waiting to speak. There are eight of these lonely spirits and yet I cannot say here, whether others will join us.

First I see the ghosts of Watson and Clarke, the Priests who suffered their fate at Winchester Castle on the 4th December 1603, when they were pronounced traitors to King James I of England and were hung drawn and quartered. Their severed heads being carried around the Castle and up into the battlements, where they were displayed, so that no other man might take it into his head to rise up against his King. On the 6th December Lord Cobham's brother, Brook, was tried and executed. On the 10th December Lord Cobham and Lord Grey were to be executed. On the 13th December, Sir Walter Raleigh was pronounced a Traitor and informed he would suffer a Traitor's death.

The Tower of London in 1603 conjures up terrible reflections in the human mind, working through the sensations best by the eye where they feed upon the imagination. What else may we rely upon, except our senses, to bring forward a picture to show us the reality of this horror?

I have often been compelled to lift the latch on the decaying wooden door, that leads me deep into my dwelling. Stepping slowly down the winding staircase, my way is lit only by the waning light of a candle, as I breathe in the damp air and walk into the cold, dark basement, where I find myself, once more filled with a fear that is brought about by distant memory. These spirits can offer no reward to my inquiring mind, and yet I long to acquaint my myself with their history. I need to show myself in their cause, for their cruel suffering, as it led them ever forward, begging the Lord to show them mercy, until they sank into their unwelcoming graves.

I have their history stored away in a great wooden chest, and must reach into it, and make it known to others, before I too fall into the spirit world, as my destiny predicts I must.

The chill of the basement causes me to fear its very existence. It is my secret place, where all the history I am to speak of is hidden away. I fear it is an unapproachable place, where I must cause myself to be among those ghosts if I am to finish this work. It is a place where, upon opening the door, the grey stone walls light up the faces of the ghostly images of those men, who trick my eyes into believing that they are still living. They Leap swiftly forward, rushing toward me, aided by the reflection of the moonlight; until my wits cause me to realize that the full moon cannot be found in the sky, as I advance to the window and peer out into the blackness that descends from a Winter sky. I find that I have caused them to wake by the light of my own burning tallow and my longing to bring their history to life. Then my mind is filled with the terrible and ghastly fate of Raleigh's friend, the Dramatist, Christopherus Marlowe. I find myself crossing the room to the old wooden chest, kept beneath the small window of that otherwise cold and dark place, where I might delve into the reasons for his murder. I desire to approach him and yet beside him Thomas Kyd stands taller in my mind, as his fellow Dramatist since I have uncovered more of his history than was first made known to me. At least I have a mind to make him stand tall through my experiences with his father, Francis Kyd the Scrivener. The spirits of their age being Christopherus Marlowe and the said Thomas Kyd, long to lead me into their shared writing chamber of 1591 and 1592, where it is said that together they wrote Er Hamlet. Kyd was arrested and tortured at Newgate. Marlowe was stabbed through the eye. It is history to me and I know that it is contained within Raleigh's Chest of papers hidden away in the Barn at Syon House. It is a dark and dangerous history, and yet I cannot help myself, for I must have it, and fear I shall never be happy until I have completed this work.

Having approached the chest of papers, and drawing away the heavy lid, in search of the knowledge contained therein, I have determined to write about it in a manner uncommon to an uneducated man such as I would appear to the World, if it could only be brought out of me. I reach in and find two folios for comparison, one a book by Sir Walter Raleigh and two plays by William Shakespeare: but the one I draw out is not written by Shakespeare but by Thomas Kyd and yet there I find the ghoast in Actvs Primvs Scene I: Induction:

Extracts from the Dramatic works of Thomas Kyd

Enter the Ghoast of Andrea, and with him Revenge

"Ghoast. When this eternall substance of my soule
Did live imprisond in my wanton flesh,
Ech intheir function serving others need
I was a Courtier in the Spanish Court.
My name was Don Andrea; my discent,
Though not ignoble, yet inferiour far
To gratious fortunes of my tender youth:
For there in prime and pride of all my yeeres,
By duteous service and deserving love,
In secret I possest a worthy dame,
Which hight sweet Bel0imperia by name.
But in the harvest of my sommer joyes,
Deaths winter nipt the blossomes of my blisse,
Forcing divorce betwixt my love and me.
for in the late conflict with Portingale
My valour drew me into dangers mouth,
Till life to death made passage through my wounds.
When I was slaine, my soule descended straight,
To passe the flowing streame of Acheron;
But churlish Charon, only boatman there,
Said that my rites of buriall not performde,
I might not sit amongst his passengers.
Ere Sol had slept three nights in Thetis lap,
And slakte his smoaking charriot in her floud,
By Don Horatio, our Knight Marshals sonne,

HIC JACET: SIR WALTER RALEIGH

My funerals and obsequies were done.
Then was the Feriman of Hell content
To passe me over to the slimie strond
That leades to fell Avernus ougly waves.
There, pleasing Cerberus with honied speech,
I past the perils of the formost porch.
Not farre from hence, amidst ten thousand soules,
Sat Minor, Eacus, and Rhadamant,
To whome no sonner gan I make approch,
To crave a pasport for my wandring Ghost,
But Minos, in graven leaves of Lotterie,
Drew forth manner of my life and death.
[6]This Knight (quoth he) both liv'd and died in love,
And for his love tried fortune to the warres,
And, by warres fortune, lost both love and life.
Why then, said Eacus, convay him hence,
To walke with lovers in our fieldes of love,
And spend the course of everlasting time
Under greene mirtle tress and Cipresse shades.
No, no, said Rhadamant, it were not well
With loving soules to place a Martialist:
He died in warre, and must to Martiall fields,
Where wounded Hector lives in lasting paine,
And Achilles Mermedons do scoure the plaine.
Then Minos, mildest censor of the three,
Made this device to end the difference:
To dome him as best seemes his Majestie.
To this effect my pasport straight was drawne.
In keeping on my way to Plutos Court,
Through dreadfull shades of ever glooming night,
 I saw more sights then thousand tongues can tell,

---

[6]Sir Philip Sidney

Or pennes can write, or mortall harts can think.
Three waies there were: that on the right hand side
Was ready way unto the foresaid fields,
Where lovers lieve and bloudie Martialists;
But either sort contain within his bounds.
The left hand path, declining fearefully,
Was ready dounfall to the deepest hell,
where bloudie furies shakes their whips of steele,
and poore Ixion turnes an endles wheele;
Where usurers are choakt with melting golde,
And wantons are imbraste with ouglie Snakes,
And murderes grone with never killing wounds,
And [7] perjurde wights scalded in boyling lead,
Twixt these two waies I trod the middle path,
Which brought me to the faire Elizian greene,
In midst whereof there standes a stately Towre,
The walles of brasse, the gates of adamant.
Heere finding Pluto with his Proserpine,
I shewed my passport humbled on my knee;
Whereaft faire Proserpine began to smile,
And begd that onely she might give my domme.
Pluto was pleasd, and sealde it with a kisse.
Forthwith, [8] Revenge, she rounded thee in th'eare,
And bad thee lead me through the gates of Horn,
Where dreames have passage in the silent night.
No sooner had she spoke, but we were heere,
I wot not how, in twinkling of an eye.
Revenge. Then know, Andrea, that thou art ariv'd
Where thou shalt see the author of thy death,
Don Balthazar, the Prince of Portingale,

---

[7] perjured wits

[8] Sir Walter Raleigh's ship: 'Revenge' in memory of Christopher Marlowe who wrote these lines.

Depriv'd of life by Bel-imperia.
Heere sit we downe to see the misterie,
And serve for Chorus in this Tragedie.

****

The second parchment I had drawn from the chest was that by the hand of Sir Walter Raleigh himself concerning his first voyage to Guiana.

The Great Rich and Beautiful Empire of Guiana 1596 - Sir Walter Raleigh – a letter

Thursday 6th February 1595 : Guiana
 K3[p.69/70 "Next unto Arui there are two rivers Atoica and Caora, and on that braunch which is called Caora are a nation of people, whose heads appeare not above their shoulders, which though it may be thought a meere fable, yet for mine owne part I am resolved it is true, because every child in the provinces of Arromaia and Carwri affirme the same: *they are called Ewaiponma: they are reported to have their eyes in their shoulders, and their mouths in the middle of their breasts, and that a long train of haire groweth backward between their shoulders."*

I left behind me Francis Sparrow (Captain Gifford's Servant) to draw the countryside and Hugh Goodwin to learn the language.

I took back to England the only son of King Topiawari whom I called Othello the Moor.

These lines I had read before I realised that before me stood the headless men contained in Shakespeare's Othello and again in the Tempest:

Shakespeare's Othello (1604)

In Act 1, scene iii refers to the "Anthropophagi, and men whose heads do grow beneath their shoulders"

"whose heads appear not above their shoulders they are called Ewaipanoma; they are reported to have their eyes in their shoulders and their mouths in the middle of their breasts, and that long train of hair growing backward between their shoulders".

And in the Tempest (1611)

Gon: "Gaith Sir, you need not fear: when we were boys, who believe that there were mountaineers dew-lapped like bulls, whose throats had hanging at them wallets of flesh? ... or that there were such men whose heads stood in their breasts which we now find, each putter out of five for one will bring us good warrant."

In my rising anger I drew the remainder of the text of 'The Great Rich and Beautiful Empire of Guiana, 1596'" from the chest and once again I return slowly to the warmth of my fireside in the middle of the house that I call my haven of sanity, only to find that I have brought with me not only the old parchments, but the very spirit of the man whose history I must record, standing beside me. Only one has followed me into the room and I feel his presence all about me, until when I close my eyes, I see a picture of him clearly in my mind and it becomes so vivid that I see him approaching my desk. I am forced to leap from my chair and return the parchments in a great hurry and in fear of my life. Not least because I sense that he is looking over my shoulder and breathing upon me, and I feel my bones are numbed with cold even in this warm room, so that if I do not cease this work then I shall die before my grave calls me to everlasting sleep. I am undeterred. I tell myself that it is through no fear of mine that my work has been halted again for that night, because I would have no intruder read my unfinished lines until I can prepare myself to reveal them. I return the papers safely to the wooden chest, with a chill in my bones that only leaves me when I am alone beside my fire, and I continue to gaze into it until it reveals its mystery to me.

HIC JACET: SIR WALTER RALEIGH

How many times I have performed that act over the years I cannot say, except to the approaching ghosts that haunts me in my waking and in my sleep, for they are with me only one at a time, urging each other forward to speak. If I sense that my former guide is looking over my shoulder as I write, then I must welcome him as a friend and ask his forgiveness for disturbing him in the beginning of my work, as I sought out only Sir Walter Raleigh in my childhood, and believed that only he would come forward to speak to me. I understand now that his friends were beside him as I questioned my mind for his history.

Book 1 1595
The Discoverie of Guiana, 1596 Sir Walter Raleigh

On Thursday 6th February 1595 we departed England, and the Sunday
following had sight of the North cape of Spayne, the winde for the
most part continuing prosperous: we passed in sight of the Burlings,
and the rocke and lo onwardes for the Canaries, and fell with Fuerte
ventura the 17. of the same moneth, where we spent two or three daies,
and relieved our companies with some fresh meate. From thence wee
coasted by the Gran Canaria   , and so to Tenerife, and staied there for
the Lyons whelp your Lordships ship, and for captaine Amys Preston
and the rest: But when after 7. or 8. daies we found them not, wee
departed and directed our course for Trinedado with mine own shippe,
and a small barke of Captaine Crosses onely (for we had before lost
sight of a small Galleo on the coast of Spayne, which came with us
from Plymouth:) wee arrived at Trinedado the 22. of March, casting
ancour at point Curiapan, which the Spanyards call punto de Gallo,
which is situate in 8. degrees or there abouts: we abode there 4. or 5.
daies, and in all that time we came not to the speach of anie Indian or
Spaniard: on the coast we saw a fire, as we sailed from the point Carao
towards Curiapan, but for feare of the Spaniards, none durst come to
speake with us. I my selfe coasted it in my barge close abord the shore
and landed in every Cove, the better to know the lland, while the ships
kept the chanell. From Curiapan after a fewe daies we turned up
Northeast to recover that place which the Spaniards cal puerto de los
Hispanioles, and the inhabitants Conquerabia, and as before
(revictualing my barge) I left the shippes and kept by the shore, the
better to come to speach with some of the inhabitantes, and also to
speach with some of the inhabitantes, and also to understand the rivers,
watring places and portes of the Iland which (as it is rudely done) my
purpose is to send your Lordship after a few daies. From Curiapan I
came to a port & seat of Indians call Parico where we found a fresh-
water river, but sawe no people. From thence I rowed to another port,
called by the naturals Piche, and by the Spaniardes Tierra de Brea: In
the way betweene both were divers little brooks of fresh water, & one
salt river that had store of oisters upon the branches of the trees, &
were very salt and well tasted. Al their oisters grow upon those

boughs and spraies, and not on the ground: the like is commonlie seene in the West Indies and else where. This tree is described by Andrew Theuet in his french Antartique, and the forme figures in his booke as a plante verye straunge, and by Plinie in his XII. booke of his naturall historie. But in this Ilande, as also in Guiana there are verie manie of them.

At this point called Tierra de Brea or Piche there is that abundance of stone pitch, that all the ships of the world may be therewith loden from thence, and wee made triall of it in trimming our ships to be most excellent good, and melteth not with the sunne as the pitch of Norway, and therefore for ships trading the south partes very profitable. From thence we went to the moutaine foote called Annaperima, and so passed the river Carone on which the Spanish Citie was seated, we met with our ships at puerto de los Hispanioles or Conquerabia.

This Iland of Trinedado hath the forme of a sheepehook, and is but narrow, the north part is very mounteynous, the soile is very excellent and will beare sugar, ginger, or any other commodity that the Indies yeeld. It hath store of deare, wyld porks, fruits, fish & fowle: It hath also for bread sufficient Mais, Cassaui, and of those roots and fruits which are common every where in the west indies. It hath divers beasts, which the Indies have not: the Spaniards confessed that they found grains of gold in some of the rivers, but they having a purpose to enter Guiana (the Magazin of all rich mettels) cared not to spend time in the search thereof any farther. This Iland is called by the people thereof Cairi, and in it are divers nations: those about Parico are called Iaio, those at Punto Carao are of the Arwacas, and between Carao and Curiapan they are called Salvaios, betweene Carao and punto Galera are the Nepoios, and those about the spanish Citie tearme themselves Carinepagots: Of the rest of the nations, and of the other portes and rivers I leave to speake heere, beeing impertinent to my purpose, and meane to describe them as they are situate in the particular plot and description of the Iland, three partes whereof I coasted with my barge, that I might the better discribe it.

Meeting with the ships at puerto de los Hispanioles, we found at the landing place a company spanyards who kept a guard at the descent, and they offering a signe of peace I sent Captaine Whiddon to speake with them, whome afterward to my great griefe I left buried in the said Iland after my returne from Guiana, beeing a man most honest and valiant. The Spanyards seemed to be desirous to trade with us, and to enter into tearms of peace, more of doubt of their own strength then for ought else, and in the end upon pledge, some of them came abord: the same evening there stale also abord us in a small Canoa two Indians, the one of them being a Casique or Lord of people called Cantyman, who had the yeare before beene with Captaine Widdon, and was of his acquaintance. By this Cantyman wee understood what strength the spaniardes had, how farre it was to their Citie, and of Don Anthonio de Berreo the governour, who was said to be slaine in his second attempt of Guiana, but was not.

While we remained at puerto de los Hispanioles some Spaniardes came abord us to buy lynnen of the company, and such other thinges as they wanted, and also to view our shippes and company, all which I entertained kindly and feasted after our manner: by meanes whereof I learned of one and another as much of the estate of Guiana as I could, or as they knew, for those poore souldiers having beene many yeares without wine, a fewe draughts made them merry, in which moode they vaunted to Guiana and of the riches thereof, and all what they knew of the waies and passages, myself seeming to purpose nothing lesse then the entrance or discoverie thereof, but bred in them an opinion that I was bound onely for the reliefe of those english, which I had planted in Virginia, whereof the brute was come among them, which I had performed in my returne if extremity of weather had not forst me from the said coast.

I found occasions of staying in this place for two causes: the one was to be revenged of Berro, who the yeare before betraied 8. of Captaine Widdons men, and tooke them while he departed from them to seeke the E. Bonaventure, which arrived at Trinedado the day before from the East Indies: in whose absence Berreo sent a Canoa abord the pinnace onely with Indians and dogs inviting the company to goe with them into the woods to kill a deare, who like wise men in the absence of their Captaine followed the Indians but were no sooner one harquebush short from the shore, but Berreos souldeirs lying in ambush had them all, notwithstanding that he had given his worde to Captaine Whiddon that they should take water and wood safelie: the other cause of my stay was, for that by discourse with the Spaniards I daily learned more and more of Guiana, of the rivers and passages, and of the enterprize of Berro, by what meanes or fault he failed, and how he meant to prosecute the same.

While we thus spent the time I was assured by another Casigne of the north side of the Iland, that Berreo had sent to Marguerita & to Cassado at parting, if it had bin possible. For although he had given order through all the Iland that no Indian should come aborde to trade with me upon paine of hanging and quartering, (having executed two of them for the same which I afterwardes found, yet every night there came some with most lamentable complaints of his cruelty, how he had devided the Iland & given to every soldier a part, that he made the ancient Casiqui which were lordes of the country to be their slaves, that he kept them in chains, & dropped their naked bodies with burning bacon, & other torments, which I found afterwards to be true: for in the city after I entred the same there were 5. of the Lords or little kings (which they cal Casiqui in the West Indies) in one chaine almost dead of famine, and wasted with torments: these are called in their own language Acarewana, and now of late since English, French & Spanish are come among them, they cal themselves Capitaynes, because they perceive that the chiefest of every ship is called by that name Those five Capitaynes in the chaine were called Wannawanare, Carotori, Maquarima, Tarroopanama, & Alterima. so as both to be revenged of the former wrong, as also considering that to enter Guiana by small boats, to depart 400. or 500 miles from my ships, and to leave a garrison in my backe interested in the same enterprize, who also daily expected supplies out of Spaine, I should have savoured very much the Asse (else?): and therefore taking a time of most advantage,

I set upon the Corp du guard in the evening, and having put them to the sword, sente Captaine Calforld onwards with 60. soldiers, & my self followed with 40. more & so took their new city which they called S. Joseph, by breake of day: they abode not any fight after a few shot, & al being dismissed but onely Berro and his companion, I brought them with me abord, and at the instance of the Indians I set their new City of S. Josephs on fire.

The same day arrived Captaine George Gifford with your Lord ships ship, & Captaine Keymis whom I lost on the coast of Spaine, with the Gallego, and in them divers Gent. and others, which to our little army was a great comfort and supply.

We then hastened away towards our purposed discovery, and first I called all the Captaines of the Iland together that were enemies to the spaniards, for there were some which Berreo had brought out of other countries, & planted there to eat out & wast those that were natural of the place, & by my indian interpreter, which I carried out of England, I made them understand that I was the servant of a Queene, who was the great Casique of the north, and a virgin, and had more Casiqui under her than there were trees in their Iland: that she was an enemy to the Castellans in respect of their tyrannie and oppression, and that she delivered all such nations about her, as were by them oppressed, and having freed all the coast of the northern world from their servitude had sent me to free them also, and with al to defend the countrey of Guiana from their invasion and conquest. I shewed them her majesties picture which they so admired and honored, as it had beene easie to have brought them Idolatrous thereof.

The like & more large discourse I made to the rest of the nations both in my passing to Guiana, & to those of the borders, so as in that part of the world her majesty is very famous and admirable, whom they now call Ezrabeta Cassipuna Aquerewana, which is as much as Elizabeth, the great princesse or greatest commander. This done wee left puerto de los Hispanioles, and returned to Curiapan, and having Berreo my prisonour I gathered from him as much of Guiana as he knew.

HIC JACET: SIR WALTER RALEIGH

This Berreo is a gent. well descended, and had long served the spanish king in Millain, Naples, the low Countries and else where, very valiant and liberall, and a Gent. of great assurednes, and of a great heart: I used him according to his estate and worth in all things I could, according to the small meanes I had.

I sent Captain Whiddon the yeare before to get what knowledge he could of guiana, and the end of my journey at this time was to discover and enter the same, but my intelligence was farre from trueth, for the country is situate above 600. English miles further from the sea, then I was made beleeve it had beene, which afterward understanding to be true by Berro, I kept it from the knowledge of my companies, who else woulde never have beene brought to attempt the same: of which 600. miles I passed 400. leaving my shippes so farre from me at anchor in the sea, which was more of desire to performe that discovery, then of reason, especially having such poore & weake vessels to transport ourselves in; for in the bottom of an old Gallego which I caused to be fashioned like a Galley, and in one barge, two wherries, and a ship bote of the Lyons whelpe, we carried 100 persons and their victuals for a moneth in the same, being al driven to lie in the raine and wether, in the open aire, in the burning sunne, & upon the hard bords, and to dresse our meat, and to carry all manner of furniture in them, wherewith they were so pestred and unsavery, that what with victuals, being most fish, with the wet cloths of so many men thrust together and the heate of the sunne, I will undertake there was never any prison in England, that coulde be founde more unsavory and lothsome, especially to my selfe, who had for many yeares before beene dieted and cared for in a sort farre differing.

If Captaine Preston had not beene perswaded that he should have come too late Trinedado to have found us there (for the moneth was expired which I promised to tarry for him there were he could recover the coast of Spain) but that I had pleased god he might have joyned with us, and that wee had entred the countrey some ten daies sooner ere the rivers were overflowing, we had adventured either to have gone to the great city of Monoa, or at least taken so many of the other Cities and townes neerer at hand, as would have made a royall returne: But it pleased not God so much to favour me at this time: if it shall be my lot to prosecute the same, I shall willingly spend my life therein, and if any else shall be enabled thereunto, and conquere the same, I assure him thus much, he shall performe more than ever was done in Mexico by Cortez, or in Peru by Pacaro, whereof the one conquered the Empire of Muntezuma, the other Guascar, and Atabalipa, and whatsoever Prince shall prossess it, that Prince shall be Lorde of more Gold, and of a more beautifull Empire, and of more Cities and people, then eyther the king of Spayne, or the great Turke.

But because there may arise many doubtes, and how this Empire of Guania is becoming so populous, and adorned with so manie greate Cities, Townes, Temples, and treasures, I thought good to make it knowen, that the Emperour now raigning is descended from those magnifient Princes of Peru of whose large territories, of whose pollicies, conquests, edifices, and riches Pedro de Cieza, Franciso Lopez, and others have written large discourses: for when Francisco Pacaro, Diego Almagro and other conquered the said Empire of Peru, and had put to death Atabalipa sonne to Guaynacapa, which Atabalipa had formerly caused his eldest brother Guascar to be slaine, one of the younger sonnes of Guaynacapa fled out of Peru, and tooke with him many thousandes of those souldiers of the Empyre called Oreiones, and with those and many others which followed him, he vanquished al that tract and valley of America which is situate betweene the great rivers of Amazones, and Baraquan, otherwise called Orenoke and Maranion.

The Empyre of Guiana is directly east from Peru towards the sea, and lieth under the Equinoctial line, and it hath more abundance of Golde then any part of Peru, and as many or more great Cities then ever Peru had when it florished most: it is governed by the same lawes, and the Emprour and people observe the same religion, and the same forme and pollicies in government as was used in Peru, yet differing in any part: and as I have beene assured by such of the Spanyardes as have seene Manoa the emperiall Citie of Guiana, which the Spanyardes cal el Dorado, that for the greatness, for the riches, and for the excellent seate, it farre exceedeth any of the world, at least of so much of the world as it knowen to the Spanish nation: it is founded upon a lake of salt water of 200 leagues long like unto mare capiu. and if we compare it to that of Peru, & but reade the report of [9] Franciso Lopez & others, it will seeme more than credible, and because we may judge of the one by the other, I thought good to insert part of the 120. chapter of Lopez in his general historie of the Indies, wherein he discribeth the court and magnifience of Guaynacapa, ancestor of the Emperour of Guiana, whose very words are these. Todo el servicio de su case, mesa, y cozina era de oro, y de plaza, y quando menos de plata, y cobre por murezio. Tenia en su recamara estatuas buccas de ore que pareciangigantes y lu figuras al propio: y tamano de quantos animales, aues, arboles, y yeruas prozue le tierra,y de quantos peces cria la mar y aguas de sui reynos. Tenia assi mesmo sogas, costales, cestuas, y toroxes de oro y plata, rimeros de palos de oro, que pareciessen lenna raiada para quemar. En fin no avia cosa en suitierra, que no la tuuiesse de oro conirahecha : y aun dizen, que tenian los Ingas un vergel en una Isla cerca de la Puna, donde se yuan a holgar, quando querian mar, que tenia la ortaliza, las flores, yarboles de oro y plat a, inuencion y grandeza hasta entonces nunca vista. Alleude de todo esto tenia infinitismia cantidad de plat, y oro por labrar en el Cuzco, u se perdio por la muerte de Guascar, ca los Indios lo escondicron, viendo que los espanioles se lo tomauan, y embiatutu a Espania.

That is, all the vessels of his house, table, and kitchin were of Gold

---

[9] Lopez: 1509 : Lopez di Sequira visits Mallaca. Alfonso de Albuquereu, a Portuguese, becomes Governor of India, and kes great conquests and discoveries from this time until his death in 1515.

1531 Pizarro conquers Peru.

and Silver, and the meanest of silver and copper for strength and hardnes of the metal.* See new Atlantis [10] (he spoke in Spanish of the School): He had in his wardroppe hollow statues of golde which seemed giants, and the figures in proportion and bignes of all the beastes, birdes, trees and hearbes, that the earth bringeth forth: and of all the fishes that the sea or waters of his kingdome breedeth. He had also ropes, budgets, chestes and troughts of golde and silver, heapes of billets of golde that seemed woode, marked out to burne. Finally there was nothing in his countrey, whereof hee had not the counterfeat in gold. Yea and they say, The Ingas had a garden of pleasure in an Iland neere Puna, where they went to recreate themselves, when they would take the ayre of the Sea, which had all kind of garden hearbes, flowers and trees of Gold and silver, an invention, & magnificence til then never seen: Besides all this, he had an infinite quantitie of silver and gold unwrought in Cuzco which was lost by the death of Guascar, for the Indians hid it, seeing that the spaniards tooke it, and sent it into Spayne.

And in the 117. Chapter Franciso Picarro caused the Golde and Silver of Atabalipa to bee weyed, after he had taken it, which Lopez setteth downe in these wordes following.

Hallaron cinquenta y dos mil marcos de buera plata, y un million y trezientos y veinte y seys mil, y quinientos pesos de oro, which is: They founde fiftie and two thousand markes of good silver, and one million, and three hundred twentie and sixe thousand and five hundred posoes of golde.

Nowe although these reportes may seeme straunge, yet if wee consider

---

[10] New Atlantis: "In which scroll were written in ancient Hebrew, and in ancient Greek, and in good Latin of the School, and in Spanish, these words; 'Land ye not, none of you; and provide to be gone from this coast within sixteen days, except you have further time given you. Meanwhile, if you want fresh water, or victual, or help for your sick, or that your ship needeth repair, write down your wants, and you shall have that which belongeth to mercy."

the many millions which are daily brought out of Peru into Spaine, wee may easely beleeve the same, for wee finde that by the abundant treasure of that countrey, the Spanish King vexeth all the Princes of Europe, and is become in a fewe yeares from a poore king of Castile the greatest monarke of this part of the worlde, and likelie every day to increase, if other Princes forsloe the good occasions offered, and suffer him to adde this Emp8ire to the rest, which by farre exceedeth all the rest: if his golde now in daunger us, hee will then be unresistable. Such of the spaniards as afterwarde undevoured the conquest thereof (whereof there have beene many as shall bee declared heereafter) thought that this Inga, (of whome this Emperor now living is descended) tooke his way by the river of Amazones, by that braunch which is called Papamene, for by that way followed Oreliano (by the commandement of the Marquis Pacarro in the yeare 1542.) whose name the river also beareth this day, which is also by others called Maragnon, although Andrew Thevet doth affirm that between Maragnon and Amazones there are 120. leagues: but sure it is that those rivers have one head & beginning, and that Maragnon which Thenet describeth is but a braunch of Amazones or Oreliano, of which I wil speake more in an other place. It was also attempted by Diego Ordace, but whether before Oreliano or after I knowe not: but it is now little lesse then 70. yeares since that Ordace a knight of the order of Saint Iago [11] attempted the same: and it was in the yeare 1542. that Oreliano discovered the river of Amazones; but the first that eer sawe Manoa was Johannes Martines master of the munition to Ordace. At a porte called Morequito in Guiana there lyeth at this daie a great anchor or Ordaces shippe, and this porte is some 300 miles within the lande, upon the greate river of Orenoque.

I rested at this port fowre daies: twentie daies after I left the shippes at Curiapan. the relation of this Martynes (who was the first that

---

[11] Read Othello

discovered Manoa) his successe & end is to be seene in the Chauncery of Saint Inan de puerto rico, whereof Berreo had a coppie, which appeared to be the greatest incouragement as well to Berreo as to others that formerly attempted the discovery and conquest. Oreliano after he sailed to the discoverie of Guiana by the said river of Amazones, passed into Spaine, and there obtained a patent of the king of the invasion and conquest, but died by sea about the Ilands, and his fleet beeing severed by [12]*tempest, the action for that time proceeded not. Diego Ordace followed the enterprize, and departed Spaine with 600. soldiers and 30. horse, who arriving on the coast of Guiana was slaine in a muteny with the most part of such as favoured him, as also of the rebellious part of such as favoured him, as also of the rebellious part, in so much as his ships perished, and few or none returned, neither was it certainely knowen what became of the said Odace, untill Berreo found the anchor of his ship in the river of Orenoque; but it was supposed, and so it is written by Lopez that he perished on the seas, and of other writers diversly conceived & reported. And heerof it came that Martynes entred so farre within the lande and arrived at that Citie of Inga the Empoeror, for it chaunced that while Ordace with his armie restedat the port of Morequito (who was either the first or second that attempted Guiana) by some negligence the whole store of powder provided for the service, was set on fire, & Martines having the chief charge was condemned by the generall Ordace to be executed forthwith: Martines being much favoured by the soldiers had all the meane possible procured for his life, but it could not be obtained in other sort then this. That he should be set into a Canoa alone without any victual, onely with his armes, and so turned loose into the great river: but it pleased God that the Conoa was carried downe the streame, & that certain of the Guianians met it the same evening, & having not at any time sene any Christian, nor any man of that colour, they carried Martynes into the land to be wondred at, and so from towne to towne, untill he came to the great Citie of Manoa, the seate and residence of Inga the Emperor. The Emperor after he had beheld

---

[12] The Tempest - the Storm. Oreliano (Corelianos) : Read

him, knew him to be a Christian (for it was not long before that his brethren Guascar and Atabalipa were vanquishd by the spaniards in Peru) and caused him to be lodged in his pallace, and well entertained: hee lived 7. months in Manoa, but not sufferd to wander into the country any where: hee was also brought thither all the waie blindfield, led by the Indians, until he came to the entrance of Manoa itself, and was 14. or 1 daies in the passage: he allowed at his death that he entred the City at Noon, & then they uncovered his face, and that he travelled al that daie til night thorow the Citie, and the next day from sun rising to sun setting, ere he came to the pallace of Inga. After that Marthynes had lived 7. months in Manoa, and began to understand the language of the countrey, Inga asked him whether he desired to returne into his own countrey, or would willingly abide with him: but Martynes not desirous to stay, obtained the favour of Inga to depart, with whom he sent diver Guianians to conduct him to the river of Orenoque all loden with as much gold as they could carrie, which he gave to Martines at his departure. but when he was arrived neere the rivers side, the borderers which are called Orenoqueponi robbed him and his Guianians of all the treasure (the borderers beeing at that time at warres which Inga, and not conquered) save onely of two great bottels of gords, which were filled with beads of gold curiously wrought, which those Orenqueponi thought had been no other thing then his drink or meate or grain for foode with which Martynes had libertie to passe, and so in Canoas he fell down by the river of Orenoque to Trinedado, and from thence to Marguerita, and so to Saint Juan de puerto rico, where remaining a long tyme for passage into Spayne he died. In the time of his extreme sickness, and when he was without hope of life, receaving the Sacrament at the handes of his Confessor, he delivered these thinges, with the relation of his travels, and also called for his Calabaza or gords of the beades which he gave to the Church & friers to be praied for. This Martynes was he that christened the Citie of Manoa, by the name of El Dorado, and as Berreo informed me upon this occasion. Those Guianians and also the borderers, and all others in that tract which I have seen are marveylous great drunkardes, in which vice I think no nation can compare with them and at the times of their solemne feats when the Emperor carowseth with his Captayns, tributories, & governours, the manner is thus. All those that pledge him are first stripped naked, & their bodies annoynted al over with a kinde of white Balsanum: by them called Curcai) of which there is great plenty and yet very deare amongst them, and it is of all other the most precious, whereof we have had good experience: when they are annointed all over, certain servants of the Emperor having prepared gold made into fine powder blow it thorow hollow canes upon their naked bodies, untill they be al shining from the foote to the head, & in this sort they sit drinking by twenties and hundreds & continue in drunkennes sometimes sixe or seven daies together: the same is also confirmed by a letter written into Spaine which was intercepted, which master Robert Dudley told me he had seen. Upon this sight, and for the abundance of gold which he saw in the citie, the Images of gold in their Temples, the plates, armors, and shields of gold which they use in the wars, he called it El Dorado. After Oreliano who was emploied by Pacaro afterwards Marques Pacaro conqueror and governor of Peru, and the death of Ordace and Marthynes, one Pedro de Osua, a knight of Navarre attempted Guiana, taking his way from Peru, and built his brigandines upon a river called Oia, which riseth to the southward of quito, and is very great: this river falleth into Amazones, by which Osua with his companies descended, and came out of that Province which is called Mutylones: and it seemeth to me that this Empire is reserved for her Majestie and the English nation, by reason of the hard successe which all these & other Spaniards found in attempting the same, whereof I will speake brieflie, though impertinent in some sort to my purpose. This Pedro de Osua had among his troupes a Biscayn called Agiri, a man meanlie borne, & bare no other office than a Sergeant or Alferes: but after certaine months, when the soldiers were grieved with travels and consumed with famine, and that no entrance could be found by the branches or body of Amazones, this Agiri raised a muteny, of which hee made himselfe the head, and so prevailed as he put Osua to the Sword, and all his followers, taking on him the whole charge and commandement with a purpose not onely to make himselfe Emperror of Guiana, but also of Peru, and of all that side of the West Indies: he had of his partie seven hundred soldiers, and of those many promised to draw in other captains and companies to deliver up towns and forests in Peru, but neither finding by the saide river any passage into Guiana, nor any possibilitie to returne towards Peru by the same Amazones, by reason that the descent of the river made so great a currant, he was inforced to desembarque at the mouth of the said Amazones, which cannot be lesse than a thousand leagues from the place where they imbarqued: from thence he coasted the land till he arrived at Marguerita to the North of Mompata, which is at this daie called Puerto de Tyranno, for that he there slue Don Juan de villa Andreda, governor of Marguerita, who was father to Don Juan Sermiento governor of Marguerita when Sir John Burgh landed there, and attempted the Iland. Agiri put to the sword all others in the Iland that refused to be of his partie, and tooke with him certain Cemerones, and other desperate companions: From thence he went to Cumana, and there slew the Governor, and dealt in all as at Marguerita: he spoiled all the coast of Caracas, and the province of Vensuello, and of Rio de bache, and as I remember it was the same year that Sir John Hawking sailed to Saint Juan de Lua in the Jesiu of Lubeck, for himselfe told me that he met with such a one upon the coast that rebelled, and had sailed downe all the river of Amazones. Agiri from hence landed about Sancta Marta, and sacked it also, putting to death so many as refused to be his followers, purposing to invade Nuevo reygno de Granada, & and to sack Pampelone, Merida, Lagrita Tuuis, & the rest of the cities of Nuevo reygno, and from thence againe to enter Peru: but in a fight in the said Nuevo reygno he was overthrowne, & finding no way to escape, he first put to the sword his own children, foretelling them that they should not live to be defamed or upbraid by the Spaniards after his death, who would have tearmed them the children of a Traytor or Tyrant, and that since he could not make them Princes, he woulde yet deliver them from shame and reproch: These were the ends and tragedies of Oreliano, Ordace, Osua, Martynes, and Agiri.

After these followed Heronimo Ortal de Saragosa with 130 soldiers, who failing his entrance by sea was cast with the currant on the coast of Paria, and peopled about S. Miguell de Nevueri. It was then attempted by Don Pedro de Sylua a Portugues of the familie of

Rigomes de Sylva, and by the favour which Rigomes had with the king, he was set out, but he also shot wide of the mark, for being departed from Spaines with his fleete, he entered by Maragnon or Amazones, where by the nations of the river, and by the Amazones he was utterly overthrowen, and himselfe and all his armie defeated, onely seven escaped, and of those but two returned.

After him came Pedro Hernandes de Serpa, and landed at Cumana in the West Indies, taking his journey by land towards Orenoque, which may bee some 120. leagues, but ere he came to the borders of the said river, he was set upon by a nation of Indians called Wikiri, and overthrowen in sort, that of 300 soldiers, horsemen, many Indians, and Negros, there returned but 18: others affirm that he was defeated in the very entrance of Guiana, at the first civill towne of the Empire called Macureguarai. Captaine Preston in taking S. Iago de Leon (which was by him and his companies very resolutely performed, being a great towne, and far within the land) held a gentleman prisoner who died in his ship, that was one of the companie of Hernandes de Serpa, and saved among those that escaped, who witnessed what opinion is held among the spaniards thereabouts of the great riches of Guiana, and El Dorado the citie of Inga. Another Spaniard was brought aboard me by Captaine Preston, who told me in the hearing of himselfe and divers other gentlemen, that he met with Berreos Campmaster at Caracas, when he came from the borders of Guiana, and that he saw with him fortie of most pure plates of golde curiously wrought, and swords of Guiana decked with inlaid golde, feathers garnished with golde, and divers rarities which he carried to the Spanish king.

After Hernandes de Serpa it was undertaken by the Adelantado, Don Gonzales Cemenes de Casada, who was one of the chiefest in the conquest of Nuevo reyno, whose daughter & heire Don Anthonio de Berreo married: Gonzales sought the passage also by the river called Papameno, which riseth by Quito in Peru, & runneth southeast 100. leagues, & then falleth into Amazones, but he also sailing the entrance, returned with the losse of much labour and cost: I tooke one captaine George a Spaniard that followed Gonzales in this enterprise. Gonzales gave his daughter to Berreo taking his oath and honor, to follow the enterprise to the last of his substance and life, who since as he hath sworne to me hath spent 300000. ducates in the same, and yet never could enter so far into the land as my selfe with that poore troupe or rather a handfull of men, being in all about 100 gentlemen, soldiers, rowers, bote-keepers, boies, and of all sorts: neither could any of the forepassed undertakers, nor Berreo himselfe discover the country, till now lately by conference with an ancient king called Carapana he got the true light thereof: for Berreo came above 1500 miles, ere he understood ought, or could finde any passage or entrance into any part thereof, yet he had experience of all these forenamed, and divers others, and was perswaded of their errors and mistakings. Berreo sought it by the river assanar, which falleth into a great river called Pato, Pato falleth into Meta, and Meta into Baranquan, which is also called Orenoque.

He tooke his journey from Neuvo reyno de Granada where he dwelt, having the inheritance of Gonzales Cemes in those parts: he was followed with 700. horse, he drave with him 1000. head of cattell, he had also many women, Indians, and slaves. How all these rivers crosse and encounter, how the countrie lieth and is bordred, the passage of Cemes, and of Berreo, mine owne discouverie, and the way that Ientred, with all the rest of the nations and rivers, your Lordship shall receive in a large Chart or Map, which I have not yet finished, and which I shall most humbly pray your Lo. to secret, and not to suffer it to passe your own hands; for by a draught thereof all may bee prevented by other nations. For I know it is this very yeere sought by the French, although by the way that they now take, I feare it not much. It was also told me ere I departed England, that Villiers the Admirall was in preparation for the planting of Amazones, to which river the French have made divers voiages, and returned much gold and other rarities. I spake with a Captaine of a French ship that came from thence, his ship riding in Falmouth, the same yeere that my ships came first from Virginia.

there was another this yeere in Helford that also came from thence, and had been 14. months at an ancor in Amazones, which were both very rich. Although as I am perswaded, Guana cannot be entred that way, yet no doubt the trade of gold from thence passeth by branches of rivers into the river of Amazones, and so it doth on every hand farre from the countrey it selfe, for those Indians of Trenedado have plates of gold from Guiana, and those Canibals of Dominca which dwell in the Ilands by which our ships passe yeerly to the West Indies, also the Indians of Paria, those Indians called Tucaris, Chochi, Apotomios, Cumanagots, and all those other nations inhabiting nere about the mountaines that run from Paria thorow the Province of Vensuello, and in Maracapana, and the Canibals of Guinipa, the Indians called Assawai, Coaca, Aiai, and the rest (all which shall be described in my description as they are situate) have plates of gold of Guiana. And upon the river of Amazones Thevet writeth that the people weare Coissants of gold, for of that form the Guianians most commonly make them: So as from Dominica to Amazones which is abouve 250 leagues, all the chiefe Indians in al parts weare of those plates of Guiana, undoubtedly those that trade Amazones returne much gold, which (as is aforesaid) commeth by trade from Guina, by some branch of a river that falleth from the countrey into Amazones, and either it is by the river which passeth by the nations called Tisnados, or by Carepuna. I made inquirie amongst the most ancient and best traveled of the Ortenoqueponi, & I had knowledge of all the rivers between Orenoque and Amazones, and was desirous to understand the truth of those warlike women, because of some it is beleeved, of others not: And though I digresse from my purpose, yet I will set downe what hath been delivered me for the truth of those women, and I spake with a Casique or Lord of people that told me he had been in the river, and beyond it also. The nations of these women are on the south side of the river in the Provinces of Topago, and their chiefest strengths and retraicts are in the Ilands scituate on the south side of the entrance, some 60. leagues within the mouth of the said river. The memories of the like women are very ancient as well in Africa as in Asia: In Africa those that had Medusa for Queene: others in Scithia neere the rivers of Tanais and Thermadon: we find also that Lampedo and Marthesia were Queens of the Amazones: in many histories they are verified to have been, and in divers ages and Provinces: But they which are not far from Guiana do accompanie with men but once in a yeere, and for the time of one moneth, which I gather by their relation to be in Aprill. At that time all the Kings of the borders assemble, and the Queenes of the Amazones, and after the Queens have chosen, the rest cast lots for their Valentines. This one moneth, they feast, daunce & drinke of their wines in abundance, & the Moone being downe, they all depart to their owne Provinces. If they conceive, and be delivered of a sonne, they returne him to the father, if of a daughter they nourish it, and retain it, and as many as have daughters send unto the begetters a Present, all being desirous to increase their one sex and kinde, but that the cut of the right dug of the breast I do not finde to be true. It was farther told me, that if in the wars they tooke any prisoners that they used to accompany with those also at what time soever, but in the end for certaine they put them to death: for they are said to be very cruell and bloodthirsty, especially to such as offer to invade their territories. These Amazones have likewise great store of these plates of golde, which they recover by exchange chiefly for a kinde of greene stones, which the Spaniards called Piedras Hijadas, and we use for spleene stones, and for the disease of the stone we also esteeme them: of these I saw divers in Guiana, and commonly every kind or Casique hath one, which their wives for the most part weare, and they esteeme them as great jewels.

But to returne to the enterprise of Berreo, who (as I have said) departed from Nuevo reyno with 700. horse, besides the provisions above rehearsed; he descended by the river called Cassanar, which riseth in Nueno reyno out of the mountaines by the citie of Tuuia, from which mountaine also springeth Pato, both which fall into the great river of Meta, and Meta riseth from a mountaine joining to Pampelone in the same Nuevo reyno de Granada: these as also uaiare, which issueth out of the mountains by Timana fall all into Baraisan, and are but of his heads, for at their coming together they lose their names, and Barquan farther down is also re-baptized by the name of Orenoque. On the other side of the citie and hills of Timana riseth rio grande, which falleth into the sea by Sancta Marta. By Cassonar first, and so into Meta Berreo passed, keeping his horsemen on the banks, where the countrie served them for to march, and where otherwise he was driven to embarque them in botes which he bulded for the purpose, and so came with the currant down the river of Meta, and so into Baraquan. After he entred that great and mightie river, he began dailie to loose of his companies both men and horse, for it is in many places violentlie swift, and hath forcible eddies, many sands, and divers Ilands sharpe pointed with rocks: but after one whole yeere, journeying for the most part by river, and the rest by land he grew dailie to fewer numbers, for both by sickness, and by encountring with the people of of those regions, through which he travelled, his companies were much wasted, especially by divers incounters with the Amapaiens: And in all this time he never could learne of any passage into guiana, nor any newes or same thereof, untill he came to the farther border of the said Amapaia, eight daies journey from the river Caroli, which was the farthest river that we entred. Among those of Amapaia, guiuana was famous, but few of these people accosted Berreo, or would trade with him the first three months of the six which he sojourned there. This Amapaia is also marvelous rich in gold (as both Berreo confessed, and those of Guiana with whom I had most conference) and is situate upon Orenoke also. In this countrey Berreo lost 60. of his best soldiers, and most of all his horse that remained of his former yeeres travell: but in the end after divers encounters with those nations they grew to peace, and they presented Berreo with 10 Images of fine gold among divers other plates and and Coissants, which as he sware to me and divers other gentlemen were so curiouslie wrought, as he had not seene the like either in Italy, Spaine, or the Lowe Countries: and he was resolved that when they came to the hands of the Spanish king, to whom he had sent them by his Campmaster, they would appeer very admirable, especially being wrought by such a nation as had no Iron instrument at all, nor anie of those helps which our goldsmiths have to worke withall. The particular name of the people in Amapaia which gave him these peeces are called Anebas, and the river of Orenoque at that place is above 12. English miles brode, which may be from his out fall into the sea 700. or 800. miles.

This Province of Amapaia is a verie low and marish ground neere the river, and by reason of the red water which issueth out in small branches thorow the fenn7y and boggie ground there breed divers poysonfull wormes and serpents, and the Spaniards no suspecting, nor in anie sort foreknowing the danger were infected with a greevous kind of flux by drinking thereof, and even the very horses poisoned therewith: In so much as at the end of the six months that they abode there, of all there troops, there were not left above 120 soldiers, and neither horse nor cattle. For Berreo hoped to have found Guiana by 10000. miles neerer than it fell out to be in the end, by means whereof they sustained much want and much hunger, oppressed with greevous diseases, and all the miseries that could be imagined. I demanded of those in Guiana that had travelled Amapaia how they lived with that tawnie or red water when they travelled thither, and they told me that after the Sun was neere the middle of the skie, they used to fill their pots and pitchers with that water, but either before that time, or towards the setting of the Sun it was dangerous to drinke of, and in the night strong poison. I learned also of divers other rivers of that nature among them which were also (while the Sun was in the Meridian) verie safe to drink, and in the morning, evening, and night, wonderful dangerous and infective. From this Province Berreo hasted away as soon as the Spring and beginning of Summer appeared, and sought his entrance on the borders of Orenoque on the south side, but there ran a ledge of so high & impassable mountaines as he was not able by any means to march over them, continuing for the east sea into which Orenoque falleth, even to Quito in Peru: neither had he means to carrie victuall or munition over those craggie, high, and fast hills, being all woody, and those so thicke and spiny, and so full of prickles, thorns, and briers, as it is impossible to creepe thorow them: he had also neither friendship among the people, nor any interpreter to perswade or treate with them, and more to his disadvantage, the casique and Kings of amapaia had given knowledge of his purpose to the Guianians, and that he sought to sacke and conquer the Emprie, for the hope of their so great abundance and quantities of gold: he passed by the mouths of many great rives, which fell into Orenoque both from the north and south, which I forbeare to name for tediousnes, because they are more pleasing in describing than reading.

Berreo affirmed that there fell an hundred rivers into Orenoque from the north and south, whereof the lest was a big as Rio grande, that passeth between Popayan, and Nuevo reyno de granada (Rio grande being esteemed one of the renowmed rivers in al the west Indies, & numbered among the great rivers of the world:) But he knew not the names of any of these, but Caroli only, neither from what nations they descended, neither to what Provinces they led, for he had no meanes to discourse with the inhabitants at any time: neither was he curious in these things, being utterlie unlearned, & not knowing the east from the west. But of al these I got some knowledge, & of manie more, partly by mine own travel, & the rest by conference: of some one I learned one, of others the rest, having with me an Indian that spake many languages, & that of Guiana naturally. I sought out al the aged men, & such as were greatest travelers, and by the one & the other I came to understand the situations, the rivers, the kingdoms from the east sea to the borders of Peru, & from Orenoque southward as far as Amazones or Maragnon, and the regions of Maria Tamball, and of all the kings of Provinces and captains of townes and villages, how they stood in tearms of peace or war, and which were friends or enemies the one with the other, without which there can be neither entrance nor conquest in those parts, nor else where: Fro by the dissention between Guascar and Atabalipa, Pacaro conquered Peru, and by the hatred that the Traxcallians bare to Mutezuma, Cortez was victorious over Mexico, without which both the one and the other had failed of their enterprize, and of the great honor and riches, which they attained unto.

Now Berreo began to grow into despaire, and looked for no other success than his predecessors in this enterprize, untill such time as he arrived at the Province of Emeria towards the east sea and mought of the river, where he found a nation of people very favourable, and the countrey full of all manner of victual. The king of this land is called Carapana, a mana very subtill, and of great experience, being little lesse than 100. yeeres old: In his youth he was sent by his father into the Iland of Trinedado, by reason of civill warre among themselves, and was bred at a village, in that Iland, called Parico: at that place in his youth he had seene many Christians both French and Spanish, and went divers times with the Indians of Trinedado to Marguerita and Cumana in the west Indies, (for both those places have ever been releeved with victuall from Trinedado) by reason whereof he grew of more understanding, and noted the difference of the nations, comparing the strength and armes of his country with those of the Christians, and ever after temporized so, as whosoever else did amisse, or was wasted by contention, Carapana kept himself and his country in quiet and plentie: he also held peace with Caribas or Canibals his neighbors, and had free trade with all nations whosoever else had war.

Berreo soujourned and rested his weake troupe in the towne of Carapana six weeks, and from him learned the way and passage to Guiana, and the riches & magnificence thereof: but being then utterly disable to proceed, he determined to trie his fortune another yeere, when he had renewed his provisions, and regathered more force, which he hoped for as well out of Spain, as from Nuevo reyno, where he had left his son Don Anthonio Xemenes to second him upon the first notice given of his entrance, & so for the present embarqued himselfe in Canoas, & by the branches of Orenoque arrived at Trinedado, having from Carapana sufficient Pilots to conduct him. From Trinedado he coasted Paria, and so recovered Marguerita: and having made relation to Don Juan Sermiento the Governour of his proceeding, and perswaded him of the riches of Guiana, he obtained from thence 50 soldiers, promising presentlie to returne to Carapana, and so into Guiana. But Berreo meant nothing lesse at that time, for he wanted manie provisions necessarie for such an enterprize, and therefore departing from Marguerita seated himselfe in Trinedado, and from thence sent his Campmaster, and his Sargenant major back to the borders to discover the neerest passage, into the Emprie, as also to treat with the borderers, and to drawe them to his partie and love, without which, he knew he could neither passe safelie, nor in anie sort be releeved with victuall or ought else. Carapana directed this companie to a king called Morequito, assuring them that no man could deliver so much of Guiana as Morequito could, and that his dwelling was but five daies journey from Macureguarai, the first civill towne of Guiana.

Now your Lordship shall understand that this Morequito, one of the greatest Lords or Kings of the borders of Guiana, had two or three yeeres before beene at Cumana, and at Marguerita, in the west Indies, with great store of plates of gold, which he carried to exchange for such other things as he wanted in his owne countrey, and was dailie feasted, and presented by the governors of those places, and held amongst them some two months, in which time one Vides governor of Cuman wan him to be his conductor into Guiana, being allured by those Croissants and Images of gold which he brought with him to trade, as also by the ancient fame and magnificence of El Dorado: whereupon Vides sent into Spaine for a Patent to discover and conquer Guiana, not knowing of the precedence of Berreos patent, which as Berreo affirmeth was signed before that of Vides: so as when Vides understood of Berreo, and that he had made entrance into that territorie, and foregone his desire and hope, it was verilie thought that Vides practised with Morequito to hinder and disturbe Berreo in all he could, and not to suffer him to enter through his Seignory, nor anie of his companies, neither to victuall, nor guide them in anie sort; for Vides governor of Cumana, and Berreo were become mortall enemies, as well for that berreo had gotten Trinedado into his Patent with Guiana, as also in that he was by Berreo prevented in the journey of guiana itselfe: howsoever it was I know not, but orequito for a time disssembled his disposition, suffered Spaniards, and a Frier(which Berreo had sent to discover Manoa) to travell through his countrey, gave them a guide for Macureguarai the first towne of civill and apparelled people, from whence they had other guides to bring them to Manoa the great citie of Inga: and being furnished with those things, which they had learned of Carapana, were of most price in Guiana, went onward, and in eleven daies arrived at Manoa, as Berreo affirmeth for certain: although I could not be assured thereof by the Lord which now governeth the Province of Morequito, for he told me that they got all the gold they had, in other townes on this side Manoa, there being many very great and rich, and (as he said) built like the townes of Christians, with many roomes.

When these ten Spaniards were returned, and readie to put out of the border of Arromaia, the people of Morequito set upon them, & slew them all but one that swam the river, and tooke from them to the value of 40000.pesoes of golde, and as it is written in the storie of Job, one onelie lived to bring the newes to Berreo, that both his nine soldiers and holie father were benighted in the saide Province. I my selfe spake with the Captaines of Morequito that slew them, and was at the place where it was expectued. Berreo inraged heerewithall sent all the strength he could make into Arromaia, to be revenged of him, his people, and countrey: but Morequito suspecting the same fled over Orenoque, and thorow the territories of the Saima, and Wikiri, recovered Cumana, where he thought himselfe very safe with Vides the governor: But Berreo sending for him in the kings name, and his messengers finding him in the house of one Fashardo on the sudden ere it was suspected, so as he could not then be conveied away, Vides durst not deny him, as well to avoide the suspicion of the practise, as also for that an holy father was slaine by him and his people. Morequito offred Fashardo the weight of three quintals in gold, to let him escape, but the poore Guianian betraid of all sides was delivered to the Campmaster of Berreo, and was presented executed.

After the death of this Morequito, the soldiers of Berreo spoiled his territorie, & tooke divers prisoners, among others they tooke the uncle of Morequito called *Topiawari,* who is now king of Arromaia, (whose sonne I brought with me into England) and is a man of great understanding and pollicie: he is above 1`00. yeeres old, and yet of a very able bodie: the Spaniards led him in a chain 17. daies, and made him their guide from place to place betweene his countrey & Emeria the province of Carapana aforesaid, and was at last redeemed for 100. plates of gold, and divers stones called Piedras Hijada, or spleen stones. Now Berreo for executing of Morequito and other cruelties, spoiles, and slaughters done in Arromaia hath lost the love of the Orenoqueponi, and of all the borderers, and dare not send any of his soldiers any father into the land than to Carapana, which he calleth the port of Guiana: but from thence by the helpe of Carapana he had trade farther into the countrey, and alwaies appointed 10. Spaniards to reside in Carapanas towne, by whose favor and by being conducted by his people, those ten searched the countrey thereabouts as well for mines, as for other trades and commodities.

they have also gotten a nephew of Morequito, whom they have Christened and named Don Juan, of whom they have great hope, endeavouring by all means to establish him in the said province. Among manie other trades of those Spaniards used in Canoas to passe to the rivers of Barema, Pawroma, and Dissequebe, which are on the south side of the mouth of Orenoque, and there buy women and children from the Canibals, which are of that barbarous nature, as they will for 3. or 4. hatchets sell the sonnes and daughters of their owne brethren and sisters, and for somewhat more even their own daughters: heerof the Spaniards make great profit, for buying a maid of 12. or 13. yeeres for three or four hatchets, they sell them againe at Marguerita in the west Indies for 50. and 100. pesoes, which is so many crownes.

the master of my shipo Io. Douglas tooke one of the Canoas which came loden from thence with people to be sold, and the most of them escaped, yet of those hee brought, there was one as well favored, and as well shaped as ever I saw anie in England, and afterward I sawe many of them, which but for their tawnie colour may bee compared to anie of Europe. They also trade in those rivers for bread of Cassani, of which they buy an hundred pound weight for a knife, and sell it at Marguerita for ten pesoes. They also recover great store of cotten, brasill wood, and those beds which they call [13] Hamacas or brasill beds wherein in hot countries all the spaniards use to lie commonlie, and in no other, neither did we ourselves while we were there: By means of which trades, for ransom of divers of the Guianians, and for exchange of hatchets and knives, Berreo recovered some store of gold plates,

---

[13] Hammocks

eagles of gold, and Images of men and divers birds, and dispatched his Campmaster for Spaine with all that he had gathered, therewith to levy soldiers, and by the shew therof to draw others to the love of the enterprize: and having sent divers Images as well of men as beasts, birds and fishes so curiouslie wrought in gold, doubted not but to perswade the king to yeeld to him some further helpe, especiallie for that this land hath never been sacked, the mines never wrought, and in the Indies their works were well spent, and the gold drawn out with great labor and charge: he also dispatched messengers to his son in Nuevo reyno to levy all the forces he could, and to come down the river of Orenoque to Emeria, the province of Carapana, to meet him: he had also sent to **Sant** [14]**Iago de Leon** pm to the coast of the Caracas to buy horses and mules.

After I had thus learned of his proceedings past & purposes: I told him that I had resolved to see Guiana, and that it was the end of my journey, & the cause of my coming to Trinedado, as it was indeed, (& for that purpose I sent Ia. Whiddon the yeere before to get intelligence, with whom Berreo himselfe had speech at that time, and remembered how inquisitive Ia. Whiddon was of his proceedings, and of the countrey of Guiana,) Berreo was stricken into a great melancholoie and sadness, and used all the arguments he could to disswade me, and also assured the gentlemen of my company that it would be labor lost: and that they should suffer many miseries if they proceeded: And first he delivered that I could not enter anie of the rivers with any barke or pinace, nor hardly with anie ships bote, it was so low, sandie, and full of flats, and that his companies were daily grounded in their Canoas which drew but twelve inches water: he further saide that none of the countrey would come to speake with us, but would all flie, and if we followed them to their dwellings, they would burne their owne townes, and besides that the way was long, the winter at hand, and that the

---

[14] Othello

rivers beginning once to swell, it was impossible to stem the currant, and that we could not in those small botes by any means carry victuall for halfe the time, and that (which indeed most discouraged my company) the Kings and Lords of all the borders and of Guiana had decreed, that none of them should trade with any Christians for gold, because the same would be their owne overthrow, and that for the love of gold the Christians meant to conquer and dispossesse them of all together.

Many and the most of these I found to be true, but yet I resolving to make
rial of all whatsoever happened, directed Captaine George Gifford my Vice-admirall to take the Lions Whelpe, and Captaine Calfield his barke to turne to the eastward, against the brize what they could possible, to recover the mouth of a river called Capuri, whose entrance I had before sent Captaine Whiddon and Io. Douglas the master, to discover, who founde some nine foote water or better upon the flood, and five at lowe water, to whom I had given instructions that they shoulde ancor at the edge of the should, and upon the best of the flood to thrust over, which should John Douglas boyed and bekonned for them before: but they laboured in vain, for neither could they turne it up altogether so farre to the east, neither did the flood continue so long, but the water fell ere they coulde have passed the sands, as we after founde by a second experience: so as now we must either give over our enterprize, or leaving our ships at adventure 400. mile behind us, to run up in our ships botes, one barge, and two wherries, but being doubtfull how to carrie victuals for so long a time in such bables, or anie strength of men, especiallie for that Berreo assured us that his sonne must be by that time come downe with manie soldiers, I sent away one King master of the Lions whelp with his ships bote to trie another branch of a river in the bottome of the Bay of Guanipa, which was called Amana, to prove if there were water to be found for either of the small ships to enter: But when he came to the mouth of Amana, he found it as the rest, but staied not to discover it throughlie, because he was assured by an Indian his guide that the Canibals of Guanipa would assaile them with many Canoas, and that they shot poisoned arrowes, so as if he hasted not backe they should all be lost.

In the mean time fearing the worst I caused all the Carpenters we had to cut down a Gallego bote, which we meant to cast off, and to fit her with banks to row on, and in all things to prepare her the best they could, so as she might be brought to drawe but five foote, for so much we had on the bar of Capuri at lowe water: And doubting of Kings return I sent Io. Douglas againe in my long barge, as well to relieve him as also to make a perfect search in the bottom of that baie: For it hath been held for infallible that whatsoever ship or bote shall fall therein, can never dessemboque againe, by reason of the violent currant which setteth into the said bay, as also for that the brize and easterly wind bloweth directlie into the same, of which opinion I have heard John Hampton of Plimmouth one of the greatest experience of England, & divers others besides that have traded Trinedado.

I sent with John Douglas an old Cassique of Trinedado for a Pilot, who tolde us that we could not returne again by the bay or gulfe, but that he knew a by branch which ran within the land to the Eastward, and that he thought by it we might fall into Caupir, and so returne in fower daies: John Dowglas searched those rivers, and found fower goodly entrances, whereof the least was as bigge as the Thames at Woolwich, but in the baie thitherward it was shole and but six foote water, so as we were now without hope of any ship or barke to passe over, and therefore resolved to go on with the botes, and the bottome of the Gallego, in which we thrust 60. men: In the Lions whelps bote and wherrie we carried 20. Captaine Calfield in his wherrie carried ten more, and in my barge other ten, which made up a hundred: we had no other meanes but to carrie victuall for a moneth in the same, and also to lodge therein as we could, and to boile and dresse our meat. Captaine Gifford had with him Master Edw. Porter, captaine Eynos, and eight more in his wherrie with all their victuall, weapons, and provisions: Captain Calfield had with him my cosen Butshead Gorges and eight more. In the galley, of gent. and officers my selfe had Captaine Thyn, my cosen John Greenvile, my nephew John Gilbert, captaine whiddon, captaine Keymis, Edw. Hancocke, captaine Clarke, lieutenant Hewes, Tho. Upton, captaine Facy, Jerome Ferrar, Antho. Wells, Will. Connock and about 50. more. We could not learne of Berreo any other waie to enter but in branches, so farre to the windeward as it was impossible for us to recover: for we had as much sea to crosse over in our wherries as betweene Dover and Callys, and in a great billow, the winde and currant being both very strong, so as we were driven to go in those small botes directly before the winde into the bottome of the baie of Guanipa, and form thence to enter the mouth of some one of those rivers, which Io. Dowglas has last discovered, and had with us for Pilote an Indian of Barema, a river to the south of Orenoque, betweene that an Amazones, whose Canoas we had formerlie taken as he was going from the said Barema, laden with Cassui bread to sell at Marguerita: this Arwacan promised to bring me into the great river of Orenoque, but indeed of that which we entred he was utterly ignorant, for he had not seene it in twelve yeeres before, at which time he was very yoong, and of no judgement, and if God had not sentus another helpe, we might have wandred a whole yeere in that baorinth of rivers, ere we had found anyway, either out or in, especiallie after we were past the ebbing and flowing, which was in fower daies: for I know all the earth doth not yeeld the like confluence of streames and branches, the one crossing the other so many times, and all so faire and large, and so like one anther, as no man can tell which to take: and if we went by the Sun or compasse hoping thereby to go directly one way or other, yet that waie we were also carried in a circle amongst multitudes of Ilands, and every Iland so bordered with high trees, as no man could see any further than the breadth of the river, or length of the breach: But this it chanced that entering into a river, (which because it had no name we called the river of the Red Crosse, our selves being the first Christians that ever came therein:) the 22. of May as we were rowing up the same, we espied a small canoa with three Indians, which (by the swiftness of my barge, rowing with eight oares) I overtooke ere they could cross the river, the rest of the people on the banks shadowed under the thicke wood gazed on with a doubtfull conceit what might befall those three which we had taken: But when they perceived that we offred them no violence, neither entred their Canoa with any of ours, nor tooke out of the Canoa any of theirs, they then began to shew themselves on the banks side, and offred to traffique with us for such things as they had, and as we drewe neere they all staide, and we came with our barge to the mouth of a little creeke which came from their towne into the great river.

As we abode there a while, our Indian Pilot called Ferdinando would needs go ashore to their village to fetch some fruites, and to drinke of their artificiall wines, and also to see the place, and to know the Lord of it against another time, and tooke with him a brother of his which he had with him in the journey: when they came to the village of these people, the Lord of the Iland offred to lay hands on them, purposing to have slaine them both, yeelding for reason that this Indian of ours had brought a strange nation into their territorie to spoyle and destroy them: But the Pilot being quicke and of a disposed body slipt their fingers, and ran into the woods, and his brother being the better footman of the two, recovered the creekes mouth, where we staied in our barge, crying out that his brother was slaine, with that we set hands on one of them that was next us, a very old man, and brought him into the barge, assuring him that if we had not our Pilot againe, we would presently cut off his head. this old man being resolved that he should apie the losse of the other, cried out to those in the woods to save Ferdinando our Pilot, but they followed him notwithstanding, and hunted after him upon the foote with their Deere dogs, and with so maine a crie that all the woods eckoed with the shouted they made, but at last this poore chased Indian recovered the river side, and got upon a tree, and as w were coasting, leaped down and swam to the barge halfe dead with feare; but our good hap was, that we kept the other old Indian, which we handfasted to redeeme our Pilot withall, for being naturall of those rivers, we assured our selves he knew the way better than any stranger could, and indeed, but for this chance I thinke we had never founde the way either to Guiana, or backe to our ships: for Ferdinando after a few daies knew nothing at all, nor which way to turne, yea and many times the old man himselfe was in great doubt which river to take. those people which dwell in these broken Ilands & drowned lands are generally called Tiuitiuas, there are of them two sorts, the one called Ciawani, and the other Waraweete.

The great river of Orenoque or Baraquan hath nine branches which fall out on the north side of his owne maine mouth: on the south side it hath seven other fallings into the sea, so it desemboketh by 16. armes in al, betweene Ilands and broken ground, but the Ilands are verie great, manie of them as bigge as the Isle of Wight and bigger, and many lesse: from the first branch on the north to the last of the south it is as lest 100. leagues, so as the rivers mouth is no lesse than 300. miles wide at his entrance into the Sea, which I take to be farre bigger than that of Amazones: al those that inhabite in the mouth of this river upon the severall north branches are the these Tiuitiuas, of which there are two chiefe Lords which have continuall warres one with the other: the Ilands which lie on the right hand are called Pallamos, and the land on the lest Horotomaka, and the river by which John Dowglas returned within the land from Amana to Capuri, they call Macuri.

These Tiuitiuas are a verie goodlie people and verie valiant, and have the most manlie speech and most deliberate that ever I heard of what nation soever. In the summer they have houses on the ground as in other places: In the winter they dwell upon the trees, where they build very artificiall townes and villages, as it is written in the Spanish storie of the West Indies, that those people do in the low lands neere the gulfe of Uraba: for betweene May and September the river of Orenoke riseth thirtie foote upright, and then are those Ilands overflowen twentie foote high above the levell of the ground, saving some few raised grounds in the middle of them: and for this cause they are enforced to live in this manner. They never eate of anie thing that is set or sowen, and as at home they use neither planting nor other manurance, so when they come abroad they refuse to feede of ought, but of that which nature without labor bring either foorth. They use the tops of Palmitos for bread, and kill Deere, fish and porks for the rest of their sustenance, they have also manie sorts of fruits that grow in the woods, and great varietie of birds and foule.

And if to speake of them were not tedious and vulgare, surely we sawe in those passages of very rare colours & forms, not else where to be found, for as much as I have either seen or read. Of those people those that dwell upon the branches of Orenoque called Capuri and Macureo, are for the most part Carpenters of Canoas, for they make the most and fairest houses, and sell them into Guiana for gold, and into Trinedado for Tobacco, in the excessive taking whereof, they exceede all nations, and notwithstanding the moistness of the aire in which they live, the hardnes of their diet, and the great labors they suffer to hunt, fish, and foule for their living, in all my life either in the Indies or in Europe did I never behold a more goodlie or better favoured people, or a more manlie. They were woont to make warre upon all nations, and especially on the Canibals, so as none durst without a good strength trade by those rivers, but of late they are at peace with their neighbors, all holding the spaniards for a common enimie. When their commanders die, they use great lamentation, and when they thinke the flesh of their bodies is putrified, and fallen from the bones, then they take up the carcase againe, and hag it in the Caiquies house that died, and decke his skull with feathers of all colours, and hang all his gold plates about the bones of his armes, thighes, and legges. Those nations which are called Arwacas which dwell on the south of Orenoque, (of which place and nation our Indian Pilot was) are dispersed in manie other places, and do use to beate the bones of their Lords into powder, and their wives and friends drinke it all in their severall sorts of drinks.

After we departed from the port of these Ciawani, we passed up the river with the flood, and ancored the ebbe, and in this sort we went onward. The third daie that we entred the river our Calley came on ground and stuck so fast, as we thought that even there our discovery had ended, and that we must have left 60. of our men to have inhabited like rookes upon trees with those nations: but the next morning, after we had cast out all her ballast, with tugging and hauling to and fro, we got her afloate, and went on: At fower daies ende wee fell into as goodlie a river a ever I beheld, which was called the great Amana, which ran more directlie without winding sand turnings than the other. But soone after the flood of the sea left us, and we enforced either by maine strength to row against a violent currant, or to returne as wise as we went out, we had then no shift but to perswade the companies that it was but two or thee daies worke, and therefore desired them to take paines, every gentleman and others taking their turns to row, and to spell one the other at the hours end. Everie daie we passed by goodlie branches of rivers, some falling form the west, others from the east into Amana, but those I leave to the description in the Chart of discoverie, where everie shall be named with his rising and descent. When three daies more were overgone, our companies began to despaire, the weather being extreame hot, the river bordered with verie high trees that kept away the aire, and the currant against us every daie stronger than the other: But we evermore commanded our Pilots to promise an end the next daie, and used it so long as we were driven to assure them from fower reaches of the river to three, and so to two, and so to the next reach: but so log we laboured as many daies were spent, and so driven to draw ourselves to harder allowance, our bread even at the last, and no drinke at all: our men and our selves so wearied and scorched, and doubtfull withall whether we should ever performe it or no, the heat encreasing as we drew towards the line; for wee were now in five degrees.

The farther we went on (our victuall decreasing and the aire breeding great faintness) we grew weaker and weaker when we had most need of strength and abilitie, for howerlie the river ran more violently than other against us, and the barge, wherries, the ships bote of Captaine Gifford, and Captain Calfied, had spent all their provisions, so as wee were brought into despaire and discomfort, had we not perswaded all the companie that it was but onlie one daies worke more to attaine the lande where we should ... 17z [p45 l]:

If my tears are shed as I sit alone and weep for them, then it is out of a love that cannot be repaid and I seek no reward. I cannot pity those men who died in innocence because their spirits are still among us, and if the thought of them causes a man to wake from his sleep through fear of his own conscience then it is just.

Some Extracts of Entries from Henslowe's Diaries

And here [15]"The entries, in [16]Henslowe's diary beginning on February 23, 1591-2, when Lord Strange's men were performing, are as follows (the Spanish Tragedie (according to Schick):- (s.d. Shillings and Pennies).

[R{eceive}d at spanes comodye donne oracoe, the 23 of February

xiiis dvi

Rd at the comodey of done oracio, the 13 of marche 1591   xxixs

Rd at [17]Jeronymo, the 14 of marche 1591   £iii vis

---

[15]From The Works of Thomas Kyd by Frederick S. Boas OBE, MA HON, LLD., HON. D.LITT., F.R.S.L. 1954

[16]Henslowe's diary records 2 lost plays March 1588/9 £6.00 to dramatists Chettle and Porter for a play called "The Spencers". See Non-Shakespearean table of plays

Sir Walter Raleigh on the other hand, was the Twel*fth* Knight, because he was knighted on 12th Night at the Feast of the Epiphany on the 12th January 1585: at Hampton Court, and there he was honoured for his bravery at the Battles of Montconteur and Jarnac; for his former bravery in Ireland under the Leadership of Lord Grey in 1581 and Queen Elizabeth I awarded and rewarded him with 40,000 acres in Ireland and Lismore Castle: where he penned such lines as 'the face that launched a thousand ships' and thereafer Walter Ralegh introduced Edumund Spenser to Court and the Queen she cried: 'Ralegh! when will you cease to be a beggar': and he replied : 'When your Majesty ceases to be a Patron!'

+The most interesting and beautiful of all Shakespeare's works are the Sonnets. His passion for soniteering withered out of fashion after the Sonnets were published; and yet Sir Philip Sidney was the greatest Elizabethan poet and soniteer: Sir Philip Sidney, was two years younger than Raleigh born in 1554 and Raleigh survived him by 22 years. Sidney died at Arhnem after an attack on a food convoy, in Flanders, after the battle of Zutphen and his father in law, Sir Francis Walsingham the 'Spymaster' of the Catholics, together with the Earl of Essex, brought home the personal effects of Sir Philip Sidney, including his sword, which he bequeathed to The Second Earl of Essex, Robert Devereux. Essex married Sir Philip Sidney's widow, Frances Walsingham in the year 1589 and Essex incurred the Wrath of the Queen.

Rd at Jeronymo, the 20 of marche 1591 xxxciiis
Rd at done oracio, the 30 marche 1591   xxxviiis
Rd at Jeronymo, the 31 of marche 1591   £iii
Rd at Jeronymo, the 7 of aprell 1591   xxvis
Rd at the comedey of Jeronymo, the 10 of aprell 1591   xxviiis
Rd at Jeronymo, the 14 aprell 1591   xxxiiis
Rd at the comodey Jeronymo, the 22 of aprell 1591   xviis
Rd at Jeronymo, the 24 of aprell 1592   xxviiis
Rd at Jeronymo, the 2 of maye 1592   xxxivs
Rd at Jeronymo, the 9 ofo maye 1592   xxvis
Whittson-tyde. Rd at Jeronymo, the 13 of maye 1592   £111 ivs

Rd at the comodey of Jeronymo, the 21 of maye 1592   xxviiis
Rd at Jeronymo, the 22 of maye 1592   xxviis
Rd at Jeronymo, the 27 of maye 1592   xxiiis
Rd at Jeronymo, the 9 of june 1592   xxviiis
Rd at Jeronymo, the 18 of june 1592   xxivs
Rd at the comodey of Jeronymo, the 20 of June 1592   xivs
Rd at Jeronymo, the 30 of desembr 1592   £111 viiis
Rd at Jeronymo, the 8 of janeary 1593   xxiis
Rd at Jeronymo, the 22 of jeneway 1593   xxs

From January 23, 1593, there is no record by Henslowe of any representation
of 'Jeronymo' or 'done oracio' till January 7, 1597, when the Lord Admiral's
players were performing. During 1597 the following entries appear in the
Diary.

7 of jeneway 1597 Rd at Joronymo   £iii
11 of jeneway 1597 Rd at Joranymo   xxxxs
17 of jeneway 1597 Rd at Joronymo   xixs
Janeary 31, Rd at Joronymo   1 04/01 15 06
Febreary 9,Rd at Joronymo   00 17/04 15 02
Marche 8, Rd at Joronymo   01 01/00 03 04
Aprille 21, Rd at Jeronymo   00 17/00 03 04
Maye 4, Rd at Joronymo   00 11/07 14 00
Maye 25, Rd at Joronymo   00 19/00 14 06
June 20, Rd at Joronemo   00 14/00 00 00
July 19, Rd at Jeronemo   01 00/01 13 01
October 11, Rd at Jeroneymo   02 00/01 13 00

Sir Walter Raleigh arrives at Queen Elizabeth's Court, 1581

During the Summer of 1581 Queen Elizabeth and her courtiers were in residence at Hampton Court.

Walter Raleigh had left his home in Islington which he had shared with Thomas Harriott in a mood of great excitement.

Raleigh, at the age of 29 was not a wealthy man and he therefore possessed no expensive clothing or jewellery with which he could hope to impress the aristocracy at Court. He still spoke with a Devonshire accent and had retained his country manners to a certain extent. Nevertheless, the Earl of Leicester had assured Raleigh that he would be a great asset to the Queen's Court and that he could hope for a position of some importance after a suitable period of time had elapsed: perhaps finding a place in the Queen's diplomatic service. Raleigh had gained a knowledge of English law at Middle Temple, which he had just left. Perhaps he could join the Queen's bodyguard and put to good use the knowledge he had gained during his military service in France under his cousin Arthur Champernoun, during the French religious civil wars and then in Ireland, where he had served under Lord Grey and now he had an intense dislike for Grey.

The Queen had already heard of Walter Raleigh through reports from Kate Ashley, Raleigh's Great Aunt, and no sooner had the Queen been reminded that Raleigh's mother was a Champernoun, Elizabeth had warmed immediately to the suggestion that Raleigh should be invited to join the Court.

Another member of that well loved family, Kate Champernoun, had been Queen Elizabeth's governess when she was a child and her father, King Henry VIII had sent her as a child to live at Hatfield House in Hertfordshire. There, Kate had helped to educate the future Queen of England in the classical style which had included being taught to dance, ride horses, play the virginals and to take part in archery; in addition of course to lessons in needlework, which had been Elizabeth's least favourite pastime, which she had endeavored to avoid wherever possible even to the extent of feigning illness. But Kate had always been kind to her, and understood her likes and dislikes, and she had therefore been firm but kind to Elizabeth. Frequent reports of Elizabeth's progress had been sent to King Henry VIII at Hampton Court and because Elizabeth had always adored her Father, she had therefore, tried extremely hard to impress him, right up until his death in 1547, when she had been just 14 years old.

As Raleigh continued on his journey in the hired shining black coach drawn by two black, one dappled and one brown horse, he had decided that the interior of the coach was not well matched to its appearance on the outside, since it was cold and draughty. He felt uncomfortable as the coach bumped and swayed along the winding lanes leading to Richmond and his long legs were becoming stiff because he could not stretch them out and his feet were already numb, despite his thick leather boots and woollen stockings. He looked down again at his hands and noticed that they were turning a combination of reddish and mottled blue, because he had failed to find his leather gloves among his luggage and must have left them in Islington because he had left in such a rush that morning. It all seemed such a long time ago. He was sure they would be adopted by Thomas Harriott quite readily. And yet only a few short hours had passed by. As he rubbed his hands together in an effort to warm them he turned his mind away from his present discomfort and began thinking excitedly about his future.

What would life be like at Court? Would he enjoy living among those great men, such as the Earl of Oxford and the Earl of Leicester? Or the more difficult personalities, such as Sir Francis Walsingham who had been nicknamed the Queen's spy or was more popularly known as the "Great Spymaster of the Catholics" because of his efforts to counteract Catholic worship; was it really true that Walsingham had devised a system of counter espionage against the Catholics, after he had witnessed the Massacre of the Huguenot's from the French

HIC JACET: SIR WALTER RALEIGH

Embassy at Paris? Those thoughts belonged to the darker side of life at Queen Elizabeth's court and Raleigh would not permit his mind to dwell upon them for too long.

There were, indeed, more interesting personalities at Court, such as Christopherus Hatton, one of the Queen's favorites. Raleigh had heard that Christopherus Hatton was in love with the Queen with such an intensity of feeling that he had sworn never to marry! Hatton was, by all accounts, a very talented dancer, and it was said that the Queen chose him as a dancing partner at all the Balls and Masques which were frequently held at Court and whilst the court was in progress.

These thoughts which occupied Raleigh's mind were mere snippets of information which he had heard second hand. And yet, soon enough he would be able to call upon his own senses to vouchsafe their truth or otherwise. His experiences would then become as a mirror to his soul and would be recorded there for time itself to call upon.

As the coach finally entered the great gates of Hampton Court Raleigh suddenly felt apprehensive as he saw in the distance the ladies and courtiers walking in the grounds dressed in their magnificent attire and he knew that he knew that his own dark clothing looked shabby in comparison.

The coach in which he travelled brought him unwanted attention, and he knew that he would have to face the crowds of inquisitive courtiers before he felt ready to do so. As he climbed down from his carriage and was greeted by several bystanders, one of whom was a young and impudent youth who pointed down at Raleigh's boots which were muddied and stained with wear, he and started to laugh and nudged the lady standing next to him, who hid her smiles behind her hand.

"Are you on an errand Sir? May we assist you?"

"I am newly arrived at Court and in search of my great aunt, Kate Ashley".

"Ah, a Devon man! mimmicked the youth, (and he turned to the lady and said "He need not have brought half of it with him on the soles of his boots!)"

"And you Sir, are no doubt the Court wit!"

"I Sir! Am I Francis Bacon, the son of the late Nicholas Bacon once Keeper of the Great Seal of England".

"Then you are indeed honored!" said Raleigh angrily and just as he was about to say more, a tall and elegant looking man approached him and said he was Lord Cumberland.

"Pay no attention to young Bacon, he is trying to impress the ladies"

"Well he certainly would not do so by looks alone" replied Raleigh, and they walked together into Hampton Court.

As Raleigh moved away from the crowd and went in search of his Great Aunt, but he knew that his pride would get the better of him unless he could rapidly improve his situation at the Court and so he resolved to do so.

Here he would meet Lord Burleigh - The Queen's "spirit", the Earl of Leicester her "eyes", the Duke of Anjou "her Frog" and Sir Francis Walsingham "her Spy".

As the years passed by ad Raleigh became familiar with the ways of the court life, he grew wiser by design. Her Majesty, Queen Elizabeth, through her own wisdom had taught him to be seen to comply with her Ministers for effect. And this he became rather good at.

One of the many interesting events which took place at Hampton Court will be described below.

It had all begun when the Queen had woken in a peculiar mood the morning before, and had shown her obstinacy to her Ladies in Waiting, by refusing to leave her bed until she had been brought a bowl of comfits, having no regard for her teeth whatsoever. As the Queen lay propped u-pon her feather pillows, an idea came swiftly into her mind, as she enjoyed her comfits, putting them into her mouth one after another, and chewing vigorously, her jaw pausing while she paused for thought every now and then, as she began to dwell upon this idea:

Perhaps she would knight Walter Raleigh - he had shown great skill as a politician and possessed a great wit. Moreover he was a man of great courage which had displayed at the Battles of Jarnac and Montcontour and in Ireland. His courage in its turn, gave her courage.

Therefore the Queen was determined to knight him in the face of opposition. Of course, she knew that Raleigh adhered to the Roman Catholic faith (and she herself still retained fond memories of her instruction in that religion, which she had received through her sister, Mary Tudor, who had imprisoned her in the White Tower at the Tower of London until she had relinquished her Protestant faith, after the death of her father.

Queen Mary had tried to unit Spain and England, wishing only to bring the country back to a peaceful Realm and Mary had been the wife of King Philip of Spain who had appeared to live only to worship his faith and count his treasure. If only her father, King Henry VIII had not broken with Rome ... then she too would still be able to worship in the Roman Catholic faith. Her mother, Anne Boleyn would still be alive and would never have married King Henry ... instead she would have married Henry Percy of Syon.

The Queen shivered suddenly and began to feel a chill as the room seemed to cool. Was it her imagination, or did the room darken slightly and as these thoughts passed through her mind? Wat is that the spirit of her poor father was here with her now, watching over her?

Putting these thoughts into her mind. Perhaps he was unable to rest because of the wrong he had done to his people and to his wives and to her poor mother.

The Queen sighed miserably, and lay back against her pillows, casting aside her half eaten bowl of comfits, which her lady took from her, putting them on a small wooden table near the huge window.

The Queen then felt suddenly agitated and fell into a mood of complainment. She proceeded in the first instance to complain of a pain in the left side of her neck and ordered that the room be warmed immediately for her before she could leave her bed.

Bess Throckmorton, her Maid of Honour who had arrived at the court the year before, arranged for the fire to be lit and when the room was warm enough she assisted the Queen as she dressed. Still the Queen complained. Her ruff, she said was too sharp and stiff and in future she would have her own court ruffmaker to live at the Palace, to design and make her ruffs. If such a ruffmaker could not be found in London then one must be brought to her from Holland.

"Bess! This ruff is too stiff and itchy and I will not entertain it about my neck. It is not at all what I had in mind. Neither is it white enough - being so dully that it looks as if it were washed in ditchwater. I will have the Professor of Ruffmaking brought to me. Have you arranged for Mistress Dingham Vander Plasse to instruct my ruffmaker on how to make a tolerable ruff? I asked you to do that last week. Have you made enquiries for me? I just don't know why I didn't think of it before: Ruffs made from a material called holland by a woman from Holland, that will be fun won't it?"

"Yes your majesty" said Bess, trying to sound as enthusiastic as possible but she was beginning to tire of the complaints far too quickly, considering it was so early in the morning.

I know that Mistress Dingham has set herself up in a little shop in Cheapside and is renowned throughout London." continued Bess as she began removing the ruff from the Queen's neck. "And I understand that Mistress Vander Plasse charges four to five pounds for the instruction of ruffmaking, and another twenty shillings if the ruffmakers are to be instructed on how to make the starch for the completed ruffs. I thought perhaps it was a little expensive and I was trying to procure information on another ruffmaker before I presented you with the final figures in comparison, your majesty".

"Do not keep calling me Majesty!" shouted the Queen as she stamped her foot and turned round to face Bess. "I would ask you to call me Bess, but you are Bess, and therefore I am Elizabeth, because that is after all my name, except in company of course. You know how to observe etiquette and therefore I do not have to explain to you that it is of immense importance to me that my servants and friends alike must show me the respect worthy of my position."

Anyway, the expense of the ruffs is of no concern to me. Well, I mean it is of concern to me if others spend my money without my knowledge, but not if I wish my money to be spent on myself to bring me comfort" and then the Queen giggled at her use of the word comfort when she had just finished a bowl of comfits. "Just arrange it with Mistress Dingham Vander Plasse and all will be well. I must have a new ruff to wear for the Banquet on the 12th Night! It will be pure white and laced with golden threads and sparkling with tiny diamonds."

Mistress Dingham Vander Plasse
and her shop at Cheapside, London - 1564

Young Mistress Angelique Dingham Vander Plasse, a poor, headstrong and very talented Flemish ruff maker, sailed for England in 1564. She was a short lady with keen eyesight and a shock of blonde curls which framed her otherwise plain face. Even though she had reached the somewhat mature age of 28, she had not been enticed into marriage or even considered for the role of a wife by any young man who had taken it upon himself to know more of her character. her temperament was such that many who knew her well, avoided upsetting her for fear that she would fly into a violent rage, where her face would become so red with anger that they feared for their own safety. The reason for her great anger, stemmed mainly from the death of her beloved father when she had been 13 years old. This came at a time when she had been receiving tuition from him in the highly esteemed art of ruffmaking. he often referred to a book which he brought down from a high shelf in his shop, with great frequency, written in his own fine handwriting. That book contained his own secret and very successful recipes for the making of a fine startch, and the methods he used to weave gold and silver threads for the ruffs which he exported to London, and sold to the Royal Court. Her father had often told her that one day it would all be passed to her and upon his death, Mistress Dingham had thought the book so precious that she had named it her own book of secrets and she had hidden it away from her mother, fomerly Mistress Arabelle Vrillon a French woman, realising that one day it would make her own fortune, when she was old enought to put it to good use.

Her father's untimely death had necessitated the shop being closed for two years, whilst her moth continued to mourn her husband. This action by Arabelle Vrillon, had caused her young daughter to go without the pleasant aspects of life, such as riding in the carriage with a little silver bell dangling from its roof, that had previously chimed to amuse her and had been put there by her father, when she was a child of 8 years old to mark her birthday. It was not long after the carriage had been disposed of, that their grand house near the river was sold.

All that the young Mistress Dingham had left was the little silver bell and the hidden book of secrets. Gone were the fine gowns she had been used to wearing, and the soft fur lined slippers that had once warmed her feet. When she complained about her lack, her mother would tell her that her father had been over indulgent with her and that she must make the best of things as they were.

It was true that her mother had tried to continue making the ruffs that her father had once produced. But without the book of secrets her starch was too heavy and lumpy, the threads of silver and gold could not be made and the customers ceased to recommend their friends and neighbours to the Dingham Vander Plasse business. Her mother appeared to have no control over a needle and thread the way her father had. Her mother would not allow her to assit with the family business in any way, in order to perform the tasks of her dead father. The result was that faults and errors were found in her work, time and again and the unhappy customers came in their droves to angrily demand their money back from her tearful and weak-willed mother.

As the Dingham family fortune dwindled to dangerously low proportions, causing them to live in reduced circumstances, young Mistress Dingham found that with each passing year, her love for her mother decreased and Angelique's temper grew more intolerable. She had never forgivewn her mother for her failings and it was not too soon for her when her mother passed away. No tears were shed upon her death, and since she had waited patiently for the day when she could leave Holland and make her way into London, she wasted no time in booking a passage for herself on the first ship that was due to leave her homeland. She had heard that a fortune was to be made for the talented among her own profession. She had remembered all that she had been taught by her father, and even though her mother had refused to allower her to work as a ruffmaker, young Angelique soon found that her skills returned and she even told herself that she possessed a fine gift indeed.

She carried with her on her voyage, the carefully preserved stock, which she proudly called her inheritance from her mother, and that being no more than 12 large rolls of the precious material known as white lawn. With this cache of material, she meant to make her fortune and she saw to it that they were carefully laid down and covered securely in the hold of the ship. Many who sailed to foreign lands had lost their fortunes through storm damage to their goods upon the ships, but Mistress Dingham was one of the more fortunate beings of those times. As she waited for her goods to be unloaded, she held her breath. Seeing that all was safe, she let out a great sigh of relief and hailed a carriage for herself in Portsmouth.

Mistress Van der Plasse, as she later became known, made her way into London by coach, which she managed to pay for, by pinching a penny or two from the dwindlingn funds in her purse, which she had brought with her after a long period of careful saving for that very day. She resolved to take to take great care when chosing a location for her future business, and settled upon the idea of renting a handsome shop with a bow fronted leaded window in Cheapside, where she could display her fine handiwork.

Thereafter, she found it to be the best possible place to make, display and sell her own ruffs. Cheapside was indeed, as she had noted immediately upon her arrival, the most fashionable area to buy clothing in London. She had taken a great interest in studying the rows of bow fronted shops and noted with great satisfaction the inferior ruffs on display. She gave a hearty chuckle toherself and moved along.

As Mistress Dingham walked slowly along Cheapside, she found that the shopkeepers displayed their goods to their own great advantage, and colourful velvet suits, trimmed with silver jewellery were displayed in this shop and the delicate silk hats to be worn indoors and out, in that shop. Breeches that buttoned at the knee, others that tied below the knee and were to be worn with stockings. Some stockings, she noted, were even sewn to the breeches and were known as wholehose. There were fine Doublets, slashed to show a second colour of silk beneath, indicating wealth, just as she had heard that they were the fashion in the days of King Henry VIII.

If she had been poor upon her arrival in London, she soon found that her fortune had changed within a very short time. Dutch women were sent for and put to work in her workroom in Cheapside, it being a shop of great proportions with room enough at the front and rear to fulfill all her expectations.

Up until the second year of Queen Elizabeth's reign, all ruffs were made froma material known as holland and they were over stiff, too full of starch and very plain.

With the appearance of Mistress Dingham Vander Plasse, who proclaimed herself as a Professor of her art, she changed the style of ruff-making in England and her elegant ruffs were in great demand with the most popular ladies and Earls, the Lords and highly esteemed gentlemen aliek. None wishing to appear in public dressed in the old fashioned style of ruff.

Mistress Dingham grew so famous that within a very short time, the Queen herself had heard of her, and would thereafter, have no ruff made by any other than Mistress Angelique Dingham Vander Plasse, who visited Hampton Court Palace to measure the proportions of the Queen herself.

Mistress Dingham was indeed a notable lady and could be seen at the London Bourse conducting her financial business at the Royal Exchange where she flourished into a leading business women of her age.

Another Scene at the Palace of Hampton Court

Returning to Hampton Court, it was to be noted by the Court Reporter of her time, Mr Henry Wootton, that the Queen proceeded to complain that her hair was too short to be dressed with the jewels which she desired to wear to the Banquet on the Feast of the Ephiphany and that her teeth were in need of attention if she were to smile freely at her admirers and never to hide behind her waving fan.

Bess Throckmorton felt that she could speak plainly to the Queen and suppressing her former annoyance at the Queen's earlier complainments, enjoyed this opportunity to say "You must not forget to rub your teeth with your solution! Remember, Sir Hugh Platt said that 'Men must not clean their teeth with Aqua fortis, lest within a few dressings they would probably be forced to borrow a rank!' - Instead, you must rub gently with a mixture of powdered pumice stone and brick and coral which will remove the stain effectively. It will after all add to your comfort if you must enjoy your comfits"

The Queen was not amused at Bess's forthrightness and replied grumpily "If I continue to rub with the apothecary's concoction I will indeed borrow a rank before the Banquet and instead of my comfort my mouth will bleed again."

"But your Majesty, you must look to your teeth and take care not to entertain your liking for too many sweet foods - they will do you ill."

"How dare you tell me that my teeth will make me look ill. How dare you! You are a mere servant to me and you will observe your place in my Court, lest you find yourself relegated to my kitchens. Do you hear me. Answer me directly."

Bess turned away slowly because she was crying. It had all become too much for her and she did not know how to please the Queen on such a morning. Everything she said was wrong. Everything she did was wrong when the Queen was in a contrary mood.

HIC JACET: SIR WALTER RALEIGH

The Queen turned to look at Bess and noticed that she was crying silently and pretending that she was pinning up her dark braided hair, which had tumbled loose and was starting to fall about her shoulders.

"Oh Bess! I am sorry! Please don't cry. You know how it upsets me. Do you know that of all my Ladies in Waiting, my liking for you is greater than the rest of the Court ladies together. And if I am sharp with you, then remember that I do not mean to be so. It is just that I have so many things to bother me, and I know not how to express my discomfort at them. I hate Banquets but I love them as much again. I love the attention, but I hate my appearance now and then. You speak too freely sometimes, and I like not the truth!"

Then the Queen stood up and started to pace the room as excitedly as a young girl of sixteen. "Listen Bess! I have a wonderful idea and it is but playing on a pun! I aim to knight Walter Raleigh on Twelfth Knight and he will be my Twelfth Knight."

"But that is the Feast of the Epiphany ... please do not reveal Walter Raleigh's religion to the Court! It will put him in great danger with Sir Francis Walsingham."

And then the Queen sat down so that Bess could continue to dress the Queen's hair with pearls.

"Come now Bess, there is nothing to worry about. How many of the Lords and Ladies of my court will connect a pun with the Holy day of Obligation? Anyway, by the time the night of the Banquet arrives there will be no turning back and no will one dare to interfere. I am in the good for gaiety and I will have preparations made for the greatest Banquet this Court has ever seen. In the meantime I wish to see no more tears fall from your eyes. It saddens me."

"Remember, it is our secret until the very night. Only you and I alone will know of it. You can keep a secret can't you Bess?"

Bess composed herself, being of a complacent nature and luckily for her, Penelope Rich (or Lady Perrott), who was also in the room, but standing on the other side, stepped forward to speak to the Queen.

Lady Perrott had been busy arranging a vase of flowers, containing freesias and nasturtiums, which she brought forward to show to the Queen, setting them down before her with great pride, to display her own handiwork. She had also been listening to the conversation which had taken place regarding Walter Raleigh, since she could not tolerate his presence even in the smallest of measures, and thought him far too proud and too full of wit that had made him the Queen's favourite. Not to mention his Devon accent! In view of the Queen's fond attention to her brother, the 20 year old Robert Devereux, the 2nd Earl of Essex, Raleigh could only be seen as a threat to their secret designs upon the Queen's favour. Raleigh had no blood connections with the Queen as her brother did, being the Queen's second cousin. Raleigh's constant quips about her brother being the poorest Earl in England had irked her beyond words and she therefore sought any opportunity to bring him into disfavor with the Queen. It would take time perhaps but she would work towards her goal by subtle means as all important ladies of the Court must do.

At the very moment that the Queen's eyes beheld Lady Perrott, her mood lightened considerably, since they were firm friends and the Queen readily accepted her advice, partially because she could not decide whether she loved Walter Raleigh more than the Earl of Essex of vice versa. Today she was in a mood to tease them both! She remembered how the poverty stricken Earl would fly into a rage when she last called him to her side and complained of his crumpled clothing and lack of bejewelled attire, as she whispered into his ear the words:

"Earl of March"

to remind him of his descent in the Royal line and through the victory of Crecy the longevity of the 100 year War which brought about his ruin in that line of descent.

"If you live for 100 years, my dear Lord of Essex, you will still be my Earl of March."

The Queen also noticed that Bess was becoming increasingly interested in Walter Raleigh and therefore she must work her designs to find out as much as possible by taking Bess into her confidence.

"Oh, I could not help overhearing your sharpness to Bess, Elizabeth! It is most unfair. You must rid yourself of your gloomy mood. Did I hear the word Banquet mentioned? How I adore such pass-times. If you are worried about your teeth then I will find Sir Hugh Platt - he has a recipe which will interest you." said Lady Perrot

"Yes, you are right, since I am in no mood for any more of these preparations. I will have a rest now and you may go and amuse yourself Bess."

The Queen then turned all her attention to Lady Perrott and asked "Have you seen Robert this morning? What is he doing? Go and find him for me Penelope would you? And send him to me quickly if you will. Oh, and tell him to send Sir Hugh Platt promptly, when he has found him.

Now go! Leave me in peace both of you. Amuse yourselves elsewhere said the Queen as she waved her hand to dismiss them."

Bess Throckmorton and Lady Perrott left the room and both of them breathed a sign of relief behind the closed doors of the Queen's apartment. They hurried through the Halls of Hampton Court, their long dresses rustling behind them, in their efforts to seek out Robert Devereux. And yet it was not difficult to locate him, since they had only to ask where all the prettiest ladies of the Court were occupying themselves, and they were promptly directed to the Music Hall. Once they had entered the hall they found themselves weaving in and out of the crowd of spectators.

As they walked through the Hall Bess noticed Sir Francis Walsingham and Francis Bacon standing together in the background observing the crowd as patiently as hawks, as they usually did, in order to see what they might otherwise miss in the way of court intrigue. Bess reminded herself that she must keep a watchful eye on Walsingham from now on since Walter Raleigh was about to become one his enemies.

Then they passed Lord Grey and his entourage, where Sir Philip Sidney stood enduringly, as he felt it was his duty to know the present political climate within the Court. There he appeared to official observers, such as Walsingham, bored with the conversation going on around him and he wore a sad countenance which was typically noticed.

Sidney seemed as though he were detached and in another world entirely: as he stood tall, and tapping his foot to the music so well that we may find if we search his mind entirely, thoughts of Mary Queen of Scots as he repeated to himself the words from his sonnets "XXX ... 'If in the Scotch Court be no weltring yet: These questions busy wits to me do frame; I, cumbred with good manners, answer do, But know not how. For still I think of you'. Sidney continued to ponder how he may continue to write his Sonnets perhaps for dear Queen Mary of Scots the prisoner of vicious malice and hatred of the Roman religion and yet still remain annonymous to the Court:

"And Love doth hold my hand and makes me write... to XLV: Of lovers' ruin some thrice tragedy, I am not I, pity the tale of me." Sir Philip Sidney, Sonnets

(Iago: "In compliment externitis not long after but I will wear my heart upon my sleeve for Daws to peck at: I am not what I am." William Shakespeare

See Raleigh's account of Guiana : *Iago*)

The musicians who were organized into groups, were practising the harpsichord and the virginals, the spinet, and the viol - under the tuition of the great Master of music of their age: William Byrd, who was himself an organist and composer {1543 to 1623}, who had been awarded the Monopoly of Royal Grant for printing music and music papers for 21 years. Also instructing the musicians was John Bull, who had been brought in from Gresham College where he served as a Professor of Music {1562 to 1628}, in order that he give expert tuition. Bull was a musician and an organist and had once been a chorister at the Chapel Royal at the age of 9.

And then of course John Dowland, who had just returned to London for the occasion, and he was indeed a famous lutist who had spread the fame of English music throughout Europe, having travelled to Brunswick, Hesse, Venice, Florence, Bologna and Nurnberg.

William Byrd was commanding the largest audience and he walked among the players he was tutoring, who sat in a wide circle holding their instruments - or they were sitting at their instruments. He was giving them instruction and a little of the history of the viol (the ancestor to the violin) which he took care to mention in order to entertain the interested spectators to whom he now spoke in a raised voice so that all could hear him.

"Viols are four of a type:

First we have the Treble, or Descant Viol. Stand up Master Harris and display your instrument to the interested Ladies and Gentlemen of the Court! Hold it up higher so that they can view it!"

Byrd then turned to the rest of the musicians who waited patiently for his instruction, and he continued:

"As I call out in order to name the instrument which you are about to play, you should do as Master Harris is doing, and walk within this circle (and he moved his arm wide to outline the movement), and thus you will display your instrument when I tell you to do so, which will be when I have finished speaking!

Next we have the Tenor Viol or Viola da Braccio

Then as you will see, the Bass Viol or Viola da Gamba, and finally the Double Bass Viol or Violone!

All these instruments possess of six strings and tuning is done with fourths, with a one-third between the third and fourth strings.

Please be seated and tune your instruments, then let practice begin."

One by one the players stood, holding up their instruments, and walking to and fro to display them proudly to the interested onlookers who were the bored Knights and Ladies of the Court, in the habit of walking through the Palace to observe the scenes within and if nothing interesting should present itself to them, then they would walk through the Palace grounds to amuse themselves fully and to the greatest extent perhaps within the Maze or strolling in the beautiful gardens.

The young Earl of Essex stood with his ever increasing entourage of admiring ladies who crowded about him with excitement, and hung upon his every word, as he made attempts at witty comments regarding the unknown skill of the musicians and the daintiness with which they players walked about and how long and delicate their fingers were. To the annoyance of the great lover of music and dance, the shy, sad and retiring Christopher Hatton who had his path blocked by Essex and the ladies, as he meekly complained that he could not see what was taking place within the circle of musicians, no matter how much he bobbed and weaved about in an effort to achieve a more prominent position. Essex, being in a belligerent mood or affecting to be so to impress the ladies, refused to budge and feigned deafness.

Hatton was shy because he had always been shy - he was sad because he was in love with the Queen even though she was older by far, and he was of a retiring nature because he had lost all his confidence when he had asked the Queen to marry him and she had laughed at him and rushed about the Court to display her merriment at such a match. And she had told all who cared to listen (which was everyone present) that she had refused Hatton's proposal of marriage. Hatton had vowed never to marry anyone (a vow which he kept throughout his lifetime). It would seem that he was genuinely in love. Hatton had proceeded to tell everyone who had paid attention to the Queen's amusing story (one by one, because he was not given to great displays of courage such as it took to rush through company, shouting at the top of one's voice), that he still considered himself the Queen's favourite, albeit known affectionately as her 'skipping sheep'. The little jeweled bodkin and bucket which the Queen had presented to him after the above event, (when he had been walking in the grounds and she had been out riding), proved to him at least that all was well, and in order to keep water (Water or Warter being the Queen's pet name for Raleigh - since she loved to mimic his Devon accent), then one must have a bucket in which to keep water. This to his mind put him in higher favour with the Queen that Raleigh. But when Walter Raleigh had heard this tale from Hatton's lips he had laughed heartily at such trivialities and said that he would console himself with the fact that the Queen had given Hatton those little trinkets to keep him amused as one would amuse a child.

Hatton knew that the queen would dance with him at the Banquet and then it would be the Earl of Essex who would be vexed - since he hated the ladies and above all the Queen to show affection to anyone else but himself. Raleigh would look on in awe at the great display, because Raleigh was not a nimble dancer, having a great likeness for ale and wine, which tended to make him clumsy and sarcastic.

How did he know that the Queen would choose him as a dancing partner? He knew because he was the best dancer at the Court and that was something to be very proud of. Of course, first he would have to let the Queen know that he was upset at the attention she paid to Raleigh and Essex, and he had learned through experience, that the best way to let the Queen know this was to quietly and unobtrusively sulk for attention. It had worked before and it would work again. The Queen after all was a very kind-hearted person and that was why he loved her. She had genuine feelings for him. But she also held other men in high regard and sought out their company in favour of his own. This filled him with sadness but he had resigned himself to the fact that there were Court favorites who were intellectually his superior. Everyone was good at something and he knew that his dancing would keep him in a prominent position within the Queen Court throughout her lifetime.

In the midst of these amusements, Raleigh stood back and looked on with great interest at the antics of these great Lords and Ladies who behaved as children, and because a great observer of human nature can always see more by standing back a little, and reflecting the mind, he stood away from the crowd. He was watching Sir Philip Sidney in particular, who appeared to be staring longingly at Lady Perrott who had just entered the hall, and had indeed noticed that Sidney was watching her, and this she had observed from the corner of her eye, but of course, she pretended not to notice him in order to hurt him more, since she loathed him. Lady Perrott did not however, notice Raleigh, who looked across at her with a knowing smirk upon his face. Sir Philip Sidney was everything that her brother would never be, perhaps a little too kind, far too sympathetic and definitely too gifted. It created a frenzy in her mind as she observed Sidney in the same light that she observed every other person at Court, a pride she took in her ability to recognise the good souls from the bad as her brother had taught her. But in Sidney she saw a man who was not quite human because he appeared to have an ethereal quality to his personality. He never seemed to allow anger to take hold of him and yet he was always so compliantly strong in his will. And even apologetic to his antagonists that she felt he mocked her and all around him. Such were his parts and yet she dared not speak of them for he was revered at Court for his Sonnets. Many asked for whom they were composed and he feigned deceit and said 'To all ladies': And yet, the undercurrent of his writing told her that they were composed for one alone. Perhaps she would determine the cause of his embroiled mind and declare all to the Court. And yet she felt that she for once was foxed by him. Perhaps it had been his strict upbringing - but he was in short, far too cultured for her own brasher tastes in respect of his manners, his inherent love of nature and his kindness towards others.

These were qualities that Lady Perrott did not possess and yet she misled her friends into believing that she was as kind and considerate as her brother had always been, and when she had led them into a blind alley she turned them across to Walsingham: For to her the intrigue of Court life was to ensnare the deceiver, since she had once been deceived so terribly that it had made a dark mark upon her soul .

Lady Perrott pushed her way through the ladies in an effort to reach her brother and nudged particularly hard at the ones she most disliked, being nearly all of them. How she detested the conceit and jealousy which manifested in these women who vied for the attention of her brother, being in her opinion, one of the most handsome young men of the Court, and one of the most eligible. It was understandable that these women wanted attention but their painted smiling lips and false temperaments sickened her and she had no time for them. Sidney's wife, Frances Walsingham was as usual standing beside Essex and if ever there had been a mismatch of a marriage it had been between Sidney and Walsingham. That was probably why Sidney spent so much time abroad volunteering to go to war with his father in law, Sir Francis Walsingham. She pulled at her brother's sleeve but he shrugged her off, not realizing that it was she, and instead thinking it was Frances Walsingham, and he wished he to think that he was out to impress another great lady. Lady Perrott however, would not be put off in such a manner, and promptly raised her arm and pinched at his left ear very sharply. He turned about quickly, and was greatly surprised to turn and see that his supposed admirer was his own sister.

"Don't ignore me in your efforts to impress the ladies of the Court and prove yourself worthy of your own vanity, Robert."

"I am sorry, but I didn't realize it was you worrying away at the sleeve of my doublet. What is it. Can you not see how deep I am into this amusement?"

"You are to go to the Queen's chamber immediately and don't tarry. She is not in a good humor even though I have tried to cheer her with flowers, but she is in no mood for them and would have you for company. Oh, and leave your pride and obstinancy here for it has no place in the Queen's chamber."

Bess spoke up suddenly "The Queen also want you take Sir Hugh Platt with you. She seeks something from him."

"I do not know where Sir Hugh Platt is so how can I take him? answered Essex irritably.

"I think Sir Hugh is playing tennis in King Henry's old court with Lord Cumberland, because I overheard them talking earlier", said one of the ladies.

"I will go myself and try to calm her although I cannot say I am pleased to be taken away from my pleasures." and with this Essex bid farewell to his company, and stormed off to the Queen's chamber, but as he approached her door he could hear a conversation going on within and not wishing to interrupt, he stood outside very quietly and listened.

The Queen was speaking in a shrill voice and sounded agitated.

"Just look at my hair - what is to be done with it! I shall never manage to wear all those jewels and yet I want to. In fact I will, and if I cannot do so, then I shall wear them upon my dress" said the Queen to her hairdresser, as she fingered a large golden trinket box. "I need more hair! Arrange for a wigmaker to be sent to me.

HIC JACET: SIR WALTER RALEIGH

And now I will have my dressmaker step forward. and to her dressmaker she said "Ah! there you are! What kept you so long? I will have that large pearl and this even larger diamond sewn on to that gorgeous purple silk gown - you know the one I mean don't you? The one I had made and was going to wear, but decided not to because I was in favour of the black velvet gown at the last moment, and then I fell ill and cold not attend the Ball at all." and then the Queen stopped to think to herself ('or was I really ill or just in poor humor as I am today?) "Oh let me see the dress again! Fetch it here for me.

I am going to impress Walter Raleigh. Raleigh will then cause Essex to become jealous by paying too much attention to me and Christopherus Hatton will fly off into a corner as usual and sulk, until Philip Sidney takes pity on him and consoles him. I will then seek them out and dance with them one by one, and last of all with Hatton to make him happy again. It will all be such fun for everyone to watch. After that perhaps a quarrel will break out and that will give me the opportunity to escape, having had more fun that I have had for some long time past. I will have to sit down and devise a variety of pass times to keep myself and everyone else amused."

At this convenient point, Essex rapped at the door and entered before being told to do so, and gave no hint that he had overheard the conversation since matters had been of a delicate nature.

"My dear cousin Elizabeth, you called for me? he said as he bent to kiss her on the cheek. I understand you wish the recipe from Sir Hugh Platt for your teeth? Are they troubling you again? I could not find him and I understand he is engaged in a game of tennis on your father's old court. I will send for him if I may ... and yet I have it here if you need it before he arrives."

The Queen looked blankly back at him,

"Where? I see nothing!"

"Here! In here!" he said as he pointed to his head and the dark curls that bobbed upon it. "I have memorized it, for I employ it myself."

"I will give you pen and paper directly then and you must write it down for me".

"My own teeth are not as they were and yet I have not the liking for sweetmeats that you have!" Retorted Essex with a sly smile, as the Queen turned to pick up her pen and paper.

"Give me the pen then I will record Platt's recipe for you"

And he began to write as he said the words out loud:

"Take a quart of honey, as much vinegar, half so much wine and after they have been boiled together, then wash the teeth therewith now and then!

There! It is easy to remember, being so short and yet I will say again that to my mind and those I have told of it, agree with me that it makes sound sense and they advocate its efficiency. And yet, I still value the gold tooth pick that you presented to me at last Summer's Banquet and I will always treasure it. Look! I wear it around my neck on a long gold chain - See! I have it about me now."

Do not forget cousin Elizabeth, that I keep my toothpick well occupied lest I should find that I have no teeth to pick! Now I know you have a tooth pick and now you also have Platt's recipe. The two combined have served me well as they shall in future serve you. There! Now do you feel better?"

"Yes Robert, now that you are here I feel much better. Tell me what you have been doing today?"

"Oh just fencing lessons, and then archery early this morning; and later to the music hall where they are practising the viol. Let us talk of other matters. Is there any news from the French court of Queen Mary of Scots. Or of Lord Bothwell? Has he been found?"

"Why do you always enquire of my cousin Mary? You know how it irks me. The French court are still furious about the death of Mary's husband. Why Mary married the Earl of Bothwell, I shall never understand. He fled abroad to enlist support for Mary and was been captured and taken prisoner to Dragsholm Castle in Denmark where he had died chained to a pillar half his height so that he may never stand up again. He went mad and then died insane in 1578. I am sorry to give you such sad news Robert, and I have kept it from you for as long as possible."

Then all fell silent between them and Robert Devereux stood and knew not what to do, before he left the room and so he cried out in a passion: "Remember these words cousin Elizabeth for they will haunt you to your grave, and I cannot stop the words nor the mind from which they come, for so in love with Queen Mary is he that he writes lines so memorable that they will live for an eternity : "Of lovers' ruin some thrice tragedy, I am not I, pity the tale of me."

And as he tricked his feet to walk forward, he did so in haste and he did not want the Queen to see the tears that had filled his eyes.

The Palace was still alive with activity that day, but for the Earl of Essex the day had been marred and his route was swiftly to Essex House to be alone and ponder on the fate of the Earl of Bothwell and all that he had set out to do for his wife, and once again, as he followed the path of so many before him, he had failed Mary Queen of Scots, for she was still a prisoner of the Queen his own second cousin and her cursed advisers.

Hampton Court 1585

Preparations are in Progress for a Great Banquet to be held in Honour of Sir Walter Raleigh who is to be Knighted on Twelfth Night at the Feast of the Epiphany on 12th January 1585 By Queen Elizabeth I

Sir Walter Raleigh spent this particular afternoon secretly playing cards in a quiet chamber of Hampton Court Palace with Elizabeth Throckmorton, the Queen's Maid of Honour, with whom he had fallen in love but he had not as yet declared his feelings for her. They appeared unaware that they were being quietly observed through a hole which had previously been bored into the wooden wall of their secret chamber, under the instructions of Sir Francis Walsingham. Walsingham had gained his information about the secret meetings of this couple on a daily basis from his own daughter, the wife of Sir Philip Sidney, Francis Sidney who appeared not to love her husband at all but instead pursued the Earl of Essex for all he was worth, in the most shameless fashion about the Court.

Bess had joined the Queen's Court in 1584 and her friendship with Raleigh had grown into mutual love during that time. Raleigh did not declare his feelings for her and so she would not declare hers for him. And this is how the romance developed. Raleigh was aware that interest had been excited in connection with their relationship but Bess appeared to have no knowledge of Walsingham and his devious activities, and so they sat happily enjoying their own company. Or so they thought! But every word they uttered was listened to, and nothing escaped the ears of Sir Francis Walsingham.

All was not well in this respect but now we must leave them to their privacy and explore a far away and more industrious area of the Palace.

We go to a place where gossip was rife among the young kitchen maids and the scullery maids, some of them pretty and some fat and dumpy but all professed to have knowledge of what went on between the lords and ladies whose very meals they were busy preparing. Where the young lads listened to this gossip as they were turning the spits to roast the lamb and the pork, the oxen and beef, and watching the roaring flames of the huge fires which lit up their eyes and faces as they stared at the charred red bricks of the chimney breasts. If they felt that they were being roasted alive and in despair, then they did not complain.

Opposite the warmth of those great kitchens in another little room, we may observe the elderly grey haired man named Samuel Giulio, whose father was of Italian descent. Samuel who suffered miserably from failing eyesight and chronic rheumatism brought about by his diligent occupation.

In the small and dimly lit room in which he worked, he was surrounded by four brick walls, which had been painted white long ago, and a cold grey flagstone floor. The room was furnished with no more than the immediate necessities, being two long shelves which had been joined to the wall for the purpose of holding the several huge and heavy leather bound books of royal accounts dating back 10 years, which always stood neatly upright when not in use, and kept above the left hand side of the tall, heavy oak desk which slanted conveniently forward at a 45 degree angle, to assist the writer, who sat on a high stool.

This little room was reached by walking down a narrow red brick corridor adjacent to the great kitchens of Hampton Court, and was occupied on a daily basis by Samuel as described above, who was employed as the assistant to the Master of the Queen's kitchens. The master himself rarely made an appearance except to inspect the accounts and chide poor Samuel for being too extravagant with the Queen's finances.

Samuel sat hunched over his wooden desk which had become so familiar with his own use over the previous long years, that as he gazed down upon it he could remember every scratch and nick and how it had been formed during the course of his work. These were among his fond memories as he stopped to ponder and he tried to imagine who would sit and continue his work when he no longer occupied this seat or indeed when he had passed into the next world.

As usual he felt cold and tugged again at his heavy dark woollen jacket, which had become worn with an age as great as his own, and seemed to mould comfortably to his body but he was determined in his effort to pull it closer to his shoulders. He stood up and shuffled about to look for some fresh firewood to rescue the faint glimmer in the hearth, being all that was left of the fire, but he could find no more wood in the woodbox beside the hearth and he could spare no time to go in search of more, because he felt that his time was too precious. He went back to his seat and picked up his quill. Even when Samuel did have firewood he found that the smoke always managed to get into his lungs and caused him to cough uncontrollably. Samuel could not decide whether it was better to remain cold, or to be warm and spend his time coughing. In his opinion the chimney was blocked up and he would have it attended to.

For the last six weeks from dawn until dusk Samuel had spent his time in the performance of his duties which were connected with arrangements for the forthcoming Banquet and thereafter meticulously writing up the accounts in his neat handwriting. This he did on a daily basis except for the Sabbath day, usually returning home slightly earlier on a Saturday.

Upon returning home at night to his little cottage just over the bridge in Hampton, he would often spend his evenings sitting beside the warmth of the fireplace, in his favourite chair, sipping mulled wine laced with spices, because it reminded him of the Palace, but his wife Amelia Guilio always watered it down for him because she said it would cause him to develop gout.

Samuel frequently complained bitterly to his wife that he seemed to have spent the best years of his life working at Hampton Court Palace

HIC JACET: SIR WALTER RALEIGH

where he had worked his way up from stable boy at 12, to herb gardener at 15, after which he had been employed as a kitchen hand from the ages of 22 to 30. And that is where he had met Amelia. There had been some gossip connected to their romance and Amelia had been obliged to leave her employment and so now she wished for news on a daily basis, of all that she had left behind her in her youth.

Now as Samuel he sat and continued the work his father had done before him during the early reign of Queen Elizabeth, he knew that he longed for some rest and a little comfort in his old age, and this was to be the last Banquet he prepared for as he was about to retire. And he wanted to make a great success of it. He was determined that nothing should escape his attention and he was adamant that no one should assist him in his work.

Samuel knew a great deal about what went on at the Palace on a day by day basis, some of it good and some of it bad, but he always ensured that he told his wife all he heard in an effort to bring some cheer to her evenings, which she later recorded in her Book of Court Gossip, known as 'Amelia Guilio's Court Secrets - 1509 to 1603'. Never forgetting to add that all he knew and told her, together with all that his father had told him of King Henry VIII's Court gossip, was to be regarded as private to themselves and should not be uttered outside the walls of their cottage for fear of creating extremes of paradox. Samuel told her of the affairs that went on between the Lords and the Ladies at Court, and the love matches which ensued between the French Court and the Queen. He told her of the threats of War from Europe connected with Mary Queen of Scots and her supporters who tried to rescue her from imprisonment and of the sad and lonely life that Mary had led since her return to Scotland from France. Secretly Samuel and his wife were in support of Mary but they dared not to speak out, just as others would never do such a thing, unless his name were Sir Walter Raleigh.

Samuel was now once again fully absorbed in his work as he sorted methodically through the papers containing lists of the supplies he had ordered from the meat markets, the fish markets, the brewers and the vintners as he was in charge of the major preparations for the forthcoming Banquet to be held on the day of the Feast of the Epiphany.

First he checked the quantities of lambs and calves already ordered, then the beef and lean oxen to be brought from the butchers in Eastcheap, St. Nicholas' Shambles and the Stock Market. He had been particularly careful to request that the livestock be selected from the best herds which he knew were reared in the Castle Meadows.

On the other hand, the fish must come from the best fish markets in London, and those were the Stock Fishmongers at Thames Street, where he must be sure to buy in the stock fish and salt fish; and then he would have wet fish only from Knightrider Street and Bridge Street.

His problem at the moment was in deciding whether 9 barrels of white herrings at 10s a barrel would be sufficient? and then how many cades of red herring at 6s 8d per cade should he order? (A cade containing 500), the sprats at 2s per cade (a cade containing 1,000 fish), and 200 salmon at 6d each were very expensive he thought, but then if there were not enough to go round he would be blamed for scrimping.

Then on to the vegetables and the fruits from Sopers Lane; the finest selection of wines and ales from the Vintners in the Vintry and the Brewers at the riverside. And finally all the Poultry would be bought from Poultry in the City. He must not forget the wheat and malt, the hops and the flour.

As Samuel entered the quantities of all the above goods into the Royal household books, he wrote with great urgency because he was aware that time was running out and he had only a week left before the great day itself would be here to release him from his work and he would pass all the responsibility on to the very Master of the Queen's Kitchens himself and to the Chefs who would be responsible for preparing the food.

All his careful preparations must be put into practice and he had been told that no expense should be spared and this was to ensure that all provisions ordered must be of the best quality since the Queen meant to impress her 1,000 guests.

The Banquet was to honour Sir Walter Raleigh, who was to be knighted, although he did not know about it, since it would be a surprise for him. It was to be remembered at all times that the Queen's hospitality was the hall-mark of her Court.

Samuel was thus engaged when he was interrupted by one of the Cooks who called in to see him from the Great Kitchen.

"Ah Samuel, I have brought you a glass of mulled wine, piping hot and full of good spices to warm you on this cold afternoon! I am here to remind you that I must have more galagals, turnfole and saunders for my exquisite recipes. Have you ordered them for me? Do you remember me asking you about them last week?"

Samuel turned to look into the pleasing and welcome face of the young French cook, named Andre-Phillipe, who had recently been recommended by several of the Queen's courtiers, after they had visited Paris and then came back to tell Queen Elizabeth of his culinary expertise. Queen Catherine of Aragon had been delighted to release him from her employment since she said, she still had many talented cooks to delight her Court, and so Andre-Phillipe had been hastily brought over by boat from French Court where he had won notoriety as one of the most splendid Chefs in the royal kitchens of Fontainbleau, as the creator of fine sweetmeats, delicate pastries and exquisite puddings which were a great favourite with Queen Elizabeth, due to her liking for such foods. The Queen had not been disappointed.

"Thank you for the wine Andre, it is kind of you to think of me when you need not, and it is most welcome as my hands feel as if they are frozen to the bone. Could you ask one of the lads in the kitchen to bring me some more logs for my little fire? Why there's barely a flicker left in the ashes! Oh, and some more tallow candles for the lantern. I meant to bring some with me as I noticed yesterday that there is only half a candle left to burn and it will be pitch dark in just over an hour."

"Yes Samuel, I will arrange it as soon as I go back into the Kitchen. But why don't you come back with me. Bring your books and papers with you? There the huge fire burns like a furnace and you can pull up one of the little tables and sit beside the warmth of the chimney breast. I can never understand why you have to sit in this cold and miserable little room all alone."

"I'll be in when I've finished writing up my accounts of these orders. Otherwise I'll get nothing done listening to all the gossiping kitchen maids and cooks and the smell of your delicious pastries cooking always puts me off my work and makes me want to eat, and then after I've had my fill, I feel tired and want to fall asleep. I am so tired already, and there is little time left to spare. Why, the important day will be here before we know where we are and so many of the orders are still undelivered. I will have to send a messenger into the city first thing in the morning to see what is causing the delay.

Now tell me Andre, what exactly are Galagals, and the Saunders? Indeed I do not remember you asking me for them before. If you did ask then I confess I did not hear you."

"Well, there is still time to get them. The galagals or galengals are an Asiatic plant, the root of which has an impressive aromatic smell. We used them all the time at the Palace of Fontainbleu and I have recommended them to the Poultry Chef, and I have told him that they give the chicken a grand taste." He said in his French accent. "Then we come to the saunders - they are the product of a tall Indian tree and I use if for coloring the little sweetmeats which I then form into delicate shapes to please the Queen and her important guests. The turnfole or turnsole, I know you have ordered for me before! You remember, it is the violet blue coloring matter from the leaves of that plant which turns to face the Sun as it grows. It is such a pretty little plant and I use the colour to make the almond cakes. They are one of the Queen's favourites and we cannot disappoint her can we? But then she has so many favourites!

Why Samuel! The pepperers in Soper's Lane is the place to find them all in one go. There they stock the finest herbs and spices in London and all in one shop. Most of their goods are imported from overseas. I went there once, just after I arrived at Court, in order to seek out the very best of the many different flavourings for my new recipes. There they have many shelves lined with row upon row of small and colourful bottles. Peppercorns and ginger, mace and cloves, cinnamon and blanch powder. Oh! and I nearly forgot to tell you - more nutmeg! We need more nutmeg!." Said Andrew who was laughing cheerfully as he patted Samuel on the shoulder playfully, on the shoulder and then he turned and made ready to depart."

"Since you know the shop so well you can go first thing in the morning and collect all you need for yourself. I think that would be best don't you? I do fear if I send one of those Maids she will come back with all the wrong things and I will be blamed again."

"As you wish! And now I must get back to work."

Samuel was alone again and he turned his attention to the crockery which had been stored away since the last great Banquet held to honour Le Duc d'Alencon the French prince, also popularly known as the Frog Prince, and once engaged to Queen Elizabeth, but the engagement had not lasted long and now the Prince was married to the daughter of the King of Spain and the Queen was left all alone to weep her tears of loneliness.

Of course, thought Samuel, there were always Banquets held each year or even twice a year but none so special as this Banquet was to be.

They would be needing more silver salvers, plates and pewter mugs, and finger bowls, (the Lords and Ladies must bring their own forks): No doubt they would all try to outdo one another and have special jeweled varieties to wave about among the important guests.

There would be Peacocks for decoration of the tables and arrangements of flowers - but that was not for him to arrange. Annes, comfits of sweetmeats (fruits or root preserved with sugar and dried) - Prepared by Andre ...

Suddenly Samuel was interrupted once more as a youth named Stephen called to him from the doorway:

"Samuel! Oh Samuel - the wagons are here Master! It was Stephen's job to arrange the safe unloading of the wagons and to see that the food was safely stored away as Samuel checked them off his lists."

Samuel stood and walked slowly, or as quickly as he was able to move his stiff body, tugging at his heavy dark jacket and pulling it about himself as protection from the cold Winter air. He shivered as he walked down the alley and the cold winter wind bit into his face and blew against his body, but on he went, in spite of this, his hair being blown about furiously by the wind. Past the kitchens and into the great Courtyard. He squinted as he looked towards the great Gates, the rain blurring his view, but sure enough, the wagons were being drawn along one by one by the powerful carthorses and they were laden with the food and drinks for the Banquet."

Sir Walter Raleigh's Patent to Discover the Land of Virginia, 1584

Sir Walter Raleigh's half brother, Sir Humphrey Gilbert was born in Devonshire in 1539. He was educated at Eton and Oxford. It had been intended that Sir Humphrey Gilbert become a lawyer but Gilbert had a natural leaning towards military life and after being introduced to the Court of Queen Elizabeth by Catherine Ashley. The Queen introduced him to [18] Sir Philip Sidney who gave him an appointment in Ireland. The Queen was well pleased with Gilbert's service and she knighted him in 1570 and gave him command of Munster. Gilbert was also the first English colonel to command English forces in the Netherlands.

In 1578 Gilbert 'received letters patent authorizing him and his heirs to discover, occupy and possess such remote and heathen lands not actually possessed of an Christian prince or people, as should deem good to him or them."

Gilbert's first Expedition in the Summer of 1578 comprised of eleven ships and was manned by 400 seamen but it was doomed, when fights broke out on board one of the ships and murder was committed at Plymouth. There remained only 7 ships for the expedition and it set sail with only 150 men. Gilbert returned in 1579 but had lost his bravest Captain Miles Morgan, who had gone missing and also his best ships.

[Raleigh at the age of 27 and in command of the "Falcon", together with his half brother, Sir Humphrey Gilbert, set out for North America in September 1578 but were driven back to Plymouth by storms. They set out again in November but this time were met by Spaniards and attacked off Cape Verde].

Gilbert's fleet this time comprised of five ships, and Sir Walter Raleigh

---

[18] See Sir Philip Sidney's Sonnets and compare with those of William Shakespeare.

had commissioned and paid for a ship named the Ark Raleigh for this expedition, but on the 13th June, the Ark Raleigh deserted. Gilbert was furious about the desertion and wrote to Sir George Peckham asking him to persuade Raleigh to make an example of the crew. Upon enquiry it had been found that the ships crew had been stricken with a contagious illness which had necessitated their swift return to England.

Raleigh's letter to Sir Humphrey Gilbert
As he set sail for Virginia from Plymouth on the 11th June 1584

[("I have sent you a token from Her Majesty, an anchor guided by a lady, as you see; and farther, Her Highness willed me to send you word that she wished you as great good hap, and safety to your ship, as if her self were there in person; desiring you to have care of yourself, as of that which she tendereth; and therefore for her sake you must provide for it accordingly. Further, she commandeth me that you leave your picture with me. For the rest, I leave till our meeting, or to the report of this bearer, who would needs be messenger of this good news. So I commit you to the will and protection of God, who sends us life or death as he shall please or hath appointed".)]

Your true brother,
Walter Raleigh, 11th June 1583

Sir Humphrey Gilbert landed in Newfoundland on the 5th August, 1583 and took possession of that territory in the name of the Queen of England. On the 9th September as the two remaining ships, the 'Golden Hind' and the 'Squirrel' were sailing southward for their return to England, they encountered storms and Gilbert cried out "We are as near to heaven by sea as by land," and that night his ships lights were seen to go out and his ship went down with all hands on board:

In 1584 Raleigh received the patent to discover America and sent a party to explore the Atlantic Coast from Florida to North Carolina and the Queen granted him the original patent upon the death of his half brother Gilbert, 'Walter Ralegh Militis - Domini et Gubernatoria Virginiae'.

The Capture of the Matre de Dios
And Sir Walter Raleigh's Secret Marriage November 1591

He was a discoverer and a privateer, daring to sail into Spanish waters
and waylay the fleets of ships belonging to King Philip of Spain which
were filled with silver from his portuguese mines.   Raleigh had fought
at the Battle of Cadiz in 1596 and had fired the "St Philip" in revenge
for the death of his cousin Sir Richard Grenville in 1591 at the Battle
of the Azores, where he died on board that great ship as a prisoner of
Spain. Raleigh remembered the letter he had written to Sir Humphrey
Gilbert just before he had set sail for Spain:

"I have sent you a token from Her Majesty, an anchor guided by a
lady, as you see; and farther, Her Highness willed me to send you
word that she wished you as great good hap, and safety to your ship, as
if her self were there in person; desiring you to have care of yourself,
as of that which she tendereth; and therefore for her sake you must
provide for it accordingly. Further, she commandeth me that you
leave your picture with me.   For the rest, I leave till our meeting, or to
the report of this bearer, who would needs be messenger of this good
news. So I commit you to the will and protection of God, who sends
us life or death as he shall please or hath appointed".
Your true brother.
Walter Raleigh, 1591.

Raleigh had sworn to be avenged for the "Revenge". Raleigh had
sustained a great injury to his right leg, during that terrible Battle and
had from that day forward, walked with the aid of a stick to hold him
upright because his leg had been maimed for life.

Sir Walter had been the favourite Knight of Queen Elizabeth and lived
at her Court for ten years before she banished him for daring to seduce
and marry Bess Throckmorton the Queen's own Maid of Honour.

The marriage had taken place in November 1591 at a little parish church in Lillington, Dorset, without the Queen's knowledge and Bess had been five months with child. Their child, a boy, whom they named Damerei Raleigh had been born to them on the 29th March 1592, but died shortly after his arrival into this world and was buried in Dorset. The Earl of Essex, had stood as Godfather to the child and when the Queen learned of this news through a court letter writer named [19] she read his letter:

"S.W.R., as it seemeth, hath been too inward with one of Her Majesty's Maids; I fear to say who, but if you should guess at E.T. you may not be far wrong. The matter hath only now been apparent to all eyes, and the lady hath been sent away, but nobody believes it can end there. S.W.R. hath escaped from London for a time; he will be speedily sent for and brought back, where what awaiteth him nobody knoweth, save by conjecture. All think the Tower will be his dwelling, like a hermit poor in pensive place, where he may spend his endless days in doubt. It is affirmed that they are married; but the Queen is most fiercely incensed, and, as the bruit goes, threateneth the most bitter punishment to both the offenders. S.W.R will lose, it is thought, all his places and preferments at Court, with the Queen's favour; such will be the end of his speedy rising, and now he must fall as low as he was high, at the which many will rejoice. I can write no more at this time, and do not care to send this, only you will hear it from others. All is alarm and confusion at this discovery of the discoverer, and not indeed of a new continent, but of a new incontinent'.

Raleigh, who had set out on a privateering expedition on the 6th May 1592 as an Admiral, was ordered back to Court, having been previously told by the Queen that he must relinquish his position to Frobisher. Frobisher overtook him on the 7th May and Raleigh held on until Cape Finistere.

---

[19] Sir Henry Wooten put Raleigh on Marshall Law (at Cadiz 1596)

HIC JACET: SIR WALTER RALEIGH

As the Spanish Admiral eyed Frobisher he forgot to keep sight of his treasure ship and Sir John Burroughs and his men of war waited patiently at Sancta Cruce being a little town off the Azores, for their chance to capture the 'Portugees' and Burroughs was briskly pursued by the seething Earl of Cumberland who kicked his heels because he had been kept at a distance due to calm weather. A storm approached overnight and was welcomed by Cumberland and Burroughs and they had no alternative but to weigh anchor, and the sailors aboard the 'Portugees' were unlading their goods as swiftly as any men might at Flores, but being approached by the English they fired their Carrack and the English designs were lost as to that ship. Some of the prisoners they had taken, had given them fresh hope, telling them that several other Merchant-men approached behind them and Sir John Burroughs put his Men of War at several distances and waited.

The "Madre de Dios" (Mother of God) approached, being a ship 165 foot long from head to stern, seven decks high and laden with goods to the value of £150,000 'besides what the seamen took for their own use'.

Immediately he returned to the court, he and Bess Throckmorton his new wife were carried off to the Tower of London on the 7th August 1592 and held in the Brick Tower.

Secretary Burleigh's son Cecil was sent to quell the riot and calm the looters but he could do little except send for Raleigh who was brought to the scene accompanied by his Tower Keeper, and as Cecil observed the reaction of his sailors who cried out for him. Cecil wrote a letter to the Queen's Privy Councillor, recording and relaying what he had seen:

"I assure you Sir, his poor servants, to the number of 140 godly men, and all the mariners came to him with such shouts of joy as I never heard a man more troubled to quiet them in my life. But his heart is broken for he is very extreme pensive, longer than he is busied, in which he can toil terribly. The meeting between him and Sir John Gilbert [Raleigh's half brother Sir Humphrey Gilbert] was with tears on Sir John's part. Whensoever he is saluted with congratulations for liberty, he doth answer: "No, I am still the Queen of England's poor captive".

Sir Walter was released in September 1592 to quell the rebellious sailors who were looting the East Indian Carrack, the "Madre de Dios", a treasure ship which Raleigh's expedition had captured. She was a 'floating castle' with 800 inhabitants'. Among the great cargo were pepper, cloves, and cinnamon, cochineal, mace, nugmegs and musk. The pepper among the loot was worth £102,000. There were chests of precious stones, pearls, amber and ebony; satins, tapestries and silks. It took ten English ships to carry the cargo from Dartmouth to London. The sailors in the West Country went mad and started looting the ship when they heard that Raleigh was held in the Tower. One sailor alone was found to have in his possession 'a chain of orient pearls, two chains of gold, four great pearls of the bigness of a fair pea, four forks of crystal and four spoons of crystal set with gold and stones, and two cords of musk, and rushing to meet them were 2000 merchants. In one deal with a merchant, 1,800 diamonds and 300 rubies were purchased for £130.'

Raleigh wrote a letter to Burleigh and said 'in particular how Her Majesty might be profited by the Carrack, according to the offer I made. My promise was not to buy my bondage but my liberty, and I hope, of Her Majesty's favour. Fourscore thousand pounds is more than ever a man presented Her Majesty as yet. If God have sent it for my ransom, I hope Her Majesty will accept it'. The Queen in the end claimed half the treasure and Raleigh was rewarded with nothing more than his Freedom.

Bess was still held captive until the end of 1592 after which they moved to Sherborne Castle in Dorset. In January 1592 the Queen had given Raleigh Sherborne Castle

Their second son, Wat Raleigh was born in late October and on the 1st

November, 1593 he was baptised at a little church in the Hamlet of Lillington.

Robert Devereux, being the Second Earl of Essex, the Queen's cousin once removed, became the new favourite at Court, introduced by the Earl of Leicester and Lettice Knollys his mother.

PARIS, FRANCE - DAYBREAK
AUGUST 24TH 1572

In 1568 when Walter Raleigh was just 16 years old he sailed from England to serve under one of his cousins, Sir Arthur Champernoun, Vice Admiral of the West commanding at Plymouth. Raleigh as a soldier, was to fight in the religious Civil Wars at the Battles of Montcontour and Jarnac. Raleigh had taken the decision to desert Oriel College in Oxford, his academic studies waiting in the wings for his return, and temporarily relinquished in favour of soldiering as he determined to join the 100 Devon Volunteers.20

Raleigh's cousin Champernoun was the son in law of the Huguenot leader Mongomeri. Whilst at Languedoc, Raleigh wrote an account of the smoking out of a band of Catholics in the caves:

'We know not how to enter by any ladder or engine, till at last, by certain bundles of lighted straw let down by an iron chain with a weighty stone in the midst, those that defended it were so smothered that they surrendered themselves, with their plate, money and other goods therein hidden, or they must have died like bees that are smoked out of their hives.'

Elsewhere, bands of English and French Huguenot privateers were provided with Commissions from the Prince of Conde or from Admiral Coligny, to set sailed and to track down the Spanish silver fleets.

20
  He took with him as a souvenir, a black gown from Oriel College in fond memory of the time he had spent there and could never quite bear to part with that Gown which he kept among his personal possessions, throughout his lifetime (and bequeathed it to Thomas Harriot in his last Will and Testament, when he said: ["Moreover I geve to the said Thomas Harryott all my bookes & the furniture in his owne Chamber and in my bedchamber in Durham house togeather with all such blacke suites of apparell as I have in the same house.' "and the raising of funds from the sale of 'the shippe called the Robucke with her Ancores Tackle & furniture & all my Artylerye and great ordinance'. and he decreed 'my reputed daughter begotten on the bodye of Alice Goold now in Ireland shall have the soome of ffive hundreth Markes (333 6s 8d)]';

The King of Spain who had gone to a great deal of trouble in order to negotiate a loan in silver coin from Genoese bankers, had made arrangements for the money to be sent off by ship to pay Alva's troops, but the money never reached Antwerp because the Huguenot privateers had intercepted the ship and promptly removed the silver coin. These events coincided with those in London, where Coligny's brother in law, the Cardinal de Chatillon was also issuing commissions to privateers to 'capture at sea all the enemies of God otherwise called Papists'.

During 1569 Raleigh had been present at the Battles of Montcontour and Jarnac in Western France, a war which lasted for two years, and the Duke of Anjou who was 20 years old at this time, (Charles IX's younger brother), also fought at these battles. It was at the Battle of Jarnac that Conde was taken prisoner and murdered by Anjou's Captains of the Guard.

The French Treaty of Blois was signed in April 1572 as England and France had pledged to aid one another in times of conflict, but the keeping of the pledge and the prevailing peace and tolerance between Catholics and Protestants was to be short-lived.

Just four months had passed after the signing of the Treaty before Catherine de Medici and Charles IX had purportedly consented to a plan that the leader of the French Huguenot's should be assassinated for his part in a conspiracy against the Catholics. News of this conspiracy had very quickly reached the Queen Mother and her son Charles IX and their seemingly ruthless decision concerning Admiral Coligny had sparked of the beginning of what was to become the most terrible Massacre and religious civil war that France had ever seen, which very quickly turned France into an almighty bloodbath.

Coligny, who had been invited to the French Court, was planning an attack on Spain at the time of the marriage of Henry of Navarre to

Margaret of Valois, which was celebrated at Notre Dame in the square. The Council of Ministers called together by Catherine de Medici, informed Coligny that they preferred the threat of civil war to a prospective war with Spain, and when the Guises heard this news they intervened personally by hiring an assassin named Maurevert to kill Coligny. Maurevert shot at Coligny with a crossbow on the 20th August 1572, which wounded him and cut off one of his fingers. Charles IX then visited Coligny who had advised him to rule without the aid of his mother, and Catherine de Medici became very worried and used her powerful influence to convince her son that the Huguenots were planning to seize power. The Queen urged her son in a meeting lasting for several hours, to have Coligny and his Protestant accomplices murdered. Charles gave his consent and told his mother 'Kill them all, so that none will be left to reproach me for it'.

St. Bartholomew's Day Massacre suddenly began at daybreak on the 24th August 1572 and as dawn began to brighten the little streets of Paris, the killing began which was to spark off the fourth of the religious civil wars in France.

The leader of the French troops of Henri, Duc de Guise and other Catholic extremists had secretly made their preparations for the onslaught on the unarmed Protestants. The Duc's troops began marching into the Streets of Paris from their camp just outside the town where they had been massing, as the unsuspecting and unprepared men, women and children slept peacefully in their beds unaware of the impending danger, unarmed and helpless. Admiral Coligny the leader of the French Protestants, was one of the first Huguenot victims. Coligny was brutally murdered by four Catholic extremists who had suddenly broken into his home and cut him down with their swords in cold blood, and his body was thrown out of the window. There had been no time for him to raise the alarm or to call for assistance.

Henri, Duc de Guise signaled for the Massacre of all known Huguenots to begin. The Duc's soldiers, who were armed with Pikes, Staffs, large wooden clubs, Arquebuses and swords, began dragging the Huguenots from their beds and some were thrown from their windows of their bedrooms, the soldiers not wishing to take the trouble to convey them down the stairs. Once seized the Huguenots were stripped of their clothing and tied up with rope about their ankles only to be dragged through the streets of Paris by the Duc's vicious soldiers. Others were hung from gibbets or decapitated. Desperate women and toddlers attempted to flee the City in search of a safe place to hide, some were carrying their infants in their arms, as they were pursued and waylaid by the soldiers and cut down as they cried out and screamed for mercy. Even those who climbed on the roofs of their houses could not escape the massacre as the soldiers followed them in their flight. The fresh red blood of the Huguenot victims of the Massacre of St Bartholomew began seeping into the brown earth of Paris in the name of religion.

Some of the Huguenots were lucky enough to find boats to convey them along the river but the soldiers were also vigilant along the riverbanks and were seen throwing people headlong into the river, Some were left to drown while others were dead before they entered the water. The slaughter continued until all known Protestants had been eliminated, after which the homes of the victims were looted.

Sir Francis Walsingham, who was at that time the English Ambassador to Paris, could only watch in great alarm and horror from the window in the French Embassy, and the events which he witnessed bred in him a ruthless and fanatical hatred of the Catholics in France and England and he was to become known as the 'Spymaster of the Catholics'.

Sir Philip Sidney [born at Penshurst Kent in 1554 and educated at Christchurch, Oxford in 1568-1571], soldier and sonneteer, was certainly in Paris at the age of 18, on the night of St Bartholomew's Massacre, as was probably Raleigh. Marlowe still only aged 8, was too young and tender to have been there, and therefore someone else recorded the events of the Massacre, for Marlowe's play 'The Massacre at Paris', published in and he was later murdered by Walsingham's servant, Robert Poley.

News of the Massacre of Paris was very quickly carried abroad and it was being said that 2,000 Huguenots had been murdered in the Capital alone. Fierce retaliatory fighting soon extended to other parts of France and spread rapidly throughout the Provinces.

Royal orders were issued to have the War stopped immediately, to no avail and the final death toll was estimated at 50,000.

The actions of Henri, Duc de Guise, the powerful noble of the House of Lorraine did not go unpunished and he was also assassinated 16 years later in the Chateau de Blois in 1588 on the orders of King Henri III.

After the Massacre, the French Ambassador Fenelon reached the Court at Woodstock after three days of waiting to be received by the Queen. As he walked through the halls and chambers on his way to speak to the queen he noted that all the Courtiers were silent and dressed entirely in black mourning, and were all deeply saddened and affected by news of the Massacre which had taken place in Paris. Fenelon, amidst the fierce and tearful anger of the Queen, tried his utmost to defend the actions of the Queen Mother, Catherine de Medici and her son Charles IX and their supposed joint decision to condone the murder of Admiral Coligny, and he explained at great length that a Protestant conspiracy had been uncovered which had brought about the decision for the severe reprisals which had taken place in Paris and it was with regret that the fighting had spread throughout France and was now out of all control.

Queen Elizabeth and her ministers viewed the activities of the Catholics as a threat to the State and the old legislation which had been drafted in Parliament, stating that all Englishmen be forced to pay £20 per month if they failed to attend the Anglican services and to be seen to be supporting queen and Church, was still in force in England. Because of the Pope's Bull of Excommunication against Queen Elizabeth I, it was deemed high treason to promote Papal theology.

Prior to St. Bartholomew's Massacre, Queen Elizabeth had been in the midst of marriage negotiations with King Charles IX and Catherine de Medici for her marriage to Le Duc d'Alencon, Catherine's youngest son, who was almost twenty years younger than Elizabeth. Although Elizabeth wanted to put her Court into mourning in the wake of St Bartholomew's Massacre, this would have meant that she would have had to cease negotiations for she was keen to have her 'Frog Prince' visit her in England and the Queen had been receiving letters from Alencon regularly. Plans had to be put off yet again, as Elizabeth received news that Alencon had been imprisoned in France for conspiring with the Huguenots and that his brother, the Duke of Anjou had been elected King of Poland, in preference to Ivan the Terrible.

Charles IX's cousin, the King of Navarre was being held captive at Court, after the Massacre and had been lured to Court by Charles IX who said it had been his intention to marry Navarre to his sister Margaret of Valois. Navarre had made attempts to escape with the assistance of Le mole and Coconnas who were beheaded when the Plot was uncovered.

In England, John Stubbs wrote a Tract entitled 'The Gaping Gulf' complaining against the marriage negotiations between Queen Elizabeth I and Le Duc d'Alencon in which he recorded his opinion that Alencon was 'the old serpent himself come to seduce the English Eve and to ruin the English Paradise'. Stubbs then went on to say 'the Roman mass would return in Alencon's private Chapel to silence God's word' because Catherine de Medici had during their protracted marriage negotiations, informed Queen Elizabeth that Le Duc d'Alencon and his entourage must be allowed to worship in his own Catholic religion and unfortunately for Stubbs, Preachers in London and elsewhere took up the Tract and gave feverish sermons in order to promote ill feeling toward the brother of the French King and stirred up intense public reaction which necessitated a proclamation forbidding further reading of Stubbs tract. Stubbs was later sent for trial on the accusation of sedition and sentence was pronounced by the Court that he should lose his right hand so that he may write no more Tracts of this or any other nature. 'When Stubbs right hand was amputated he took off his hat with his left hand and cried bravely, '"God save the Queen" before he fell to the ground in a faint'. As Stubbs was carried off to the Tower of London, he was heard to say 'left there is a true Englishman's hand'. And sadly, no more was heard of poor Thomas Stubbs after he entered the Tower because he contracted gangrene in what remained of his right arm and he died in his filthy Tower cell shortly afterwards in great agony and without medical assistance being afforded to him.

The health of Charles IX worsened and it was thought that he was suffering from Tuberculosis as he took to his bed and he repented for the blood he had shed and exclaimed to his nurse 'Nurse, Nurse! so much blood all around me! Is it that which I have shed?" He died on 31st May 1574.

It was not until the 16th June 1574 that the heir to the throne of France, Duke of Anjou who had been elected as the King of Poland a year earlier, in preference to Ivan the Terrible, suddenly received news from his mother Catherine de Medici that he must return to France as his brother Charles IX had died. The Duke fled Poland secretly during the night and headed for Austria. There he received a magnificent reception from the Emperor of Vienna after which he spent a splendid week in Venice enjoying the festivals which were being held.

And so, the Duke of Anjou who had once wooed Queen Elizabeth I was crowned King of France on the 13th and 14th February and he married Louise of Lorraine. His younger brother, Le Duc d'Alencon then inherited the title of the Duke of Anjou, and began courting the daughter of Philip of Spain, forgetting about the marriage negotiations between himself and Queen Elizabeth I of England and the Queen of England wept once more at her plight, and a broken love affair brought about by her Advisers.

The long years which Raleigh had spent in battle torn France as a soldier during the terrible French religious civil wars were drawing to a close and had taught Raleigh some very harsh lessons, in addition to which he had also developed an in depth understanding of the futility of civil war. His experiences in France also stood him in good stead in later years, when he was able to call upon his knowledge of military strategy and put it to good use in Ireland for which he was awarded Lismore Castle and 40,000 acres by the Queen of England in 158[ ]

Upon his return to England, Walter Raleigh may have acquired an edge of ruthlessness but he had also gained a tremendous strength of character which was to remain with him for the rest of his life and he had received an extreme and profound grounding as a soldier whilst serving under his cousin Champernoun.

Queen Catherine de Medici and the French Court -1536 - 1562

Catherine de Medici stood in front of the open window of her bed chamber in the Royal apartments and sighed miserably as she gazed out upon the beautiful gardens surrounding the Palace of Fountainbleu. She felt so completely alone and was hoping to catch sight of her husband on the lawns which were crowded with courtiers and court ladies who were walking hand in hand or standing in small groups and discussing life at the French court.

Catherine wanted to speak to her husband on a matter of great importance but be never seemed to have time to talk to her. She had been married to the French King, Henri II, for nine years and she was still only 23 years old. During that time she had been forced to endure the humiliation of her husband's continuing affair with Diane of Potiers, who had captured the King's heart when he had been just 17 years old and Diane had been 37. The King spent at least 7 hours of the day and most of his nights with Diane and discussed all affairs of State with her whilst Catherine was left in the background and she was neither invited to meetings, nor informed of forthcoming events or decisions which had been taken concerning the Royal Court. The King had always treated her with indifference throughout their marriage and it was quite obvious that he preferred the company of Diane to anyone else at court and left no-one in any doubt as to who occupied the place nearest to his heart as he continued to bestow titles and honours upon Diane and awarded her huge sums of money to swell her already massive private fortune.

As Catherine watched her husband walking towards the Palace with his arm around Diane, she tried very hard to suppress the familiar feelings of hurt and anger which she had always felt when she saw them together. She knew that she had no alternative but to accept the situation she found herself in and resolved to wait for things to change, and one day they surely would change.

Catherine started to cry as her eyes followed them. They both looked so happy together and they were obviously enjoying their walk in the sunshine, whilst she preferred to remain within the confines of the Palace because she felt herself to be the object of ridicule among the courtiers. Sometimes Catherine would join the Hunt or go on the royal walks with her ladies, through the forest or the grounds, but Diane was always beside the King and Catherine had no alternative but to remain in the background, following along behind them.

Catherine had just finished her private prayers at her little alter, and her prayers were always on the same subject - asking God to grant her the child she longer for. Perhaps then the King would give up his mistress, she thought to herself.

The King had already fathered a daughter by Phillipa Ducci, although some said that the real mother was Diane of Poitiers. The child had even been named Diane and had promptly been brought to Court where she was treated with great tenderness by everyone, including King Henri, as he had proudly announced to Catherine that the fault of childlessness within their marriage did not lie with him and he had proved it. This news and the sight of the baby girl had only reinforced Catherine's suspicions that she was probably barren.

Although Catherine had been waiting and praying for a child of her own, every day during the nine years of her marriage, she had painstakingly followed the advice of her physicians and had resolved never to give up hope. Only recently, one of her doctors had suggested that she should try tablets of myrrh, informing her that the tablets had proved to be a perfect remedy for childless women and the he had administered them on many occasions with great success. Of course, she had been tempted to try the tablets and wondered whether she should have told her husband of her decision. It was too late now because she thought she was at last pregnant and was longing to inform the King. Catherine had worn a very uncomfortable belt of woven goat's hair next to her body because she had been told it would bring her a child and around her neck she still wore a necklace containing ashes of a large frog as a symbol of fertility, but these charms had not seemed to work for her. She had also taken heed of advice to bathe regularly in hot water to which had been added the perfumes of juniper, laurel, basil, rosemary, thyme and bayleaf and had accumulated boxes full of amulets and charms.

Catherine abruptly from the window because she could not bear to watch her husband and Diane any long. As the warm tears rolled down her sad face she thought to herself - this should have been the happiest day of my life, but instead I must endure further anguish and humiliation. She walked slowly across the huge room and sat down heavily in a velvet chair and immediately closed her eyes, allowing her mind to drift away into the past as her thoughts traced back over the long years she had spent at the French Court and how much she had grown to love her husband to despise the woman who stood in the way of her happiness.

Catherine had endured a terrible loneliness since leaving Florence at the age of 14, in order to marry one of the French princes and she now realised that she had been used as a pawn in a political game. Her parents had died shortly after she was born and at the age of 8 she had been sent to live in a convent, Santissima Annuziata delle Murate, where she had remained for three years, being educated by the Nuns and even now she always kept up a regular correspondence with the sisters at the convent and remembered them all with great fondness. Those years at the convent had probably been the happiest of her life, but she did not wish herself back there.

By the time Catherine had arrived at the French Court, Diane had already been firmly established as a favourite mistress with Prince Henri's father, King Francis, and even now that Catherine had become the Queen of France, she realised that Diane of Poitiers, as the new King's mistress, was the real power behind the King and probably would be for the remainder of her lifetime. Diane was the widow of Louis de Breze and she had been present at the French court since her marriage at the age of 15 to the 56 year old Grand Seneschal of Normandy, an ugly humpbacked man who had held the post of first lieutenant to King Francis, and he had been the natural grandson of Charles VII and Agnes Sorel.

King Francis and the Grand Seneschal had intervened in 1523 to save Diane's father, Saint-Vallier, from the scaffold after he had been accused of treason against the Constable of Bourbon, and Saint-Vallier had been quickly tried, found guilty and sentenced to death. Upon her father's release, Diane had offered herself to King Francis to show her gratitude and had from that moment established herself as one of the King's mistresses and quickly became one of his favourites. The King in turn became very good friends with Diane and her husband and used to visit them at Chateau Anet until the Seneschal's death in 1531 at the age of 72. After the funeral of her husband, Diane had taken to wearing widows weeds at all times and black had only served to enhance her appearance, since she had been blessed with a fair complexion.

Catherine remembered when she had thrown herself at the feet of King Francis and wept, begging him not to send her back to Florence because she had not fulfilled her duty as a wife and had been unsuccessful in producing children. King Francis had comforted her by saying that as God had chosen to send her to be the wife of his son, then he was happy to accept her as such. King Francis had helped Catherine to understand the strong ties which bound Diane and Henri together, and he had carefully explained that Henri and his brother Francis had lost their mother when they were just 5 and 6 years old, and Diane had, even then, filled a place in their hearts, although of course she could never take the place of their mother.

King Francis had gone on to tell the anxious Catherine of how Diane had accompanied Henry as a 7 year old child, when he had been forced to travel with the Court ladies on his way to Bayonne with his 8 year old brother, the Dauphin Francis where they were to be exchanged as hostages for their Father, who had been held prisoner in Spain. They were met by a Spanish officer and 10 gentlemen all armed with swords and daggers. King Francis was released on the promise that he would restore the Constable of Bourbon's titles, and return to him the region of Burgundy and join the two French families together by marrying his sister Eleanor. In addition to which he must hand over his sons as hostages. King Francis had agreed to all these demands as he had been kept in such harsh conditions in the Alcazar prison in Madrid by Charles of Bourbon Montpensier, that he would have agreed to almost anything to regain his liberty at that time. A ransom of 2 million ECU's had been paid in exchange for his liberty whilst his sons were led away and immediately imprisoned for four years. They were kept in severe conditions under heavy armed guard in a small cell with bare walls and no light, fresh air or sunshine. Their cell had been furnished only with stone seats to sit on and iron bars to look at. Henri had never fully recovered from his childhood ordeal and at the time of his release he had almost forgotten his native French and it was frequently remarked upon that he was never seen to smile again at Court as a child. Any love of learning that Henri may have had before his imprisonment quickly left him during those four years and was never to return and his father later rejected him, calling him slow-witted.

King Francis had not expected Henri to succeed to the throne because that honour should have gone to his brother the Dauphin Francis, who had been the King's favourite son and he had held a command in the Army. He had died on the 15th May 1536, under mysterious circumstances after a day playing ball games in the forest, and having exhausted himself he had retired to his bed chamber to lie down and rest. He had called for his Page, Sebastiano de Montecuculli, and asked him to take a little earthenware pitcher and fill it with cold water. The vase had been a gift to Francis from Donna Agnese and after Sebastiano had brought the water back to the Dauphin's chamber the young Prince had immediately drained its contents and upon doing so he had fallen ill. The mysterious illness had lasted for four days, after which the Dauphin had died and everyone assumed that the Dauphin had been poisoned. Sebastiano was immediately accused of poisoning the Dauphin on the orders of Charles V, because the Duke of Ferrara had sent Sebastiano to the Court. The wretched Page was immediately taken away, questioned and tortured to extract a confession from him. The torture did not cease until the poor youth had given the answers to the questions which his tormentors wished to hear and unable to bear the terrible torture any longer, he confessed that there had been a plot to poison the Dauphin. He was sentenced to the terrible death of being tied by the arms and legs to four horses and was pulled apart whilst still alive. The four parts of his body were hung outside the Palace gates and his head was mounted on a pike.

Catherine shuddered as she recounted her memories of the long conversations which had taken place between her and King Francis. The King had been very kind to her and she missed him terribly since he had always made time to talk to her.

Catherine was beginning to put her emotions in order and although she was not happy with the situation she found herself in, she did nevertheless, accept that her husband would always love Diane. King Henri had recently announced Diane as the Duchess of Valentinois and Diane was in the process of building yet another chateau for herself - this time it was to be in Chaumont. As if the Chateux of Anet and Chenonceaux were not enough for her.

Only once had Catherine ever given way to her own curiosity, as to what her husband and his mistress did in private and this had happened when she had been staying in a room directly above her husband and Diane, and she had ordered one of her attendants to drill a small hole in the ceiling so that she could peer through it and watch them in the room below. What Catherine had observed had been so painful to her as she saw them caressing each other on the bed and then falling down together on the floor, never releasing their hold upon one another and kissing each other in a way that the King had never kissed her, and she had resolved never again to degrade herself by allowing her curiosity to become excited regarding her husband and his mistress.

All Catherine really had to comfort her was her belief in her own religion. As the niece of Pope Clement VII she had been brought up very strictly and instructed in the Catholic faith. She still enjoyed her times at prayer and found that it helped her troubled mind, especially when she was faced with thoughts of her husband's infidelities.

Catherine was tired of trying to think of solutions to her problems and she allowed her mind to clear and her thoughts to drift away to happier times as she wished herself back at the Convent again. She closed her eyes and fell into a deep sleep as she sand further into her comfortable chair.

When she awoke it was growing dark and one of her ladies in waiting stood before her, explaining that the King was now ready to see her.

In January 1544 Catherine de Medici and King Henri II rejoiced at the birth of their son Francis, after they had been childless for 10 years.

Four years later, yet another English Army was on its way to Scotland and the life of Princess Mary Stuart was again under threat, the Scots realised that an allegiance with France was their only hope of salvation and when in the Spring of that year, the French King, Henri II, put forward a suggestion to the widowed Mary of Guise, that France and Scotland should be united through the marriage of their son Francis (at that time aged four) to Mary Queen of Scots aged 6, and the proposal was eagerly accepted as it brought with it the promise of military assistance for Scotland. The Scots willingly accepted and by June the French fleet of over one hundred vessels, including sixteen galleys, a brigantine and three great ships, were sighted off Dunbar and landed their men at Leith. They immediately marched on Haddington which had been occupied by the English Army.

Mary of Guise was delighted that her daughter was to marry into the French royal family and on the 6th July 1548 at a Nunnery at Haddington the Treaty was signed which would unite Scotland and France.

Mary's hand had once been promised to Henry VIII's son, Edward VI of England.

HIC JACET: SIR WALTER RALEIGH

To celebrate the recapture of Calais by the Duke of Guise (Mary Queen of Scots uncle), on the 8th January 1558, which had been lost to France for 211 years, thereby destroying the English stronghold and domination of that town, marriage preparations were made for the dauphin Francis to marry Mary Queen of Scots, and Henri II's daughter married the widower King Philip II of Spain after the death of his wife, Mary Tudor.

In 1559 King Henri II had organized and attended various festivals and tournaments which were being held to celebrate new found peace in France. It was at one of these tournaments that King Henri II had his eye put out by Gabriel de Montgomery's lance. After an agonizing ten days of suffering the 41 year old King died and France was again on the brink of Civil War. The King had ignored the warnings of Nostradamus who had predicted that he would die in this way, be he had refused to believe it.

Catherine de Medici could not, as she had hoped, rule France as regent because the former Dauphin, now King Francis II, was already 15 years. The young King was too inexperienced to rule France himself and as a result Mary Queen of Scots and her husband were influenced by her uncle Francis, the Duke of Guise and his brother Cardinal de Lorraine. The Guises opposed leniency towards the Protestants and as Henri II's old favourite adviser Anne de Bourg had taken it upon himself to speak out against the intolerance shown towards the Protestants, he was condemned as a heretic and burned at the stake. The effects of this atrocity and the murder of Montmorency generated extreme hatred which was directed towards the Guises and marked Francis II, who had been ill advised to sanction such measures, as a cruel and intolerant King.

At this time the Prince of Conde, and his younger brother Antoine, the head of the House of Bourbon, became the King of Navarre through his marriage to Joan d'Albret, and was installed at the impregnable

Chateau d'Amboise. An assault was planned and led by the Protestant La Renaudie and his troops for an attack on Blois which was to take place on the 15th March 1560.

Unbeknown to La Reanudie, the Guises had already received information concerning their preparations and on the 17th March, as the assault was about to commence, the Guises were well prepared with artillery and managed to quell the seige which resulted in the death of Renaudie. As La Renaudie's accomplices attempted to escape, it was inevitable that some of these men met their deaths instantly as their throats were cut one by one, while others were selected and taken prisoner and put on trial, after which they were hung from the castle battlements as a deterrent against further plots.

King Francis II blamed the Prince of Conde as the chief instigator of the plot and saw it as a direct threat to dethrone him. This prompted the Prince to approach King Francis himself and he went to Amboise to try to reason with King Francis, but the Prince quickly realised that he had acted rashly in trying to approach the King and fled immediately, realizing that he was about to be arrested.

King Francis was continually ill, and as a result was unable to govern effectively. Catherine de Medici took matters into her own hands and as she was aware that the Guises were becoming increasingly unpopular with the citizens of France, she took steps to quell the unrest by appointing Michel de l'Hospital as Chancellor and at his request, a meeting of the Estates-General was called to Orleans to which the King of Navarre and the Prince of Conde were invited. This had been a ploy to arrest the Prince of Conde, and on the orders of King Francis, and at the instigation of the Guises, Conde was tried and condemned to death. Mercifully, Michel de L'Hospital repealed the order for Conde's execution and he was set free.

The Court were residing at Vespers and in November, the King who had been out hunting with a party of courtiers had upon his return, complained bitterly of experiencing violent pains in his ear. Unfortunately, because he had often complained of earache these complaints were not taken too seriously, until he fainted the following evening. His doctors could do nothing to ease his painful headaches and his festering ear infection. The young King grew progressively worse and as he lay in his bed screaming and crying out in agony, his mother Queen Catherine, and his wife Mary Queen of Scots, were at his bedside constantly, but he died on the 5th December 1560 of meningitis and what was thought to be infected adenoidal growths. He had been King of France for just nineteen months and the religious civil wars had gripped France throughout his lifetime. During their short marriage the French King and Mary Queen of Scots had quartered the arms of England with those of France to the fury of Queen Elizabeth I and it was to this climate that his brave young widow Mary Queen of Scots at the tender age of 18 was forced to leave the French Court which had been her home since the age of 6 and return to rule Scotland. Mary had already been crowned in the Chapel Royal at Sterling on the 9th September 1543 when she was just nine months old. Mary realised that she faced opposition to her Catholic religion from the English and Scottish Protestants who continued to protest against the ancient Roman religion and the Pope of Rome, and in the years that followed, Mary became the prisoner of her own cousin, Queen Elizabeth I of England and Elizabeth's advisers, for almost twenty years, because Mary was seen as a threat to the English throne because she insisted that she had a rightful claim to the Throne of England through the marriage of her Grandfather King James IV of Scotland to Margaret Tudor, the sister of Henry VIII. Mary Queen of Scots reminded Queen Elizabeth that her father King Henry VIII had signed the Treaty of Greenwich on the 1st July 1542 after it had been read in the Scottish Parliament so that Scotland and England would become United. To which Queen Elizabeth had promptly replied that Parliament had denounced the Treaties of Greenwich in December of the same year and that it had been declared null and void upon her betrothal to the Dauphin Francis.

Charles IX became King of France in 1561 at the age of 10 and his mother Catherine De Medici demanded and ruled as regent for her son until he reached the age of majority after the sudden death of King Francis. Catherine allowed the King of Navarre, Antoine de Bourbon the Lieutenancy of the Kingdom of France although he should have ruled France.

Initially, Catherine had tried to reconcile the Catholics and Protestants during the religious civil wars, and showed her leniency towards them by calling together the Representatives of the Estates General in an effort to bring about peace. By the Ordinance of Orleans held on the 31st January 1561 and the religious persecutions brought about under conditions which had been laid down by Henri II of France, due to and in retaliation for the death of Anne du Bourg had finally ceased as a result of which Protestants imprisoned in France were released. Catherine De Medici and Michel de l'Hospital brought together the Protestant and Catholic theologians at the Colloquy of Poissy which was held from September to October 1561 and there the theologians debated their religious differences after which they were still unable to reach agreement and settle their religious differences, and as a result the Protestants were permitted to worship on specified conditions after the Edict of Saint Germain was passed on the 17th January 1562.

Queen Elizabeth had urged Mary to marry the Earl of Leicester but Mary had refused, and had instead married first Henry Lord Darnley, who was murdered. Mary was blamed for his murder.

Mary then married the Earl of Bothwell, who had fled abroad to enlist support for Mary and had been captured and taken prisoner to Dragsholm Castle in Denmark where he had died chained to a pillar half his height so that he may never stand up again. He went mad and then died insane in 1578.

Mary Queen of Scots was executed (beheaded) on the 7th February 1587 at Fotheringay Castle. Her son, who was to become James I of England, was crowned on the 29th July as Prince James (aged 13 months) at Stirling Castle in the Protestant Church beside the Castle. Mary Queen of Scots was moved into the Medieval Tower of the Castle. The Earl of Moray was appointed Regent to Prince James and

Mary Queen of Scots said "He who does not keep faith where it is due will hardly keep it where it is not due". He took possession of Mary's private and priceless jewels which were gifts to her from King Francis II of France and his Father (these included the famous Hanoverian Pearls, given by Pope Clement VII to Queen Catherine de Medici and by her to Mary Queen of Scots. The Earl of Moray presented some of the jewels to his wife and the rest he prepared to sell). Mary wrote to France and to Elizabeth in protest that everything had been taken from her. Catherine de Medici and Queen Elizabeth made bids for the black pearls (but Elizabeth bid more and secured them for her personal collection from Moray).

Mary Queen of Scots wore her gold rosary to her execution and took with her the Prayer book which had been given to her by Lord Herries (this rosary and prayer book (which were probably belonging to Lady Jane Grey before Mary Queen of Scots) are now at Sion House. The Pencuik jewels were said to have been given by Mary to her serving woman Giles Mowbray just before Mary was executed.

Background of the French Civil Wars
Queen Catherine de Medici and the French Court : 1536 - 1562

Catherine de Medici stood in front of the open window of her bed chamber in the Royal apartments and sighed miserably as she gazed out upon the beautiful gardens surrounding the Palace of Fountainbleu. She felt so completely alone and was hoping to catch sight of her husband on the lawns which were crowded with courtiers and court ladies who were walking hand in hand or standing in small groups and discussing life at the French court.

Catherine wanted to Nostradamus concerning her husband on a matter of great importance and she waited for him to enter her bedchamber, her mind fell into a state of calm as her mind led her slowly through the record of her lifetime. All Catherine really had to comfort her was her belief in her own religion. As the niece of Pope Clement VII she had been brought up very strictly and instructed in the Roman Catholic faith. She still enjoyed her times at prayer and found that it helped her troubled mind, especially when she was faced with thoughts of her husband's infidelities.

Catherine was tired of trying to think of solutions to her problems and she allowed her mind to clear and her thoughts to drift away to happier times as she wished herself back at the Convent again. She closed her eyes and fell into a deep sleep as she sank further into her comfortable Burgundy velvet chair.

[21]Cathereine de Medici was born at 11 am on Wednesday April 13th, 1519 and named Caterina Maria Romola. Her mother, Madelaine de La Tour d'Auvergne, her father Lorenzo, Duke of Urbino, a Medici. Her mother died of puerperal fever on April 28th 1519. Her father died five days later. They had married at Fortress of Amboise, overlooking the Loire, on the April 28th 1518.

---

[21]The Kings and Queens of France

After the death of her parents, Catherine lived at the Palazzo on the via Larga in Florence with her Governor, Messer Rosso Ridolfi and her two illegitimate Medici cousins, Ippolito and Alessandro. Later, when she was eight years old she was moved to Santisima Annunziata delle Murate, a Convent where she remained for three years. Even after she left the Convent, she maintained correspondence with the sisters there until 1588, (a year before her death).

She had been married to the French King, Henri II, for nine years and she was still only 23 years old. During that time she had been forced to endure the humiliation of her husband's continuing affair with Diane of Potiers, who had captured the King's heart when he had been just 17 years old and Diane had been 37. The King spent at least 7 hours of the day and most of his nights with Diane and discussed all affairs of State with her, whilst Catherine was left in the background. She was neither invited to meetings, nor informed of forthcoming events or decisions which had been taken concerning the Royal Court. The King had always treated her with indifference throughout their marriage and it was quite obvious that he preferred the company of Diane to anyone else at court and left no-one in any doubt as to who occupied the place nearest to his heart as he continued to bestow titles and honours upon Diane and awarded her huge sums of money to swell her already massive private fortune.

As Catherine watched her husband walking towards the Palace with his arm around Diane, she tried very hard to suppress the familiar feelings of hurt and anger which she had always felt when she saw them together. She knew that she had no alternative but to accept the situation she found herself in and resolved to wait for things to change, and one day they surely would change.

Catherine started to cry as her eyes followed them. They both looked so happy together and they were obviously enjoying their walk in the sunshine, whilst she preferred to remain within the confines of the

Palace because she felt herself to be the object of ridicule among the courtiers. Sometimes Catherine would join the Hung or go on the royal walks with her ladies, through the forest or the grounds, but Diane was always beside the King and Catherine had no alternative but to remain in the background, following along behind them.

Catherine had just finished her private prayers at her little alter, and her prayers were always on the same subject - asking God to grant her the child she longer for. Perhaps then the King would give up his mistress, she thought to herself.

The King had already fathered a daughter by Phillipa Ducci, although some said that the real mother was Diane of Poitiers. The child had even been named Diane and had promptly been brought to Court where she was treated with great tenderness by everyone, including King Henri, as he had proudly announced to Catherine that the fault of childlessness within their marriage did not lie with him and he had proved it. This news and the sight of the baby girl had only reinforced Catherine's suspicions that she was probably barren.

Although Catherine had been waiting and praying for a child of her own, every day during the nine years of her marriage, she had painstakingly followed the advice of her physicians and had resolved never to give up hope. Only recently, one of her doctors had suggested that she should try tablets of myrrh, informing her that the tablets had proved to be a perfect remedy for childless women and the he had administered them on many occasions with great success. Of course, she had been tempted to try the tablets and wondered whether she should have told her husband of her decision. It was too late now because she thought she was at last pregnant and was longing to inform the King. Catherine had worn a very uncomfortable belt of woven goat's hair next to her body because she had been told it would bring her a child and around her neck she still wore a necklace containing ashes of a large frog as a symbol of fertility, but these charms had not seemed to work for her. She had also taken heed of advice to bathe regularly in hot water to which had been added the perfumes of juniper, laurel, basil, rosemary, thyme and bayleaf and had accumulated boxes full of amulets and charms.

Catherine abruptly from the window because she could not bear to watch her husband and Diane any longer. As the warm tears rolled down her sad face she thought to herself - this should have been the happiest day of my life, but instead I must endure further anguish and humiliation. She walked slowly across the huge room and sat down heavily in a velvet chair and immediately closed her eyes, allowing her mind to drift away into the past as her thoughts traced back over the long years she had spent at the French Court and how much she had grown to love her husband to despise the woman who stood in the way of her happiness.

Catherine had endured a terrible loneliness since leaving Florence at the age of 14, in order to marry one of the French princes and she now realised that she had been used as a pawn in a political game. Her parents had died shortly after she was born and at the age of 8 she had been sent to live in a convent, Santissima Annuziata delle Murate, where she had remained for three years, being educated by the Nuns and even now she always kept up a regular correspondence with the sisters at the convent and remembered them all with great fondness. Those years at the convent had probably been the happiest of her life, but she did not wish herself back there.

By the time Catherine had arrived at the French Court, Diane had already been firmly established as a favourite mistress with Prince Henri's father, King Francis, and even now that Catherine had become the Queen of France, she realised that Diane of Poitiers, as the new King's mistress, was the real power behind the King and probably would be for the remainder of her lifetime. Diane was the widow of Louis de Breze and she had been present at the French court since her marriage at the age of 15 to the 56 year old Grand Seneschal of Normandy, an ugly humpbacked man who had held the post of first lieutenant to King Francis, and he had been the natural grandson of Charles VII and Agnes Sorel.

King Francis and the Grand Seneschal had intervened in 1523 to save Diane's father, Saint-Vallier, from the scaffold after he had been accused of treason against the Constable of Bourbon, and Saint-Vallier had been quickly tried, found guilty and sentenced to death. Upon her father's release, Diane had offered herself to King Francis to show her gratitude and had from that moment established herself as one of the King's mistresses and quickly became one of his favourites. The King in turn became very good friends with Diane and her husband and used to visit them at Chateau Anet until the Seneschal's death in 1531 at the age of 72. After the funeral of her husband, Diane had taken to wearing widows [22] weeds at all times and black had only served to enhance her appearance, since she had been blessed with a fair complexion.

Catherine remembered when she had thrown herself at the feet of King Francis and wept, begging him not to send her back to Florence because she had not fulfilled her duty as a wife and had been unsuccessful in producing children. King Francis had comforted her by saying that as God had chosen to send her to be the wife of his son, then he was happy to accept her as such. King Francis had helped Catherine to understand the strong ties which bound Diane and Henri together, and he had carefully explained that Henri and his brother Francis had lost their mother when they were just 5 and 6 years old, and Diane had, even then, filled a place in their hearts, although of course she could never take the place of their mother.

King Francis had gone on to tell the anxious Catherine of how Diane had accompanied Henry as a 7 year old child, when he had been forced to travel with the Court ladies on his way to Bayonne with his 8 year old brother, the Dauphin Francis where they were to be exchanged as hostages for their Father, who had been held prisoner in Spain. They were met by a Spanish officer and 10 gentlemen all armed with swords

---

[22] Widows Weeds as referred to in William Shakespeare's Sonnets: Mary Queen of Scots was influenced by her life at the French Court - Sir Philip Sidney

and daggers. King Francis was released on the promise that he would restore the Constable of Bourbon's titles, and return to him the region of Burgundy and join the two French families together by marrying his sister Eleanor. In addition to which he must hand over his sons as hostages. King Francis had agreed to all these demands as he had been kept in such harsh conditions in the Alcazar prison in Madrid by Charles of Bourbon Montpensier, that he would have agreed to almost anything to regain his liberty at that time. A ransom of 2 million Ecus had been paid in exchange for his liberty whilst his sons were led away and immediately imprisoned for four years. They were kept in severe conditions under heavy armed guard in a small cell with bare walls and no light, fresh air or sunshine. Their cell had been furnished only with stone seats to sit on and iron bars to look at. Henri had never fully recovered from his childhood ordeal and at the time of his release he had almost forgotten his native French and it was frequently remarked upon that he was never seen to smile again at Court as a child. Any love of learning that Henri may have had before his imprisonment quickly left him during those four years and was never to return and his father later rejected him, calling him slow-witted.

King Francis had not expected Henri to succeed to the throne because that honour should have gone to his brother the Dauphin Francis, who had been the King's favourite son and he had held a command in the Army. He had died on the 15th May 1536, under mysterious circumstances after a day playing ball games in the forest, and having exhausted himself he had retired to his bed chamber to lie down and rest. "He had called for his Page, Sebastiano de Montecuculli, and asked him to take a little earthenware pitcher and fill it with cold water." The vase had been a gift to Francis from Donna Agnese and after Sebastiano had brought the water back to the Dauphin's chamber the young Prince had immediately drained its contents and upon doing so he had fallen ill. The mysterious illness had lasted for four days, after which the Dauphin had died and everyone assumed that the Dauphin had been poisoned. Sebastiano was immediately accused of poisoning the Dauphin on the orders of Charles V, because the Duke of Ferrara had sent Sebastiano to the Court. The wretched Page was immediately taken away, questioned and tortured to extract a confession from him. The torture did not cease until the poor youth had given the answers to the questions which his tormentors wished to hear and unable to bear the terrible torture any longer, he confessed that there had been a plot to poison the Dauphin. He was sentenced to the terrible death of being tied by the arms and legs to four horses and was pulled apart whilst still alive. The four parts of his body were hung outside the Palace gates and his head was mounted on a pike.

Catherine shuddered as she recounted her memories of the long conversations which had taken place between her and King Francis. The King had been very kind to her and she missed him terribly since he had always made time to talk to her.

Catherine was beginning to put her emotions in order and although she was not happy with the situation she found herself in, she did nevertheless, accept that her husband would always love Diane. King Henri had recently announced Diane as the Duchess of Valentinois and Diane was in the process of building yet another chateau for herself - this time it was to be in Chaumont. As if the Chateux of Anet and Chenonceaux were not enough for her.

Only once had Catherine ever given way to her own curiosity, as to what her husband and his mistress did in private and this had happened when she had been staying in a room directly above her husband and Diane, and she had ordered one of her attendants to drill a small hole in the ceiling so that she could peer through it and watch them in the room below. What Catherine had observed had been so painful to her as she saw them caressing each other on the bed and then falling down together on the floor, never releasing their hold upon one another and kissing each other in a way the King had never kissed her, and she had resolved never again to degrade herself by allowing her curiosity to become excited regarding her husband and his mistress.

When she awoke it was growing dark and one of her ladies in waiting stood before her, explaining that the King was now ready to see her.

In January 1544 Catherine de Medici and King Henri II rejoiced at the birth of their son Francis, after they had been childless for 10 years.

Four years later, yet another English Army was on its way to Scotland and the life of Princess Mary Stuart was again under threat, the Scots realised that an allegiance with France was their only hope of salvation and when in the Spring of that year, the French King, Henri II, put forward a suggestion to the widowed Mary of Guise, that France and Scotland should be united through the marriage of their son Francis (at that time aged four) to Mary Queen of Scots aged 6, and the proposal was eagerly accepted as it brought with it the promise of military assistance for Scotland. The Scots willingly accepted and by June the French fleet of over one hundred vessels, including sixteen galleys, a brigantine and three great ships, were sighted off Dunbar and landed their men at Leith. They marched on Haddington which had been occupied by the English Army.

Mary of Guise was delighted that her daughter was to marry into the French royal family and on the 6th July 1548 at a Nunnery at Haddington the Treaty was signed which would unite Scotland and France.

Mary's hand had once been promised to Henry VIII's son, Edward VI of England.

To celebrate the recapture of Calais by the Duke of Guise (Mary Queen of Scots uncle), on the 8th January 1558, which had been lost to France for 211 years, thereby destroying the English stronghold and domination of that town, marriage preparations were made for the dauphin Francis to marry Mary Queen of Scots, and Henri II's daughter married the widower King Philip II of Spain after the death of his wife, Mary Tudor.

In 1559 King Henri II had organized and attended various festivals and tournaments which were being held to celebrate new found peace in France. It was at one of these tournaments that King Henri II had his eye put out by Gabriel de Montgomery's lance. After an agonizing ten days of suffering the 41 year old King died and France was again on the brink of Civil War. The King had ignored the warnings of Nostradamus who had predicted that he would die in this way, be he had refused to believe it.

Catherine de Medici could not, as she had hoped, rule France as regent because the former Dauphin, now King Francis II, was already 15 years. The young King was too inexperienced to rule France himself and as a result Mary Queen of Scots and her husband were influenced by her uncle Francis, the Duke of Guise and his brother Cardinal de Lorraine (Claude duc of Guise?). The Guises opposed leniency towards the Protestants and as Henri II's old favourite adviser Anne de Bourg had taken it upon himself to speak out against the intolerance shown towards the Protestants, he was condemned as a heretic and burned at the stake. The effects of this atrocity and the murder of Montmorency generated extreme hatred which was directed towards the Guises and marked Francis II, who had been ill advised to sanction such measures, as a cruel and intolerant King.

At this time the Prince of Conde, and his younger brother Antoine, the head of the House of Bourbon, became the King of Navarre through his marriage to Joan d'Albret, and was installed at the impregnable Chateau d'Amboise. An assault was planned and led by the Protestant La Renaudie and his troops for an attack on Blois which was to take place on the 15th March 1560.

Unbeknown to La Reanudie, the Guises had already received information concerning their preparations and on the 17th March, as the assault was about to commence, the Guises were well prepared with artillery and managed to quell the seige which resulted in the death of Renaudie. As La Renaudie's accomplices attempted to escape, it was inevitable that some of these men met their deaths instantly as their throats were cut one by one, while others were selected and taken prisoner and put on trial, after which they were hung from the castle battlements as a deterrent against further plots.

King Francis II blamed the Prince of Conde as the chief instigator of the plot and saw it as a direct threat to dethrone him. This prompted the Prince to approach King Francis himself and he went to Amboise to try to reason with King Francis, but the Prince quickly realised that he had acted rashly in trying to approach the King and fled immediately, realizing that he was about to be arrested.

King Francis was continually ill, and as a result was unable to govern effectively. Catherine de Medici took matters into her own hands and as she was aware that the Guises were becoming increasingly unpopular with the citizens of France, she took steps to quell the unrest by appointing Michel de l'Hospital as Chancellor and at his request, a meeting of the Estates-General was called to Orleans to which the King of Navarre and the Prince of Conde were invited. This had been a ploy to arrest the Prince of Conde, and on the orders of King Francis, and at the instigation of the Guises, Conde was tried and condemned to death. Mercifully, Michel de L'Hospital repealed the order for Conde's execution and he was set free.

The Court were residing at Vespers and in November, the King who had been out hunting with a party of courtiers had upon his return, complained bitterly of experiencing violent pains in his ear. Unfortunately, because he had often complained of earache these complaints were not taken too seriously, until he fainted the following evening. His doctors could do nothing to ease his painful headaches and his festering ear infection. The young King grew progressively worse and as he lay in his bed screaming and crying out in agony, his mother Queen Catherine, and his wife Mary Queen of Scots, were at his bedside constantly, but he died on the 5th December 1560 of meningitis and what was thought to be infected adenoidal growths. He had been King of France for just nineteen months and the religious civil wars had gripped France throughout his lifetime. During their short marriage the French King and Mary Queen of Scots had

quartered the arms of England with those of France to the fury of
Queen Elizabeth I and it was to this climate that his brave young
widow Mary Queen of Scots at the tender age of 18 was forced to
leave the French Court which had been her home since the age of 6
and return to rule Scotland. Mary had already been crowned in the
Chapel Royal at Sterling on the 9th September 1543 when she was just
nine months old. Mary realised that she faced opposition to her
Catholic religion from the English and Scottish Protestants who
continued to protest against the ancient Roman religion and the Pope
of Rome, and in the years that followed, Mary became the prisoner of
her own cousin, Queen Elizabeth I of England and Elizabeth's
advisers, for almost twenty years, because Mary was seen as a threat to
the English throne because she insisted that she had a rightful claim to
the Throne of England through the marriage of her Grandfather King
James IV of Scotland to Margaret Tudor, the sister of Henry VIII.
Mary Queen of Scots reminded Queen Elizabeth that her father King
Henry VIII had signed the Treaty of Greenwich on the 1st July 1542
after it had been read in the Scottish Parliament so that Scotland and
England would become United. To which Queen Elizabeth had
promptly replied that Parliament had denounced the Treaties of
Greenwich in December of the same year and that it had been declared
null and void upon her betrothal to the Dauphin Francis.

Charles IX became King of France in 1561 at the age of 10 and his
mother Catherine De Medici demanded and ruled as regent for her son
until he reached the age of majority after the sudden death of King
Francis. Catherine allowed the King of Navarre, Antoine de Bourbon
the Lieutenancy of the Kingdom of France although he should have
ruled France.

Initially, Catherine had tried to reconcile the Catholics and Protestants
during the religious civil wars, and showed her leniency towards them
by calling together the Representatives of the Estates General in an
effort to bring about peace. By the Ordinance of Orleans held on the
31st January 1561 and the religious persecutions brought about under
conditions which had been laid down by Henri II of France, due to and
in retaliation for the death of Anne du Bourg had finally ceased as a

result of which Protestants imprisoned in France were released.
Catherine De Medici and Michel de l'Hospital brought together the
Protestant and Catholic theologians at the Colloquy of Poissy which
was held from September to October 1561 and there the theologians
debated their religious differences after which they were still unable to
reach agreement and settle their religious differences, and as a result
the Protestants were permitted to worship on specified conditions after
the Edict of Saint Germain was passed on the 17th January 1562.

Queen Elizabeth had urged Mary to marry the [23] Earl of Leicester but
Mary had refused, and had instead married first Henry Lord Darnley,
who was murdered. Mary was blamed for his murder.

Mary then married the Earl of Bothwell, who had fled abroad to enlist
support for Mary and had been captured and taken prisoner to
Dragsholm Castle in Denmark where he had died chained to a pillar
half his height so that he may never stand up again. He went mad and
then died insane in 1578.

Mary Queen of Scots was beheaded on the 7th February 1587 at
Fotheringay Castle. It was said that her Death Warrant, signed by
Queen Elizabeth I of England on 1st February 1587, had been cast in
amongst her daily papers for signing and that she knew nothing of a
Scrivener's hand and could not read the words upon the fated
parchment.   Queen Elizabeth I always maintained her innocency and
on her death bed said to [24] Lady [25] Scrope 'May God forgive you for I

---

[23] The Earl of Leicester, Patron to William Shakespeare - see The Table of Elizabethan
Theatres and Dramatists

[24] Lady Scrope was the sister of the 2nd Lord Hunsdon who succeeded as Chamberlain after
the death of Lord Cobham in March 1597. Lady Mary Hoby (1582) was the daughter of Lord
Hunsdon and married Edward Hoby the son of Sir Thomas Hoby Diplomat and Linguist.

never shall.'

Mary's son, who was to become James I of England, was crowned on the 29th July as Prince James (aged 13 months) at Stirling Castle in the Protestant Church beside the Castle. Mary Queen of Scots was moved into the Medieval Tower of the Castle. The Earl of Moray was appointed Regent to Prince James and Mary Queen of Scots said "He who does not keep faith where it is due will hardly keep it where it is not due". He took possession of Mary's private and priceless jewels which were gifts to her from King Francis II of France and his Father (these included the famous Hanoverian Pearls, given by Pope Clement VII to Queen Catherine de Medici and by her to Mary Queen of Scots. The Earl of Moray presented some of the jewels to his wife and the rest he prepared to sell). Mary wrote to France and to Elizabeth in protest that everything had been taken from her. Catherine de Medici and Queen Elizabeth made bids for the black pearls (but Elizabeth bid more and secured them for her personal collection from Moray).

Mary Queen of Scots wore her gold rosary to her execution and took with her the Prayer book which had been given to her by Lord Herries (this rosary and prayer book (which were probably belonging to Lady Jane Grey before Mary Queen of Scots) are now at Sion House. The Pencuik jewels were said to have been given by Mary to her serving woman Giles Mowbray just before Mary was executed.

---

[25] After Richard II of Bordeaux 1377-1399, was displaced by King Henry IV (1399-1413) 'the northern barons rose against him and were defeated' - Richard Scrope Archbishop of York was executed and this action was condemned.

HIC JACET: SIR WALTER RALEIGH

St. Bartholowmew's Day Massacre at Paris
France - Daybreak, August 24th, 1572

In 1568 when Walter Raleigh was just 16 years old he sailed from England to serve under one of his cousins, Sir Arthur Champernoun, Vice Admiral of the West commanding at Plymouth. Raleigh as a soldier, was to fight in the religious Civil Wars at the Battles of Montcontour and Jarnac. Raleigh had taken the decision to desert Oriel College in Oxford, and he left his academic studies waiting in the wings for his return, temporarily relinquishing them in favour of soldiering, as he determined to join the 100 Devon Volunteers.

Raleigh's cousin Champernoun was the son in law of the Huguenot leader Mongomeri. Whilst at Languedoc, Raleigh wrote an account of the smoking out of a band of Catholics in the caves:

'We know not how to enter by any ladder or engine, till at last, by certain bundles of lighted straw let down by an iron chain with a weighty stone in the midst, those that defended it were so smothered that they surrendered themselves, with their plate, money and other goods therein hidden, or they must have died like bees that are smoked out of their hives.'

Elsewhere, bands of English and French Huguenot privateers were provided with Commissions from the Prince of Conde or from Admiral Coligny, to set sailed and to track down the Spanish silver fleets.

The King of Spain who had gone to a great deal of trouble in order to negotiate a loan in silver coin from Genoese bankers, had made arrangements for the money to be sent off by ship to pay Alva's troops, but the money never reached Antwerp because the Huguenot privateers had intercepted the ship and promptly removed the silver coin. These events coincided with those in London, where Coligny's brother in law, the Cardinal de Chatillon was also issuing commissions to privateers to 'capture at sea all the enemies of God otherwise called Papists'.

During 1569 Raleigh had been present at the Battles of Montcontour and Jarnac in Western France, a war which lasted for two years, and the Duke of Anjou who was 20 years old at this time, (Charles IX's younger brother), also fought at these battles. It was at the Battle of Jarnac that Conde was taken prisoner and murdered by Anjou's Captains of the Guard.

The French Treaty of Blois was signed in April 1572 as England and France had pledged to aid one another in times of conflict, but the keeping of the pledge and the prevailing peace and tolerance between Catholics and Protestants was to be short-lived.

Just four months had passed after the signing of the Treaty before Catherine de Medici and Charles IX had purportedly consented to a plan that the leader of the French Huguenot's should be assassinated for his part in a conspiracy against the Catholics. News of this conspiracy had very quickly reached the Queen Mother and her son Charles IX and their seemingly ruthless decision concerning Admiral Coligny had sparked of the beginning of what was to become the most terrible Massacre and religious civil war that France had ever seen, which very quickly turned France into an almighty bloodbath.

Coligny, who had been invited to the French Court, was planning an attack on Spain at the time of the marriage of Henry of Navarre to Margaret of Valois, which was celebrated at Notre Dame in the square. The Council of Ministers called together by Catherine de Medici, informed Coligny that they preferred the threat of civil war to a prospective war with Spain, and when the Guises heard this news they intervened personally by hiring an assassin named Maurevert to kill Coligny. Maurevert shot at Coligny with a crossbow on the 20th August 1572, which wounded him and cut off one of his fingers. Charles IX then visited Coligny who had advised him to rule without the aid of his mother, and Catherine de Medici became very worried and used her powerful influence to convince her son that the

Huguenots were planning to seize power. The Queen urged her son in a meeting lasting for several hours, to have Coligny and his Protestant accomplices murdered. Charles gave his consent and told his mother 'Kill them all, so that none will be left to reproach me for it'.

St. Bartholomew's Day Massacre suddenly began at daybreak on the 24th August 1572 and as dawn began to brighten the little streets of Paris, the killing began which was to spark off the fourth of the religious civil wars in France.

The leader of the French troops of Henri, Duc de Guise, Mary Queen of Scots maternal Uncle, and other Catholic supporters, had secretly made their preparations for the onslaught on the offending Protestants. The Duc's troops began marching into the Streets of Paris from their camp just outside the town where they had been massing, as the unsuspecting and unprepared men, women and children slept peacefully in their beds unaware of impending danger.

Admiral Coligny the leader of the French Protestants was one of the first Huguenot victims. Coligny was brutally murdered by four Catholic extremists who had suddenly broken into his home and cut him down with their swords in cold blood, and his body was thrown out of the window. There had been no time for him to raise the alarm or to call for assistance.

Henri, Duc de Guise signaled for the Massacre of all known Huguenots to begin. The Duc's soldiers, who were armed with Pikes, Staffs, large wooden clubs, Arquebuses and swords, began dragging the Huguenots from their beds and some were thrown from their windows of their bedrooms, the soldiers not wishing to take the trouble to convey them down the stairs. Once seized, the Huguenots were stripped of their clothing and tied up with rope about their ankles only to be dragged through the streets of Paris by the Duc's vicious soldiers. Others were hung from gibbets or decapitated. Desperate women and toddlers attempted to flee the City in search of a safe place to hide, some were carrying their infants in their arms, as they were pursued and waylaid by the soldiers and cut down as they cried out and screamed for mercy. Even those who climbed on the roofs of their houses could not escape the massacre as the soldiers followed them in their flight. The fresh red blood of the Huguenot victims of the Massacre of St Bartholomew began seeping into the brown earth of Paris in the name of religion.

Some of the Huguenots were lucky enough to find boats to convey them along the river but the soldiers were also vigilant along the riverbanks and were seen throwing people headlong into the river; some were left to drown while others were dead before they entered the water. The slaughter continued until all known Protestants had been eliminated, after which the homes of the victims were looted.

Sir Francis Walsingham[26], who was at that time the English Ambassador to Paris, could only watch in great alarm and horror from the window in the French Embassy, and the events which he witnessed bred in him a ruthless and fanatical hatred of the Catholics in France and England and he was later to become known as the 'Spymaster of the Catholics'.

Sir Philip Sidney [born at Penshurst Kent in 1554 and educated at Christchurch, Oxford in 1568-1571], soldier and sonneteer, was certainly in Paris at the age of 18, on the night of St Bartholomew's Massacre, as well as Sir Walter Raleigh. Marlowe still only aged 8, was too young and tender to have been there, and therefore someone else (probably Sir Philip Sidney) recorded the events of the Massacre, for Marlowe's play 'The Massacre at Paris', published in [see ref

---

[26] "Sir Francis Walsingham was appointed as Printer to the Queen when he received a Monopoly to print Bibles, service-books, statutes, and proclamations as well as books to be licensed by the Queen or Parliament. He was licenced by seven Privy Councillors to print the Geneva Bible and New Testament in 1599".

notes] and he was later murdered by Ingram Frizer in the company of Walsingham's servant, Robert Poley.

News of the Massacre of Paris was very quickly carried abroad and it was being said that 2,000 Huguenots had been murdered in the Capital alone. Fierce retaliatory fighting soon extended to other parts of France and spread rapidly throughout the Provinces.

Royal orders were issued to have the War stopped immediately, to no avail and the final death toll was estimated at 50,000.

The actions of Henri, Duc de Guise, the powerful noble of the House of Lorraine did not go unpunished and he was also assassinated 16 years later in the Chateau de Blois in 1588 on the orders of King Henri III.

After the Massacre, the French Ambassador Fenelon reached the Court at Woodstock after three days of waiting to be received by the Queen. As he walked through the halls and chambers on his way to speak to the queen he noted that all the Courtiers were silent and dressed entirely in black to indicate their mourning, and all were deeply saddened and affected by news of the Massacre which had taken place in Paris. Fenelon, amidst the fierce and tearful anger of the Queen, tried his utmost to defend the actions of the Queen Mother, Catherine de Medici and her son Charles IX and their supposed joint decision to condone the murder of Admiral Coligny, and he explained at great length that a Protestant conspiracy had been uncovered which had brought about the decision for the severe reprisals which had taken place in Paris and it was with regret that the fighting had spread throughout France and was now out of all control.

Queen Elizabeth and her ministers viewed the activities of the Catholics as a threat to the State and the old legislation which had been drafted in Parliament, stating that all Englishmen be forced to pay £20 per month if they failed to attend the Anglican services and to be seen to be supporting Queen and Church, was still in force in England. Because of the Pope's Bill of Excommunication against Queen Elizabeth I, it was deemed high treason to promote Papal theology or to embrace the doctrines of the ancient Roman religeon.

Prior to St. Bartholomew's Massacre, Queen Elizabeth had been in the midst of marriage negotiations with King Charles IX and Catherine de Medici for her marriage to Le Duc d'Alencon, Catherine's youngest son, who was almost twenty years younger than Elizabeth. Although Elizabeth wanted to put her Court into mourning in the wake of St Bartholomew's Massacre, this would have meant that she would have had to cease negotiations for she was keen to have her 'Frog Prince' visit her in England and the Queen had been receiving letters from Alencon regularly. Plans had to be put off yet again, as Elizabeth received news that Alencon had been imprisoned in France for conspiring with the Huguenots and that his brother, the Duke of Anjou had been elected King of Poland, in preference to Ivan the Terrible.

Charles IX's cousin, the King of Navarre was being held captive at Court, after the Massacre and had been lured to Court by Charles IX who said it had been his intention to marry Navarre to his sister Margaret of Valois. Navarre had made attempts to escape with the assistance of Le mole and Coconnas who were beheaded when the Plot was uncovered.

In England, John Stubbs wrote a Tract entitled 'The Gaping Gulf' complaining against the marriage negotiations between Queen Elizabeth I and Le Duc d'Alencon in which he recorded his opinion that Alencon was 'the old serpent himself come to seduce the English Eve and to ruin the English Paradise'. Stubbs then went on to say 'the Roman mass would return in Alencon's private Chapel to silence God's word' because Catherine de Medici had during their protracted marriage negotiations, informed Queen Elizabeth that Le Duc d'Alencon and his entourage must be allowed to worship in his own Catholic religion and unfortunately for Stubbs, Preachers in London and elsewhere took up the Tract and gave feverish sermons in order to promote ill feeling toward the brother of the French King and stirred up intense public reaction which necessitated a proclamation forbidding further reading of Stubbs tract. Stubbs was later sent for trial on the accusation of sedition and sentence was pronounced by the Court that he should lose his right hand so that he may write no more Tracts of this or any other nature. 'When Stubbs right hand was amputated he took off his hat with his left hand and cried bravely, '"God save the Queen" before he fell to the ground in a faint'. As Stubbs was carried off to the Tower of London, he was heard to say 'left there is a true Englishman's hand'. And sadly, no more was heard of poor Thomas Stubbs after he entered the Tower because he contracted gangrene in what remained of his right arm and he died in his filthy Tower cell shortly afterwards in great agony and without medical assistance being afforded to him.

The health of Charles IX worsened and it was thought that he was suffering from Tuberculosis as he took to his bed and he repented for the blood he had shed and exclaimed to his nurse 'Nurse, Nurse! so much blood all around me! Is it that which I have shed?" He died on 31st May 1574.

It was not until the 16th June 1574 that the heir to the throne of France, Duke of Anjou who had been elected as the King of Poland a year earlier, in preference to Ivan the Terrible, suddenly received news from his mother Catherine de Medici that he must return to France as his brother Charles IX had died. The Duke fled Poland secretly during the night and headed for Austria. There he received a magnificent reception from the Emperor of Vienna after which he spent a splendid week in Venice enjoying the festivals which were being held.

And so, the Duke of Anjou who had once wooed Queen Elizabeth I was crowned King of France on the 13th and 14th February and he married Louise of Lorraine. His younger brother, Le Duc d'Alencon then inherited the title of the Duke of Anjou, and began courting the daughter of Philip of Spain, forgetting about the marriage negotiations between himself and Queen Elizabeth I of England and the Queen of

England wept once more at her plight, and a broken love affair brought about by her Advisers.

The long years which Raleigh had spent in battle torn France as a soldier during the terrible French religious civil wars were drawing to a close and had taught Raleigh some very harsh lessons, in addition to which he had also developed an in depth understanding of the futility of civil war. His experiences in France also stood him in good stead in later years, when he was able to call upon his knowledge of military strategy and put it to good use in Ireland for which he was awarded Lismore Castle and 40,000 acres by the Queen of England in 1580. He spent three years there with Edmund Spencer from 1586 to 1589.

"Upon his return to England, Walter Raleigh may have acquired an edge of ruthlessness but he had also gained a tremendous strength of character which was to remain with him for the rest of his life and he had received an extreme and profound grounding as a soldier whilst serving under his cousin Champernoun." – Hugh Ross Williamson.

King James I of England was a Protestant although his mother Mary Queen of Scots remained a Catholic all her life until she was beheaded at Fotheringay Castle, and had suffered twenty years of imprisonment.

Mary's three marriages were all doomed to fail.

Her only child James had been taken from her as a baby and brought up under the strict confines of the English Court. If she ever saw him again I do not know, but she wrote often to him and in her letters she described to him her terrible life but if he received her letters I do not know of it in any history I have found, and would not hear of the toleration of Catholic worship returning to his Kingdom.

HIC JACET: SIR WALTER RALEIGH

Winter 1626
at 5 Bell Yard, London

As I now make haste to step forward in so humble a manner, I will say to my reader that I carry with me some embarrassment in the presentation of Sir Walter Raleigh's history, because I am an uneducated servant he was a skilled orator and writer during his own lifetime and I cannot bear to look further than my own mind for a criticism of my work. To criticise it would be to damn my attempt to prove that he was no traitor to his King, nor to his country. I declare that if I find criticism from any quarter, then my work has been halted before I begin. In that event I say that no eyes shall meet with my words and that they will be buried with his truth, since to seek out the truth and then find it condemned, is to find malice and betrayal a second time, heaped upon the first. That is too much for an old man such as myself to bear for the sake of Sir Walter's innocence. If my soul could induce me to work so hard that I might urge others to learn of Sir Walter Raleigh's downfall and the reasons for his execution, then I will rest peacefully in the cold and dark clay that waits to claim me.

I wish that I could draw you into a story of happiness and gaiety, since I know that it would please you, but that story has already been told and I find that I cannot offer it to you again. If you seek a true account of Sir Walter Raleigh's trial at Winchester Castle in 1603 then you will find it faithfully recorded here. As we progress, it is my promise that I will reveal important documents to you, concerning his downfall

I now suffer extreme anguish as I sit alone at my old wooden desk, placed near the window in a room overlooking a narrow alleyway, known to Londoners as 5 Bell Yard. How many long and miserable years I have endured in gathering up this history and as to the bleak and lonely path it has led me down, I cannot say within these pages, because this is not the place to reveal it.

I find myself well prepared, and have before me ink, parchment and several new feather quills which I brought with me from Lombard Street. I take little account of the hourglass as it spills its fine grains of sand with each passing moment, because darkness turns to light readily enough as I work and I need never cause myself to count time in that way.

As the words of the Scrivener's Apprentice unfold from my mind and are recorded within these pages, then I will be guided by the hushed voices of ancient men. They in their turn will kindly raise their lanterns for us so that we may look into their anxious faces, made bright by the burning of tallow candles. Then our way is already lit and will lead on our journey for the truth about Sir Walter Raleigh's downfall.

It is necessary that at times our journey will lead us down narrow streets as we pass the cramped rows of gabled houses with their leaded, misty glass window panes, not daring to peer into them, and we will experience a feeling of being watched by these ghosts of ancient times, but as we are only viewing them through our own minds, they will not be disturbed by us so very much. We will see the inhabitants of London dashing out of their houses and into our path because they are anxious to stop and speak to us as we slowly make our way forward. Some will merely seek to beg an old penny from us to buy their bread, since they are poor and trapped within their own memories of poverty. Then we must be kind and humble to them, as we can do little to assist them, since they are left only with the will to lead or follow us as they choose.

When we meet with these spirits as they walk ahead of us, over the egg shaped cobbles of ancient London, we will view it through their eyes, so that they might come alive in the mind of the reader who attention they wish to capture. They will be dressed in their long black cloaks as they lead us forward in search truth, and they will speak, but sometimes it will barely be a whisper, and yet what they utter we must hear, for it is history to us and their misery must never be forgotten. If they fear to tell us their story then it is because their memories are awakened to the true horror of their times and they may hesitate to step forward. They will walk among the rats in the narrow streets of the plague infested City of London of 1603, and the rats will scurry for their lives because the ghosts of these men disturb them as they walk among us once more.

If my tears are shed as I sit alone and weep for them, then it is out of a love that cannot be repaid and I seek no reward. I cannot pity those men who died in innocence because their spirits are still among us, and if the thought of them causes a man to wake from his sleep through fear of his own conscience then it is just.

As I stare into the glowing embers of the fire, I am aware that the room is warm and yet I shiver. The walls lighted by the bright glow of the burning wood, reveal to my eyes, the otherwise darkened room, and all about me I see the dark shadows of the past rising up from the depths of my mind as I am cast back into the year 1603. The shadows are horrible as they dance across the walls, waiting to speak. There are eight of these lonely spirits and yet I cannot say whether others will join us. First I see the ghosts of Watson and Clarke, the Priests who suffered their fate at Winchester Castle on the 4th December 1603, when they were pronounced traitors to King James I of England and were hung drawn and quartered. Their severed heads being carried around the Castle and up into the battlements, where they were displayed, so that no other man might take it into his head to rise up against his King. On the 6th December Lord Cobham's brother, Brook, was tried and executed. On the 10th December Lord Cobham and Lord Grey were to be executed. On the 13th December, Sir Walter Raleigh was to die.

Elizabethan Calendar 1603
A Plague Year

Deaths from the Plague in this year were between 1,500 and 2,500 per week. In the first week of September 3,000 people died of the Plague

January 1603

M	T	W	TH	F	S	S
					1	2
3	4	5	6	7	8	9
10	11	12	13	14	15	16
17	18	19	20	21	22	23
24	25	26	27	28	29	30
31						

February 1603

M	T	W	TH	F	S	S
	1	2	3	4	5	6
7	8	9	10	11	12	13
14	15	16	17	18	19	20
21	22	23	24	25	26	27
28						

March 1603

M	T	W	TH	F	S	S
	1	2	3	4	5	6
7	8	9	10	11	12	13
14	15	16	17	18	19	20
21	22	23	24	25	26	27
28	29	30	31			

The Queen cannot sleep for 20 days

Queen Elizabeth dies at 2 am

King James VI of Scotland becomes King James I of England. Three days before the Queen's funeral, James ordered that Lord Mountjoy, Lord Thos. Howard and the Earls of Cumberland and to his Privy Council.

Northumberland were to be sworn

April 1603

M	T	W	TH	F	S	S
				1	2	3

```
4   5   6   7   8   9  10
11  12  13  14  15  16  17
18  19  20  21  22  23  24
25  26  27  28   29  30
```

May 1603

M	T	W	TH	F	S	S
						1
2	3	4	5	6	7	8

7th Sir Walter Raleigh arrives in London from Jersey

M	T	W	TH	F	S	S
9	10	11	12	13	14	15

On 8th May Raleigh is called before James I and told that the King is pleased to inform him that his position as Captain of the Guard is to go to Sir Thomas Irskine.

```
16  17  18  19  20  21  22
23  24  25  26  27  28  29
30 31
```

June 1603

M	T	W	TH	F	S	S
		1	2	3	4	5
6	7	8	9	10	11	12

King James visits Henry Percy, 9th Earl of Northumberland, "Wizard Earl" at Syon House

M	T	W	TH	F	S	S
13	14	15	16	17	18	19

9th June Lord Cobham:Conference with Raleigh at Durham Hse

M	T	W	TH	F	S	S
20	21	22	23	24	25	26

9th June Cobham goes to his brother George Brook to tell all.

M	T	W	TH	F	S	S
27	28	29	30			

14th June Cobham delivers Raleigh's book to Brook

On the 8th June Raleigh is told that King James wishes Durham House in the Strand, London, to be made over to the Bishop of Durham The Raleighs are to vacate the property by 24th June. It had been the home of Sir Walter Raleigh since 1583, and overlooked the River Thames, and a short distance away was Essex House, which had been the home of Robert Devereux, the Second Earl of Essex, who in earlier times had been a friend to Raleigh, and had even stood as godfather to his son Damerei, who had died in infancy. A rivalry had sprung up between them, perhaps vying for the Queen's affections, or perhaps it

was for dramatic patronage reasons.

July 1603

M	T	W	TH	F	S	S
				1	2	3
4	5	6	7	8	9	10
11	12	13	14	15	16	17
18	19	20	21	22	23	24
25	26	27	28	29	30	31

5th July Antony Copley arrested, carried to the Tower of London Gorges, Grey and Brook arrested
14 th July Raleigh, Kemys and Lord Cobham are arrested

August 1603

M	T	W	TH	F	S	S
1	2		3	4	5	6	7
8	9		10	11	12	13	14
15	16	17	18	19	20	21
22	23	24	25	26	27	28
29	30	31				

September 1603

M	T	W	TH	F	S	S
			1	2	3	4
5	6	7	8	9	10	11
12	13	14	15	16	17	18
19	20	21	22	23	24	25
26	27	28	29	30		

Report of the Special Commissioners. Judges meet at Maidenhead
All prisoners are isolated

October 1603

M	T	W	TH	F	S	S
					1	2
3	4	5	6	7	8	9
10	11	12	13	14	15	16
17	18	19	20	21	22	23
24	25	26	27	28	29	30
31						

November 1603

M	T	W	TH	F	S	S
	1	2	3	4	5	6
7	8	9	10	11	12	13
14	15	16	17	18	19	20
21	22	23	24	25	26	27
28	29	30				

17th Raleigh's trial begins at Winchester

December 1603

M	T	W	TH	F	S	S
			1	2	3	4
5	6	7	8	9	10	11
12	13	14	15	16	17	18
19	20	21	22	23	24	25
26	27	28	29	30	31	

4th Priests Clarke and Watson executed Their heads displayed on the attlements of Winchester Castle

6thCobham's brother, Brook tried and Executed

10th Markham, Cobham and Grey to die

13th Raleigh is sentenced to be hung drawn and quartered

7th December the King sends Warrants remitting the sentences of Raleigh, Cobham, Markham and Grey, but keeps it a secret from the Prisoners.

Each man is brought to the Scaffold, released for prayer, brought back to the Scaffold and told their sentences have been remitted by the King. They are then told they are all sentenced to life imprisonment in the Tower of London.

1603
Queen Elizabeth I of England is about to Die

Queen Elizabeth I lay on her death bed in March 1603. She was 70 years old. Several of her advisers gathered about her bedside, pondering upon the best course of action befitting their rank and honesty. She would push them away with disdain since through her eyes, blurred by her own illness and her sadness, and brought about through age, she saw only the shadows of her youth approaching her in near death. They mean to lead her away to a hall of judgement in the next Word, where she will meet, not her father, King Henry VIII of England but the King of Kings. Lord Burleigh (her 'eyes') is dead. Approaching her bed is her cousin, Mary Queen of Scots and then she turns in her bed and cries out that she did not sign the death Warrant. Then her second cousin, Robert Devereux, the Second Earl of Essex stands behind Mary, her beloved Robert lost his head in Ash Wednesday 1601 for raising an army against her to claim the throne upon her death, and yet his heritage had dated back to King [27] I of England. 'Raleigh!' cried the Queen. 'Raleigh' - I must warn him against the future King for I have caused the events of history to be changed by my own actions. 'Raleigh'.

Few were surprised that the Queen, who had been unable to sleep for

---

[27] the play Edward II acted by the Earl of Pembroke's Men on the 30th January 1593. [Revived by Queen Anne's men at the Red Bull in St. John's Streete.

20 days had not stirred from her bed for many days, and yet the son of Mary Queen of Scots waited to claim her throne.

King James VI of Scotland waited outside London.

Durham House, The Strand, London
8th June, 1603

Sir Walter Raleigh, with his son Wat Raleigh

It was still early in the morning when Raleigh had climbed the old wooden staircase on his way to the turret, and he stopped suddenly on the second floor landing of Durham House and opened the windows in order to observe the scenes upon the River Thames. This had been his home since 1583 when the Queen had granted him the use of it. He cast his eyes upon the effects of the brilliant sunshine that cast a golden shimmer upon the surface of the otherwise dark water, as far as his eye could see. The reflection upon the river lit up the magnificent houses in the Parish of St. Martin's in the Fields. Then a dark cloud fell upon him as he turned his eyes toward Essex House, where Robert Devereux, the Second Earl of Essex had once lived, and where he had barricaded himself before his arrest and execution, for his planned Rebellion against Queen Elizabeth, after his return from the war in Ireland.

As Raleigh made his way up the final flight of stairs, he paused outside the empty room opposite his own study, and remembered how his dear friend Thomas Harriot had once occupied this room after he had arrived in London from Oxford University at the age of 24, and looking for a place to live and continue his studies concerning astronomy and mathematics. Harriot had shown signs of becoming a brilliant scientist and mathematician.

As Raleigh entered the empty room and looked around him, a scene presented itself to his mind as he remembered how excited Harriot had been to tell him of his new experiment to measure rainfall.

First, Harriot had measured his study room and found it to be 21 1/2 feet by 12 1/2 feet and had said he wished to know how much rain it would take to fill the entire room. He set out to perform his experiment with the aid of a cube and having ascertained that it was capable of holding exactly 9 cubic inches, he set about measuring rainfall using his pulse as one beat per second. By this method Harriot calculated that the rain fell at a rate of 8 1/2 inches during a twenty four hour period. Harriot had then shown Raleigh a drawing of a parellelogram to indicate that his room contained 268 3/4 square feet or 38,700 square inches and had remarked that by this calculation he would find the answer.

Harriot now lived at Syon House in Brentford, with the Wizard Earl, Henry Percy the Ninth Earl of Northumberland, who shared his interest in science and had been introduced to the Earl by Raleigh himself. Nevertheless, Harriot still remained a true friend and companion to Raleigh and continued as Raleigh's auditor and performed clerical duties, keeping records of his Estates in Ireland and at Sherborne, which were stored in the Chest that was hidden at the great Barn on the Syon Estate.

Raleigh sighed and closed the door to Harriot's old room and crossed the wide square hall as he made his way into his own white walled study. He closed the door behind him and as he leaned back against it he, resolved to spend the rest of his day there, being eager to take up his quill again and write. Since it was something he had neglected to do for quite some time.

He immediately pulled up his chair and seated himself at his old wooden desk beneath the open window and commenced writing, amidst the pleasing sound of birds singing in the distance and this brought him comfort to soothe his mind.

Raleigh, who was 6 feet tall, had with the assistance of one of his servants, dressed in a plain grey shirt, buttoned up to his neck with small darker grey buttons. Over his shirt he wore a beige and brown embroidered thigh length padded doublet with sleeves capped at his broad shoulders, which attached to his grey breeches by tags and laces or points, and a white starched lace ruff around his neck. His dark brown wavy hair was slightly tousled because he had been leaning on his left elbow upon the desk and the fingers of his left hand were resting upon his head. He was writing meticulously with brown ink which he had applied to the stiff parchment with a freshly sharpened quill, topped with a snowy white feather. He leaned forward intermittently to dip his quill into the highly polished silver inkstand, taking great care not to take more ink than he needed, by running the tip of the quill against the rim of the inkwell. As he completed each new page of writing, he carefully applied fine grains of white sand to the parchment in order to dry it thoroughly. He was writing an Essay on his Estate at Sherborne and how he would improve the gardens and plant beautiful plants and trees to form a pleasing aspect from the windows of his Castle.

The Sun's rays seemed to travel up through the humid morning air, and as they struck the small diamond shaped glass and pierced in through the windows of the little turret the light created an ethereal effect within the room. The resultant golden glow seemed to produce a magical effect as it fell sparkling upon the various objects in the room, such as the steel mirror hanging on the wall. There was a noticeable silence in the room except for the scratching of his quill, moving slowly and carefully across the parchment as he formed his beautiful script.

Raleigh was sitting in a comfortable chair, leaning back against a large deep red tapestry cushion which he had propped up behind himself. His old wooden desk, scratched and battered by time, was conveniently placed in front of the small leaded window. A silver inkstand stood on the table in front of him and had been a gift from the Queen and as he looked upon it he remembered how pleased he had been to receive it on his birthday in 1598. On the left hand side of the desk stood a bundle of cream coloured parchment together with several new and brightly coloured feather quills which stood upright in a pewter mug. The hourglass on the table containing white sand was trickling steadily through and he noticed that it was almost time to turn it again. He had been writing for three hours and he stood to look at the sundial outside, which told him it was almost noon. He stood up and made ready to pour himself a goblet of red wine and then turned as there was a slight tap at the door.

He turned and saw that it was one of his young servant's, Peter Dean, who hurried into the room, and wore an extremely worried expression. He was carrying a letter which he was so anxious to hand to Raleigh that he tripped over the leg of the chair that Raleigh had just sat back into. The brimming goblet of wine fell from his hand before he had taken more than a sip, and as the red stain sank into his expensive doublet he spoke sharply:

"What ails you man that you deprive me of my wine and almost knock me from my seat?"

Peter, a tall blonde youth of 20, stood before him dressed in a plain Navy blue doublet of heavy cotton which had been half unbuttoned to show a white shirt beneath pale blue knee length hose and highly polished black leather shoes. His face was flushed with colour because he had been running through the house and up the stairs and as he tripped he had crumpled the letter he had been holding. He handed the letter to Raleigh and said:

"This letter has just been delivered to the main door by your son, Wat, and I am told it contains harsh news".

As Raleigh took the letter, not noticing its condition, he said "My son is but 10 years old and I forbade him to accompany his mother this morning. Where is he now?"

"He ran swiftly away from the door, and down the Strand, closely chased by Ben Johnson who had accompanied him back from the Hampton Court".

"Then he will be found in a nearby alehouse I have no doubt!. And my wife? Where is she now? What the devil has happened?"

Wasting no more time, Raleigh tore open the letter and noted it had been dated the 8th June, 1603 and as he read the contents, tears sprang too readily to his eyes. It was from his wife, who not being able to carry the news quickly enough from the Court had scribbled this hasty note:

On the 8th June Raleigh is told that King James wishes Durham House
to be made over to the Bishop of Durham
The Raleighs are to vacate the property by 24th June. It had been the
home of Sir Walter Raleigh since 1583

'Prepare yourself my husband, since we are required to vacate Durham
House by the end of June. King James has deemed it so. We are
found to be unfit tenants since the fire. The house is to pass to the
Bishop of Durham and we must vacate our home by the 24th June,
since Cecil finds us unfit tenants since the fire, albeit the Queen's
desire that you should remain in residence for your lifetime and thus
mine.'

Signed, Bess

"Your wife has requested a conference with Lord Cobham at Court
and will make her way back presently. She seems to think that he may
intervene through his father, Lord Cecil and can use his influence with
the King."

Raleigh cast his mind back to that very morning, calling to mind how
he and his wife had argued about the new King and his motives. And
he had tried to explain to her that there was trouble afoot concerning
Essex, beheaded on Ash Wednesday 1601. Bess had cried out in
anger that since Essex was a Traitor to the Queen then he had died for
his cause. And then she had announced that she would take herself off
to Hampton Court and enquire about the cause of the fire that had
taken place at Durham House on the 1st May 1603, feeling that it was
her duty, since she had been present at the house at the time, and
Raleigh had been abroad in Jersey. It had taken place late at night she
had said, and therefore she had not been responsible. Raleigh had
strongly suspected that a servant had caused it, and that the servant
was Peter Dean who stood before him now. His suspicion was so,
since it had taken place near to the quarters in which he lodged
himself. His son Wat had been present and he had taken his mother's
side on the matter.

HIC JACET: SIR WALTER RALEIGH

His wife, Bess Throckmorton, Lady Raleigh, had left the house later that morning, and made her way hastily by carriage to the King's Court. There she resolved that she would be received for a second interview with Lord Cecil, (the first having been in May when the fire had taken place), in an effort to procure for them more than a leasehold interest in Durham House, since the expense of the repairs to the house after the fire damage would be tremendous.

The mysterious fire which had taken place at Durham House in May had necessitated Raleigh being called back from his official duties in Jersey. Many of his official papers had vanished, and were purported to have been burned in the blaze, and yet he felt uneasy about them. They had been kept under lock and key in the strong wooden chest in the attic and the fire had not touched that part of the house. Among the missing papers had been his personal letters to the Queen in 1601, concerning the Earl of Essex and his conduct in Ireland during that year. Her had also given the Queen his own opinion of the Earl's planned rebellion against her and his advice had been harsh, and yet strangely, though understandably misinterpreted by friends of the Earl.

It had been no easy task to retrieve those letters from the Queen and yet she had reluctantly agreed to return them to him, when he had told her that he feared the Privy Councillors would seek them out to honour the Earl. Since they had been written in confidence to her he had them in his possession again. Until the night of the fire.

"You may go now Peter since I have no further need".

He turned and looked about the room for some comfort. His mind seemed to carry him back and forth until he found a comfortable situation in which to place it.
In this study he had never hidden himself away. Yet here he had always found comfort and solace.

He would take some time to stand and reflect at his steel mirror. The very mirror he requested to be made in honour of his cousin, the poet, George Gasgoine, and now when he looked into it he saw an ancient mirror and it produced pictures from his mind.

He considered himself intently and gazed deeply into his own grey eyes and they flashed back at him dispassionately. For inspiration he picked up his treasured, jeweled comb from the table and his memory was immediately brought to life.

The jeweled comb containing emeralds, diamonds, rubies and sapphires, had been a present from the Queen when he was in great favour with her after a day at the Hunt in the meadows of Hampton Court. Her father had spent his time hunting and she had wished to observe the men of Court at their hunting. That she had not dressed accordingly, had brought about a situation of great merit for himself. It had not been his plan to display his chivalry toward her and yet upon that day, it had been seen as a show of great arrogance on the part of the great Lords and Earls of the Court, who could not have been expected to act thus:

He had taken off and laid down his magnificent cloak of pearls, being of great expense to him, and there upon the mud it was left for her to tread upon, because she had hesitated to move forward and her Lords had stood idly by and watched the scene. Why said the Lords did you dress for evening Court for a daytime Hunt? Because the Queen dressed so and I desired to please her".

It had come about because the evening before, after being invited to play cards with the Queen, he had stayed too long, until Dawn and upon leaving, and having written upon her window pane with a diamond at Hampton Court 'Fain would I climb, yet I fear to fall'...; the Queen had replied 'If thy heart fail thee, then climb not at all!".

The diamond with which he had written had been a gift from the Queen. Not because he had excelled at cards or dice, but because he had won through the skill of his own mind.

HIC JACET: SIR WALTER RALEIGH

There, in her chamber, as the cold grey Dawn had approached, the Queen had complained when he took out his wooden pipe and filled it with tobacco. The smoke she had said, filled her with great anguish, since he burned his money from inside himself and did himself damage, callously if he put himself up as a chimney for her. He had explained that it was a substance from America, and since she would not let him go there himself he must sample the delights it had to offer.

"Tobacco! It is tobacco! And I have a mind for it!"

"Then your mind deceives you if you think I am able to endure the smell, and nor can I breathe the air it makes for."

"But if I empty my pipe and show you the content, will you see Gold?"

"If I seek gold and see the colour of mud I will see no Gold!"

"Then heed this":

Raleigh had taken from beneath his doublet, a small black leather packet, and filled his rusting silver pipe and began to smoke it. He emptied the contents of his pipe into a double weighing scale and asked the Queen to place a diamond into the opposite scale.

And this is what he said:

As we sit at a wooden table
It will be an Elizabethan fable;
I will make a claim of olde
To know the weight of smoke;
If Queen Elizabeth will concede
And move a little forward
My proof will be that other men
Through gain turn gold to smoke
But I turn smoke to gold.

I weigh the ashes sure and just
To prove I know the weight of smoke!"

And if yesterday had much to tell now, then he would tell it. One
story and yet these men and women, they are legends. One mind
speaking for many. So it is with history, and it brings us closer.

He slowly began to comb his hair, which fell in waves from his
temples.

He was 52 years old and his ambitious mind had been stayed. He no
longer saw the dark trailing curls nor the clear grey eyes that he had
once looked upon in this mirror long ago.   Now he saw a reflection of
his past and it brought him pain from his own soul. As he combed his
hair, he noticed the thin silvered strands and he recognised that it was
no longer vanity that caused him to do this, but he wished his mind to
take him to what was past and not to leave him in his present state.
What he saw did not please him, indeed it was his own way of
marveling at the passing of time itself and marking it in a moment of
reflection. Perhaps it was a trick of the sunlight, but he also noticed
the deep lines that had not been there a few short months ago, when
the Queen was still alive. He turned his head slowly from side to side
to examine their progress, and reflected that he would be a fortunate
man indeed if he lived long enough to see a full head of silver hair
grow upon his head and the lined face of an old man stare back at
himself in the future, from this very mirror.

He turned his attention to his grey eyes and looked deeply into them as
if he expected to find some hidden secret which would reveal itself
from deep within his soul if he could stay long enough to discover
what this was.

In this very study, his dear friend Christopher Marlowe had sat beside
him and announced that he had sold his work to the [
company] for £10 per play.

Marlowe at the age of 29 had been murdered by Ingram Frizer, at the home of Mistress Eleanor Bull and yet Frizer had walked free. Poley and Skeres knew more and he had resolved to find the cause. If the cause had been found then he was yet to comprehend its meaning. A literary warfare? His friend Marlowe had been the most accomplished Dramatist; he had skills far greater than young William Shakespeare and yet he had been misinterpreted for his work concerning St. Bartholomew's Massacre and the Duke of Guise, The Uncle of Mary Queen of Scots. Marlowe had made enemies at Court and none greater than Sir Francis Walsingham, the 'Spymaster of the Catholics", present at the massacre. And then Marlowe was lured to the place of his death by Nicholas Walsingham's servant. If two witnesses are proof to the murder, then the murder took place. The Inquest on Marlowe found a verdict of self defence since they were urged that it was self defence, and yet Marlowe had arrived at 10 in the morning to that house and he had drunk too much to fight and draw his poniard. He had not received any money for his plays since his co-dramatist Thomas Kyd,

So intent was he before the steel mirror, that Raleigh did not hear the door open as Lord Cobham entered the room.

The Conspirators to the Spanish Bye and Main Plot, 1603

I am led to tell you now of the discontented men who were involved in the Spanish Bye Plot and the Main Plot.

The curious Sir Walter Raleigh was attracted like a moth to a flame as he overheard a conversation which had taken place in a dark courtyard outside Durham House and when Sir Walter peered through the silence and the darkness, he saw that it was between Lawrency and the Lord Cobham.

Sir Walter waited for his moment and then immediately searched out Cobham and resolved to learn news of the Plot against the King, but he was himself drawn into what can only be described as a trap, and he was immediately ensnared and swiftly betrayed by [28] Cobham.

This is known as 'Sir Walter's Treason' and the following men were involved:

William Watson A secular priest
Clarke A secular priest
Anthony Copley
Sir Arthur Gorges
The Count of Aremberg   Ambassador to the Arch Duke
Lord Cobham, a Protestant,
George Brook, a Protestant
Henry Brook
Parham who brought in,
Lord Grey of Wilton, a Puritan
Sir Griffin Markham
Mr Lawrency an Antwerp Merchant and friend to Lord Cobham
Sir Walter Raleigh

---

[28] See Cobham's letters to Raleigh

There designs were:

(i)   To set the Crown on the [29] Lady Arabella; or to seize the King and make him grant their desires and a pardon.

(ii)   To have a toleration of religion.

(iii)   To procure aid and assistance from foreign princes.

(iv)   To turn out of the court such as they disliked and   desired to place themselves in the following offices:

The Priest Watson	-	to be Lord Chancellor
George Brook -		Lord-Treasurer
Sir Griffin Markham	-	Secretary of State
Lord Grey	-	Master of the Horse and Earl-Marshal of England

Priest Watson drew up an Oath of secrecy, but as no provision for future office was made for Sir Walter we may be sure of his innocence, as his trial will indicate to the reader.

Anthony Copley was the first to be arrested on the 5th July 1603, and having been carried off to the Tower of London where he was questioned and tortured he confessed the entire plot to murder the King and proceeded to implicate Sir Griffin Markham, William Watson and George Brook.

By the 14th July as events moved forward Gorges, Lord Grey and

---

[29] Lady Arabella Stuart by descent Charles Stuart 6th Earl of Lennox and Elizabeth daught of Sir William Cavendish (Arabella d.1615) 1st wife of William Seymour (Duke of Somerset, K.G. d. 1660 (and then married Frances daughter of Robert Devereux, Earl of Essex (2nd wife d. 1674 (the Earl of Essex had married Frances Walsingham the widow of Sir Philip Sidney)

George Brook were arrested and taken to the Tower.

Lord Cobham and Sir Walter Raleigh were taken into custody without having been formally charged and a Special Commission was called to the Tower of London where each of the Prisoners would be examined in turn. It was ordered that they should all be kept in strict isolation and questioned intensively.

After his arrest on the 14th July 1603, Raleigh and Lawrence Kemys were committed to the Tower. During his imprisonment in the Bloody Tower, Raleigh saw that the actions of his enemies were about to destroy him and seeking to put his Estate in order before his death he wrote a letter to his dear wife Besse:

1.   You shall now receive (my dear Wife) my last Words in these my last Lines. My Love I send you, that you may keep it when I am dead; and my Counsel, that you may remember it when I am no more. I would not by my Will present you with Sorrows (Dear Besse) let them go into the Grave with me, and be buried in the Dust. And seeing that it is not God's Will that I should see you any more in this Life, bear it patiently, and with a Heart like thy self. First I send you all the Thanks which my Heart can conceive, or my Words can rehearse, for your many Travails, and Care taken for me; which though they have not taken effect as you wished, yet my Debt to you is not the less; but pay it I never shall in this world. Secondly, I beseech you, for the Love you bare me living, do not hide your self many Days, but by your Travels seek to help your miserable Fortunes, and the right of your poor Child. Thy Mourning cannot avail me, I am but Dust. Thirdly, you shall understand that my Land was conveyed bona fide to my child: The Writings were drawn at Midsummer was twelve Months, my honest Cousin Brett can testify so much, and Dolberry too can remember somewhat therein. And I trust my Blood will quench their Malice that have cruelly murdered me, and that they will not seek also to kill thee and thine with extreme Poverty. To what Friend to direct thee I know not, for all mine have left me in the true time of Trial. And I perceive that my Death was determined from the first Day. Most sorry I am, God knows, that having been surprised with

Death that I can leave you in no better Estate. God is my Witness, I meant you all my Office of Wines, or all that I could have purchased by selling it, half my Stuff and all my Jewels, but some one for the Boy; but God hath prevented all my Resolutions, that great God that ruleth all in all; but if you can live free from Want, care for no more, the rest is but Vanity. Love God, and begin betimes to repose your self upon him, and therein shall you find true and lasting Riches, and endless Comfort: for the rest, when you have travelled and wearied your Thoughts over all sorts of worldly Cogitations, you shall but sit down by Sorrow in the end Teach your Son also to love and fear God whilst he is yet young, that the Fear of God may grow with him; and then God will be a Husband to you, and a Father to him; a Husband and a Father which cannot be taken from you. Baily oweth me 2001. and Adrian 6001. in Jersey. I also have much owing me besides.. The Arrearages of the Wines will pay your Debts. And howsoever you do, for my Soul's sake pay all poor Men. When I am gone no doubt you shall be sought to, for the World thinks that I was very rich. [30]But *take heed of the Pretenses of Men, and their Affections, for they last not but in honest and worthy Men; and no greater Misery can befall you in this Life than to become a Prey, and afterwards to be despised.* I speak not this (God knows) to dissuade you from Marriage, for it will be best for you both in respect of the World and of God. As for me, I am no more yours, nor you mine, Death hath cut us asunder; and God hath divided me from the World, and you from me. Remember your poor Child for his Father's sake, who chose you, and loved you in his happiest Times. Get those Letters (if it be possible) which I writ to the Lords, wherein I sued for Life: God is my Witness it was for you and yours that I desired Life; but it is true that I disdain'd my self for begging of it: for know it, (my dear Wife) that your Son is the Son of a true Man, and who, in his own respect, despiseth Death, *and all his misshapen and ugly Forms.* I cannot write much, God knows how

---

[30] Essays: Sir Francis Bacon

hardly I steal this Time while others sleep, and it is also time that I should separate my Thoughts from the World, Beg my dead Body, which living was denied thee; and either lay it at Sherburne (and if the Land continue) or in Exeter-Church by my Father and Mother. I can say no more, Time and Death call me away; the everlasting, powerful, infinite, and omnipotent God, that Almighty God, who is Goodness it self, the true Life and the true Light, keep thee and thine, have Mercy on me, and teach me to forgive my Persecutors and Accusers, and send us to meet in his glorious Kingdom. My dear Wife, farewell. Bless my poor Boy. Pray for me, and let my good God hold you both in his Arms. Written with the dying Hand of sometime thy Husband, but now alas overthrown.

2.   [("Receive from they unfortunate husband these his last lines; these the last words that ever thou shalt receive from him. that I can live never to see thee and my child more! - I cannot ....'(and urge you to marry again 'not to please sense, but to avoid poverty, and to preserve thy child. For myself, I am left of all men that have done good to many. All my good turns forgotten; all my errors revived and expounded to all extremity of ill. All my services, hazards, and expenses for my country - plantings, discoveries, fights, councils, and whatsoever else - malice hath now covered over. I am now made an enemy and traitor by the word of an unworthy man. He (Cobham) hath proclaimed me to be a partaker of his vain imaginations, notwithstanding the whole course of my life hath approved the contrary, as my death shall approve it. Woe, woe, woe be unto him by whose falsehood we are lost. He hath separated us asunder. He hath slain my *honor*; my *fortune*. He hath robbed thee of thy husband, thy child of his father, and me of you both.

Oh intolerable infamy! O God! I cannot resist these thoughts. I cannot live to think how I am derided, to think of the expectation of my enemies, the scorns I shall receive, the cruel words of lawyers, the infamous taunts and despites, to be made a wonder and a spectacle! ... O Death! destroy my memory which is my tormentor; my thoughts and my life cannot dwell in one body...

HIC JACET: SIR WALTER RALEIGH

I bless my poor child, and let him know his father was no traitor. Be bold of my innocence, for God - to whom I offer life and soul - knows it. And whosoever thou choose again after me, let him be but thy politique husband. But let my son be thy beloved, for he is part of me and I live in him; and the difference is but in the number and not in the kind. And the Lord for ever keep thee and them, and give thee comfort in both worlds."

Walter Raleigh
28th October, 1618

[31] Sir Walter Raleigh's (Indenture 1 August 1599

"[("This Indenture made the first day of August in the one & fforteth yeare of the Raigne of our soveraigne ladie Elizabeth by the grace of god of England ffrance & Ireland Queen defender of the faith &c Betweene the honorable Sir Walter Ralegh knight Captaine of her majesties guard & lo: warden of the Stannaries in the Counties of Devon & Cornewall of the one party And Sir George Carew & Thomas Heriott gentleman of the other party Witnesseth that the said Sir George Carew & Thomas Heriott gentleman of the other party Witnesseth that the said Sir George Carew & Thomas Heriott for diverse good causes & consideracions them hereunto movinge & especially for performance [of] the trust reposed in them have devised graunted assigned & sett over & by these presente doe demise graunte assigne & sett over unto the said Sir Walter Ralegh All that there Castle, mannors Lordshippes Landes Tenementes & hereditamentes Rentes Revercions service advousones patronages ffranchises liberties Royalties Jurisdicions & hereditamentes whatsoever within the hundred of Sherborne & yetminister in the County of Dorset To have & to hold all & singuler the premisses with the appurtenances unto the said Sir Walter Ralegh his Executors & assignes for all the tyme & tearme yett to Come & unexpired which some tymes was graunted by John Gouldwell late Bishop of Sarum unto the Queens most Excellent

---

[31] Sir Walter Raleigh's Indenture 1 August 1599 [Thomas Harriot John Shirley :1983

Majestie In witness whereof the [parties first above have to these present Indentures Interchangeably sett ther names and seales the day & yeare first above writtten:/

[Signed]   George Carewe   [Signed]   Tho: Harriots

(Obverse/Reverse)   Signed sealed & delivered in the presence of

        Howard   Henry sothar   Welighe Elbert
                        'releas from Sir G. Carew
                        & T. Herriotts'

                                                    ").]

"In 1609 when the Crown was attempting to take over the properties as part of the actions of attainder, Ralegh made a formal statement to the Attorney-General regarding his negotiations with respect to his Dorset properties. As his account is reported by his biographer [32]Edwards:

[("   'I conveyed the same estates to my son, twice, as I remember, by certain grants to certain persons and friends in trust. Those conveyances were revocable, and I did afterwards revoke them For, finding my fortune at Court towards the end of her late Majesty's reign to be at a stand, and that I daily attended dangerous employments against her late Majesty's enemies, and had not in the said former grants made any provision for my wife, I made the former grants void; and then afterwards, for the natural love and affection which I bare to the aid Walter Ralegh, then my one son, and still being desirous, as well to settle and establish some estate of and in the said castles and manors, and also some livelihood and provision for my wife, to be had thereout during her nature life, I made a new grant which last-

---

[32] Edward Edwards, The Life of Sir Walter Ralegh, 2 vols., Macmillan, 1868. Vol 1, pp 466-7

mentioned deed was made not many months before the now Bishop [Cotton] was consecrated, as I verily believe ... But by reasonn of my manifold troubles, I do not know where the said deed is, or in whose hands or custody.' Its purport, it is further said, was to convey the estates to his son, subject to a rent-charge of two hundred pounds a year for Lady Ralegh during her life. 'Her late Majesty,' proceeds Sir Walter, 'having afterwards procured form the said now Bishop the inheritance of the said lordship, castles, and manors, it pleased her to give me the same by a sufficient conveyance in law ... and afterwards I did intend to settle the inheritance of the same upon my said son ...'

).]

33

(Indenture 1 August 1599

"[("This Indenture made the first day of August in the one & fforteth yeare of the Raigne of our soveraigne ladie Elizabeth by the grace of god of England ffrance & Ireland Queen defender of the faith &c Betweene the honorable Sir Walter Ralegh knight Captaine of her majesties guard & lo: warden of the Stannaries in the Counties of Devon & Cornewall of the one party And Sir George Carew & Thomas Heriott gentleman of the other party Witnesseth that the said Sir George Carew & Thomas Heriott gentleman of the other party Witnesseth that the said Sir George Carew & Thomas Heriott for diverse good causes & consideracions them hereunto movinge & especially for performance [of] the trust reposed in them have devised graunted assigned & sett over & by these presente doe demise graunte assigne & sett over unto the said Sir Walter Ralegh All that ther Castle, mannors Lordshippes Landes Tenementes & hereditamentes Rentes Revercions service advousones patronages ffranchises liberties Royalties Jurisdicions & hereditamentes whatsoever within the hundred of Sherborne & yetminister in the County of Dorset To have & to hold all & singuler the premisses with the appurtenances unto the said Sir Walter Ralegh his Executors & assignes for all the tyme &

---

33 Sir Walter Raleigh's Last Will and Testament Indenture 1 August 1599 [Thomas Harriot John Shirley : 1983

tearme yett to Come & unexpired which some tymes was graunted by John Gouldwell late Bishop of Sarum unto the Queens most Excellent Majestie In witness whereof the [parties first above have to these present Indentures Interchangeably sett ther names and seales the day & yeare first above writtten:
[Signed]   George Carewe   [Signed]   Tho:
Harriots

[Obverse]   Signed sealed & delivered in the presence of

         Howard   Henry sothar   Welighe Elbert
                        'releas from Sir G. Carew
                        & T. Herriotts'
                                                    ").]

"In 1609 when the Crown was attempting to take over the properties as part of the actions of attainder, Ralegh made a formal statement to the Attorney-General regarding his negotiations with respect to his Dorset properties. As his account is reported by his biographer [34] Edwards:

[("   'I conveyed the same estates to my son, ... twice, as I remember, by certain grants to certain persons and friends in trust. Those conveyances were revocable, and I did afterwards revoke them ... For, finding my fortune at Court towards the end of her late Majesty's reign to be at a stand, and that I daily attended dangerous employments against her late Majesty's enemies, and had not in the said former grants made any provision for my wife, I made the former grants void; and then afterwards, for the natural love and affection which I bare to the aid Walter Ralegh, then my one son, and still being desirous, as well to settle and establish some estate of and in the said castles and manors, and also some livelihood and provision for my

_____

[34] Edward Edwards, The Life of Sir Walter Ralegh, 2 vols., Macmillan, 1868. Vol 1, pp 466-7

wife, to be had thereout during her nature life, I made a new grant ...
which last-mentioned deed was made not many months before the now
Bishop [Cotton] was consecrated, as I verily believe ... But by reasonn
of my manifold troubles, I do not know where the said deed is, or in
whose hands or custody.' Its purport, it is further said, was to convey
the estates to his son, subject to a rent-charge of two hundred pounds a
year for Lady Ralegh during her life. 'Her late Majesty,' proceeds Sir
Walter, 'having afterwards procured form the said now Bishop the
inheritance of the said lordship, castles, and manors, it pleased her to
give me the same by a sufficient conveyance in law ... and afterwards I
did intend to settle the inheritance of the same upon my said
son ...'

).]

1603

After his arrest on the 14th July 1603, Raleigh and Lawrence Kemys
were committed to the Tower. During his imprisonment in the Bloody
Tower, Raleigh saw that the actions of his enemies were about to
destroy him and seeking to put his Estate in order before his death he
wrote a letter to his dear wife Bess:

Raleigh's Arrest Draws Near
1603

Sir Walter knew that Anthony Copley had been arrested on the 5th July and that it was a matter of time before they would seek him out for questioning in connection with the Bye and Main Plot against King James I.   He knew that the King's Guards would not seize him yet, and so he had some time left to reflect. Perhaps a matter of days were all that were left to him, and then what would time bring him?

He would be confined to house arrest as they searched for their proof and invention stripped away from fact would be found elsewhere. Just as it had been for the Earl of Essex, so it would be for him.

That is why they sought him out and would eventually succeed and destroy him. Since Essex had died at the scaffold then he must die at the scaffold. A fire took place at Essex House in 1601 when he had been arrested, and so a fire had taken place his own home, Durham House during his short absence.

The Queen had signed his death warrant with her last breath because she had refused to destroy his letters to her, concerning Essex. Lord Burleigh would never have revealed them, and yet now that she was dead, King James and his Privy Councillors had found them. And rather like a play being reenacted they would make him suffer unto his last breath.

The King would be triumphant and he was already found guilty. If there were a trial it would be decided before he had spoken, since there would be no defence and no truth.

[35] The Arraignment of Sir Walter Raleigh, Knight At Winton, on Thursday the 17th November, 1603

Before the Right Honourable, the Earl of Suffolk, Lord Chamberlain.

Earl of Devon
Lord Henry Howard
Lord Cecil, Earl of Shrewsbury
Lord Wotton
Sir John Stanhope, Vice Chamberlain
Lord Chief-Justice of the Common Pleas, Anderson
Justice Gaudie
Justice Warburton
Sir William Wade Commissioners

First, the commission of Oyer and Terminer was read by the Clerk of the Crown-Office; and the Prisoner bid hold up his hand.

And then presently the Indictment was in effect as followeth:

That he did conspire, and go about to deprive the King of his Government;
To raise up Sedition within the Realm;
To alter Religion, to bring in the Roman Superstition, and to procure Foreign enemies to invade the Kingdoms. That the Lord Cobham [36], the

---

[35] for his part in proclaiming Lady Arabella Stewart next in line of succession to the Throne of England after the death of Queen Elizabeth I: Mary Queen of Scots had married Henry Lord Darnley who had been murdered and Mary blamed and imprisoned. Lady Arabella Stewart descended from that line: Charles Earl of Lennox = Lady Arabella Stewart .see footnote and so the Devereuxs' are by descent the rightful heirs to the Scottish throne when it is proved that Queen Elizabeth I did not know that she had signed the Death Warrant of Mary Queen of Scots since it had been written in a Secretary's hand - Queen Elizabeth I only keeping Mary under close guard because she would have had Elizabeth's throne from her during her own lifetime by her direct descent from Henry Vii/Henry VIII and Margaret Tudor.

[36] Lord Cobham was Cecil's Nephew. Lord Cecil was Queen Elizabeth I's former Secretary,

nine of June last, did meet with the said Sir Walter Raleigh in Durham House, in the Parish of St. Martins in the Fields, and then and there had Conference with him, how to advance Arabella Stuart to the Crown and Royal Throne of this Kingdom; and that then and there it was agreed, that Cobham should treat with Aremberg, Ambassador from the Arch-Duke of Austria, to obtain of him 600,000 Crowns, to bring to pass their intended Treasons. It was agreed that Cobham should go to the Arch-Duke Albert, to procure him to advance the pretended title of Arabella: from thence knowing that Albert had not sufficient means to maintain his own army in the Low countries, Cobham should go to Spain to procure the King to assist and further her pretended title.

It was agreed, the better to effect all this Conspiracy, that Arabella should write three letters, one to the Arch-Duke, another to the King of Spain, and a third to the Duke of Savoy, and promise three things:

Firstly, to establish firm Peace between England and Spain.
Secondly, to tolerate the Popish and Roman superstition.
Thirdly, to be ruled by them in contracting of her marriage.

And for the effecting these traitorous purposes, Cobham should return to the Isle of Jersey, and should find Sir Walter Raleigh Captain of the said Isle there, and take Counsel of Raleigh for the distributing of the aforesaid Crowns, as the occasion or discontentment of the subjects should give cause and way.

And further, that Cobham and his brother Brook met on the 9th June last, and Cobham told Brook all these Treasons: To the which Treasons Brook gave his assent, and did join himself to all these; and after on the Thursday following, Cobham and Brook did speak these words:

---

and was Chancellor Burleigh's second son, and a former friend of Sir Walter Raleigh.

That there would never be a good World in England, till the King (meaning our Sovereign Lord) and his Cubs (meaning his Royal issue) were taken away.

And the more to disable and deprive the King of his Crown, and to confirm the said Cobham in his intents, Raleigh did publish a book, falsely written against the most just and Royal title of the King, knowing the said book to be written against the just title of the King; which book Cobham after that received of him. Further, for the better effecting these traitorous purposes, and to establish the said Brook in his intent, the said Cobham did deliver the said book unto him the 14th June. And further on the 16th June, for the accomplishment of the said Conference, and by the traitorous instigation of Raleigh, did move Brook to incite Arabella to write to the three forenamed Princes, to procure them to advance her title, and that she, after she had obtained the Crown, should promise to perform three things, viz.[37]

1.   Peace between England and Spain.

2.   To tolerate with impunity the Popish and Roman superstitions.

3.   To be ruled by them three in the contracting of her marriage.

To these motions the said Brook gave his assent. And for the better effecting of the said Treasons, Cobham on the 17th of June,[38] by the

---

[37] On the 14th June Cobham delivers Raleigh's book to his brother Brook.

On the 16th June Cobham pursuades Brook to incite Arabella to write to the three Princes.

[38] Cobham wrote Letters to Count Aremberg and delivered the letters to Matthew de Lawrency, to be delivered to the said Count, for the obtaining of 600,000 Crowns. Count Aremberg replied in a letter to Cobham, which he received on the 18th June. Cobham then promised Raleigh that when he received the money he would deliver 8,000 Crowns to him. Cobham promised his brother Brook 10,000 Crowns.

instigation of Raleigh, did write letters to Count Aremberg, and did deliver the said letters to one Matthew de Lawrency, to be delivered to the said Count: which he did deliver for the obtaining of the 600,000 Crowns; which money by other letter Count Aremberg did promise to perform the payment of; and this letter Cobham received the eighteenth of June. And then did Cobham promise to Raleigh, that when he had received the said money, he would deliver 8,000 Crowns to him: to which motion he did consent; and afterwards Cobham offered Brook, that after he should receive the said Crowns, he would give to him 10,000 thereof; to which motion Brook did assent.

To the indictment Sir Walter Raleigh pleaded not guilty.

Sir Walter Raleigh's Trial at Winchester Castle
The Jury

Sir Ralph Conisby	- Knight
Sir Thomas Fowler	- Knight
Sir Edward Peacock	- Knight
Sir William Rowe	- Knight
Henry Goodyer	- Esquire
Roger Wood	- Esquire
Thomas Walker	- Esquire
Thomas Whitby	- Esquire
Thomas Highgate	- Gentleman
Robert Kemthon	- Gentleman
John Chawkey	- Gentleman
Robert Brumley	- Gentleman

Sir Walter Raleigh prisoner, was asked, whether he would take exceptions to any of the Jury?

Raleigh: I know none of them; they are all Christians, and honest Gentlemen, I except against none.

E. Suffolk. You Gentlemen of the Kings Learned Counsel, follow the same course as you did the other day.

Raleigh: My Lord, I pray you I may answer the Points particularly as they are delivered, by reason of the weakness of my memory and sickness.

Popham, Chief Justice: After the Kings Learned Counsel have delivered all the Evidence, Sir Walter, you may answer particularly to what you will.

Heale, the King's Sergeant at Law: You have heard of Raleigh's bloody Attempts to kill the King and his Royal Progeny, and in place thereof to advance one Arabella Stuart: The particulars of the Indictment are these. First, that Raleigh met with Cobham the ninth June and had Conference of an Invasion , of a Rebellion, and an Insurrection, to be made by the King's Subjects, to depose the King, and to kill his children, poor babes that never gave offense: Here is Blood, here is a new King and Governor. In our King consists all our happiness, and the true use of the Gospel, a thing which we all wished to be settled after the death of the Queen. Here must be money to do this, for money is the Sinew of War. Where should that he had? Count Aremberg must procure it of Philip King of Spain, five or six hundred thousand Crowns, and out of this sum Raleigh must have eight thousand. But what is that Count Aremberg? though I am no good Frenchman, yet it is as much as to say in English, Earl of Aremberg. Then there must be Friends to effect this: Cobham must go to Albert Arch-Duke of Austria, for whom Aremberg was Ambassador at that time in England. And what then? He must persuade the Duke to assist the pretended Title of Arabella. From thence Cobham must go to the King of Spain, and persuade him to assist the said title. Since the Conquest there was never the like Treason. But out of whose head came it? Out of Raleigh's, who must also advise Cobham to use his brother Brook to incite the Lady Arabella to write three several letters, as aforesaid in the Indictment; all this was on the ninth of June. Then three days after Brook was acquainted with it: After this Cobham said to Brook, it will never be well in England till the King and his Cubs are taken away. Afterwards Raleigh delivered a book to Cobham, treacherously written against the title of the King. It appears that Cobham took Raleigh to be either a God, or an Idol. Cobham endeavors to set up a new King, or Governor. God forbid mine eyes should ever see so unhappy a change. As for the Lady Arabella, she upon my conscience hath no more title to the Crown than I have, which before God I utterly renounce. Cobham a man bred in England, hath no experience abroad: but Raleigh, a man of great wit, military, and a swordsman. Now whether these things were bred in a hollow tree, I leave to them to speak of, who can speak far better than my self. And so sat him down again.

Sir Edward Cook, the King's Attorney: I must first, my Lords, before I come to the cause give one caution, because we shall often mention persons of eminent places, some of them great Monarchs: What ever we say of them, we shall but repeat what others have said of them; I mean the Capital Offenders in their Confessions: We professing law, must speak reverently of Kings and Potentates. I perceive these honourable Lords, and the rest of this great Assembly, are come to hear what hath been scattered upon the Wrack of Report. We carry a just mind, to condemn no man but upon plain Evidence. Here is mischief, Mischief in Summo Gradu, exorbitant Mischief. My speech shall chiefly touch these three Points: Imitation, Supportation, and Defence.

The imitation of Evil ever exceeds the Precedent; as on the contrary imitation of good ever comes short. Mischief cannot be supported but by mischief; yea, it will so multiply, that it will bring all to confusion. Mischief is ever underprop'd by falsehood of foul practices. And because all these things did concur in this Treason, you shall understand the Main, as before you did the Bye.

The Treason of the Bye, consisteth in these Points: First, that the Lords Grey, Brook, Markham, and the rest, intended by Force in the Night to surprise the King's Court: which was a Rebellion in the Heart of the Realm, yea in the Heart of the Heart, in the Court. They intended to take him that is a Sovereign, to make him subject to their power, purposing to open the doors with Muzquets and Calievers, and to take also the Prince and Council. Then under the King's Authority to carry the King to the Tower; and to make a stale of the Admiral. When they had the King there, to extort three things from him: First, a Pardon for all their Treasons. Secondly, a toleration of the Roman superstition: which, their eyes shall sooner fall out than they shall ever see; for the King hath spoken these words in the hearing of many, I will lose the Crown, and my life, before ever I will alter religion. And, thirdly, to remove counsellors:

In the room of the Lord Chancellor, they would have placed one Watson a Priest, absurd in humanity, and ignorant in Divinity.

Brook, of whom I will speak nothing, Lord-Treasurer. The great Secretary must be Markham, oculus patriae. A hole must be found in my Lord Chief Justice's coat. Grey must be Earl-Marshal, and Master of the Horse, because he would have a table in the Court. marry, he would advance the Earl of Worcester to an higher place. All this cannot be done without a multitude. Therefore Watson the Priest tells a resolute man that the King was in danger of Puritans and Jesuites; so to bring him in blindfold into the action, saying, that the King is no King till he be crowned; therefore every man might right his own wrongs: but he is Rex natus, his dignity descends as well as yours, my Lords. Then Watson imposeth a blasphemous Oath, they should swear to defend the King's person; to keep secret what was given them in charge, and seek all ways and means to advance the Catholic religion. Then they intend to send for the Lord Mayor and the Aldermen, in the King's name, to the Tower, lest they should make any resistance, and then to take hostages of them; and to enjoyn them to provide for them Victuals and munition. Grey, because the King removed before Midsummer, had a further reach, to get a company of sword-men to assist the action: Therefore he would stay till he had obtained a regiment from Ostend, or Austria. So you see these Treasons were like Sampson's foxes, which were joyned in their Tails, though their heads were severed.

Raleigh: You Gentlemen of the Jury, I pray you remember I am not charged with the Bye, being the Treason of the Priest.

Attorney: You are not. My Lords, you shall observe three things in the Treasons: First, they had a watchword (the King's safety) their presence was Bonum in se, their intent was Malum in se. Secondly, they avouched scripture; both the Priests had Scriptum est; perverting and ignorantly mistaking the scriptures. Thirdly, they avouched the Common Law, to prove that he was non King till he was crowned;

alleging a Statute of Eliz. 13.

This by way of imitation, hath been the course of all traitors.

In the 20th of Edw. the 2d., Isabella the Queen, and the Lord Mortimer, gave out, that the King's person was not safe, for the good of the Church and Commonwealth.

The Bishop of Carlisle did preach on this text, my head is grieved: meaning by the Head, the King; that when the Head began to be negligent, the people might reform what is amiss.

In the 3d Hen. 4. Sir Roger Clarington accompanied with two priests, gave out, that Richard the Second was alive, when he was dead.

Edward the 3rd caused Mortimer's head to be cut off, for giving counsel to murther the King.

The 3. Henry 7. sir Henry Stanly found the Crown in the dust, and set it on the King's Head; when Fitzwater and Garret told him that Edward the 5th was alive, he said, if I be alive, I will assist him. But this cost him his head.

Edmond de la Pool, Duke of Suffolk, killed a man in the reign of King Henry the 7th, for which the King would have him hold up his hand at the Bar, and then Pardoned him. Yet he took such an offence thereat, that he sent to the Noblemen, to help to reform the Common-wealth; and then said, he would go to France, and get power there. Sir Roger Compton knew all the Treason, and discovered Windon and others, that were attainted.

He aid there was another thing that would be stood upon, namely, that they had but one witness. Then he vouched one Appleyard's Case, a Traytor in Norfolk, who said a man must have two accusers. Helms was the man that accused him; but Mr Just. Catlin said, that Statute was not in force at that day. His words [thrust her into the Ditch.]

Then he went on speaking of accusers, and made this difference: An accuser is a speaker by report, when a witness is he that upon his Oath shall speak his knowledge of any man.

A third sort of Evidence there is likewise, and this is held more forcible than either of the other two; and that is, when a man by his accusation of another, shall by the same accusation also condemn himself, and make himself liable to the same fault and punishment: this is more forcible than many witnesses. So then so much by way of imitation. Then he defined Treason; there is Treason in the Heart, in the Hand, in the Mouth, in Consummation: comparing that in Corde to the Root of a Tree; in Ore, to the Bud; in Manu, to the Blossom; and that which is in Consummatione, to the Fruit.

Now I come to your Charge, you of the Jury. the greatness of Treason is to be considered in these two things, Determinatione finis, and Electione mediorum. this Treason excelleth in both, for that it was to destroy the King and his progeny. these Treasons are said to be Crimen laesae Majestatis; this goeth further, and may be term'd Crimen exterpandae Regiae Majestaatis, and totius Progeniei Suae. I shall not need, my Lords, to speak any thing concerning the King, nor of the bounty and sweetness of his nature, whose thoughts are innocent, whose words are full of wisdom and learning, and whose works are full of honour; although it be a true saying Nunquam nimis quod nunquam satis. But to whom do you bear your malice? to the children?

Raleigh: To whom speak you this? You tell me news I never heard of.

Attorney: Oh Sir, do I? I will prove you the Notoriousest Traytor that ever came to the Bar. After you have taken away the King, you would alter Religion: as you, Sir Walter Raleigh, have followed them of the Bye in imitation; for I will charge you with the words.

Raleigh: Your words cannot condemn me, my innocency is my Defence. Prove one of these things wherewith you have charged me, and I will confess the whole Indictment, and that I am the horriblest Traytor that ever lived, and worthy to be crucified with a thousand thousand torments.

Attorney: Nay, I will prove all: Thou art a monster, thou hast an English face, but a Spanish heart. Now you must have money: Aremberg was no sooner in England (I charge thee Raleigh) but thou incitedst Cobham to go unto him, and to deal with him for money, to bestow on discontented persons, to raise Rebellion on the Kingdom.

Raleigh: Let me answer for my self.

Attorney: Thou shalt not.

Raleigh: It concerneth my life.

Lord Chief Justice Popham: Sir Walter Raleigh, Mr Attorney is but yet in the General, but when the King's Counsel have given the evidence wholly, you shall answer every particular.

Attorney: Oh! do I touch you.

Lord Cecil: Mr Attorney, when you have done with this General Chargee, do you not mean to let him answer to every particular?

Attorney: Yes, when we deliver the Proofs to be read. Raleigh procured Cobham to go to Aremberg, which he did by his instigation: Raleigh supped with Cobham before he went to Aremberg; after supper, Raleigh conducted him to Durham House; from whence Cobham went with Lawrency, a Servant of Aremberg's, unto him, and went in by a back way. Cobham could never be quiet until he had entertained this motion, for he had four letters from Raleigh. Aremberg answered, the money should be performed, but knew not to whom it should be distributed. Then Cobham and Lawrency came back to Durham House, where they found Raleigh. Cobham and

Raleigh went up, and left Lawrency below, where they had secret Conference in a Gallery, and after Cobham and Lawrency departed from Raleigh. Your jargon was Peace! What is that? Spanish invasion, Scottish subversion. And again, you are not a fit man to take so much money for procuring of a lawful peace, for peace procured by money is dishonourable. Then Cobham must go to Spain, and return by Jersey, where you were Captain: And then because Cobham had not so much Policy, or at least wickedness as you, he must go to Spain, and return by Jersey, where you were Captain: And then because Cobham had not so much Policy, or at least wickedness as you, he must have your advice for the distribution of the money. Would you have deposed so good a King, lineally descended of Elizabeth, eldest daughter of Edward 4th? why then must you set up another? I think you meant to make Arabella a Titular Queen, of whose Title I will speak nothing, but sure you meant to make her a Stale: Ah good Lady! you could mean her no good.

Raleigh: You tell me news, Mr Attorney.

Attorney: Oh Sir! I am the more large, because I know with whom I deal: for we have to deal to day with a Man of Wit.

Raleigh: Did I ever speak with this Lady?

Attorney: I will track you out before I have done: English-men will not be led by persuasion of words, but they must have books to persuade.

Raleigh: The book was written by a man of your profession, Mr Attorney.

Attorney: I would not have you impatient.

Raleigh: Methinks you fall out with yourself, I say nothing.

Attorney: By this book you would persuade men that he is not the lawful King. Now let us consider some circumstances: My lords, you know my Lord Cobham (for whom we all lament, and rejoice; Lament in that his house, which hath stood so long unspotted, is now ruinated; Rejoyce, in that his Treasons are revealed): he is neither Politician nor Sword-man; Raleigh was both, united in the cause with him, and therefore cause of his destruction. Another circumstance is the secret contriving of it. Humphry Stafford claimed sanctuary for Treason. Raleigh in his machivilian policy hath made a sanctuary for Treason. He must talk with none but Cobham, because (saith he) one witness can never condemn me. For Brook said unto Sir Griffith Markham, take heed how you do make my Lord Cobham acquainted; for whatsoever he knoweth, Raleigh the Witch will get it out of him. As soon as Raleigh was examined on one point of treason concerning my Lord Cobham, he wrote to him thus; I have been examined of you, and confessed nothing. Further you sent to him by your trusty Francis Kemish, that one witness, that one witness could not condemn; and therefore bad his Lordship be of good Courage. Came this out of Cobham's Quiver? No: But out of Raleigh's Machivilian and Devilish policy. Yea, but Cobham did retract it; Why then did you urge it? Now then see the most horrible practices that ever came out of the bottomless Pit of the Lowest Hell. After that Raleigh had intelligence that Cobham had accused him, he endeavored to have Intelligence from Cobham, which he had gotten by your Sir John Payton: But I think it was the Error of his Youth.

Raleigh: The Lords told it me, or else I had not been sent to the Tower.

Attorney: Thus Cobham by the instigation of Raleigh, entered into these actions: So that the question will be, whether you are not the principal Traitor, and he would nevertheless have entered into it? Why did Cobham retract all that same? First, because Raleigh was so odious, he thought he should fare the worse for his sake. Secondly, he thought thus with himself, if he be free, I shall clear my self the better. After this Cobham asked for a Preacher to confer with, pretending to have Doctor Andrews; but indeed he meant not to have him, but Mr

Galloway; a Worthy and Reverend Preacher, who can do more with the King (as is said) than any other; that he, seeing his constant denial, might inform the King thereof. Here he plays with the Preacher. If Raleigh could persuade the Lords, that Cobham had no intent to ravel, then he thought all should be well. Here is forgery. In the Tower Cobham must write to Sir Thomas Vane, a worthy Man, that he meant not to go into Spain; which letter Raleigh devised in Cobham's name.

Raleigh: I will wash my hands of the Indictment, and die a true man to the King.

Attorney: You are the absolutest Traytor that ever was.

Raleigh: Your phrases will not prove it, Mr Attorney.

Attorney: Cobham writeth a letter to my Lord Cecil, and doth will Mella his man, to lay it in a Spanish bible and to make as though he found it by chance. This was after he had intelligence with this viper, that he was false.

Lord Cecil: You mean a letter intended to me, I never had it.

Attorney: No my Lord, you had it not. You, my masters of the Jury, respect not the wickedness and hatred of the man, respect his cause if he be guilty I know you will have care of it, for the preservation of the King, the continuance of the Gospel authorized and the good of us all.

Raleigh: I do not hear yet, that you have spoken one word against me, here is no Treason of mine done: If my Lord Cobham be a Traytor, what is that to me?

Attorney: All that he did was by thy instigation, thou viper; for I thou thee, thou Traytor.

Raleigh: It becometh not a man of quality and virtue, to call me so:

But I take comfort in it, it is all you can do.

Attorney: Have I angered you?

Raleigh: I am in no case to be angry.

Popham. Sir Walter Raleigh, Mr Attorney, I speaketh out of the zeal of his duty, for the service of the King, and you for your life; be valiant on both sides.

Now they proceed to the Reading of the Proofs.

The Lord Cobham's Examination Read.

Besides he spake of Plots and Invasions: Of the Particulars whereof he could give no account, though Raleigh and he had conferred of them. Further, he aid, he was afraid of Raleigh, that when he should return by Jersey, that he would have him and the money to the King. Being examined of Sir Arthur Gorge, he freed him, saying:

They never durst trust him, but Sir Arthur Savage they intended to use, because they thought him a fit man.

Raleigh: Let me see the accusation: This is absolutely all the Evidence can be brought against me; poor shifts! You Gentlemen of the Jury, I pray you understand this: This is that which must either condemn, or give me life; which must free me, or send my wife and children to beg their bread about the streets. This is that must prove me a notorious Traytor, or a true subject to the King. Let me see my Accusation, that I may make my answer.

Clerk of the Council: I did read it, and shew you all the Examinations.

Raleigh: At my first Examination at Windsor, my Lords asked me, what I knew of Cobham's practice with Aremberg? I answered negatively: And as concerning Arabella, I protest before God, I never heard one word of it. If that be proved, let me be guilty of ten thousand Treasons. It is a strange thing you will impute that to me, when I never heard so much as the name of Arabella Stuart, but only the name of Arabella.

After being Examined, I told my Lords, that I thought my Lord Cobham had Conference with Aremberg, I suspected his visiting of him: For after he departed from me at Durham House, I saw him pass by his own stairs, and he passed over to St. Mary's Saviours, where I knew Lawrency, a Merchant, and a follower of Aremberg, lay, and therefore likely to go unto him. My Lord Cecil asked my opinion concerning Lawrency; I said, that if you do not apprehend Lawrency, it is dangerous he will flie; if you do apprehend him, you shall give my Lord Cobham notice thereof. I was asked likewise, who was the greatest man with my Lord Cobham? I answered, I knew no man so great with him, as your Wyat of Kent.

As soon as Cobham saw my letter as had discovered his dealing with Aremberg, in his fury he accused me, but before he came to the stair-foot he repented, and said he had done me wrong. When he came to the end of his Accusation, he added, that if he had brought this money to Jersey, he feared that I would have delivered him and the money to the King. Mr Attorney, you said this never came out of Cobham's Quiver, he is a simple man. Is he so simple? No: He hath a disposition of his own, he will not easily be guided by others, but when he has once taken head in a matter, he is not easily drawn out of it; he is a babe. But it is strange for me to <u>devise</u> with Cobham, that he should go to Spain, to persuade the King to disperse so much money, he being a man of no love in England, and I having resigned my room of chiefest command, the Wardenship of the Stanneries: Is it not strange for me to make my self Robin Hood, or a Kett, or a Cade? I knowing England to be in better Estate to defend itself than ever it was. I knew Scotland United; Ireland quieted, wherein of late our Forces were dispersed; Denmark assured, which before was suspected. I knew, that having a Lady whom Time had surprised, we had now an active King, a lawful successor, who would himself be present in all his affairs. The State of Spain was not unknown to me. I had written a discourse, which I had intended to present unto the King, against peace with Spain. I knew the Spaniard had six Repulses, three in Ireland, and three at sea, and once in 1588 at Calls, by my Lord Admiral. I knew the King of Spain to be the proudest Prince IN Christendom; but now he cometh creeping to the King my Master for peace. I knew whereas before he had in his Port six or seven score sails of ships, he had now but six or seven. I knew of twenty five millions he had from his Indies, he hath scarce one left. I knew him to be so poor, that the Jesuites in Spain, who were wont to have such large allowance, were fain to beg at the Church door. Was it ever read or heard, that any Prince should disburse so much Money without a sufficient Pawn? I knew her own subjects, the Citizens of London, would not lend her Majesty money without lands in mortgage. I knew the Queen did not lend the states money without Flushing, Broil, and other towns for a Pawn. And can it be thought, that he would let Cobham have so great a sum?

I never came to the Lord Cobham's but about matters of his profit, as the ordering of his house, paying of his servants board-wages, etc. I had of his when I was examined, four thousand pounds worth of jewels for a purchase; a pearl of three thousand pound, and a ring worth five hundred pound: If he had had a fancy to run away, he would not have left so much to have purchased a Lease in fee farm. I saw him buy three hundred pounds worth of books to send to his library at Canterbury, and a cabinet of thirty pound to give to Mr Attorney, for drawing the Conveyances; and God in Heaven knoweth, not I, whether he intended to travel or no. But for that practice with Arabella, or letters to Aremberg framed, or any discourse with him, or in what language he spake unto him; if I knew of any of these things, I would absolutely confess the Indictment, and acknowledge my self worthy ten thousand deaths.

Cobham's second Examination read

"The Lord Cobham being required to subscribe to an Examination, there was shewed a Note under Sir Walter Raleigh's hand, the which when he had perused, he paused, and after brake forth into these speeches: Oh, Villain! Oh Traytor! I will now tell you all the Truth: And then said, his purpose was to go into Flanders, and into Spain, for the obtaining the aforesaid Money, and that Raleigh had appointed to meet him in Jersey as he returned home, to be advised of him about the distribution of the money."

Popham, Lord Chief Justice. When Cobham answered to the Interrogatories, he made scruple to subscribe, and being urged to it, he said, if he might hear me affirm, that a person of his degree ought to set his hand, he would, I lying then at Richmond, for fear of the Plague, was sent for, and I told he ought to subscribe; otherwise it were a contempt of a high nature: then he subscribed. The Lords questioned with him further, and he shewed them a letter, as I thought written to me, but was indeed written to my Lord Cecil: He desired to see the letter again, and then said, O Wretch! Oh Traytor! Whereby I perceived you had not performed that Trust he had reposed in you.

Raleigh: He is as passionate a Man as lives, for he hath not spared the best friends he hath in England in his passion. My Lords, I take it, he that has been examined, has ever been asked at the time of his Examination, if it be according to his meaning, and then to subscribe. Methinks, my Lords, when he accused a man, he should give some account and reason of it; it is not sufficient to say, we talked of it. If I had been the Plotter, would not I have given Cobham some arguments, whereby to persuade the King of Spain, and answer his objections. I knew Westmoreland and Bothwell, men of other understandings than Cobham, were ready to beg their bread.

Sir Thomas Fowler, one of the Jury: Did Sir Walter Raleigh write a letter to my Lord before he was examined concerning him, or not?

Attorney: Yes.

Lord Cecil: I am in great dispute with my self to speak in the case of this Gentleman: A former dearness between me and him tied so firm a know of my conceit of his virtues, now broken by a discovery of his imperfections. I protest, did I serve a King that I knew would be displeased with me for speaking, in this case I would speak whatever came of it: But seeing he is compacted of piety and justice, and that will not mislike of any man for speaking a truth, I will answer your question.

Sir Walter Raleigh was stayed by me at Windsor, upon the first News of Copley, that the Kings person should be surprised by my Lord Grey, and Mr George Brook; when I found Brook was in, I suspected Cobham, then I doubted Raleigh to be a partaker. I speak not this, that it should be thought I had greater Judgment than the rest of my Lords, making this haste to have them examined. Raleigh following to Windsor, I met with him upon the tarras, and willed him, as from the King to stay, saying, the Lords had something to say to him: then he was examined, but not concerning my Lord Cobham, but of the Surprising Treason. My Lord Grey was apprehended, and likewise Brook; by Brook we found, that he had given notice to Cobham of the surprising Treason, as he delivered it to us, but with as much spariness of a Brother as he might: we sent for my Lord Cobham to Richmond, where he stood upon his justification, and his quality; sometimes being forward, he said he was not bound to subscribe, wherewith we made the King acquainted. Cobham said, if my Lord Chief Justice would say it were a contempt, he would subscribe; whereof being resolved, he subscribed. There was a light given to Aremberg, that Lawrency was examined, but that Raleigh knew that Cobham was examined, is more than I know.

Raleigh: If my Lord Cobham had trusted me in the Main, was not I as fit a man to be trusted in the Bye?

Lord Cecil: Raleigh did by his letters acquaint us, that my Lord Cobham had sent Lawrency to Aremberg, when he knew not he had any dealings with him.

Lord Henry Howard: It made for you, if Lawrency had been only acquainted with Cobham, and not with you. But you knew his whole Estate, and were acquainted with Cobham's practice with Lawrency, and it was known to you before that Lawrency depended on Aremberg.

Attorney: 1. Raleigh protested against the surprising Treason. 2. That he knew not of the matter touching Arabella. I would not charge you, Sir Walter, with a matter of falsehood: You say, you suspected the intelligence that Cobham had with Aremberg, by Lawrency.

Raleigh: I thought it had been no other intelligence, but such as might be warranted.

Attorney: Then it was but lawful suspicion. But to that whereas you said, that Cobham had accused you in passion, I answer three ways: 1. I observed when Cobham said, 'Let me see the letter again?' he paused, and when he did see that Count Aremberg was touched, he cried out, Oh Traytor! Oh Villain! Now will I confess the whole truth. 2. The accusation of a man on hear-say, is nothing. Would he accuse himself on passion and ruinate his cause and posterity, out of malice to accuse you? 3. Could this be out of passion? Mark the manner of it: Cobham had told this at least two months before to his brother Brook, "You are fools, you are on the Bye, Raleigh and I are on the Main, we mean to take away the King and his Cubs"; this he delivered two months before. So mark the manner and the matter, he would not turn the weapon against his own bosom, and accuse himself to accuse you.

Raleigh: Hath Cobham confessed that?

Lord Chief Justice: This is spoken by Mr Attorney, to prove that Cobham's speech came not out of passion.

Raleigh: Let it be proved that Cobham said so.

Attorney: Cobham saith, he was a long time doubtful of Raleigh, that he would send him and the money to the King. Did Cobham fear lest you would betray him in Jersey? Then of necessity there must be trust between you. No man can betray a man but that he is trusted, in my understanding. This is the greatest argument to prove that he was acquainted with Cobham's proceedings. Raleigh has a deeper reach than to make himself, as he said, Robin Hood, a Kett or a Cade, yet I never heard that Robin Hood was a Traytor, they say he was an Outlaw. and whereas he saith, that our King is not only more wealthy and potent than his predecessors, but also more politick and wise, so that he would have no hope to prevail. I answer, there is no King so potent, wise and active but he may be overtaken through Treason. Whereas you said Spain is so poor, discoursing so largely thereof it had been better for you to have kept in Guiana, than to have been so well acquainted with the state of Spain. Besides, if you could have brought Spain and Scotland to have joyned, you might have hoped to prevail a great deal the better. For his six overthrows, I answer; He hath the more malice, because repulses breed desire of revenge. Then you say, you never talked with Cobham but about Leases, and letting lands, and ordering his house; I never knew you Clerk of the Kitchen, etc. If you had fallen on your knees at first, and confessed the Treason, it had been better for you. You say, he meant to have given me a Cabinet of thirty pound, perhaps he thought by those means to have anticipated me therewith. But you say, all these are circumstances. I answer, all this accusation in circumstance is true: Here now I might appeal to my Lords, that you take hold of this, that he subscribed not to the accusation.

Lord Henry Howard: Cobham was not then pressed to subscribe.

Attorney: His accusation being testified by the Lords, is of as great force, as if he had subscribed. Raleigh saith again, if the Accuser be alive, he must be brought face to face to speak, and alleges 25th Edward 3rd. That there must be two sufficient witnesses that must be brought face to face before the accused, and alledgeth 10. and 13 Eliz.

Raleigh: You try me by the Spanish Inquisition, if you proceed only by the circumstances without two witnesses.

Attorney: This is treasonable speech.

Raleigh: Overture hominem justum in cause sua injustum est: Good my Lords, let it be proved either by the laws of the land, or the laws of God, that there ought not to be two witnesses appointed; yet I will not stand to defend this point in law, if the King will have it so: it is no rare thing for a man to be falsely accused. A Judge condemned a woman in sarum for killing her husband, on the testimony of one witness; afterwards his man confessed the murder, when she was executed. Who after being touched in conscience for the judgment, was used to say, quod nunquam de hoc facto aninam in vita sua purgaret. It is also commanded by the Scripture, allocutus est Jehova Mosen, in ore duorum qut trium Testium, etc.

If Christ requireth it, as it appeareth, Matthew 18. If by the Canon, civil law, and God's word, it be required, that there must be two witnesses at the least, bear with me if I desire one.

I would not desire to live, if I were privy to Cobham's proceedings: I had been a slave, a villain, a fool, if I had endeavoured to set up Arabella and refused so gracious a Lord and Sovereign: But urge your Proofs.

Lord Chief Justice: You have offered questions on divers Statutes, all which mention two accusers in case of Indictments; you have deceived yourself, for the laws of 25 Ed. 3. and 5 Ed. 6. are released. It sufficeth now if there be Proofs made either under hand, or by testimony of witnesses or by Oaths; it needs not the subscription of the party, so there be hands of credible men to testify the Examination.

Raleigh: It may be an Error in me and if those laws be repealed, yet I hope the equity of them remains still; but if you affirm it, it must be a law to posterity. The Proof of the Common Law is by witness and Jury; Let Cobham be here, let him speak it or call my accuser before my face, and I have done.

Attorney: Scientia sceleris est mere Ignorantia: You have read the Letter of the Law, but understand it not. Here was your Anchor-hold, and your Rendevouz: You trust to Cobham, either Cobham must accuse you, or no body; if he did, then it would not hurt you, because he is but one witness; if he did not, then you are safe.

Raleigh: If ever I read word of the Law or Statute before I was prisoner in the Tower, God confound me.

Attorney: Now I come to prove the circumstances of the accusation to be true. Cobham confessed he had a passport to travel, hereby intending to present Overtures to the Arch-Duke, and from thence to go to Spain, and there to have Conference with the King for money: You say he promised to come home by Jersey, to make merry with you and your wife.

Raleigh: I said in his return from France, not Spain.

Attorney: Further, in his Examination he saith, nothing could be set down for the distribution of the money to the discontented, without conference with Raleigh. You said it should have been for procurement of Peace, but it was for raising Rebellion. Further, Cobham saith, he would never have entered into these courses, but by your instigation, and that you would never let him alone. Your Scholar was not apt enough to tell us all the Plots, that is enough for you to do, that are his Master: You intended to trust Sir Arthur Savage, whom I take to be an honest and true Gentleman, but not Sir Arthur Gorge.

Raleigh: All this is but one accusation of Cobham's, I hear no other thing; to which accusation he never subscribed nor avouched it, I beseech you, my Lords, let Cobham be sent for, charge him on his soul, on his allegiance to the King; if he affirm it, I am guilty.

Lord Cecil: It is the accusation of my Lord Cobham, it is the evidence against you, must it not be of force with his subscription? I desire to be resolved by the Judges, whether by the law it is not a forcible argument of evidence.

The Judges: My Lord it is.

Raleigh: The King at his Coronation is sworn, In omnibus Judiciis suis Aequitatem, non Rigorem Lesi, observare: By the rigour and cruelty of the law it may be a forcible Evidence.

Lord Chief Justice: That is not the Rigour of the Law, but the Justice of the Law; else when a man hath made a plain accusation, by practice he might be brought to retract it again.

Raleigh: Oh my Lord, you may use Equity.

Lord Chief Justice: That is from the King, you are to have Justice from us.

Lord Anderson: The law is, if the matter be proved to the Jury, they must find you guilty; for Cobham's accusation is n not only against you, there are other things sufficient.

Lord Cecil: Now that Sir Walter Raleigh is satisfied, that Cobham's subscription is not necessary: I pray you Mr Attorney go on.

Raleigh: Good Mr. Attorney be patient, and give me leave.

Lord Cecil: An unnecessary patience is a hindrance, let him go on with his Proofs, and then repel them.

Raleigh: I would answer particularly.

Lord Cecil: If you would have a Table, a Pen, and Ink, you shall.

Then paper, pen and ink was given him

[Here the Clerk of the Crown read the letter, which the Lord Cobham did write in July, which was to the effect of his former Examination, further saying, I have disclosed all; to accuse any one falsely, were to Burthen my own conscience].

Attorney: Read Coplies confession the 8th of June, he saith, He was offered 1000 Crowns to be in this action.

Here Watson's Additions were read.

"The great mass of money from the Count was impossible, saith Brook, etc.

Brooks Confession read:

There have letters passed, saith he, between Cobham and Aremberg, for a great sum of money, to assist a second action, for the surprising of his Majesty.

Attorney: It is not possible it was of passion; for it was in talk before three men being severally examined, who agreed in the sum to be bestowed on discontented persons. That Grey should have 12000 Crowns, and Raleigh should have 8000, or 10000 Crowns.

Cobham's Examination, July 18

If the money might be procured (saith he) then a man may give pensions. Being asked if a pension should not be given to his brother Brook, he denied it not.

Lawrency's Examination

Within five days after Aremberg arrived, Cobham resorted unto him. that night that Cobham went to Aremberg with Lawrency, Raleigh supped with him.

Attorney: Raleigh must have his part of the money, therefore now he is a traytor. The Crown shall never stand one year on the head of the King (my master) if a Traytor may not be condemned by circumstances: For if A. tells B. and B. tells C. and C. D etc. you shall never prove Treason by two witnesses.

Raleigh's Examination was read

He confesseth Cobham offered him 8000 Crowns, which he was to have for the furtherance of the peace between England and Spain; and that he should have it within three days. To which, he said, he gave this answer, When I see the money I will tell you more; for I had thought it had been one of his ordinary idle conceipts, and therefore made no accompt thereof.

Raleigh: The Attorney hath made a long narration of Copley, and the Priests, which concerns me nothing, neither know I how Cobham was altered. For he told me, if I would agree to further the peace, he would get me 8000 Crowns. I asked him, who shall have the rest of the money? He said, I will offer such a noble-,am (who was not named) some of the money. I said, he will not be persuaded by you, and he will extreamly hate you for such a motion. Let me be pinched to death with hot irons, if ever I knew there was any intention to bestow the money on discontented persons. I had made a discourse against the peace, and would have printed it: If Cobham changed his mind; if the Priests, if Brook had any such intent, what is that to me? They must answer for it. He offered me the money before Aremberg came, that is difference of time.

Serjeant Philips. Raleigh confesseth the matter, but avoideth it by distinguishing of times. You said it was offered you before the coming of Aremberg; which is false. For you being examined whether you should have such money of Cobham, or not: You said yea, and that you should have it within two or three days. nemo moriturus presumitur mentiri.

Lord Henry Howard: Allege me any ground or cause, wherefore you gave ear to my Lord Cobham for receiving pensions, in matters you had not to deal with.

Raleigh: Could I stop my Lord Cobham's mouth?

Lord Cecil: Sir Walter Raleigh presseth, that my Lord Cobham should be brought face to face. If he ask things of favour and grace, they must come only from him that can give them. If we sit here as Commissioners, how shall we be satisfied whether he ought to be brought, unless we hear the Judges speak.

Lord Chief Justice: This thing cannot be granted, for then a number of Treasons should flourish: The Accuser may be drawn by Practice, whilst he is in person.

Judge Gawdy. The Statute you speak of, concerning two witnesses in case of Treason is found to be inconvenient, therefore by another law it was taken away.

Raleigh: The common trial of England is by Jury and Witnesses.

Lord Chief Justice: No, by Examination: If three conspire a Treason, and they all confess it; he is neither a witness, yet there are condemned.

Judge Warburton. I marvel, Sir Walter, that you being of such experience and wit, should stand on this point; for so many horse-stealers may escape, if they may not be condemned without witnesses. If one should rush into the King's Privy-chamber, whilst he is alone, and kill the King (which God forbid) and this man be met coming with his sword drawn all bloody; shall not he be condemned to death? My Lord Cobham hath, perhaps, been laboured withal; and to save you, his old friend, it may be that he will deny all that which he hath said.

Raleigh. I know not how you conceive the law.

Lord Chief Justice: Nay, we do not conceive the law, but we know the law.

Raleigh: the wisdom of the law of Gob is absolute and perfect, Haec fac, et vives, etc. But now by the wisdom of the state, the wisdom of the law is uncertain. Indeed where the accuser is not to be had conveniently, I agree with you; but here my accuser may, he is alive, and in the house. Susanna had been condemned, if Daniel had not cried out: will you condemn an innocent Israelite, without examination or knowledge of the truth? Remember, it is absolutely the Commandment of God: If a false witness rise up, you shall cause him to be brought before the Judges; if he be found false, he shall have the punishment which the accused should have had. It is very sure for my Lord to accuse me is my certain danger, and it may be a means to excuse himself.

Lord Chief Justice: there must not such a gap be opened for the destruction of the King, as would be if we should grant this. You plead hard for your self, but the laws plead as hard for the thing. I did never hear that course to be taken in a case of Treason, as to write one to another, or speak one to another during the time of their imprisonment. There hath been intelligence between you, and what underhand practices there may be, I know not. If the circumstances agree not with the evidence, we will not condemn you.

Raleigh: The King desires nothing but the knowledge of the Truth, and would have no advantage taken by severity of the law. If ever we had a gracious King, now we have; I hope, as he is, such are his ministers. If there be but a trial of five Marks at common law, a witness must be deposed. Good my Lords, let my accuser come face to face, and be deposed.

Lord Chief Justice: You have no law for it: God forbid any man should accuse himself upon his Oath.

Attorney: The law presumes, a man will not accuse himself to accuse another. You are an odious man: For Cobham thinks his cause the worse that you are in it. Now you shall hear of some stirs to be raised in Scotland.

Parts of Copley's Examination

"Also Watson told me, that a special person told him, that Aremberg offered to him a thousand Crowns to be in that Action, and that Brook said, the stirs in Scotland came out of Rawleigh's head".

Raleigh: Brook hath been taught his lesson.

Lord Henry Howard: This Examination was taken before me; Did I teach him his lesson?

Raleigh: I protest before God, I meant it not by any Privy Counsellor but because money is scant, he will juggle on both sides.

Raleigh's Examination:

"The way to invade England, were to begin with stirs in Scotland".

Raleigh: I think so still: I have spoken it to divers of the Lords of the council, by way of discourse and opinion.

Attorney: Now let us come to those words of destroying the King and his Cubs.

Raleigh: O barbarous! If they, like unnatural villains, should use those words, shall I be charged with them? I will not hear it, I was never any Plotter with them against my country, I was never false to the Crown of England. I have spent 4000 Pounds of my own against the Spanish Faction, for the good of my country. Do you bring the words of these hellish spiders, Clark, Watson, and others against me?

Attorney: Thou hast a Spanish heart, and thy self art a Spider of Hell; for thou confesseth the King to be a most sweet and gracious prince, and yet hast conspired against him.

Watson's Examination Read:

"He said, that George Brook told him twice, that his brother, the Lord Cobham, said to him, that you are but on the Bye, but Raleigh and I are on the Main".

Brook's Examination read

"Being asked what was meant by this jargon the Bye and the Main? He said, that the Lord Cobham told him, that Grey and others were in the Bye, he and Raleigh were on the Main. Being asked what Exposition his brother made of these words? he said, he is loth to repeat it. And after saith, by the Main was meant the taking away of the King and his issue; and thinks on his conscience, it was infused into his Brother's Head by Raleigh."

Cobham's Examination read

"Being asked, if ever he had said, "It will never be well in England, till the King and his Cubs were taken away. He said, he had answered before, and that he would answer no more to that point.

Raleigh: I am not named in all this: there is a law of two sorts of accusers, one of his own knowledge, another by hear-say.

Earl of Suffolk: See the case of Arnold.

Lord Chief Justice: It is the case of Sir William Thomas, and Sir Nicholas Arnold.

Raleigh: I this may be, you will have any mans life in a week.

Attorney: Raleigh saith, that Cobham was in a passion when he said so. Would he tell his brother any thing of malice against Raleigh, whom he loved as his life.

Raleigh: Brook never loved me; until his brother had accused me, he said nothing.

Lord Cecil: We have heard nothing that might lead us to think that Brook accused you, he was only in the Surprising Treason: for by accusing you he should accuse his brother.

Raleigh: He doth not care much for that.

Lord Cecil: I must judge the best. The accusation of his brother was not voluntary; he pared every thing as much as he could, to save his brother.

Cobham's Examination read:

"He saith he had a book written against the title of the King, which he had of Raleigh, and that he gave it to his brother Brook: and Raleigh said it was foolishly written".

Attorney: After the King came within twelve miles of London, Cobham never came to see him; and intended to travel without seeing the Queen and the Prince. Now in this discontentment, you gave him the book, and he gave it to his brother.

Raleigh: I never gave it him, he took it off my table.

HIC JACET: SIR WALTER RALEIGH

Lord Howard: Where had you this book?

Raleigh: In the old Lord Treasurers study, after his death.

Lord Cecil: did you ever shew or make known the book to me?

Raleigh: No, my Lord.

Lord Cecil: My Father being employed in the Affairs of State at that time, it was like enough, he had many books and papers written against the Queen and State, which might come to his hands by the discovery of such offences.

Attorney. I observe there was intelligence between you and Cobham in the Tower; for after he said, it was against the King's title, he denied it again.

Sir William Wade. First my lord Cobham confesseth it, and after he had subscribed it, he revoked it again: to me he always said, that the drift of it was against the King's Title.

Raleigh: I protest before God, and all his works, I gave him not the book.

nota: Sir Robert Wroth speaketh, or whispereth something secretly:

Attorney: My Lords, I must complain of Sir Robert Wroth, he says this evidence is not material.

Sir Robert Wroth. I never spake the words.

Attorney: Let Mr Serjeant Philips testify, whether he heard him say the words or no.

Lord Cecil: I will give my word for Sir Robert Wroth.

Sir Robert Wroth: I will speak as truly as you, Mr Attorney, for by God, I never spake it.

Lord Chief Justice. Wherefore should this book be burnt?

Raleigh: I burned it not.

Serjeant Philips: You presented your friend with it, when he was discontented. If it had been before the Queen's death it had been a less matter; but you gave it him presently when he came from the King, which was the time of his discontentment.

Raleigh: Here is a book supposed to be Treasonable; I never read it, commended it, or delivered it, nor urged it.

Attorney: Why this is cunning.

Raleigh: Every thing that doth make for me is cunning, and every thing that maketh against me is probable.

Attorney. Lord Cobham saith, that Kemish came to him with a letter torn, and did with him not to be dismayed, for one witness could not hurt him.

Raleigh: this poor man hath been close prisoner these eighteen weeks; he was offered the rack to make him confess. I never sent any such message by him, I only writ to him, to tell him what I had done with Mr Attorney; having of his at that time a great pearl and a diamond.

Lord Henry Howard: No circumstance moveth me more than this. Kemish was never on the rack, the King gave charge that no rigour should be used.

Commissioners: We protest before God, there was no such matter intended to our knowledges.

Raleigh: Was not the Keeper of the Rack sent for, and he threatened with it?

Sir William Wade: When Mr Solicitor and myself examined Kemish, we told him he deserved the Rack, but did not threaten him with it.

Commissioners: It was more than we knew.

Cobham's Examination Read:

"He saith, Kemish brought him a letter from Raleigh, and that part which was concerning the Lords of the Council, was rent out; the letter contained, that he was examined and cleared himself of all; and that the Lord Henry Howard said, because he was discontent, he was fit to be in the Action. And further, that Kemish said to him from Raleigh, that he should be of good comfort, for one witness could not condemn a man for Treason".

Lord Cecil: Cobham was asked, whether and when he heard from you? he said, every day.

Raleigh: Kemish added more, I never bade him speak those words.

> Nota.   Mr Attorney here offered to interrupt
> him.

Lord Cecil: It is his last discourse. Give him leave Mr. Attorney.

Raleigh: I am accused concerning Arabella, concerning money out of Spain. My Lord Chief Justice saith, a man may be condemned with one witness, yea, without any witness. Cobham is guilty of many things, conscientia mille tests; he hath accused himself, what can he hope for but mercy? My Lords vouchsafe me this grace. Let him be brought, being alive, and in the house; let him avouch any of these things, I will confess the whole Indictment, and renounce the King's mercy.

Lord Cecil: Here hath been a touch of the Lady Arabella Stuart, a near Kingswoman of the Kings. Let us not scandal the innocent by confusion of speech: She is as innocent of all these things as I, or any man here; only she received a letter from my Lord Cobham, to prepare her; which she laughed at, and immediately sent it to the King. So far was she from discontentment that she laughed him to scorn. But you see how far the Count of Aremberg did consent.

The Lord Admiral (Nottingham) being in a standing, with the Lady Arabella, spake to the Court.

The Lady doth here protest upon her salvation, that she never dealt in any of these things; and so she willed me to tell the Court.

Lord Cecil: The Lord Cobham wrote to my Lady Arabella, to know if he might come to speak with her, and gave her to understand, that there were some about the King, that laboured to disgrace her; she doubted it was but a trick. But Brook saith, his brother moved him to procure Arabella to write letters to the King of Spain, but he saith, he never did it.

Raleigh: The Lord Cobham hath accused me, you see in what manner he hath forsworn it. Were it not for his accusation, all this were nothing. Let him be asked, if I knew of the letter which Lawrency brought to him from Aremberg. Let me speak for my life, it can be no hurt for him to be brought; he dares not accuse me. If you grant me not this favour, I am strangely used. Campian was not denied to have his accusers face to face.

Lord Chief Justice: Since he must needs have justice, the acquitting of his old friend may move him to speak otherwise than the Truth.

Raleigh: If I had been the infuser of all these Treasons into him. You Gentlemen of the Jury, mark this, he said I have been the cause of all his miseries, and the destruction of his house, and that all evil hath happened unto him, by my wicked counsel. If this be true, whom hath he cause to accuse, and to be revenged on, but on me? And I know him to be as revengeful as any man on Earth.

Attorney: He is a party, and may not come, the law is against it.

Raleigh: It is a Toy to tell me of such law. I defy such law, I stand on the fact.

Lord Cecil: I am afraid my often speaking (who am inferior to my Lords here present) will make the World think I delight to hear my self talk. My affection to you, Sir Walter Raleigh, was not extinguished, but slaked, in regard of your deserts. You know the Law of the Realm (to which your mind doth not contest) that my Lord Cobham cannot be brought.

Raleigh: He may be, my Lord.

Lord Cecil: But dare you challenge it?

Raleigh: No.

Lord Cecil: You say that my Lord Cobham, your main accuser, must come to accuse you. You say, he hath retracted: I say, many particulars are not retracted. What the validity of all this is, is merely left to the Jury. Let me ask you this, If my Lord Cobham will say you were the only instigator of him to proceed in the Treason's, dare you put yourself on this?

Raleigh: If he will speak it before God and the King, that ever I knew of Arabella's matter, or the money out of Spain, or of the Surprising Treason; I will put myself on it. God's Will and the King's be done with me.

Lord Henry Howard: How if he speak things equivalent to that you have said.

Raleigh: Yes, in a main point.

Lord Cecil; If he say, you have been the Instigator of him to deal with the Spanish King, had not the Council cause to draw you hither?

Raleigh: I put my self on it.

Lord Cecil: then Sir Walter Raleigh, call upon God, and prepare your self for I do verily believe my Lords will prove this. Excepting your faults (I call them no worse) by God, I am your friend. The heat and passion in you and the Attorney's zeal in the King's service make me speak this.

Raleigh: Whosoever is the workman, it is reason he should give account of his work to the work-master. But let it be proved that he acquainted me with any of his conferences with Aremberg: he would surely have given me some account.

Lord Cecil: That follows not. If I set you on wok, and you give me no account am I therefore innocent?

Attorney: For the Lady Arabella, I said she was never acquainted with the matter. Now that Raleigh had Conference in all these Treasons, it is manifest; the Jury hath heard the matter. There is one Dyer, a Pilot, that being in Lisbon, met with a Portugal Gentleman, who asked him if the King of England was crowned yet? To whom he answered, I think not yet, but he shall be shortly. Nay, saith the Portugal, that shall never be, for his throat will be cut by Don Raleigh and Don Cobham before he be crowned.

Dyer was called and sworn, and delivered this Evidence.

Dyer: I came to a Merchants house in Lisbon, to see a boy that I had there; there came a gentleman into the house, and enquiring what countryman I was? I said, an Englishman. Whereupon he asked me, if the King was crowned? And I answered, No, but that I hoped he should be so shortly. Nay, saith he, he shall never be crowned; for Don Raleigh and Don Cobham will cut his throat ere that day come.

Raleigh: What infer you upon this?

Attorney: that your treason hath wings.

Raleigh: If Cobham did practice with Aremberg, how could it not but be known in Spain? Why did they name the Duke of Buckingham with Jack Straw's Treason, and the Duke of York with Jack Cade, but that it was to countenance his Treason?

Consider you Gentlemen of the Jury, there is no cause so doubtful which the Kings Counsel cannot make good against the Law. Consider my disability, and their ability: they prove nothing against me, only they bring the Accusation of my Lord Cobham, which he hath lamented and repented as heartily, as if it had been for an horrible murther: for he knew that all this sorrow which should come to me, is by his means. Presumptions must proceed from precedent or subsequent facts. I have spent 40000 Crowns against the Spaniard. I had not purchased 40 pound a year. If I had died in Guiana, I had not left 300 Marks a year to my wife and son. I that have always condemned the Spanish faction, methinks it is a strange thing that now I should affect it! Remember what St. Austin says, sic judicate tanqwuam ab alio mox judicandi; unus julex, unum tribunal. If you would be contented on presumptions to be delivered up to be slaughtered, to have your wives and children turned into the streets to beg their bread; if you would be contented to be so judged, judge so of me.

Serjeant Phillips: I hope to make this so clear, as that the wit of man shall have no colour to answer it. The matter is treason in the highest degree, the end to deprive the King of his Crown. The particular Treasons are these: First, to raise up Rebellion, and to effect that, to procure money; to raise up tumults in Scotland, by divulging a treasonable book against the Kings right to the Crown; the purpose, to take away the life of his majesty and his issue. My Lord Cobham confesseth Sir Walter Raleigh to be guilty of all these treasons. The question is, whether he be guilty as joining with him, or instigating of him? The course to prove this was by my Lord Cobham's accusation. If that be true, he is guilty; if not, he is clear. So whether Cobham say true, or Raleigh? That is the Question. Raleigh hath no Answer, but the Shadow of as much Wit, as the Wit of Man can devise. He useth his bare denial; the denial of a defendant must not move the Jury. In the Star Chamber, or in the Chancery, for matter of Title, if the Defendant be called in question, his denial on his oath is no evidence to the Court to clear him, he doth it in propria cause; therefore much else in matters of treason. Cobham's testification against him before then, and since, hath been largely discoursed.

Raleigh: If truth be constant, and constancy be in truth, why hath he forsworn that he hath said? You have not proved any one thing against me by direct Proofs, but all by circumstances.

Attorney: Have you done? The King must have the last.

Raleigh: Nay, Mr Attorney, he which speaketh for his life, must speak last. False repetitions and mistakings must not mar my cause. You should speak secundum allegata et probata. I appeal to you and the King in this point, whether Cobham's accusation be sufficient to condemn me?

Attorney: The King's safety and your clearing cannot agree. I protest before God, I never knew a clearer Treason.

Raleigh: I never had intelligence with Cobham since I came to the Tower.

Attorney: Go too, I will lay thee upon thy back, for the confidentest Traytor that ever came at a Bar. Why should you take 8000 crowns for a peace?

Lord Cecil: Be not so impatient, good Mr Attorney, give him leave to speak.

Attorney: If I may not be patiently heard, you will encourage Traytors, and discourage us. I am the King's sworn servant, and must speak: If he be guilty, he is a Traytor, if not deliver him.

Nota: Here Mr Attorney sat down in a chafe, and would speak no more, until the Commissioners urged and intreated him. After much ado he went on, and made a long Repetition of all the Evidence, for the direction of the Jury; and at the repeating of some things, Sir Walter Raleigh interrupted him,, and said, he did him wrong.

Attorney: Thou are the most vile and execrable Traytor that ever lived.

Raleigh: You speak indiscreetly, barbarously and uncivilly.

Attorney: I want words sufficient to express thy viperous treasons.

Raleigh: I think you want words indeed, for you have spoken one thing half a dozen times.

Attorney: Thou art an odious fellow, thy name is hateful to all the Realm of England for thy Pride.

Raleigh: It will go near to prove a measuring cast between you and me, Mr Attorney.

Attorney: Well, I will now make it appear to the World, that there never lived a viler viper upon the face of the Earth than thou, and therewithal he drew a letter out of his pocket, saying further, My Lords, you shall see, this is an Agent that hat writ a Treatise against the Spaniard, and hath ever so detested him; this is he that hath spent so much money against him in service; and yet you shall all see whether his heart be not wholly spanish. The Lord Cobham, who of his own nature was a good and honourable Gentleman, till overtaken by this Wretch, now finding his conscience heavily burthened with some courses which the subtilty of this Traytor had drawn him into, my Lords, he could be at no rest with himself, not quiet in his thoughts, until he was eased of that heavy weight; out of which passion of his mind, and discharge of his duty to his Prince, and his conscience to God, taking it upon his salvation that he wrote nothing but the Truth, with his own hands he wrote this letter. Now Sir you shall see whether you had intelligence with Cobham, within four days before he came to the Tower. If he be wholly Spanish, that desired a Pension of 1500 Pound a year from Spain, that Spain by him might have intelligence, then Raleigh is a traytor. He hath taken an apple, and pinned a letter unto it, and threw it into my Lord Cobham's window; the contents whereof were this, 'It is doubtful, whether we shall be proceeded with or no, perhaps you shall not be tried. This was to get a retractation. Oh! it was Adam's Apple, whereby the Devil did deceive him. Further, he wrote thus, 'Do not as my Lord of Essex did; take heed of a Preacher; for by his persuasion he confessed, and made himself guilty. I doubt not but this day God shall have as great a conquest by this Traytor, and the Son of God shall be as much glorified, as when it was said, vicisti Galilae; you know my meaning. What though Cobham retracted, yet he could not rest nor sleep till he confirmed it again. If this be not enough to prove him a Traytor, the King my master shall not live three years to an end.

Nota. Here Mr. Attorney produced the Lord Cobham's letter, and as he read it, inserted some speeches.

 I have thought fit to set down this to my Lords, wherein I protest on my soul to write nothing but the truth. I am now come near the period of my time, therefore I confess the whole truth before God, and his Angels. Raleigh, four days before I came from the Tower caused an Apple (Eves Apple) to be thrown in at my Chamber window; the effect of it was to intreat me to right the wrong that I had done him, in saying, that I should have come home by Heresy; which under my hand to him I have retracted. His first letter I answered not, which was thrown in the same manner, wherein he prayed me to write him a letter, which I did. He sent me word that the Judges met at Mr Attorneys house, and that there was good hope the proceedings against us should be stayed; He sent me another time a little tobacco. At Aremberg's coming Raleigh was to have procured a pension of fifteen hundred pounds a year; for which he promised that no action should be against Spain, the Low-Countries, or the Indies, but he would give knowledge before hand. He told me the States had audience with the King. (Attorney. Ah! is not this a Spanish heart in an English body?) He hath been the original cause of my ruine; for I had no dealing with Aremberg, but by his instigation. He hath also been the cause of my discontentment ; he advised me, not to be overtaken with preachers, as Essex was; and that the King would better allow of a constant denial, than to accuse any.

Attorney: Oh damnable atheist! He hath learned some text of scripture to serve his own purpose, but falsely alledged. He counsels him not to be counselled by Preachers, as Essex was: He died the Child of God, God honoured him at his death; thou wast by when he died. Et Lupus et turpes instant morientibus usea. He died indeed for his offence. The King himself spake these words: He that shall say Essex died not for Treason is punishable.

Raleigh: You have heard a strange tale of a strange man. Now he thinks, he hath matter enough to destroy me; but the King, and all of you shall witness, by our deaths, which of us was the ruine of the other. I bid a poor fellow throw in the letter at his window, written to this purpose, 'You know you have undone me, now write three lines to justifie me'. In this I will die, that he hath done me wrong: Why did not he acquaint me with his Treasons, if I acquainted him with my dispositions?

Lord Chief Justice: But what say you now of the rest of the letter, and the Pension of £1500 per annum?

Raleigh: I say that cobham is a base, dishonourable poor soul.

Attorney. Is he base? I return it into thy throat, on his behalf: But for thee, he had been a good subject.

Lord Chief Justice: I perceive you are not so clear a man, as you have protested all this while; for you should have discovered these matters to the King.

Nota: Here Raleigh pulled a letter out of his pocket, which the Lord Cobham had written to him, and desired my Lord Cecil to read it, because he only knew his hand; the effect of it was as followeth:

Cobham's Letter of Justification to Raleigh:

'Seeing myself so near my end, for the discharge of my own conscience, and freeing myself from your blood, which else will cry vengeance against me: I protest upon my salvation, I never practised with Spain by your procurement; God so comfort me in this my affliction, as you are a true subject, for any thing that I know. I will say as Daniel, Purus sum a sanguine hujus. So God have mercy on my soul, as I know no treason by you'.

Raleigh: Now I wonder how many souls this man hath! he dams one in this letter, and another in that.

Here was much ado, Mr Attorney alleged that his last letter was polickly and cunningly urged from Lord Cobham, and that the first was simply the truth; and that lest it should seem doubtful that the fist letter was drawn from my Lord Cobham by promise of mercy, or hope of favour, the Lord Chief Justice willed that the Jury might herein be satisfied.

Whereupon the Earl of Devonshire delivered that the same was meer voluntary, and not extracted from the Lord Cobham upon any hopes or promise of Pardon.

Nota: This was the last Evidence: whereupon a Marshall was sworn to keep the Jury Private. The Jury departed and staid not a quarter of an hour, but returned, and gave their verdict:

"GUILTY".

Serjeant Heale demanded Judgment against the Prisoner:

Clerk of the Crown.

'Sir Walter Raleigh, thou hast been indicted, arraingned, and pleaded not guilty, for all these several Treasons, and for tryal thereof hast put thy self upon thy country; which country are these, who have found thee guilty. What canst thou say for thy self, why Judgment and Execution of Death should not pass against thee?

Raleigh: My Lords, the Jury have found my guilty. They must do as they are directed. I can say nothing why Judgment should not proceed. You see whereof Cobham hath accused me. You remember his protestations, that I was never guilty. I desire the King should know of the wrongs done unto me since I came hither.

Lord Chief Justice: You had no wrong, Sir Walter.

Raleigh: Yes, of Mr Attorney. I desire my lords to remember three things to the King:

1.   I was accused to be a practiser with Spain. I never knew that my Lord Cobham meant to go thither; I will ask no mercy at the Kings hands if he will affirm it.

2.   I never knew of the practice with Arabella.

3.   I never knew of my Lord Cobham's practice with Aremberg,

nor of the Surprising Treason.

Lord Chief Justice: In my conscience I am persuaded that Cobham hath accused you truly. You cannot deny but that you were dealt with to have a pension to be a spy for Spain; therefore you are not so true to the King as you have protested yourself to be.

Raleigh: I submit myself to the King's mercy; I know his mercy is greater than my offence. I recommend my wife, and son of tender years, unbrought up, to his compassion.

Lord Chief Justice: I have thought I should never had seen this day, to have stood in this place to give sentence of death against you; because I thought it impossible, that one of so great parts should have fallen so grievously. God hath bestowed on you many benefits. You had been a man fit and able to have served the King in good place. You had brought your self into a good State of Living, if you had entered into a good consideration of your Estate, and not suffered your own wit to have intrapped your self, you might have lived in good comfort. It is best for man not to seek to climb too high, lest he fall; nor yet to creep too low, lest he be trodden on. It was the posie of the wisest and greatest counsellor of our time in England, In medio spatio mediocria firma locantur.

You might have lived well with 3000 a year, for so I have heard your Revenues to be. I know nothing might move you to be discontented; but if you had been down, you know Fortunes Wheel, when it is turned about, riseth again. I never heard that the King took away anything from you, but the Captainship of the Guard, which he did with very good reason, to have one of his own knowledge, whom he might trust, in that place. You have been taken for a wise man, and so have shewed wit enough this day. Again, for Monopolies for wine, etc. If the King had said, it is a matter that offends my people, should I burthen them for your private good? I think you could not well take it hardly, that his subjects were eased, though by your private hindrance. Two vices have lodged chiefly in you; one is an eager ambition, the other corrupt covetousness. Ambition, in desiring to be advanced to equal grace and favour, as you have been before-time; that Grace you had then you got not in a day or year. For your covetousness, I am sorry to hear that a gentleman of your wealth should become a base spie for the enemy, which is the vilest of all other; wherein on my conscience Cobham hath said true: by it you would have increased your living 1500 Pound a year. This covetousness is like a canker, that eats the Iron Place where it lives. Your case being thus, let it not grieve you, if I speak a little out of zeal, and love to your good. You have been taxed by the World, with the Defence of the most heathenish and blasphemous Opinions which I list not to repeat, because Christian ears cannot endure to hear them, nor the authors and maintainers of them suffered to live in any Christian commonwealth. You know what men said of Harpool. You shall do well before you go out of the World to give satisfaction therein, and not to die with these imputations on you. Let not any Devil persuade you to think there is no Eternity in Heaven: for if you think thus, you shall find Eternity in Hell-Fire. In the first accusation of my Lord Cobham, I observed his manner of speaking; I protest before the Living God, I am persuaded he spoke nothing but the Truth. You wrote, that he should not in any case confess any thing to a Preacher, telling him an example of my Lord of Essex, that noble Earl that is gone; who if he had not been carried away with others, had lived in honour to this day among us. he confessed his offences, and obtained mercy of the Lord, for I am verily persuaded in my heart, he died a worthy servant of God. Your conceit of not confessing anything is very inhumane and wicked. In this World is the time of confessing, that we may be absolved at the day of Judgment. You have shewed a fearful sign of denying God, in advising a man not to confess the Truth. It now comes in my mind, why you may not have your accuser come face to face: for such an one is easily brought to retract, when he seeth there is no hope of his own life. It is dangerous that any Traytors should have any access to, or conference with one another; when they see themselves must die, they will think it best to have their fellow live, that he may commit the like Treason again, and so in some sort seek Revenge.

Now it resteth to pronounce the Judgement, which I wish you had not been this day to have received of me: For if the fear of God in you had been answerable to your other great parts, you might have lived to have been a singular good subject. I never saw the like Trial, and hope I shall never see the like again.

The Judgement

But since you have been found guilty of these horrible Treasons, the Judgment of this Court is, that you shall be had from hence to the place whence you came, there to remain until the Day of Execution; and from thence you shall be drawn upon a Hurdle through the open streets to the Place of Execution, there to be hanged and cut down alive, and your Body shall be opened, your Heart and Bowels pluckt out, and your Privy Members cut off, and thrown into the Fire before your Eyes; then your Head to be strucken off from your body, and your body shall be divided into four Quarters, to be disposed of at the King's Pleasure: And

"GOD HAVE MERCY ON YOUR SOUL"

Sir Walter Raleigh besought the Earl of Devonshire, and the Lords, to be suiters on his behalf to the King; that in regard of Places of Estimation he did bear in his Majesties time, the Rigour of his Judgment might be qualified, and his death honourable, and not ignominious.

Whereinafter after they had promised him to do their utmost Endeavours, the Court rose, and the Prisoner was carried up again to the Castle.

On the 4th December 1603 the priests Clarke and Watson were executed at Winchester and their executions were carried out by Titchbourne. The quarters of their bodies were displayed on the turrets of the Castle.

Watson had confessed that he had drawn the other men in to the plot and held that the King was no sovereign until he were crowned, giving instances in Saul and Jeroboam. Clarke had agreed with Watson.

Parham and Brooksby were acquitted by the Jury.

Two days after Raleigh's trial George Brook was tried and he pleaded that his only intention had been to try faithful subjects, saying that he had a commission to do so, but he could not produce it and was sentenced to die. On the 6th December when he was executed.

Markham confessed the indictment, pleaded discontent and desired mercy.

On the 10th December, Markham, Grey and Cobham were to die.

Raleigh's execution was to take place on Tuesday, 13th December. The terrible sentence of a Traitor's death was pronounced and Sir Walter Raleigh was to be hung, drawn and quartered.

King James had decided to play a cruel trick on these four men and spare their lives. On the 7th December the King had signed Warrants staying these executions and had sent his gentleman of the Bedchamber, Mr Gibbs, to deliver the letters in the King's own hand, to the Sheriff. The King had given strict orders that none of the prisoners were to be informed.

One by one Raleigh, Cobham, Markham and Grey were brought to the scaffold and one by one they were released for prayer. They were then brought back to the scaffold for final release only to hear that they were to be imprisoned for life in the Tower of London and were all taken back to London.

Sir Walter Raleigh, Lord Cobham and Lord Grey were imprisoned under the supervision of Harvey the Lieutenant of the Tower and each man was permitted two servants.

Warrants were issued and signed granting access to the prisoner Sir Walter Raleigh who was to occupy the Bloody Tower.

Lady Raleigh
Carew Raleigh
Sir George Carew
Raleigh's Physician
Alexander Brett
Mr Peter Van Lore
Mr Arthur Ashton
Mr Charles Chewt
The widow Morley
Mr Shelbury
Two Servants,
Peter Deane, and,
John Talbot, who was to remain with Raleigh until the end.

Sir Walter Raleigh remained the King's prisoner for thirteen years.

HIC JACET: SIR WALTER RALEIGH

5 Bell Yard, London - 1626
Here a Man's Soul is to be found, washed in anguish

I, John Talbot will say that I was born into this evil World in the Autumn of 1574 without ambition. I had no thought of raising myself up from my own humble background, and acknowledged with thanks all that the good Lord had to offer me when I attended Mass each Sunday at St. Bride's Church, Fleet Street in the City of London. There I knelt on the cold stone floor for an hour or more, breathing in the cold dark air as the words of the Priest filled my willing ears. I deemed that I had caused a good act to be performed upon my own soul in that Church, which would guard me from harm throughout each day until the Sunday past became the Sunday present, and then I would seek out the Church again, offering my thanks once more. Thus lived my life, and seeing that it had been caused to be divided into days and weeks I never looked for the months that would come to claim the years of my life, and turn me into an old man as I am now.

My soul became a circle of my own view of goodness and I knew that I revolved within it. My highest admiration at that time was for the Priest who spoke to us as we gathered before him, and where he preached to us of the goodness that we must search out within ourselves, and for him I would have laid down my life even as a small child, if he had been offered danger or malice from any man. I spent my Sundays with a keen eye on my prayer book and another on those that gathered about us (because I always thought of the Priest and myself as 'Us').

As a young man, I gave only the slightest thought to the misfortunes of other men, whether rich or poor, and even though I was urged to do so, I never allowed myself to dwell too long upon their fate, supposing that they had drawn their share of misery down upon their own shoulders and that they were forced to wear it like a dark cloak for the remainder of their days.

I confess that I am the former servant of Sir Walter Raleigh, known as the Twelfth Knight of Queen of Queen Elizabeth's Court because he was knighted on Twelfth Night at the Feast of the Epiphany in [   ]. He pledged to become the Captain of her Guard, shielding her from all evil unto her death. I will remember him always as the proud Knight renowned throughout this Kingdom for his pride and the great dignity which won him many enemies. He took up residence at Durham House in the Strand, London in 1585, when that mansion was leased to him by Queen Elizabeth I. That is where I served him and that is where I lived out my youth.

On the morning of the 29th October, 1618, I watched as my master was taken to the block at Westminster to meet his death. He bore his misery well, behind another countenance and by that I mean that he masked his own fear of death and carried himself with great dignity. He neither flinched nor wavered in his last intent, which was to reveal to the crowds that had gathered for the Lord Mayor's Show, and who could not be drawn away from the scene of his execution, that he was no traitor to the King of England. There, on that bitter winter morning, he read out his Apology to King James I of England, for his second voyage to Guiana. He stood upon the wooden scaffold, straining his voice so that all might hear him; but before that time came to him, he had read aloud to the waiting crowds, his great speech to the Lords, raising his voice high and walking among them, turning now and then to face his spectators, and in their view he found a great strength rising up from his spirit , which carried him through that event, even in his great affliction.

Not since Raleigh's downfall in 1603, have I enjoyed the peace of mind that was once mine, and never has my former happiness returned to me since his arrest, trial and imprisonment. I fear that it never will.

If that were the only claim I had to the history of this great man, then I should put away my quill in haste and banish myself into the darkest corner with deep embarrassment, but the servants of all great men have secrets to tell, and yet mine would have died with me if I thought that they could harm my master in any way, even after his death, and I am too concerned with his good name to allow it.

I have made my home at 5 Bell Yard in the City of London, my purpose being this work. I cannot lay claim to a great University education nor to any patronage in this work, but if I fail to please the living then I am helpless indeed to please the spirits I must speak of, and it will bring me little comfort to record these words. How many long and miserable years I have endured for Sir Walter's sake in gathering up this history in order that I might set it down for my reader, and as to the bleak and lonely path it has led me down, I cannot say within these pages, because this is not the place to reveal it.

It is true that I am an uneducated man, but those who say that I was born without ambition must judge me for this book. It is strange that a book brought about through a knowledge of history can sway a man's mind (and even if only one, then he may tell his friends) so that the word of a friend may be carried abroad and cause others to seek out the truth and turn one man's search for the truth into another man's envy when he thought to reveal it once.

Now that I draw my thoughts inward to the end of my life, as all men must, if they are well prepared to die, I can establish my early thought as ambition, and I know and describe my ambition to be like a fire that has been lit in my mind, where it has burned into my soul so that nothing will cause it to be extinguished until my work has been accomplished,

For my purpose I have caused myself to become a master of Sir Walter's history. Let no-one say that I have caused myself to be surrounded by the deepest misery that any living soul could endure as I reveal the history of Sir Walter Raleigh's downfall.

I will detain you no longer in continuing with my story, since those who wish to be heard are becoming anxious and I would not wish to delay you unduly, excepting that I must introduce myself to you, so that you may see here no hidden motives or allow you any thought which may cause you to think that this work has been a dalliance with which I sought to amuse myself with a calm mind.

I have already confessed to you that I am an old man, and although many are familiar with the portrait of Sir Walter Raleigh, very few would claim to know me. My years will betray me as such, to any who would look upon me, and if I take the trouble to describe myself to you here, it is because I fear that you would never recognise me if you saw me, when I would have you do so, not least for the sake of this history, which I am proud to record for you.

Let me say that time has caught me out, if I find that I am too old to please myself by my own reflection, through my faded blue eyes, so that I could never hope to please another. I could turn away and blame it upon the calendar and never injure my own pride. It is better that I do not look into my own face again, when all I could hope to find is an unwelcome reflection. No, it is better to dwell in ignorance, so that in future, any who have cause to seek me out, might blame themselves instead, for looking into such a book as this - where they find the spirits of ancient times rising up from their own hell to ask for justice as they step forward to speak in order to record their words on these pages. If time itself will fall backwards, then they will, through their own words come alive once more, and they will live again if only for a few short hours so that we might hear them and judge them when they were denied justice in life.

I am not so very tall as to be called remarkable, and when I attempt to stand upright I tend to stoop, when once I was proud of my strong shoulders. When I walk through the London streets in the cold air, I find that my bones ache, when once I could have said that I was proud to hold my head up and that I was handsome enough with my golden locks of hair and clear blue eyes. Then I could have called myself vain, as I took myself around London with great pride and the young ladies danced into my path to seek out my company. Now my hair is grey and thin and if my face bears the marks of my years of misery, then I can only ask that you let me reveal my story, for surely I have earned the right to do so. My fingers are gnarled with age, and my palms are no longer smooth, since great maps of wisdom may be found upon them, if I hold them to the candlelight to observe them. But I would have no pity from you at all, since my hands and my mind have served me well in my role as a servant to Sir Walter Raleigh, and after his execution, I sought a position as a Scrivener's Apprentice, where I continue to serve him through this work, which I have planned for many years. Surely one man may serve another and no longer carry the title of servant?

I am tired of playing the part of victim to all that this World calls disgrace, knowing that I have not caused it or brought it upon myself, and yet if I had not sought to become a Scrivener's Apprentice and a historian, I would surely have lived on in ignorance and might perhaps have found my own measure of happiness. As it is, I have no power to alter what I had fed my mind upon and I must complete my work, since I have caused it to surround me so entirely, that I find I have no time to spare for my own rest. I cannot say that I have fallen very low, except in my own misery, but that has been my case for many long years. I now live in a state of solitary ill-humour, and few desire to seek me out for company. No blame can fall upon them, because they cannot know that I was blessed with a carefree spirit in my youth.

[insert a list of those named on the Warrant to visit Sir Walter Raleigh at the Bloody tower after his imprisonment]

Raleigh's Second Voyage to Guiana, 1617

In March 1617 Sir Walter Raleigh was released from the Bloody Tower where he had been held as a prisoner since November 1603, and although still unpardoned, went about making the preparations for his second voyage to Guiana on a private expedition, and under the [39] Privy Seal of King James I of England in search of Gold which he intended to bring home for King James I of England:

Letters Patent to Discover Guiana granted by King James I of England

Dated this six and twentieth day of August in the fourteenth year of Our Reign of England, France, and Ireland, and of Scotland the fiftieth:

[40] ["James, by the Grace of God, &c. To all to whom these Presents shall come, to be read, heard, or seen, and to every of them greeting: Whereas Sir Walter Raleigh Knight, intendeth to undertake a Voyage by Sea and Shipping, unto the South parts of America, or elsewhere within America, possessed and inhabited by heathen and Savage people; to the end, to discover and find out some Commodities and Merchandizes in those Countries, that be necessary and profitable for the Subjects of these Duc Kingdoms and Dominions, whereof the Inhabitants there make little or no use of estimation; whereupon also may ensue by Trade and Commerce, some propagation of the Christian faith, and reformed Religion amongst those Savage and idolatrous people: And whereas we are credibly informed, that there

---

[39] HRO - 169M84W/9- See my letter of Permission to reproduce any such material in this book as is necessary to this Biography

[40] The Letters Patent granted to Sir Walter Raleigh by King James I of England - November 1617

are divers merchants and Owners of ships, and others, well disposed to assist the said Sir Walter Raleigh in this his Enterprize, had they sufficient Assurance to enjoy their due parts of the profits returned (in respect of the peril of Law wherein the said Sir Walter Raleigh now standeth:)

And whereas also We are informed, that divers other Gentlemen, the kinsmen & friends of the said Sir Walter Raleigh, and divers Captains and other Commanders, are also desirous to follow him, and to adventure their Lives with him in this his Journey, so as they might be commanded by no other than himself.

Know ye, that We, upon deliberate consideration had of the Premisses, being desirous by all ways and means to work and procure the benefit and good of Our loving Subjects, and to give our Princely furtherance to the said Sir Walter Raleigh, his friends and Associates herein, to the Incouragement of others in the like laudable Journeys and Enterprizes, to be hereafter prosecuted and pursued; and especially in advancement and furtherance, as well of the Conversion of Savage people, as of the increase of Trade, Traffique, and Merchandizes used by Our Subjects of this Our Kingdom, being most famous throughout all nations: Of our special Grace, certain knowledge, and meer motion, have given and granted, and by these presents for Us, Our heirs, and Successors, do give and grant unto the said Sir Walter Raleigh, full power and Authority, and free Licence and Liberty out of this Our Realm of England, or any other Duc Dominions, to have, carry, take, and lead, for and towards his said intended Voyage unto the said South parts, or other parts of America, (possessed and inhabited as aforesaid) and to Travel thither, all such, and so many of Our loving Subjects, or any other [41]Strangers that will become Our loving Subjects, and live under Our Obeyance and Allegiance, as shall willingly accompany

---

[41]See New Atlantis

him, with sufficient Shipping, Armour, Weapons, Ordnance, Munition, Powder, Shot, Habiliments, Victuals, and such Wares and Merchandizes, as are esteemed by the wild people in those parts, Clothing, Implements, furniture, Cattle, horses (& Mares, and all other such things as he shall think most necessary for his Voyage, and for the use and defence of him and his Company, and trade with the People there; and in passing and returning to and fro, and in those parts, to give away, Sell, Barter, Exchange, or otherwise dispose of the same Goods, Merchandizes, and Premises, to the Most benefit, and at the will and pleasure of the said Sir Walter Raleigh and his Company, and such other Person or Persons, as shall be Adventurers or Assistants with, or unto him in this his intended Voyage, and from thence to Return, Import, Conveye, and bring into this Our Kingdom, or any other Our Dominions, such Gold, Silver, Bullion, or any other Wares, or Merchandizes, or Commodities whatsoever, as they shall think most fit and convenient; and the same being so Returned, Imported, Conveyed, and Brought into this Our Kingdom, or any other Our Dominions, to have, take, keep, retain, and convert to the only proper Use, Benefit, and Behoof of the said Sir Walter Raleigh, and his said Company and other Persons Adventurers and Assistants with, or to him in his Voyage, without the Let, Interruption, Molestation, and Disturbance of Us, Our heirs or Successors, or any of the Officers, or Ministers of Us, Our heirs or Successors whatsoever; paying and Answering unto Us, Our heirs, and Successors, the full fifth part, in five parts to be divided, of all such gold, and Silver, and Bullion, and Oar of Gold, or Silver, and Pearl, and precious Stones, as shall be Imported over and besides; and together with such Customs, Subsidies, and other Duties, as shall be due for, or in respect of any other Goods, Wares, or Merchandizes whatsoever to be so Imported by the true meaning of these Presents. And to the end the said Sir Walter Raleigh may be the more Encouraged to go forward in this Enterprize, and all Our loving Subjects desirous to be Adventurers with him, or Assistant unto him, may be the more incited to further his Proceedings: We do hereby in **verbo Regio**, for us, Our heirs and Successors, Covenant, Promise, and Grant, to and with the said Sir Walter Raleigh, and all other Persons that shall accompany him, or to be attendant upon him, or to be Adventurers or Assistants with, or to him in this his

Voyage, that no Gold, Silver, Goods, Wares, or Merchandizes whatsoever, of what kind or cost soever, by him or them, or any of them to be Imported into this Duc Kingdom of England, or any other Duc Dominions, from any the said South, or other parts of America, (possessed or Inhabited, as aforesaid) shall be attached, seized, or taken by Us, Our heirs or Successors, or to the use of Us, Our heirs or Successors, or by any of the Officers or Ministers of Us, Our heirs or Successors Whatsoever, But that the Same, and every of them (the fifth part of the said Gold, Silver, or Bullion, and Oar of Gold and Silver, and Pearl, and precious Stones, and other the Customs and Duties aforesaid, being truly answered and payed) shall be, and remain to the sole and proper use and behoof of the said Sir Walter Raleigh, and his said Company, and such Persons as shall be Adventurers with him, or Assistant to him in this his Voyage; any Law, Statute, Act of Parliament, Proclamation, Provision, or Restraint, or any Right, title, or Claim of Us, Our heirs or Successors, or any other matter or thing whatsoever to the contrary in any wise notwithstanding. And further, of Our more especial Grace, certain Knowledge, and meer Motion, We do hereby for Us, Our heirs and Successors, ordain, constitute and appoint the said Sir Walter Raleigh to be the Sole Governour and Commander of all Persons that shall travel, or be with him in the said Voyage, to the said South, or other parts of America, (so possessed and inhabited as aforesaid) or in returning from thence. And we do hereby give unto him all Power and Authority to protect, Punish, Pardon, Govern, and Rule them, or any of them, according to such Order, Ordinances, Constitutions, Directions, and Instructions, as the said Sir Walter Raleigh shall be from time to time Established, as well in cases Capital and Criminal, as Civil, both Marine and other; So always as the said Statutes, Ordinances, and Proceedings (as near as conveniently may be) be agreeable to the Laws, Statutes, government and policy of this Our Realm of England, and not against the true Christian faith now professed in the Church of England. And because that in such and the like Enterprizes and Voyages, great inconveniencies have grown by the mutinous and disorderly carriage of the Mariners and Saylors employed in the same for want of sufficient Authority to punish them according to their Offences: We do therefore by these Presents for Us, Our heirs and Successors, give full power and Authority to the said Sir Walter Raleigh, in case of Rebellion or Mutiny by Sea or Land, to use and exercise Martial Law (upon just ground and apparent necessity) in as large and ample manner as our Lieutenant General by Sea or Land, or our Lieutenants in Our Counties, within Our Realm of England, have, had, or ought to have by force of their Commission of Lieutenancy.   And we do further by these Presents, give full power and Authority to the said Sir Walter Raleigh, to Collect, Nominate and Appoint such Captains, and other inferiour Commanders and Ministers under him, as shall be requisite for the better ordering and governing of his Company, and the good of the Voyage. And further, we do by these Presents, for Us, Our heirs and Successors, straightly Charge and Command the Warden of Our Cinque Ports, and all the Customers, Comptrollers, Surveyers, Searchers, Waiters, and other Officers and Ministers of Us, Our heirs and Successors, for the time being, that they and every of them do quietly permit and suffer the said Sir Walter Raleigh, and all person and persons that shall be willing to Travel and Adventure with him in this Voyage with their Ships, Munition, Goods, Wares, and Merchandizes whatsoever out of this Duc Realm, or any other Our Dominions, to pass into the said South or other parts of America, (possessed and Inhabited as aforesaid,) and from thence to return and import into this Our Realm, or any other Our Dominions, any Goods, Wares or Merchandizes Whatsoever and thereto Sell, or otherwise dispose of the same, to the best benefit and advantage, and to the only use and behoof of the said Sir Walter Raleigh, and his Company, and such other Persons as shall be Adventurers with him in this Voyage; paying the fifth part of all Gold and Silver, and Bullion, and Oar of Gold, and Silver, and of Pearl, and precious Stones imported, and other the Customs and Duties aforesaid. And these Presents, or the Inrolment thereof, shall be unto the said Wardens of the Cinque Ports, Customers, Comptrollers, and other the officers and Ministers aforesaid, for the time being, a sufficient Warrant and Discharge in that behalf. And Our Will and Pleasure is; and by these Presents, for Us, Our heirs and Successors, We do grant unto the said Sir Walter Raleigh, That these Our Letters Patents, or the Inrolment thereof and all and singular Grants, Clauses, and things therein contained, shall be firm, strong, sufficient, and effectual in Law, according to Our gracious Pleasure and Meaning herein expressed; Any Law, Statute, Act, Provision, Ordinance, or Restraint, or any other Matter or Thing to the contrary thereof in any wise notwithstanding. Although express mention, &c.

In witness whereof, &c. Witness Our Self at Westminster the Six and Twentieth Day of August, in the fourteenth Year of Our Reign of England, France, and Ireland, and of Scotland the fiftieth.

Per breve de Privato Sigillo

In Preparation for the Guiana Voyage Raleigh made the following Preparations

Raleigh had raised:

£30,000 in joint stock, chiefly from Devon.
£2,500 from Lady Raleigh's own Estate
£3,000 Sherborne Compensation money
£175 Government bounty to encourage shipbuilding

There were 7 ships of War and Three Pinnaces.
There were 1,000 men

Wat Raleigh was to sail as Captain to his Admiral in the 440 ton "Destiny".

Other Ships were:

The "Star"
The "Encounter"
The "Thunder"
The "Flying Joan"

Sir Walter Raleigh's Letter to Sir Ralph Winwood, Secretary to King James I of England revealing that he has been betrayed before he even sets foot in Guiana and the Spaniards are lying in wait for him and his men

[... On the 17th November 1617 Raleigh arrived at Guiana, having been much retarded by contrary winds, and wrote this letter to Sir Ralph Winwood, Secretary to King James I of England]

"Sir,

As I have not hitherto given you an account of our proceedings and passages towards the Indies, so have I no other subject to write of, than of the greatest misfortunes that ever befell any man. For whereas for the first, all those that navigate between Cape de Verd, and America, do pass between Fifteen or Twenty days at most, we found the wind so contrary, and (which are also contrary to Nature) so many storms and rains, as we spent six weeks in the passage; by reason whereof, and that in so great Heat, we wanted Water. For at the Isle Prano of Cape de Verd, we lost our Anchors and Cables, and our Water-Casks; and being driven from the Isle with a Hurricane, we were like all to have perished. Great sickness fell amongst us, and carried away great numbers of our ablest men, both for Sea and Land. The 17th November, we had sight of Guiana, and soon after came to Anchor in five Degrees of the River Galliano; here we staid till the fourth of December, landed our sick-men, set up our Barges and Shallops, which were brought out of England in Quarters, washed our Ships, and took in fresh-water, being fed and cherished by the Indians of my old Acquaintance, with a great deal of Love and Respect. My self being in the hands of Death this six weeks, and not able otherwise to move, than as I was carried in a chair, gave order to five small ships to sail into Orinoque, having Captain Kemish for their conductor towards the Mines: And in those five ships, five companies of fifty, under the command of Captain Parker, Captain North, Brethren to the Lord Monteage, and the Lord North, valiant Gentlemen, and of infinite Patience, for the Labour, Hunger, and Heat which they have endured:

My son had the third Company, Capt. Thornix of Kent the fourth company; Capt. Chidley, by his Lieutenant, the fifth. But as my Serjeant Major, Capt. Piggot, died in the former miserable passage; so my Lieutenant, Sir Warham Saint Leiger, lay sick without hope of Life, and the charge conferred on my Nephew, George Raleigh, who had also served long with infinite commendations; but by reason of my absence, and of Sir Warham's, was not so well obeyed as the Enterprise required. As they passed up the River, the Spaniards began the War, and shot at us, both with their Ordnance and Muskets; whereupon the Companies were forced to charge them, and soon after beat them out of the Town. In the Assault my Son (more desirous of Honour than Safety) was slain; with whom, to say truth, all the respects of this World have taken end in me; and although these five Captains had as weak companies as ever followed valiant Leaders, yet were there among them some twenty or thirty valiant adventurous Gentlemen, and of singular courage; as of my Sons Company, Mr. Knivet, Mr. Hammond, Mr. Lanworth, Mr. John Pleasington; his Officers, Sir John Hambden, Mr. Simon Leak, Corporal of the Field, Mr Hammond, the elder Brother, Mr. Nicholas of Buckingham, Mr. Roberts of Kent, Mr. Perin, Mr Tresham, Mr. Mollinax, Mr. Winter and his brother, Mr Wray, Mr. Miles Herbert, Mr Bradshaw, Captain Hall, and others.

Sir, I have set down the names of these Gentlemen, to the need that if his Majesty shall have cause to use their service, it may please you to take notice of them for very sufficient Gentlemen. The other five ships staid at Trinidado, having no other Port capable of them near Guiana. The second ship was commanded by my Vice-Admiral Capt. John Pennington, of whom (to do him right) he is one of the sufficientest Gentlemen for the Sea that England hath. The third by Sir Warham Saint-Legier, an exceeding valiant and worthy Gentleman. The fourth by Sir John Fern. The fifth by Captain Chidley of Devon. With these five ships I daily attended their Armada of Spain, which had they set upon us, our Force divided, the one half in Orinoque 150 miles from us, we had not only been torn in pieces, but all those in the

River had also perished, being of no force at all for Sea-fight. But we had resolved to be burnt by their sides, had the armada arrived: But belike they staid for us at Margaret, by which they knew we must pass to the Indies. For it pleased his Majesty to value us at so little, as to command me upon my Allegiance, to set down under my hand the Country, and River by which I was to enter it; to set down the Number of my Men, and Burthen of my Ships, and what Ordnance every Ship carried: which being known to the Spanish Ambassador, and by him unto the King of Spain, a dispatch was made, and letters sent from Madrid, before my departure out of the Thames. For his first letter, sent by a Barque of Advice, was dated the 19th March, 1617 at Madrid, which letter I have here inclosed sent to your Honour; the rest I reserve, not knowing whether they may be intercepted or not. The second by the King, dated the second of May, sent also by a colonel of Diego de Polonioque, Governour of Guiana, Elderedo, and Trinidado. The third by Bishop of Pedricho, and delivered to Prolonioque, the 15th July at Trinidado. And the fourth was sent from the Farmer and Secretary of his Customs in the Indies. At the same time by that of the Kings Hand sent by the Bishop, there was also a Commission for the speedy levying of 300 souldiers, and ten Pieces of Ordnance, to be sent from Portriche, for the Defence of Guiana. 150 from Nueno Remo de Grando, under the Command of Captain Anthony Musica; and the other 150 from Portricho, to be conducted by Captain Francis Landio.

Now Sir, if all that have traded to the Indies since his Majesties time, knew that the Spaniards have flayed alive all the poor Men which they have taken, being but Merchant Men, what Death and cruel Torment shall we expect, if they conquer us? Certainly, they have hitherto failed grossly, being set out thence as we were, both for Number, Time, and Place.

Lastly, to make an Apology for not working the Mine (though I know his Majesty expected it, whom I am to satisfie as much as my self) having lost my Son and my Estate in the Enterprize; yet it is true, that the Spaniards took more care to defend the passage leading unto it, than they did the Town, which by the King's Instructions they might easily do, the Countries being Asperra & Nemorosa.

But is it true, that when Capt. Kemish found the River low, and that he could not approach the Banks in most places near the Mine by a mile, and where he found a descent, a volley of Mussquet shot came from the Woods upon the Boat, and slew two Rowers, hurt six others, and shot a valiant Gentlemen of Capt. Thornix, of which wound he languisheth to this day. He, to wit, Capt. Kemish, following his own Advice, thought it was in vain to discover the Mine; and he gave me this for an Excuse at his return, that the companies of English in the Town of St. Thoma were not able to defend it against the daily and nightly Assaults of the Spaniards; That the Passages to the Mines were thick and unpassable Woods; and that the Mine being discovered, they had no Men to work it, did not discover it at all. For it is true, the Spaniards having two Gold Mines near the Town, the one possessed by Pedro Rorigo de Paran, the second by Harmian Frotinio, the third of silver by Capt. Francisco, are useless for want of Negroes to work them: For as the Indians cannot be constrained, by a Law of Charles the 5th, so the Spaniards will not, nor can endure the labour of those Mines, whatsoever the Bragadocio the Spanish Amabassador saith. I shall prove under the Proprietors hands, by the Custom-Book, and the King's Quinto, of which I recovered an Ingot or two: I shall also make it appear to any Prince, or State, that will undertake it, how easily those Mines, and five or six more of them, may be possessed, and the most of them in those Parts, which have never as yet been attempted by any, nor by any Passage to them, nor ever discovered by the English, French, or Dutch. But at Kemish's return from Orinoque, when I rejected his counsel and his course, and told him he had undone me, and wounded my credit with the King past recovery, he slew himself: For I told him, seeing my Son was slain, I cared not if I had lost 100 more in opening the Mine, so my credit had been saved. For I protest before God, had not Captain Whitney (to whom I gave more countenance than to all the Captains of my Fleet) run from me at the Granadoes, and carried another ship with him of Captain Wollastons, I would have left my Body, at St. Thome, by my Sons, or have brought with me out of that or other Mines, so much Gold Ore as should have satisfied the King. I propounded no vain thing, what shall become of me I know not. I am unpardoned in England, and my poor Estate consumed, and whether any Prince will give me Bread or no, I know not. I would desire your Honour to hold me in your good Opinion, to remember my Service to my Lord of Arundel and [42] Pembroke, to take some pity on my poor Wife, to whom I dare not write for renewing her sorrow for her Son. And I beseech you to give a copy of this to my Lord Carew; for to a broken Mind, a sick Body, and weak Eyes, it is a torment to write many Letters. I have found many things of Importance for discovering the State of Weakness of the Indies, which if I live I shall hereafter impart unto your Honour, to whom I shall remain a faithful Servant." ~ 17th November 1617, Walter Raleigh

---

[42] The Earl of Pembroke was the brother in law of Sir Philip Sidney whose sister was the Countess Mary of Pembroke.

Raleigh, Prisoner in the Bloody Tower, November 1618

Mr Walter Burre attended Sir Walter at the Bloody Tower, as I will relate to you below. It is no use for men to search in vain for Sir Walter's second volume of his History, because they will never find it. It is Mr Burr the publisher that we may all thank for that, although acting on the Instructions of the Privy Councillors direct from the King, we cannot blame him as he cannot find blame in himself.

As Mr Burr stood before Sir Walter and was asked how the first volume of his history had done, he replied that it had sold so slowly that it had undone him. "Ah, my friend, hath the first part undone thee?"

With the greatest resolve, Sir Walter stepped across the room, his kind face set in a keen determination to show his visitor that he was intent upon throwing open the lid of his battered Oak sea chest which he had taken with him on his many voyages and now being the place he proudly kept all his papers, it being on the opposite side of his small cell. He reached it before Mr Burr had time to fully understand or observe the actions of this man, whom he could only describe as the most interesting he had ever made acquaintance with. As Sir Walter threw open the heavy lid he did it so angrily that it banged against the wall, and then he gathered up the huge sheets of parchment all bound up with twine. This moment of passionate neglect had replaced his former anguish, but he failed to look upon his wooden writing desk, nor at his feather quills and well used ink well unless his mind informed him to cease his own action.

The second volume of Sir Walter's History of the World he wasted no time in carrying to the flaming log fire where Mr Burr still stood warming himself. Sir Walter displaced Mr Burr and flung the papers into the flames, not sparing the time to unravel the twine, thinking it better to force his heavy boot down on top of the papers and there to watch them burn away into blackened ashes. He turned to Mr Burr and said slowly through gritted teeth:

"The second part shall undo no more! This ungrateful world is unworthy of it."

All the wretched Mr Burr could do was watch as Sir Walter allowed the tears to fall slowly away from his eyes as he watched his magnificent work being devoured by the flames. Mr Burr dared not reveal to Sir Walter that King James had suppressed any further publication of Volume I of his History of the World, and that his work had been a bestseller from the moment it had come into his hands and yet he had been powerless to offer it to his willing public.

Sir Walter Raleigh is Executed
29th October 1618 - 8.30 a.m : Lord Mayor's Day

The Lord Mayor's Show was to take place in London on the very morning that Sir Walter was to be beheaded being the 29th October, 1618 and the hour after sunrise once the appointed time became nine of the clock thereafter.

I saw that Sir Walter had eaten a good breakfast, after which he smoked his last pipe, (and being sentimental he had desired me to bring him not his silver pipe but his old clay pipe. The clay pipe is still to be seen at his magnificent castle, being Sherborne Castle in Dorset and there it rests, in a glass case for the world to view with their eyes if they so desire.

As he approached the scaffold he was offered a cup of sack. He readily accepted and when asked if it was to his liking he said 'I will answer you as did the fellow who drank of St. Giles's bowl as he went to Tyburn: "It is a good drink if a man may tarry by it"'.

And so you will see that he kept his good humour until his soul left his body and he could utter no more. As he neared the Scaffold steps, I kept as near to him as I could do, but I was being pushed by his guards who were many in number and so I was held back by the crowd and became separated from him. Nevertheless, Sir Walter made his way towards me, and asked me why I had come out on such a bitter morning, because he saw the tears were ready in my eyes. Still I answered him as bravely as I could, saying that 'I wanted nothing but to see him and pray God to have mercy on his soul'. He reached up to his head and took off his lace nightcap, which he gave to me saying 'Take it, for thou hast more need of it now, friend, than I'. I took the lace night cap into my hands and it was still warm. That I did not immediately turn and flee from the scene of his execution was a matter for my own soul to describe to my conscience and had I known that it would take place then I could not bear to allow myself to watch him die. Yet I desired to witness his last speech since all the Lords had gathered to listen and knowing that King James I had already released Cobham and Markham, I could never believe that his execution would be finally carried out, not when it came to him being offered the blade of the axe reserved for Traitors, since he had earlier written his Apology to King James in defence of his Guiana actions, thus, and which I have here to read for you:

Raleigh's Apology to King James I of England concerning his Guiana voyage

"May it please your most excellent Majesty.

If in my journey outward bound, I had my men murdered at the Island, and yet spared to take Revenge. If I did discharge some Spanish Barques taken, without spoil. If I did forbear all parts of the Spanish Indies, wherein I might have taken twenty of their towns on the Sea coasts, and did only follow the Enterprise I undertook for Guiana, where without any directions from me a Spanish village was burnt, which was new set up within three miles of the Mine. By your majesties favour, I find no reason why the spanish Ambassador should complain of me. If it were lawful for the spaniards to murder Englishmen, binding them back to back, and then cutting their throats, when they had traded with them a whole month, and came to them on the land without so much as one sword; and that it may not be lawful for your Majesties subjects, being charged first by them, to repel force by force; we may justly say, O miserable English! If Parker and Metham took Campeach and other places in the Honduraes, seated in the heart of the Spanish Indies, burnt towns, killed the Spaniards, and had nothing said to them at their return, and myself forbore to look into the Indies because I would not offend; I may justly say, O miserable Sir Walter Raleigh! If I spent my poor Estate, lost my Son, suffered sickness, and otherwise a world of miseries; if I have resisted with the manifest hazard of my life, the robberies and spoils which my Company would have made; if when I was poor, I might have made my self rich; if when I had gotten my liberty, which all men, and nature itself do so much prize, I voluntarily lost it; if when I was sure of my life, I rendered it again; if I might elsewhere have sold my ship and goods, and put 5 to 6,0000 pound in my pocket, and yet have brought her in England. I beseech your Majesty to believe that all this I have done, because it should not be said to your Majesty, that your Majesty had given liberty and trust to a man whose end was but the recovery of his liberty, and who had betrayed your Majesty's trust. My Mutineers told me that if I returned for England, I should be undone; but I believed in your Majesty's goodness more than in all their arguments. Sure I am, that I am the first that being free, and able to enrich myself, have embraced poverty and peril: But your Majesties wisdom and goodness I have made my Judges, who have ever been, and shall ever be,

Your Majesties most humble vassal,

Walter Raleigh

Now that you have read Sir Walter's Apology, you will see that I had reason to believe he would receive a Pardon from the King.

As Sir Walter stepped up to the Scaffold and carried himself forward with great dignity he wore a smiling countenance to indicate that he was well pleased, and saluting the Lords, Knights and Gentlemen he indicated to an appointed Officer, who proclaimed a Silence.

Sir Walter Raleigh then composed himself for his audience and motioned to all present that he would be heard by waving his arms high in the air to gain attention, as he walked slowly to and fro across the Scaffold boards:

Raleigh's Speech at the Scaffold

'I desire to be born withal, because this is the third day of my fever; and if I shew any weakness, I beseech you attribute it to my malady, for this is the hour I look for it.'

He looked towards the place where the Lord of Arundal and the Lord of Doncaster sat among other Knights and to them he said in a loud voice:

'I thank God of his infinite Goodness that he hath sent me to die in the sight of so Honourable an Assembly, and not in darkness'.

But his voice could not be heard, for his audience were seated too far from him and he became agitated in his desire to be heard easily by all men present, who desired to listen to his speech. He raised his voice still louder and he said,

'I will strain myself, for I would willingly have your Honours hear me'.

'As I said, I thank my God heartily that he hath brought me into the light to die, and not suffered me to die in the dark prison of the Tower, where I have suffered a great deal of adversity, and a long sickness; and I thank God that my fever hath not taken me at this time, as I prayed God it might not.

There are two main points of suspicion that his Majesty hath conceived against me, wherein his Majesty cannot be satisfied, which I desire to clear and resolve you in:

One is, that his Majesty hath been informed that I have had some Plot with France, and his Majesty had some reason to induce him thereunto. One reason that his Majesty had to conjecture so, was, that when I came back from Guiana, being come to Plymouth, I endeavoured to go into Rochel; which was because I would fain have made my peace before I came to England. Another reason was, that upon my flight I did intend to fly to France for saving my life, having had some terror from above. A third reason was, the French Agent's coming to me; and it was reported I had Commission from the King of France.

But this I say, for a man to call God to witness to a falsehood at any time is a grievous sin, and what shall he hope for at the Tribunal Day of Judgement? But to call God to witness to a falsehood at the time of death, is far more grievous and impious, and there is no hope for such an one. And what should I expect that am now going to render an account of my faith?

I do therefore call the Lord to witness, as I hope to be saved, and as I hope to see him in his Kingdom, which will be within this quarter of this hour, I never had any commission from the King of France, nor any Treaty with the French agent, nor with any from the French King; neither knew I that there was an Agent, or what he was, till I met him in my Gallery at my Lodging, unlooked for. If I speak not true, O Lord, let me never come into thy Kingdom.

The second suspicion was, that his Majesty hath been informed, that I should speak dishonourably and disloyally of him. But my accuser was a base Frenchman, a kind of a cymical fellow, one whom I knew to be perfidious; for being drawn into this action at Winchester, in which my hand was touched, and he being sworn to secrecy overnight, revealed it in the morning.

But in this I speak now, what have I to do with Kings? I have nothing to do with them, neither do I fear them: I have now to do with God, therefore to tell a Lie now to get the favour of the King were in vain.

Therefore, as I hope to be saved at the last day, I never spake dishonourably, disloyally, nor dishonestly of the King; neither to this Frenchman, nor to any other; neither had I ever in all my life a thought of ill of his Majesty.

Therefore I cannot but think it strange, that this Frenchman being so base, so mean a Fellow, should be so far credited; and so much for this Point. I have dealt truly, and I hope I shall be believed. I confess, I did attempt to escape, and I did dissemble and fain my self sick at

Salisbury, but I hope it was no sin. The Prophet David did make himself a foot, and did suffer spittle to fall upon his beard, to escape the hands of his enemies, and it was not imputed to him as sin; and I did it to prolong time till his Majesty came, hoping for some commiseration from him.

I forgive this Frenchman, and Sir Lewis Stuckley, and have received the sacrament this morning of Mr Dean, and I do also forgive all the World.

But this much I am bound in charity to speak of this man, that all men may take good heed of him:

Sir Lewis Stuckley, my kinsman and Keeper, hath affirmed that I should tell him that I did tell my Lord Carew, and my Lord Doncaster of my present escape; but I protest before God, I never told Stuckley any such thing, neither did I tell my Lord Carew, or my Lord Doncaster, of my pretended escape. It was not likely that I should acquaint two Privy-Counsellors of my purpose; neither would I tell him, for he left me six, seven, eight, nine or ten days to go where I listed, while he rode about the country.

Again, he accused me, that I should tell him, that my Lord Carew, and my Lord Doncaster would meet me in France: which was never my speech or thought.

Thirdly, he accused me, that I shew'd him a letter, and that I should give him 10000 l. for my Escape: but cast my soul into everlasting fire if ever I made him offer of 10000 l. or 1000 l. but merely I shew'd him a letter, that if he would go with me, his debts should be paid when he was gone; neither had I 2000 l. for if I had had so much, I could have done better with it, and made my peace otherwise.

Fourthly, when I came to Sir Edward Pelham, who had been sometimes a follower of mine, who gave me good entertainment; he gave out that I had received some dram of poison in Sir Edward Pelham's house: when I answered, that I feared no such thing; for I was well assured of them in the house. Now God forgive him, for I do, and desire God to forgive him: I will not only say God is the God of Revenge, but I desire God to forgive him, as I hope to be forgiven."

Then he looked over his note of remembrance' before he continued

"Well thus far I have gone; now a little more, and I will have done by and by.

It was told the King I was brought per force into England, and that I did not intend to come again: Whereas Captain Charles Parker, Mr Tresham, Mr Leak, and divers others that knew how I was dealt withal, shall witness for me: for the common soldiers (which were 150) mutined, and sent for me to come into the Gun-Room to them, (for at that time they would not come to me) and there was I forced to take an Oath, that I would not come into England till they would have me, else they would cast me into the Sea and drown me; afterwards they entered my Cabin and set themselves against me. After I had taken this Oath, with Wine and other things I drew the chiefest of them to desist, and at length persuaded them to go into Ireland: Then would they have gone into the North parts of Ireland, but I told them they were Redshanks: yet at last with much ado I persuaded them to go into the South parts; promising to get their Pardons: but was forced to give them 125l. at Kinsale to bring them home, otherwise I had never got from them.

There was a Report that I meant not to go to Guiana at all; and that I knew not of any Mine, nor intended any such matter, but only to get my liberty, which I had not the wit to keep. But it was my full intent to go for Gold, for the benefit of his Majesty, and those that went with me, with the rest of my Countrymen: But he that knew the Head of the Mine, would not discover it when he saw my Son was slain, but made himself away. Then he turned to my Lord of Arundel and said, being in the Gallery in my ship at my departure, Your Honour took me by the hand, and said you would request me one thing, that was, that whether I made a good voyage or bad, yet I should return again into England; when I made you a promise, and gave you my faith that I would:

"And so you did" (answered my Lord). "It is true, they were the last works I spake unto you".

"Another Opinion was, that I carried to Sea with me 1600 Pieces, and that was all the Voyage I intended, only to get money into my hands, and that I had weighed my voyage before: whereas I protest I had had but 100 Pound in all the World, whereof I gave 25 Pounds to my wife: the reason of this speech was this; there was entered 20,000 Pound, and yet but 4,000 Pound in the Surveyors Book; now I gave my Bill for the other 16,000 Pound for divers adventurers, but I protest I had not a penny of money more than 100 Pound, as I hope to be saved.

Another slander was raised, that I would have gone away from them and left them at Guiana, but there were a great many of worthy men that accompanied me always, as my Serjeant Major George Raleigh, and divers others [and my self being in the hands of Death those six weeks, and not able otherwise to move, than as I was carried in a chair, gave order to five small ships to sail into Orinoque, having Captain Kemish for their conductor towards the Mines: And in those five ships, five companies of fifty, under the command of Captain Parker, Captain North, Brethren to the Lord Monteage, and the Lord North, valiant Gentlemen, and of infinite Patience, for the Labour, Hunger, and Heat which they have endured: My son had the third Company, Capt. Thornix of Kent the fourth company; Capt. Chidley, by his Lieutenant, the fifth. But as my Serjeant Major, Capt. Piggot, died in the former miserable passage; so my Lieutenant, Sir Warham Saint Leiger, lay sick without hope of Life, and the charge conferred on my Nephew, as I say, George Raleigh] that knew my intent was nothing so. And these be the material points I though good to speak of; I am now at this instant to render my Account to God, and I protest as I shall appear to him, this that I have spoken is true.

I will speak but a word or two more, because I will not trouble Mr

Sheriff too long.

There was a Report spread, that I should rejoice at the death of my Lord of Essex, and that I should take Tobacco in his presence; when as I protest I shed tears at his death though I was one of the contrary Faction; and at the time of his death I was all the while in the Armory at the further end, where I could but see him; I was sorry that I was not with him, for I heard he had a desire to see me, and be reconciled to me. So that I protest I lamented his death, and good cause had I, for it was the worse for me as it proved, for after he was gone I was little beloved.

And now I intreat you all to join with me in Prayer, that the great God of Heaven, whom I have grievously offended, being a man full of all vanity, and have lived a sinful life, in all sinful callings, having been a soldier, a Captain, a Sea-Captain, and a Courtier, which are all places of wickedness and Vice; that God (I say) would forgive me, and cast away my sin from me, and that he would receive me into everlasting life. So I may take my leave of you all, making my peace with God".

Sir Walter, having prepared himself to die, moved toward the Axe and Block and stood before his Executioner. He removed his hat, his gown and his doublet. Calling to the Headsman to show him the Axe, he said:

'I pray let me see it. Dost thou think I am afraid of it?' He took the axe into his hands and as he felt along its edge, he turned to the Sheriff and smiled before he said:

'This is a sharp medicine, but it is a physician for all diseases.'

He walked across the scaffold boards for the last time and in all directions, to show himself to his company and he prayed that they assist and strengthen him. When asked which way he would lay himself he replied, 'so the heart be right, it is no matter which way the head lieth.'

He forgave the Headsman and gave him a coin, as was customary. He then laid his head upon the block. The Headsman did not strike soon enough and Sir Walter cried out to him,

'What are you waiting for? Strike man! Strike!'

After two blows his head was severed from his body.

A coach arrived at the scene immediately after the execution, and Sir Walter's wife, Bess Throckmorton, stepped out with great dignity and held her head high for the Lords to see. After she had claimed her husband's head, still warm with his recent thoughts, it was wrapped in a black cloth, that the Lords recognised as the old Oriel gown that Raleigh had borrowed from Oxford University. His head was placed in a red leather bag and as Lady Raleigh made ready to depart, men wept to see her leave in her wretched state. If she saw them through her own misery, being left in this World to endure her remaining lot in life as it now stood. She did not indicate it to the crowd, being a lady who could and would bear herself with great dignity. Lady Raleigh entered her carriage and fled that terrible scene.

HIC JACET: SIR WALTER RALEIGH

John Talbot, Raleigh's Servant, 1618

Thus I continued on my way home to my lodgings and as I passed through the cobbled streets, I met an old fellow who would have me stop and listen to his urgent words, and the following story was related to me as I passed on my way home from the terrible scene which I had just left. The old man told me of a riot breaking out in the City of London as a crowd of angry young sailors who had been aboard Raleigh's ship recently back from Guiana, who rushed through the narrow alleys crying out Sir Walter's name, and would not hear the word 'Traitor' called out among them for they said it offended their ears, their minds and their hearts that the City folk would have it so.

At the front of this restless crowd, ran a strong tall youth by the name of Master Winter, not tired by life, and he being so strong and intent upon his purpose, his mind was bent upon causing a riot. He being only equipped with the knowledge of his father and his grandfather, and all that history being in his own head, he set out on his own path. He gathered followers for the man, being his father, who had sailed with Raleigh on his last voyage.

This youth then, took it into his own head, without any prompting from his aged relatives who were not present, to perform his last deed in favour of Sir Walter Raleigh and the great stories he had heard of him, and he took angry steps toward a wooden box and made ready to stand upon it in order to perform before the crowd,, which someone had made ready and set up for him in the streets of Westminster. His voice rang out so loud that none could fail to hear, and yet, as to mimic Sir Walter's frail voice upon the Scaffold, he cried louder still:

"Listen, Listen ye to me and all ye who will hear me ... Lest you fear to lose your own souls in the hereafter!

"Sir Walter Raleigh is dead this morning of a disease called the Axe of English Justice! The Queen's Favourite is dead I say! His head has been carried off by his lady, to a safe place!

A bystander being a sailor, cried out in support: "Aye! And he will want a head to dine next noon".

And now we will weep and want for him in our midst, and all to please the King of England who would please the King of Spain!

Here in our midst, as we stare about ourselves, we look for him. For the true Englishman that wanted only the glory of all England. I will not dare to speak of him. If his spirit has been carried off early to another World, then I will be his speaker. I will tell you all, of Queen Elizabeth's favourite Knight, fondly known to her as 'Water!'

And I speak now of a water so foul that you may liken it to English justice. For it runneth so freely in the name of the new King, that it could have been drawn from a City gulley and yet we would recognise it. If it is agreed then, to be such a well, and holding water, then it must be like a well of strong Water, as it greets us on this day of his Execution.

And now I will tell you all, if you would stay and listen, what the great Lords did say at his Execution. Hear me then and I will speak to you.

They said: "we have not such another head to cut off!"

They said: "I never saw the like trial and hope I shall never see the like again'

Why even Judge Gawdy confessed that "never before had the justice of England been so depraved and injured as in this trial."

And when Sir Walter Raleigh waited for the axe to fall and to sever his neck from his head, he bid his Executioner to hurry forward, and even though he who had been so firmly reminded of his duty, and so well rewarded, still hesitated, and threw down his own cloak for Sir Walter to kneel upon, as if in fear for himself and his own soul, he did bring back to the minds of all who watched, how Sir Walter had thrown his cloak down in a muddy street many years before to please the Queen of England for her to tread upon so that she might not muddy her feet.

Sir Walter, being still strong of mind, if his long time in the Tower had carried away his strength, cared not for his own safety, and cried out 'What dost thou fear? Strike man, strike!'

A man of slight build shoved himself forward as if the very devil had possessed him. His red, angry face showed his fury, as he stepped upon the box and reached up, placing his hands around the shoulders of the strong youth and displaced him from his stand. Ignoring the complaints from the crowd, which had increased twice over since the youth had first begun.

And now upon the box stood William Shakespeare at the age of 39, all dressed in black but for a grubby white collar about his neck, and muddied black boots. He cried out, as he reached his hands out before him and waved them angrily in front of the youth he had just displaced.

"You speak of a Knight you know little of, being one so young and yet you profess to know more than you ought!   In short, you know so much that you utter your words in a manner so fitting to your audience, that as you hold their attention with so riveted an application you begin to befit your method.

And yet I myself may speak as a man who truly knew Sir Walter Raleigh and if I take the stand here, it will become my stage, since I am an actor by profession. My role is before me and I will speak his true words.

If you as my audience will listen, you will enhance your own minds, and yet if you walk away you will ever wonder what I might speak of that could interest you."

Master Winter who had previously spoken, saw that his moment had passed and he stood firmly down although reluctantly, with his head hung low. He found himself being covered with great embarrassment, since he wept, for his own passion which had overtaken him to such a degree that he had wanted to say more.

But he being of so little knowledge, knew that he could say no more, since the very man who had hauled him from his stand and now stood before him and his waiting crowd was the great William Shakespeare. Since everyone present recognised that celebrated man, he felt that it was a scene set for the future stage and none would argue against it.

As William Shakespeare stood up in defence of Sir Walter Raleigh, being a man he had wronged during his early career as a Dramatist, he called forth into his own mind the plays he had written but spoke not yet of those, as he said:

"I stand before you now and you will recognise me as a great man because I am a writer and repeater of renowned words. If I convey my words to the minds of people who as an audience, choose to stand before me and listen, then I have done them a service, for which I would desire due payment.

And yet on this morning I desire no payment! When I fled Stratford Upon Avon, after falling into bad company and was prosecuted for deer stealing by Sir Thomas Lucy of Charlecote near Stratford, I came into London so poor and wretched, that I sat in the graveyard at St Paul's and begged my bread, among the other inhabitants of that place and an old man who went about gathering bones approached me and befriended me. Though it be that I kept that company not for as long a time as he, yet I recognise my humble beginnings. And such was my fate!

Yet armed with my talent and in full recognition of the great gift I carried in my head, I was brought forward and presented to great men who recognised my gift. I made the acquaintance of some of Raleigh's enemies, such as Sir Francis Bacon and Robert Devereux, the Second Earl of Essex who put me in such good situation that I found my rightful place.

An old man called out to him from the crowd: "Be it not your father the Bailiff you speak of when you say you found your place and Marlowe lost his eye and his life?"

And another called directly after him:

"And the bladder you wore upon the stage as you played Hamlet, filled with blood, was it that of Thomas Kyd?"

And the crowd roared with laughter as William Shakespeare waited for silence to fall again so that he could continue to speak.

I stand before you now and I speak as a humbled man, when I speak the name of Sir Walter Raleigh. For he was a great man. A man of such great parts that we have watched him die today to please those men who desire to be great in his long absence.

Therefore, no coins must rattle from your pockets and I will not look upon a pound weight of old standard silver, now being made into three pounds and two shillings by a tale, and that is when it is put into crowns, half-crowns, shillings, sixpences, twopences, pence or half pence. No, I desire no reward on this morning, on this day of the Lord Mayor's Show.

Cross not my palm and look not at my hand but into my heart as I speak henceforth.

For I will not stand and say that Sir Walter Raleigh was a man so wronged that he did not seek out his own justice when he wronged others who stood before him in his youth. That I speak in favour of him now is a matter for my own judgement. If I tell you that I will leave my own conscience beside me as I speak, then I will say that his story has led me to be so forward, that I would become an actor again upon the stage in order to recite his last speech: Being so moved by it as I am!

And let me tell it now. For the words I am about to recite could have been written by mine own hand and yet recognised as his, for the words I will speak to you are his own true words and I entertain you as I tell them:

Remember these words? "Never was a man so hated and so popular in so short a time." Whereas when I saw Sir Walter Raleigh first, I would have gone a hundred miles to see him hanged, I would, ere we parted, have gone a thousand to save his life".

Master Winter cried out: "But those are the words I called out at the start Mister Shakespeare"

The crowd laughed again and then an old lady called:

"Let him speak, he has need of it. His soul is burning like fire!"

Shakespeare continued: "For those of you who could not gather about him, because you were unable so to do, or were of a weak mind and cared not, Sir Walter stood before his Executioner today, upon the scaffold boards, and having removed his hat, gown and doublet, recited his great speech. He had prepared himself to die. Calling the Headsman to show him the Axe, Sir Walter said 'I pray let me see it, Dost thou think I am afraid of it? He took it in his hands and felt along its edge and turned to the Sheriff and smiled as he said "This is a sharp medicine, but it is a physician for all diseases". He then walked across the scaffold in all directions to show himself to his company and prayed they assist and strengthen him. When asked which way he would lay himself he said "So the heart be right, it is no matter which way the head lieth". He forgave the Headsman and he did not strike Sir Walter cried out "What are you waiting for, strike man strike". He took two blows and Sir Walter lost his head which was carried away in a red leather bag by his lady.

That he is dead we cannot deny. His life will become a legend and his story a schoolboy's tale. Any book of our own age, we may pick up and there we will read of him and his story will be brought to life.

And yet, if I speak of him thus, and if the Summons is brought by and by, penned in his Majesty's hand, I cannot stay it.

If, I say, I am thrown into the Fleet or Newgate Prison will I be left to fester there until my dying day. Why? May I not speak the truth on this his day of Judgement? Or must I scurry away and hide with my thoughts and record them in a secret place until my death? If I succour a man deemed a Traitor, am I to be deemed a Traitor?"

An old woman, ragged in her appearance, brought about by her solemn existence, moved forward and spoke to him in hushed tones:

"Here then Mister William, take this great dark cloak and cover yourself, minding your head, so that you will not be recognised. For we will not let any harm come to you for speaking the truth that we know none of yet. Let nothing more hold you back from it,

William Shakespeare covered himself with the black cloak and hood, to avoid being identified by any of the King's men who might pass by, and he looked about himself in distress, as he spoke to his waiting audience:

"I will let it be heard for I am anxious to be gone from this place and I will leave those in my midst with this scene:

Sir Walter Raleigh upon the Scaffold, out in a loud voice to his audience:

"There was a Report spread, that I should rejoice at the death of my Lord of Essex, and that I should take Tobacco ..."

At this moment Lord North approached the scene, red eyed and weary in his mind and bones, the recent rain having soaked through his cloak.

"We have heard it Mister Shakespeare, from the mouth of Sir Walter himself, just this morning, and will hear no more from you now. You repeat yourself often as is your want. Be gone with you and take yourself back to your stage and I wish you a more willing audience than the one I view surrounding you."

Lord North finally spoke to the crowd, "And that my friends is why Sir Walter died today. That is why he has been destroyed by Privy Councillor Cecil, who devised his own method and plot to bring Raleigh down swiftly. Something he would not have dared to do during the Queen's lifetime. Cecil has used his influence to prompt the King from the very beginning.

For those of you who do not know, Sir Robert Cecil, the Queen's former secretary and the second son of Lord Burleigh, being 11 years younger than Raleigh. Raleigh and Cecil had once been great friends, being related by marriage. When Cecil's young wife died suddenly in 1597 Raleigh had taken Cecil's young son Will to live at Sherborne Castle with him and Lady Raleigh and there they educated him alongside their own son Wat Raleigh, who died recently in Guiana at the age of [25].

Remember the letters that Raleigh wrote to the Queen against The Earl of Essex. Did not Cobham's letters bring down Sir Walter Raleigh at his trial when all at once he remembered King Edward II and the Earl of March?

Now you will remember that Lord Cobham is Cecil's nephew and it will begin to make sense to you. Cecil had suggested to King James that as Raleigh resided at Sherborne Castle and not at Court he was apparently unable to perform his duties as Captain of the Guard and should be removed from his position.

Cobham to win Raleigh's trust, sought an interview with James and complained personally on Raleigh's behalf although it had no effect. Raleigh arrived in London on the 8th May and called before King James Advisers to be told that his position as Captain of the Guard would go to Sir Thomas Erskine.

Whilst Raleigh was away on official business in Jersey, a fire had broken out in Durham House and Lady Raleigh sought an audience with Lord Cecil to ask if the Lease to that property might be made more permanent. Cecil promised to look into the matter and that he did. He suggested to King James that the Raleighs' were not suitable tenants. By June 24th Raleigh had lost his London home Durham House in the Strand, as it was taken away from him and given to the Bishop of Durham by King James. It had been Raleigh's London residence since 1581[3]".

And now I bid you all good day, for I will away home to my bed, and with this, Lord North took himself off in the direction of the City of London.

Raleigh's Letter to Charles Howard and the Admirals of England And Robert Cecyll Knight, 1618

And so, with this letter ready in my hand, I will detain you no longer ...

Since I have it now and therefore must read it entirely for it shows me a little more of the vile acts and treacherous deeds that could be done to any man, but as I show you these enemies of my master who have done him an injustice here, upon his returne from his voyage to Guiana the first time, I aske you to find patience and read it if you will in honour of his good memory:

TO THE RIGHT HONORABLE MY
Singuler good lord and kinsman,
Charles Howard, knight of the Garter,
Barron, and Counceller, and of the
Admirals of England the most renowmed:
And to the Right Honorable Sr. Robert Cecyll Knight,
Counceller in his Highnes privie Councels.

For your Honors many Honorable and friendlie parts, I have hitherto onely returned promises, and now for answeare of both your adventures, I have send you a bundle of papers which I have devided +between your Lo. & Sr. Robert Cecyl in these two respects chiefly: First for that it is reason, that wastful factors, when they have consumed such stockes as they had in trust, doe yeeld some cullor for the same in their account, secondly for that I am assured, that whatsoever shall be done, or written by me, shall neede a double protection and defence. The triall that I had of both your loues, when I was left of all, but of malice and revenge, makes me still presume that you will be pleased (knowing what little power I had to performe ought, and the great advantage of forewarned enemies) to answeare that out o knowledge, which others shall but object out of malice. In my more happy times as I did especially honour you both, so I found that your loves sought me out in the darkest shadow of adversitie, and that the same affection which accompanied my better fortune, sored not away from me in my manie miseries: all which though I cannot requite, yet I shall ever acknowledge: and the great debt which I have no power to pay, I can doe no more for a time but confesse to be due. It is true that as my errors were great, so they have yeelded very grievous effects, and if ought might have beene deserved in former times to have counterpoysed anie part of offences, the fruite thereof (as it seemeth) was long before fallen from the tree, and the dead stocke onely remained. I did therefore even in the winter of my life, undertake these travels, fitter for bodies lesse blasted with misfortunes, for men to great abilitie, and for mindes of better incouragement, that thereby if it were possible I might recover but the moderation of excess, and the least taste of the greatest plentie formerly possessed. If I had knowen other way to win, If I had imagined how grater adventures might have regained, if I could conceive what father meanes I might yet use, but even to appease so powerful a displeasure, I would not doubt but for one yeare more to hold fast my soule in my teeth, till it were performed. Of that little remaine I had, I have wasted in effect all herein, I have undergone many constructions, I have beene accompanied with many sorrows, with labor, hunger, heat, sickness, & peril: It appeareth notwithstanding that I made no other bravado of going to the sea, then was meant, and that I was neither hidden in Cornewall, or elsewhere, as was supposed. They have grossly belied me, that forejudged that I would rather become a servant to the Spanish king, then return, & the rest were much mistaken, who would have perswaded, that I was too easeful and sensuall to undertake a journey of so great travel. But, if what I have done, receive the gracious construction of a paineful pilgrimage, and purchase the least remission, I shall thinke all too little, and that there were wanting to the rest, many miseries: But if both the times past, the present, and what may be in the future, doe all by one graine of gall continue in an eternal distate, I doe not then knowe whether I should bewaile my selfe either for my too much travel and expence, or condemne my selfe for doing lesse then that, which can deserve nothing. From my selfe I have deserved no thankes, for I am returned a begger, and withered, but that I might have betted my poore estate, it shall appeare by the

following discourse, if I had not onely respected her Majesties future
Honor, and riches. It became not the former fortune in which I once
lived, to goe journeys of picorie, and it had sorted ill with the office of
Honor, which by her Majesties grace, I hold this day in England, to run
from Cape to Cape, & from place to place, for the pillage of ordinarie
prizes. Many yeares since, I had knowledge by relation, of that
mighty, rich, and beawtifull Empire of Guiana, and of that great and
Golden City, which the spanyards call El Dorado, and the naturals
Manoa, which Citie was conquered, reedified, and inlarged by a
yonger sonne of Guainacapa Emperor of Peru, at such time as
Francisco Pazaro and others conquered the saide Émpire, from his two
elder brethren Guascar, and Atabalipa, both then contending for the
same, the one being favoured by the Oreiones of Cuzco, the other by
the people of Caximalca. I sent my servant Jacob Whiddon the yeare
before, to get knowledge of the passages, and I had some light from
Captaine Parker sometime my servant, and nowe attending on your Lo.
that such a place there was to the southward of the great bay of
Charuas, or Guanipa: but I found that it was 600. miles father off, then
they supposed, and manie other impediments to them unknowen and
unheard. After I had displanted Don Anthony de Bearer, who was
upon the same enterprise, leaving my ships at Trinidad, at the port
called Curiapan, I wandred 400. miles, into the said country byland
and river: the particulers I will leave to the following discourse. The
countrey hath more quantity of Gold by manifolde, then the best
partes of the Indies, or Peru: All the most of the kings of the borders
are already become her Majesties vassals: & seeme to desire nothing
more than her Majesties protection, and the returne of the English
nation. It hath another grounde and assurance of riches and glory, then
the voyages of the west Indies, & an easier way to invade the best
parts therof, then by the common course. The king of spaine is not so
impovrished by taking 3 or 4 port townes in America as we suppose,
neyther are the riches of Peru, or Neuva Espania so left by the sea side,
as it can be easily whasht away, with a great flood, or spring tide, or
left drie upon the sandes on a lowe ebbe. the port townes are few and
poore in respect of the rest within the land, and are of little defence,
and are onely rich when the streets are to receive the treasure for
Spaine: And we might thinke the Spanyards verie simple, having so

many horses and slaves, that if they could not upon two daies warning, carrie all the Golde they have into the land, and farre enough from the reach of our footmen, especiallie the Indies beeing (as it is for the most part) so mounteynous, so full of woods, rivers, and marshes. In the port townes of the province of Vensuello, as Cumana, Coro, and S. Iago (whereof Coro and S. Iago were taken by Captaine Preston and Cumana and S. Josephus by us) we found not the value of one riall of plate in either: but the Cities of Barquasimeta, Valentia, S. Sebastian, Cororo, S. Lucia, Allenguna, Marecabo, and Truxillo, are not so easilie invaded: neither doth the burning of those on the coast impoverished the king of Spayne anie one Ducket, and if we sacke the river of Hache, S. Marta, and Cartagena, which are the portes of Nuevo reyno and Popayan. There are besides within the land which are indeed rich and populous, the townes and Cities of Merida, Lagrita, S. Christopheruso, the great Cities of Pampelone, S. Fede Bogota, Tunia and Mozo where the Emeralds are founde, the townes and Cities of Morequito, velis, la vill a de Leua, Palma, unda, Angustura, the greate Citie of Timana, Tocaima, S. Aguila, Pasto, Iuago, the greate citie of Popaian it selfe, Los Remedios, and the rest. If we take the ports and villages within the bay of Urab in the kingdom or rivers of Dariena, and Caribana, the cities and townes of S. Juan de Royda, of Cassis, of Antiocha, Caramanta, Cali, and Auserma have gold enough to pay the King part, and are not easily invaded by the way of the Ocean, or if Nombre de Dios and Panama be taken in the province of Castillo de oro, and the villages upon the rivers of Cenu and Chagre. Peru hath besides those and besides the magnificent cities of Quito and Lima so many Ilands, portes, Cities, and mines, as if I should name the with the rest, it would seeme incredible to the reader: of all which because I have written a particuler treatise of the west Indies, I will omit their repetition at this time, seeing that in the saide treatise I have anatomized the rest of the sea townes as well of Nicaragna, Iucata, Nueva Espanna, and the Isands, as those of the Inland, and by what meanes they may be beste invaded, as farre as any meane Judgement can comprehend* (his book 1596) . But I hope it shall appeare that there is a way found to answere every mans longing, a better Indies for her majestie then the King of Spaine hath any, which if it shall please her highnes to undertake, I shall most willingly end the rest of my daies in following the same: If it be left to the spoyle and sackage of common persons, if the love and service of so many nations be despised, so great riches, and so mightie an Empyre refused, I hope her Majestry will yet take my humble desire and my labour therein in gracious part, which if it had not beene in respect of her highnes future honer & riches, I could have laid hands and ransomed many of the kings & Cassiqui of the Country, & have had a reasonable proportion of gold for their redemption: But I have chosen rather to beare the burthen of poverty, then reproch, & rather to endure a second travel & the chaunces therof, then to have defaced an enterprise of so great assurance, untill I knew whether it pleased God to put a disposition in her princely and royall heart eyther to follow or foreflow the same: I wil therefore leave it to his ordinance that hath onely power in al things, and do humbly pray that your honors wil excuse such errors, as without the defence of art, overrunne in every part, the following discourse, in which I have neither studied phrase, forme, nor fashion, and that you will be pleased to essteeme me as your owne (though over dearly bought) and I shall ever remaine ready to doe you all honour and service.

Walter Raleigh
1618

1596?
[refers to first voyage to Guiana]

"Because there have been divers opinions conceived of the golde oare brought from Guiana, and for that an Alderman of London and an officer of +her majesties minte, hath given out that the same is of no price, I have thought good by the addition of these lines to give answers as well to the said malicious slaunder, as to the other objections. It was is true that while we abode at the Island of Trinedado, I was informed by an Indian, that not farre from the Port, where we ancored, there were founde certain minerall stones which they estimeed to be gold, and were thereunto perswaded the rather for that they had been both English, and French men gather, and imbarqued for quantities thereof: Uppon this liklyhood I sent 40 men and gave order that each one should bring a stone of that myne, to make triall of the goodnesse, which being performed, I assured them at their returne that the same was Marcasite, and of no riches or value: Notwithstanding divers trusting more to their owne sense, then to my opinion, kept of the said Marcasite, and have tried thereof, since my returne, in divers places. In Guiana itselfe I never sawe Marcasite, but all the rocks, mountaines, all stones in the plaines, in woodes, and by the rivers sides are in effect thorow shining, and appeare marveylous rich, which being tried to be no Marcasite, are the trew signes of rich mineralles, but are no other than El madre del oro (as the Spanyards terme them which is the mother of golde, or as it is saide by other the scum of gold: of divers sortes of these manie of my companie brought also into England, everie one taking the sayfest for the best, which is not generall for mine owne parte, I did not countermand any mans desire, or opinion, and I could have afforded them little if I shoulde have denied them the pleasing of their owne fancies therein: But I was resolved that golde must be found either in graines separate from the stone (as it is in most of al the rivers of Guiana) or else in a kinde of hard stone, which we call the white Sparre, of which I saw divers hills, and in sundrie places, but had neither tyme, nor men, nor instruments fitte to labour. Neere unto one of the rivers I found of the said white Sparre or flint a very great ledge, or banke, which I endeavored to breake by al the meanes I coulde, because there appeared on the out side some small graines of gold, but finding no meane to worke the same uppon the upper part, seeking the sides and circuite of the sayd rock, I founde a clift in the same, from whence the daggers, and with the heade of an ax, we gotte out some small quantitie thereof, of which kinde of white stone (wherein golde is engendred) we sawe silver hills and rocks in everie part of Guiana, wherein we travelled. Of this there hath beene made mainie trialls, and in London it was first assaide by Master Westwood a refiner dwelling in wood street, and it helde after the rate of 120000 or 13000 pounds a tunne. Another sort was afterward tried by Master Bulmar and Master Dimoke assay master, and it held after the rate of 23000 pounds a tunne. There was some of it againe tried by Master Palmer comptroller of the minte, and Master Dimoke in Golde Smiths hall, and it helde after 26900 pounds a tunne. There was also at the same time, and by the same persons a triall made of the dust of the said myne which held 8.pound 6.ounces weight of gold, in the hundred: there was likewise at the same time a triall made of an Image of Copper made in Guiana, which helde a third part gold, besides divers trialls made in the countrey, and by others in London. But because there came of ill with the good, and belike the said Alderman was not presented with the best, it hath pleased him therefore to scandall all the rest, and to deface the enterprise as much as in him lyeth. It hath also been concluded by divers, that if there had been anie such oare in Guiana, the same discovered, that I would have brought home a greater quantitie thereof: first I was not bounde to satisfie anie man of the quantitie, but such onely as adventured, if any store had been returned thereof: but it is verie true that had all their mountaynes beene of massive gold, it was impossible for us to have made anie longer staye to have wrought the same: and whosoever hath seene with what strength of stone, the best golde oare is invironned, hee will not thinke it easie to be had out in heaps, and especiallie by us who had neither men, instrumentes, nor time (as it is saide before) to performe the same: There were on this discoverie, no lesse than 100 personnes, who can all witnesse, that when we past any braunch of the river to vewe the land within, and staid from our boats but six houres, wee were driven to wade to the eyes, at our returne: and if we attempted the same the day following, it was impossible either to forde it, or to swim it, both by reason of the swiftnesse, and also for that the borders were so pestred with fast woods, as neither bote nor man could finde place, either to land, or to imbarque: for in June, July, August, and September, it is impossible to navigate any of those rivers, for such is the furie of the current, and there are so many trees and woods overflowne, as if anie boate but touch uppon anie tree or stake, it is impossible to save any one person therein: and were we departed the land, it ran with that swiftnesse, as we drawe downe most commonly against the winde, little lesse than one hundred miles a day: Besides our vessels were no other than wherries, one little barge, a small cockboate, and a bad Galiota, which wee framed in hast for that purpose at Trinedado, and those little boates had nyne or ten men apeece, with all their victuals, and armes. It is further true, that we were about 400. miles from our shippes, and had been a moneth from them, which also we left weakely mande in an open roade, and had promised our return in 15 dayes. Others have devised that the same oare was had from Barbery, and that we carried it with us into Guiana: surely the singularitie of that device, I do not well comprehend, for mine owne parte, I am not so much in love with these long voiages, as to devise, thereby to cozen my selfe, to lie hard, to fare worse, to be subjected to perils, to diseases, to ill favours, to be parched and withered, and withall to sustaine the care and labour of such an enterprize, excepte the same had more comfort, than the fetching of Marcasite in Guiana, or bying of gold oare in Barbery. But I hope the better sort will judge me by themselves, and that the way of deceipt is not the way of nor or good opinion; I have herein consumed much time, and many crowns, and I had no other respecte or desire then to serve her majesty and my Country thereby. If the Spanishe nation had beene of likle beleefe to these detractors, we should little have feared or doubted their attempts, wherewith we now are daily threned. but if we now consider of the actions both of Charles the fiste, who had the Maydenhead of Peru, and the aboundant treasures of Atabalipa, together with the affaires of the spanish king now living, what territories he hath purchased, what he hath added to the actes of his predecessors, how many kingdomes he hath indangered, how many armies, garrisons, and navies, he hath and doth maintaine, the greate losses which he hath repayred, as in 88 above 100 sayle of greate shippes with their artillery, and that no yere is lesse unfortunate but that many vessels, treasures, and people are devored, and yet notwithstanding he beginneth againe like a storme to threaten shipwracke to us all, we shall finde that these abilities rise not from the trades of sackes, and Civil Orenges, nor from ought else that either Spaine, Portugal, or any of his other provinces produce: It is his Indian Golde that indaungereth and disturbeth all the nations of Europe, it purchaseth intelligence, creepeth into Councils, and setteth bound loyalty at libertie, in the greatest Monarchies of Europe. If the Spanish king can keepe us from forraine enterprizes, and from the impreachment of his trades, eyther by offer of invasion, or by beseiging us in Britayne, Ireland, or elsewhere, he had then brought the worke of our perill in greate forwardness. Those princes which abound in treasure have greate advantages over the rest, if they once constraine them to a defensive warre, where they are driven once a yeare or oftner to cast [compare to Bacons Essays 'Of Princes'] lots for their own garments, and from such shall all trades, and entercouse, be taken away, to the general losse and impoverishment of the kingdom and common weale so reduced: besides when men are constrained to fight, it hath not the same hope as when they are prest and incouraged by the desire of spoyle and riches. Father it is to be doubted how those that in time of victorie seeme to affect their neighbour nations, will remaine after the first view of misfortunes, or ill success; to trust also to the doubfulness of a battel, is but a fearefull and uncertaine adventure, seeing therein fortune is as likely to prevaile as, vertue. It shall not be necessary to alleage all that might be said, and therefore I will thus conclude, that whatsoever kingdome shall be inforced to defend it selfe, may be compared to a bodie daungerouslie diseased, which for a season may be preserved with vulgar medicines, but in a short time, and by little and little, the same must needs fall to the ground, and be dissolved. I have therefore laboured all my life, both according to my small powre, and perswasion, to advance all those attempts,, that might eyther promise return of profit to our selves, or at last be a lett and impreachment to the quiet source, and plentiful trades of the Spanish nation, who in my weake judgement by such a warre were as easily indaungered and brought from his powerfulnes, as any prince in Europe, if it be considered from how many kingdomes and nationes his revenewes are gathered, and those so weake in their owne beings, and so farre severed from mutuall succor. But because such a preparation and resolution is not to be hoped for in hast, and that the time which our enemies embrace, can not be had againe to advantage, I will hope that these provinces, and that Empyre now by me discovered shall suffice to inable her Majesty, and the whole kingdome, with no lesse quantities of treasure, then the king of Spayne hath in all the Indies, east and west, which he possesseth, which if the same be considered and followed, ere the Spayards, reinforce the same, and if her Majesty will undertake it, I will be contented to lose her highnes favour and good opinion for ever, and my life withall, if the same be not found rather to exceed, then to equall whatsoever is in this discourse promised or declared. I will nowe referee the reader to the following discourse with the hope that the perilous and chargeable labors and indevours of such as thereby seeke the profit and honor of her Majesty, and the English nation, shall by mean of qualitie and vertue receive such construction, and good acceptance, as them selves would looke to be rewarded withall in the like."

Walter Raleigh

Sir Walter Raleigh : A list of his personal achievements

1.   Sir Walter Raleigh was born to the son of a Devon Yeoman in the year 1552 at Buddleigh Salterton in Devon.

2.   At the age of 16 Raleigh donned a black gown, which he never returned then he deserted Oxford University (Oriel College) in 1568 in favour of soldiering in France, under his cousin Arthur Champernoun.

3.   Raleigh returned from France in 1574.

4.   In February 1575 Raleigh's name was entered as a Member of Middle Temple as a lawyer.

5.   From 1575 to 1577 Raleigh lived at Islington and was sentenced to one week's imprisonment in the Fleet for duelling.

6.   In 1578 Raleigh was granted by the Queen's Counsel, the Patent to set out for the New World : Queen Elizabeth I gave him the Title: 'Walter Ralegh Militis - Domini et Gubernatoria Virginiae'. Raleigh at the age of 27 and in command of the "Falcon", together with his half brother, Sir Humphrey Gilbert , set out for North America in September 1578 but were driven back to Plymouth by storms. They set out again in November but this time were met by Spaniards and attacked off Cape Verde.

7.   In August [43]1580 Raleigh was appointed Captain in Ireland under the Deputy Lord Grey and said of him 'I like neither his carriage nor his company'. Raleigh wrote to Leicester - known as the Queen's

---

[43]Raleigh lived at Lismore Castle in Ireland an Estated with 40,000 acres,

1580/1 and in 1586 to 1590. He returned to England in June 1590

"Eyes": I have spent some time here under the Deputy Lord Grey in such poor place and charge, as were it not that I know him to be yours, I would disdain it as much as to keep sheep'.

8.   In December 1581 Raleigh had a personal altercation with Lord Grey and "had much the better in telling of his tale. And this so much so that the Queen and the Lords took no small mark of the man and his parts. The Queen then took him for a kind of oracle which nettled them all".

9.   Raleigh made his debut at the Court of Queen Elizabeth in the Winter of 1581[3].

10.   In 1583 Raleigh was granted the Farm of Wines and with it came the right to collect £1 per year from every vintner in the country, worth £2,000 a year.

11.   In 1583 Raleigh was granted the use of Durham House in the Strand where he kept 40 men and horse in attendance at all times. He spoke of the little study in the Turret as having the most pleasing aspect as in the World.

12.   Broadcloth which proved to be more lucrative than the wine licence, worth £3,000 per year.

13.   In 1584 Raleigh became MP for Devon.

14.   In 1585 Raleigh was knighted on 12th January, the day of the Feast of the Epiphany.

15.   In 1585 Made Lord Warden of the Stanneries as the Governor of the Devon and Cornwall Tin Mines.

16.   In 1585 granted Wardenship and Lieutenancy of the County of Cornwall and Vice Admiralship of Devon and Cornwall.

17.   In 1586 granted 5 Estates in 5 Midland counties and more than 40,000 acres in Ireland as a belated reward for his earlier service there.

18.   In 1587 appointed Captain of the Queen's Bodyguard at the age of 35.

19.   Raleigh married Bess Throckmorton in November 1591.

20.   [literary work- add]

21.   His History of the World was first published in 1614 and succeeded through three editions in 1617 and another 8 before the end of the century.

[44]THOMAS HARRIOT - 1560 to June 1621

I will tell you of Raleigh's dearest friend, the brilliant scientist, astronomer and mathematical genius, Thomas Harriot. Harriot first searched for rooms in London after leaving Oxford University and was already known to Raleigh through Richard Hakluyt. He was later to voyage to Guiana with Raleigh and they left England on the 6th February 1595. Harriot had spent the year before engrossed in research and compiled notes on the reading of the Cross staff without which their voyage would not have been such a great success, and I will tell you about this presently.

Thomas Harriot was born in or near Oxford in 1560. The Oxford matriculation record states Harriot's place of birth as Oxon. Although it is thought that he was born in the Parish of St. Mary's, Oxford. Records for that Parish were previously lost and no record dates back beyond the year of 1599.

Thomas Harriot arrived at the University of Oxford at the age of 17, and having taken up residence in Saint Mary's Hall on the 30th

---

[44] Historical information from the biographer of Thomas Harriot by John Shirley

November, 1577 (being of a plebeian family) he was entitled to a fee payment of 4 pence. His name was entered in the Buttery Book and each week the Beadles would come to visit the Halls to check the names of the residents in the books.

St Mary's Hall had a close connection with Oriel College and was the former rectory house of the Church of St. Mary the Virgin, becoming the property of Oriel in 1326.

At the time of Harriot's arrival, three halls were in use, the other two being Bedel Hall and St. Martin's Hall.

On Friday 20th December, 1577, a ceremonial day of the Hilary Term at the University of Oxford, Thomas Harriot stood among 250 candidates for the convocation which brought together all the senior members of the University where they assembled in the Church of St Mary the Virgin.

Harriot waited with 12 other students between the ages of fifteen and twenty nine, ready to take his oath to abide by the statutes governing his studies at the University after which he was led in turn, before the Proctor to give personal details of his name, age, birth and social status of his father. The students had been escorted there by the University Principal, also a fellow and sponsor of Oriel, Richard Pygott, who had been Principal at Oriel from 1570 to 1578.

Pygott was present during Raleigh's time as a student at Oriel, and retired when Harriot was in his second year of study.

The Chancellor of the University since 1564 had been Robert Dudley, the Earl of Leicester, who was represented in his absence by the Vice Chancellor, William Cole, in his capacity as president of Corpus Christi College and a Doctor of Divinity.

Of the many friendships Harriot formed at the University, one was with a Professor of Geography, [45] Richard Hakluyt, who had been elected 'as one of her Majesties scholars of Westminster' and being eight years older than Harriot, was just finishing his education at Christ Church, Oxford in 1570, and just about to begin his career as a lecturer at the University, having taken his degree as Master of Arts.

Hakluyt had upon reaching Oxford, fulfilled his childhood wish, having studied all available literature on voyages and discoveries at the University, together with numerous old and later reformed maps, globes, spheres and other instruments connected with the art of geography and navigation. Hakluyt had been moved to devote his life to these studies whilst still a pupil at the school of Westminster, when one of his cousins, also known as Richard Hakluyt of Middle Temple, had shown him books on cosmography, a universal map and the bible.

Harriot was constantly learning from Hakluyt, and was later able to read his published works, being 'A Particular Discourse concerning Western Discoveries written in the yere 1584, by Richard Hakluyt of Oxford at the requeste and direction of the right worshipful Mr Walter Raghly before the coming home of his two barkes'. In his book, Hakluyt discussed the settling of English colonists in America and his work in three volumes 'The Principal Navigations, Voyages and Traffiques and Discoveries of the English Nation' published from 1598 to 1600. In 1584 Hakluyt was presented to the Queen and by 1586 he had become the Prebend of Bristol. In 1602 he was installed as Prebendary of Westminster and was elected Archdeacon of Westminster in 1603.

Harriot studied under the severe discipline of Richard Pygott and Thomas Philipson. His life at the University was governed by strict

---

[45] Historical material from The Spacious Days of Queen Elizabeth An Elizabethan Background Book by Arthur B. Allen.

moral codes and dress sense, where it was ordered that they must wear black gowns with hoods at all times whenever they were present at the University. They must also wear a square cap, a ruff and hose. The colour of their clothing must be strictly black and no student may wear clothing made of silk or velvet. Failure to observe all the statutes of the University could lead to charges of perjury. Even after graduation Harriot only ever wore black for the rest of his lifetime.

The University at that time, had due to the reforms, instituted by new statutes, been designed to eliminate Catholic scholars, and begun turning away from the study of mathematics, science and philosophy and this would have made it difficult for Harriot to follow his chosen subjects.

It was compulsory for students to attend all prescribed lectures failing which they would incur fines. Lectures could only be missed upon submission of a supplication to the Congregation. Students were required to wait at the Gate of the College to be escorted to the lecture hall in School Street and the lecture would last between one and three hours during which time they were permitted to use fewer books during the lecture and encouraged to learn by rote method.

Harriot studied Grammar, rhetoric, dialectic (Aristotle), Arithmetic, Music, Geometry, Astronomy, Natural Philosophy and Aristotle's Metaphysics.

A student would be required to attend these compulsory lectures and participate in disputations usually for sixteen terms. Members of the nobility could sometimes reduce their terms of residence to four terms. Harriot submitted two supplications in 1579 which were approved by the congregation on 12th February and he was admitted to read in the faculty of arts, being awarded the Bachelor of Arts degree at the Easter convocation, giving him the right to be known thereafter as Master Thomas Harriot.

On the 29th June 1621, as he lay on his deathbed, suffering from cancer of the inner passages of the nose, at the home of his friend

Thomas Buckner, a mercer of St. Christopher's parish near the Royal Exchange, he sought to put his affairs in order before his death.

[46]Harriot looked again at several of the letters in his possession concerning the Gunpowder Plot and his mind was cast back into that time.

"Right honourable my very good Lord: the Earle of Salisbury, [one of his Majestyes most honourable privy counsell, and principall secretary of State':
The favour which I have already received from your lordship, I shall alwayes, as I am bounden, faythfully acknowledge. And if it may please your honor to extend it father for my release out of this dungeon of my many miseryes: the future service that you honor thereby shall enable me vnto, shall declare an other manner of dutifull thankefulnes then wordes. What my hart acknowledgeth: my hand doth signe, & my future deeds, with the leaue of god & your lordships fauour, shall seale.

> Your lordships
> humbly euer at comaundement:
> a poore prisoner:
> Tho: Harriots"

and then he took up another of his letters (from the files of Cecil at Hatfield House:

"Right honorable my very good Lordes:
The present misery I feele being truly innocent in hart and thought presseth me to be an humble suter to your lordships for favorable respect. All that know me can witnes that I was always of honest conversation and life. I was neuer any busy medler in matters of state.

---

[46]Thomas Harriot by John Shirley 1983, records full details of Harriot's lost work.

I was neuer ambitious for preferments. But contented with a priuate life for the loue of learning that I might study freely. Wherein my labours & endeauours, if I may speak it without praesumption, haue ben paynfull & great. And I hoped & do yet hope by the grace of god & your Lordships fauour that the effects shall so shew themselues shortly, to the good liking & allowance of the state & common weale. But now this misery of close imprisonement happening vnto me at the time of my sicknes, which was more then three weekes old before; being great windenes in my stomack & fumings into my head rising from my spleen, besides other infirmityes, as my Doctor knoweth & some effectes my keeper can witnes. This I say without your honours fauour wilbe my vtter vndoing, not only in respect of great charges, greater then I am able to endure: but also of being in place where I am not likely to reouer health. Therefore the innocency of my hart feeling this misery of close imprisonement with sicknes & many wantes, besides the desire of proceeding in my studyes, maketh me an humble suter to your honors for liberty in what measure your wisedomes shall think fit. So shall I with faythfull acknowledgement spend the rest of my time so, that your honours shall not think any lawfull fauouir ill bestowed. And I shall as my bounden duty is continue my dayly prayers to almighty god for the preservation of his Majesty and Royall progeny, and for the encrease of all honor and happines to your honors.

Your honors humble petitioner:
a poore prisoner in the Gatehouse
Tho: Harriots

Harriot based his study of gravity on the theories of Archimedes, "weighing his substance in air, then in water, and from the difference in the two weighings, determining the specific gravity or density of the unknown. However, instead of using the density of water as 1 as is done today, Harriot used 1,000, so that his calculations give a modern specific gravity reading to three decimal places. he accuracy of his workings can be seen by comparing modern readings with those of one of his earlier lists. [John Shirley : Thomas Harriot]

HIC JACET: SIR WALTER RALEIGH

Harriot's Observations		Modern Readings		
Aurum	19,135	Gold	19.3-	19.4
Argentum Vivum	13,554	Quicksilver		14.193
Plumbum nigrum	11,351	Lead (black)		11.3437
Argentum	10,529	Silver		10.492
Bismutum	9,755	Bismuth		9.78-9.86
Aes	8,795	Bronze		8.80
Orichalcum	8,529-8,728	Brass	8.47-8.86	
Ferrum	7,757	Iron		7.86
Chalbys	7,785	Steel	7.76-7.87	
Stannum	7,297	Tin		7.30
Aqua	1,000	Water		1.00
Crystallum	2,650	Fuzed Quartz(?)		2.20

[47] The Philosopher's Stone:

South   As Christ from earth to heavn did ascend
        In cloudes of clearnes vp to his trhone
        And raigneth there shiningn without end:
        Vnto his glory agayne is gon
        His fier possessing here in ye south
        With power to heale leapres & to renew youth.

West   As Christ the scripture making mention
        In holy wombe descended of Mary
        From his high trone for our redemption
        Working the holy ghost to be incarnate:
        So here our stone descendeth from his estate
        Into the wombe of our virgin Mercurall
        To helpe his brethern from filth originall.

---

[47] Written John Donne?

North   As Christ his godhead from our sight
When he our kind to him did take:
Euen so our sonne his beames of light
As for a time hath him forsake
Vnder the winges of his make
The mone he hideth his glory
And bodily dieth in kind that he may multiply.

East   As Christ our sauiour was tumulate
After his passion and eath on tree.
And after his body was glorificate
Vprose endued with mortality
So here our stone buried after penalty
Vpriseth from death darkens & solors variable
Appearing in the east with clearnes incomparable.

South   The altitude of the stone, fiery in quality, shining more then perfect quintessence, and end of ye practice, speculative, tenet ignem [gold holds fire].

West   The first or west Latitude of ye stone. And entring into the practice [practical] pole & earthly in quality occasionate. Saturne [lead] holdeth the earth.

North   The dark profundity of the stone in ye north purgatory all imperfect watry in quality, variable in colour ye eclipse of ye sonne. Tenet aquam [mercury holds water].

East   The east latitude of ye stone and entring into ye speculatiue aier of ye full moone. Jupiter [tin] holdeth the ayer.

Here the red man [sulphur] & his white wife [mercury]
Be spoused [united] with the spirity of life.

Into paradise here we go
There to be purged of payn and woe

Here be they passed there payns all
Shining brighter then the Christall

From paradise they go to heven to wonne [dwell]
Shining brighter then doth the sonne.

Harriot still had many powerful and influencial friends but he had been closest to his two patrons, The Earl of Northumberland, the Wizard Earl; and Sir Walter Raleigh, for whom Harriot had researched the material for Raleigh's monumental publication the History of the World, and earlier for Raleigh's trial in Winchester in 1603.

The Wizard Earl still lingered in the Tower of London under charges of treason after being implicated in the [48]Gunpowder Plot in 1605

The Wizard Earl and Thomas Harriott were arrested as suspected conspirators in the Gunpowder Plot. The Earl had appointed his cousin, Thomas Percy, a staunch catholic, to be constable of Alnwick Castle, being another of the Earl's stately homes. One dark evening as Harriott and the Wizard Earl had been enjoying their dinner with the family at Syon House, in Brentford and then Thomas Percy, one of the principal conspirators in the Gunpowder Plot, called suddenly at Syon House and by doing so, he immediately put the Earl and Harriott under great suspicion, although the Earl was innocent of any crime. Thomas Percy was pursued and shot in the head at Holbeach in Staffordshire and with him died all the evidence, and this left the poor Earl with no answer as to why his cousin had called upon him and the Earl's innocence nor guilt could be proven and so he remained a prisoner in

---

[48] Sir Robert Throckmorton of Coughton Hall to Elizabeth Hussey; to sir Thomas Tresham of Rushton Hall - papers hidden in the wall (he took part in the Essex Conspiracy in 1601 and the Gunpowder Plot and also his son Thomas Tresham; Lord Henry Hunsdon Lord Chamberlain - Patron of Lord Chamberlain's Men.

the Martin Tower for 17 years from November 1605 until the Summer of 1621.

Conspirators in the Gunpowder Plot, 1605

The rest of the conspirators of the Gunpowder Plot were rounded up and taken to the Tower of London and they were:

Lord Monteagle,
Francis Tresham
Robert Catesby,
Robert Winter
Thomas Winter
John Winter
John Grant,
Christopher and John Wright,
Robert Keyes
and Guido Fawkes.

The Winter Brothers were the sons of Jane Ingleby and George Winter. George Winter was the son of Robert Winter and Katherine Throckmorton.

The Wizard Earl was another of Sir Walter Raleigh's eminent friends 'Wizard Earl of Syon', being Henry Percy the Ninth Earl of Northumberland. After being introduced to Harriot it did not take the like minded Earl very long before he became the Patron of Thomas Harriot and invited him to move to Syon House in the year ...., in order that Harriot could continue his experiments. Henry Percy the Ninth Earl of Northumberland, was also renowned as a scientist during his lifetime and so much so that he became known as the 'Wizard Earl'.

Hariott then, was dedicated to his friend Sir Walter, and after his arrest he neglected his experiments and set about researching the law and preparing a defence for Sir Walter at his forthcoming Winchester trial.

It remains to be said that during the trial, Harriott saw fit to record a true account of every spoken word during the proceedings. After Sir Walter's trial and sentence to life imprisonment, Hariott cast these papers among his own in despair, seeing what little good it had done his friend, he threw them into a chest at Syon House where they remained for many years.]

Henry Percy the Duke of Northumberland and a Privy Councillor became directly implicated in the Gunpowder Plot in 1605 because his cousin [[49] Thomas Percy had been shot to death after an official proclamation had been issued by the King himself, declaring:

[50] "Whereas Thomas Percy Gentleman, and some other his confederates, persons knowen to be bitterly corrupted with the superstition of the Romish Religion, as seduced with the blindness thereof, and being otherwise of lewde life, insolent disposition, and for the most part of desperate estate, have been discovered to have contrived the most horrible treason that ever entered into the hearts of men, against our Person, our Children, the whole Nobilitie, Clergie, the Commons in Parliament assembled, which howsoever cloaked with zeale of Superstitious Religion, aymed indeed at the Subversion of the State, and to induce a horrible confusion in all things..."

The proclamation, then, commanded all the King's 'Lieutenants, Deputy Lieutenants, Sheriffes, Justices of peace, Mayors, Bayliffes, Constables, and all other our officers, Ministers, and loving Subjects' to 'employ themselves for the suppressing, apprehending, deterring, and discovering of all sorts of persons any wayes likely to be privie to a Treason so hatefull to God and man, and implying in it the utter

---

[49] As from Thomas Harriot by John Shirley p.336

[50] PRO State Papers 14, vOL 16, CITED IN dURST, OP. CIT., PP. 151-3

subversion of the Realm, and dignitie thereof. Nove 5 [1605]
[[pencilled note: 'Description in proc. for his arrest.'] the said Percy is
a tall man with a great broad beard, a good Face, the colour of his
Beard & Head myngeld with white haires, but the head more white
then the beard. he stoopeth somewhat in the shoulders. Well coloured
in the Face. long footed, small legged.'

The man who performed this execution of Thomas Percy was a man
named John Streete, who was granted a lifetime pension of 2s a day
'for that extraordinary service performed in killing those two traitors,
Piercie and Catesbie, with two bullets at one shott out of his muskett.[51]

This execution had effectively sentenced the Wizard Earl, the 9th Earl
of Northumberland to a lifetime of imprisonment since all evidence
had died with his cousin and the Earl who prayed for early release had
written a letter during his confinement under house arrest on the
charge of the Archbishop of Canterbury, and to remain at the
Archbishop's home in Croydon[52] and he wrote:

[53]"I shall be gladde as matters falles out to store you with
circumstances to the ende that the bare truth may appeare ... Friday [1
Nov.] was the day hee [Thomas Percy] came to London; I, neither anie
of myne, did see him till Monday [the 4th] twelve of the clock, when
he came to Sion to me; went away presentlie after dinner, after he had
Sawsed mee with a Gudgeon [i.e. 'deceived me with a falsehood']; and
then appeared to the rest of my people at Essex House, from whence
hee was to passe as hee told me, and then told them, to Ware, that
night; givinge them all the same gudgeon that hee had bestowed on
me, before as also to my brother Charles, my brother Alan, Sir Edward

---

[51] Durst, op cit., p. 323

[52] Batho, op. cit., p. 6, no. 3

[53] Thomas Harriot by John Shirley p. 333

Ffraunces [Steward of Petworth], Edmund Powton [the Earl's Cofferer], Giles Greene [his Steward], and Captain Whitlock [pensioner], as may appeare if they be examined. Soe as, my Lords, it is probable I should not have seen him at Sion uppon Monday [4 Nov.] if one accident had not happened; and that was this: A man of his came to the Court to my lodging uppon Sonday [3rd] to enquire of Thomas Percy [gossip had it that this man was Guy Fawkes[54] alias John Johnson]; this man was a stranger to all the Companie, and never seene before by anie of them; the fashion of the man your lordships shall understande, to the ende he may bee caught hereafter. If this man by this meanes had not discovered [i.e. divulged] that his master, Thomas Percy, had byne in towne by this Accidente; and that he fownde that my followers of necessity must knowe it, I thinke I should not have seene him uppon Monday at Syon, the greatest arguments of suspition laid to my chardge. Though I be somewhat tedious in these triffles to say to your Lordships they be matters of moment to me, and I hope you will pardon me, for I saie still, the more you knowe, the better it will be for me."

---

[54] Guido Fawkes for several days after his arrest, insisted that his name was John Johnson

[55] was suspected of plotting against the King and imprisoned in the Martin Tower for 18 years.

(Testamenta et orbos tanquam indagine capi : in sudore vultus alieni: Lex Talionis [56])

During his imprisonment, the Wizard was interrogated and here I present to you this horrible interrogation by those appointed to bring about his ruin and to keep him imprisoned in the Martin Tower because he was of the Roman Catholic faith and so they destroyed them all being Raleigh's friends, and one by one:

[the Gunpowder Plot Books [57]]

---

[55]

[56] Bacon's Essays: Of Riches p 108/9

[57] PRO State Papers 14/216. These are fos. 112, 113 r&v. : Thomas Harriot by John Shirley where they appear for the first time.

The Interrogations concerning the Gunpowder Plot
Permission kindly granted to the author to reproduce here by His
Grace, The Duke of Northumberland

[58]Interrogations to be ministred to the Earle of Northumberland

1. [Q] Whither was not Thomas Percy with you by Monday the fourth
of November last, what tyme of the daye cam he unto you, and who
dined with you that daye.

At Lambeth the declaration of the Earle of Northumberland the 23 of
November 1605.

1. [A] He Confesseth that his Cosin Thomas Percey came to him on
monday the fourth of this november about eleven of the clocke in the
forenoone and there dined with him, Sir William Lowre, Thomas
Percey his younge sonne and Heriot as his lo: thinketh.

2. (Q] Whether had not Thomas Percey private conference with you on
that daye, was such conference within your house or without, who
stood by or in the viewe when you so conferred, and when did Percy
goe from you house at Sion that day.

2. [A] he sayth that betwene the said houre of eleven and twelve he
had conference with Thomas Percey in the hall and in the parlor of his
said house before dinner and had no other conference with him at any
other time that day. and only after dinner Percy came to him, to knowe
whether he would commaund him any service, and sayth that Sir
William lowre & others passed by as they were talking and about one

---

[58] His grace The Duke of Northumberland kindly granted to me permission to include
the Interrogations of Henry Percy, 9th Earl of Northumberland concerning Henry
Percy's implication in the Gunpowder Plot.

of the clock Thomas Percey went his waye.

3. [Q] what was the conference that passed between Percey and you at your house at Sion on that day?

3. [A] the conference was concerning a priest, one Parkinson, his coming downe ... the next sommer, and the entrance and taking possession of certain land ...

4. [Q] After your comming from Sion to Northumberland house on that day was not Percey there, and what tyme of the day did he goe from thence

4. [A] He knows not of his owne knowledge that percey was there after his lordship's coming to Essex house, but the next morning he heard of fraunces [Sir Edward Francis, Steward of Petworth] that percey had been there.

5. [Q] Who came with you in your Companie from Sion

5. [A] He came in his coach and with him dalevell [Robert Delaval], his Gentleman of the Horse] & Bargon [Ralph Burgoyne or Burgen, former Gentleman of the Horse] or one of them with Sir William Lowre as he remebreth.

6. [Q] How often did Percy confer with or write or send to you between Saturday and Tuesday (the fifth of November] and by whom?

6. [A] Denies any message except for conference at Syon House.

7. [Q] What was the effect of this conference at Syon House.

7. [A] This is already answered above.

8. [Q] Who brought the message that Percy was gone? When, where, and in whose presence was the message delivered?

8. [A] The Earl recalls no such message.

9. [Q] After Percy was gone, what moved you to send after him? Whom did you send after him, when, and how many?

9. [A] He had been advised by his Steward, Francis, to write to Percy about his affairs, so he had sent Wycliffe [three Wycliffe brothers, Francis, Thomas, and William, were engaged in handling Northumberland's fiscal affairs. This would undoubtedly be Francis, commissioner for the audits of the Northern properties, for which Percy collected] and later Fotherley [Thomas Fotherley, disburser for the privy purse and groom in chamber to Northumberland].

10. [Q] Why did you send after him?

10. [A] Answered above.

11. [Q] In what ways have you employed Thomas Percy in matters of trust?

11. [A] In many small ways initially; later his trust grew and he increased his duties. Finally made him Constable of Alnwick.

12. [Q] How have you benefited him or advanced him?

12. [A] Gave him a lease to a property called Wilby Park and certain demesne properties. When Percy returned from the Low Countries he had given him £200.

13. [Q} Have you at any tyme affirmed that you had any power or meanes to despose of the Catholiques of England, or that they were to be directed by you?

13. [A] [59] Absolute denial of any such statement; says this is 'an old Scotch story'.

14. [Q] Uppon what ground or warrant did you use such speaches and when, where & to whom were they spoken.

14. [A] See above.

15. [Q] Did you ever saye or affirme to any catholique or any other, that if occasion served you would winne with that partie, or partake with them, to whome said you so, and when where and uppon what occasion.

---

[59] Alnwick Castle: Seat of the Duke of Northumberland:"Thomas, 7th Earl of Northumberland (1557-1572) A devoted Roman Catholic was appointed Warden of the East and Middle Marches by Mary, and General Warden by Queen Elizabeth. He and his brother Henry were for some years constantly engaged in Scottish expeditions. His Catholic sympathies, however, rendered him an object of suspicion to Elabeth, and the treatment he ereceived compelled him in 1560 to resign the office of Lord Warden. In 1561 Lord Grey of Wilton was appointed to that office. He compalied that the earl would not allow him to occupy Alnwick Castle, and had, in order to prevent him doing so, removed "most part of the stuff there". In 1562 the Earl writes that he cannot entertain the Scottish queen at Alnwick [Mary Queen of Scots] because the Castle is "utterly unfurnished and not so much as one bed in it", and he states that he is in such need of money that he had not £40 in the world. It is probable that he had deliberately dismanted the Castle in order that it shoudl not be used as a residence for the Government's officials. Having gained this object he would seem to have refunished it, for a survey of 1567 shows that it was provided with everything required for his own residence at that date. At length the slight put upon him, and his co-religionists' desire to restore the Catholic faith and to place Mary queen of Scots on the throne, led him into the disastrous Rising of the North. In 1568 whyile the Earl was mustering his forces in Yorkshire his retainers at his order garrisoned Alnwick Castle, but Sir John forster, Warden of the Middle Marches, promptly advanced against it, and resistance being hopeless the garrison surrenderd. The Earl kept the field till Decemeber 1568. While his forces dwindled away from desertion. At length the approach of the royal army compelled him to seek refuge in Liddesdale, then regarded as a sanctuary for outlawed men. He was, however, betrayed to the Earl of Moray, Regaent of Scotland, and reamined a prisoner in that country until 1572, when he was sold for a large sum to queen Elizabeth and handed over to Hunsdon, Governor of Berwick. He was taken to Alnwick, where he was placed in charge of Sir John forster, who conveyed him to York, guarded by a large escort throughout the journey, as, owing to his great popularity in the North, an attempt at rescue, was feared. He was beheaded at York on August 22nd, 1572, declaring the realm to be in schism and his own adherence to the Church of Rome, which has numberd him among her marthyrs and has beatified him. He carried out considerable resorations at the Castle, which was evidently in a bad state of repair at this date.

15. [A] Never said so.

16. [Q] What judgment was given to your knowledge uppon the figure [horoscope] that was cast uppon the kings nativitie.

16. [A] Carleton [Dudley Carleton who had just recently resigned from his position as secretary to the 9th Earl] told him that he received a letter (which he sawe) from St Saveur of Paris that the kings nativitie was cast in [60] Paris , and that the Kinge should live many yeres and this was since the king cam in, almost three yeares sense, and denieth that he knoweth or hath seene any other fygure touching the king's nativitie since his majesties came into England but had heard (but never seene any, and) Sir Robert Carewe had tould him of one about twoo yeres past & more But his lordship never sawe it.

17. [Q] By whom and by whose meanes, and when and where was the said figure so cast.

17. [A] He knoweth not of any that was cast otherwise than as is aforesaid.

18. [Q] How long was Percy your 'Suter' in collecting rents?

18. [A] Six years; had done some collecting for sixteen.

19. [Q] Who was your former receiver, and why did you remove him?

19. [A] Felton was the former receiver; he had got into debt, first for £500, and later for £300 more.

---

[60] Nostadamus Seer to the Court of Catherine de Medici in the reign of King Henri II of France

20. [Q] Weren't you warned that Percy meant to deceive you about your rents and to flee beyond the seas? Who told you, and when?

20. [A] He denieth that any man tould him any such matter.

21. [Q] After being warned, why did you appoint him to collect rents?

21. [A] See answer to question above.

22. [Q] Whether were not you acquainted with Whitlocks going to the tower on Wednesday morninge the sixth of November.

22. [A] He denieth that he was acquainted with his goinge.

23. [Q] Did not Whitlocke returne that day from the tower to you at Northumberland house, and what did he impart unto you ther.

23. [A] he sayeth that Whitlocke returned to him at Essex house his lordship ther being walking with his brother Allen, and tould his lordship that he was in the tower, and did see John Johnson [the alias of Guido Fawkes] ther newly sent to the tower and that one of the lieutenants menne required him to stay to attend on the lords of the council which he did a good space & no man calling for him he cam away, wherewith his lordship found fault, and said it was not well done, and the said Whitlocke said divell with him and then departed.

24. [Q] What moved you to lett him passe awaye, considering he tould you that he was ronne away, being comaunded to stay by order from the lords of the councell. What was Whitlockes purpose in going that daye to the Tower.

24. [A] for that Whitlocke said he stayed there a good space & was not called for by the lords [in margin: 'and therefore thought the lords sent not for him'] his lordship made no more of it, but confesseth it was an error in him.

25. [Q] After your Servants Carleton [Dudley Carleton], Eppesley [John Hippesley, later named Gentleman of the Horse, later in the service of the Duke of Buckingham] and grene [Giles Grene, Payer of Foreign Payments and Steward] had been with ferrers [Henry Ferrers had been tenant of the Whinniard house and was induced to move so that Percy could lease the house] to persuade him to lett his house in Westminster to Percey, what relation made they to you thereof.

25. [A] he answereth that he never knew about it until after this matter was discovered.

26. [Q] When and by whom did you first knowe that Percey had hyred the house and the Cellar in Westminster.

27. [A] Se Answer above; he had not known of these things until after the Plot was discovered.

The Examination of Sir William Lower knight the 2 December 1605

1.   What companye dyned with my Lord of Northumberland at Syon on Monday before the Parliament should haue begonne.

        He answereth Master Percye, Captaine Whytlock, and himselfe and he is not suer whither Master Herior dyned ther or noe.

2.   Wither was ther any speach at the table of any matters of Parliament.

        He answereth, Ther was a discourse, but he remembreth not the particulars.

3.   Was thir no speaches of the Articles agreed on the Commissioners for   the Vnion.

He answereth. That all the discourse that was, was only vppon
those   articles of the vnion, wich Percye shewed in a paper.

4.   Whither do you know how Percye came by the Articles.

He answereth he knoweth not.

5.   To whom did Master Percye showe the Articles besydes to
your selff.

He answereth to no other bodye, but the Articles being in his
hands, My Lord of Northumberland toke them from him, and reade
them.

6.   What sayd the Earl of Northumberland when he had reade
them.

He answereth. he remembereth that ther was a discourse but no
particulars.

7.   Betwene whom, and Percye, was the discourse

He answereth. That it was at the table in generall, by those that dyned
there.

[Signed] William Lower.

It would follow then, that Harriot, because he lived at Syon House,
was also suspected and carried off for questioning. Whilst he too
endured his imprisonment, he fell ill and one of the Duke's servants at
Syon House saw fit to carry off Harriot's precious documents and
papers and hid them so well in the great stable at Syon House, far
away from the eyes and hands of the King's Commissioners and
Examiners that they were lost for many years. No matter how hard the
Lords and the servants of their Ladies searched, prompted by the Privy
Councillors, the papers just could not be found and eventually it was
assumed that they had been destroyed.

and the Earl remained there until the Summer of 1621 after payment to the King of a heavy fine of £30,000. Since the [61]Earl could only discharge £11,000, he had endured 17 years of imprisonment, and he died in 1632.

All Thomas [62]Harriot's papers were locked in a trunk in the home of his former friend and patron at Syon House in Isleworth where Harriot had worked, studied and resided with the Ninth Earl of Northumberland in happier times, before the death of Queen Elizabeth I.

His gravestone, like that of Thomas Kyd the dramatist, was destroyed by the Great Fire of London in 1666.

Although Harriot had been urged during his lifetime to give serious consideration to publishing his works on astronomy and mathematics, he had never taken time to order his mathematical papers into a publishable form, nor had he considered it a worthwhile endeavour, until he lay upon his deathbed. He had been accused of atheism for his interest in metaphysics and astronomy. He hastily sought to itemise his belongings, consisting of globes, maps, telescopes and scientific instruments. In his Will he nominated as his Executors, Thomas Aylesbury and John Protheroe. He stated that he wished his literary executor to be Nathaniel Torporley, who should if he did not understand any of the papers, seek to confer with Master Warner and

---

[61] Whilst prisoners in the Tower, Sir Walter Raleigh and the Henry Percy, Ninth Earl of Northumberland, The Wizard Earl invented tobacco curing.

[62] Thomas Harriot died on the 29th June 1621, before the release of the Earl of Northumberland Henry Percy from the Tower of London. The Earl went straight to Petworth House in Sussex

Master Hughes.

Harriot's papers were kept safely under lock and key in a trunk in the library at Syon House.

Cecil saw to it that Raleigh and the Wizard Earl remained in the Tower of London because they were the two remaining Elizabethans who could pose any threat to his position as a Privy Councillor under King James I.

Thomas Harriot, just before his death, could not have known that the Wizard Earl of Northumberland, Henry Percy, was soon to be released from the Tower of London after 18 years of imprisonment, having been implicated in the Gunpowder Plot, and how Harriot would have rejoiced at that news. However, he was dismayed to learn that the Earl, instead of returning to Syon House, had instead gone to Petworth House and there, just three months after Harriot's death, the Earl also died.

Harriot's papers were therefore, never put into order and never published. They were missing for many years and located in the stables of Syon House where they had been locked away with the Household accounts.

The bulk of Harriot's papers remained disorderly and unpublished for *centuries after his death. As a direct result of his refusal to publish during his lifetime, Harriot did not receive the recognition he deserved and many great scientists, such as Kepler, found fame and notoriety through Harriot's earlier discoveries.

Although Harriot expressed a dying wish that his work be made orderly and then published for the benefit of mankind, he left that task to his Executors, who due to a series of misfortunes and misunderstandings, were not able to fulfil his wishes.

Harriot's amazing life had taken him through a classical education at Oxford; on to London to live first with Sir Walter Raleigh at Durham

House and Sherborne Castle, and then to Syon House in Isleworth, the home of Henry Percy, Ninth Earl of Northumberland. In 1595 he spent a year in the [63] New World with Sir Walter Raleigh and then went to Ireland to become one of the colonists on Raleigh's Irish Estates Lismore Castle and its 40,000 acres.

---

[63] See "New Atlantis" written by Sir Walter Raleigh as an account of his first voyage, being The Discoverie of the Great and Bewtiful Empyre of Guiana (which must be read side by side in order to understand the background of these voyages and discoveries): "The King's Quinto by John Talbot 1618

1593

The Murder of Christopher Marlowe, Dramatist and the Arrest and Torture of Thomas Kyd, Dramatist

Thomas Kyd's Spanish Tragedy
Kyd's Patron was the Countess of Sussex

Christopher Marlowe, Dramatist
Murdered, Midnight 1st June 1593

Marlowe's Patron was Mr. Thomas Walsingham, slain by Ingram Frizer, in the company of Robert Poley, a former Spy for Francis Walsingham, Queen Elizabeth I's Spymaster.

Robert Devereux, Second Earl of Essex – The Earl of March
(His Servant, Nicholas Skeres, was present at the murder of
Christopher Marlowe, Dramatist).

Robert Devereux's sister Frances was married to Sir Philip Sidney and upon Sidney's death at the Battle of Zutphen, Robert Devereux married Sidney's widow.

Thomas Kyd Dramatist is arrested on 12 May 1593

Christopher Marlowe Dramatist is arrested on 18th May, 1593

They perhaps died for the play, Sir Thomas More (History of the Life and Death of King Edward V and of the Usurpation of Richard III).

12 May Thomas Kyd arrested and heretical papers which he attributes to Marlowe, discovered in his room. [ill May Day scenes from the play Sir Thomas More pasted to door at Dutch churchyard]
18 May Privy Council issue warrant for the arrest of Christopherus Marlowe, at the house of his patron Mr. Thomas Walsingham at Scadbury, Chislehurst, in Kent or elsewhere [Acts of Privy Council].
20 May Christopherus Marley, Gentleman of London answers the warrant and is required to remain in daily attendance [Acts of Privy Council].

Christopher Marlowe was murdered between 10am and midnight on Wednesday 30th May 1593 at the home of Mistress Eleanor Bull in Deptford, London

Slain by Ingram Frizer whilst in the company of Robert Poley (a former Spy for Sir Francis Walsingham in the Babington Plot) and Nicholas Skeres, (a Servant to the Second Earl of Essex, Robert Devereaux at a house in Deptford Strande, a few hundred yards from Deptford Bridge

The Murder of Christopherus Marlowe
Midnight 1st June 1593

Christopher Marlowe had been arrested on the 18th May 1593.
The Privy Councillors who examined Marlowe were:

Archbishop Whitgift
Sir Christopherus Hatton   [one of his servants was executed in
Babington plot]
Lord Burghley
Lord Hunsdon   [Queen Elizabeth's cousin]
Sir James Crofts

Thomas Kyd had been arrested on the 12th May last, carried off and tortured at Newgate Prison concerning certain text from the play Sir Thomas More, being a completed play to which William Shakespeare had tried to append three pages of text, copied in a scrivener's hand.

The rhyme which led to Christopher Marlowe and Thomas Kyd's arrest – from the play Sir Thomas More by William Shakespeare

The rhyme in question reads as follows:

[64] [("A Rhime set up against the Wall of the Dutch churchyard, on Thursday May the 5th, between Eleven and Twelve at night. And there found by some of the Inhabitants of that Place; and brought to the Constable, and the rest of the Watch. beginning,

"You, Strangers, that inhabit in this Land,
Note this same Writing, do it understand.

---

[64]

Conceive it well, for Safe-guard of your Lives,
Your Goods, your Children and your dearest Wives.)].

The Privy Council decided that immediate action must be taken in
order to prevent riot or insurrection, and appointed Sir Julius Caesar,
Sir Henry Killgrew and Sir Thomas Wilkes to seek out and examine
by secret means, all persons suspected as being responsible and they
were given leave to search the premises of any writers thought to be
involved in the above plots. It was directed that a search be made for
any papers or writings which may lead to the guilty persons being
identified, after which they should be put to torture until they
confessed and revealed all they knew of the matter.

Thomas Kyd had volunteered information to the Privy Councillors
during his torture when he admitted to his tormentors that certain
heretical papers had been cast in amongst his own and therefore they
must have belonged to Christopherus Marlowe, with whom Kyd had
once shared a writing chamber in the year 1592.

Thomas Kyd was the author of the Spanish Tragedy pre-1587, a
forerunner to Hamlet, and by the year 1591 Kyd had been introduced
to Christopherus Marlowe and they had resolved to work together in
perfecting the Spanish Tragedie a forerunner to Hamlet, and during
this time they shared a writing chamber and were engaged to write for
the Earl of Sussex Players. The Spanish Tragedie was not entered for
publication until the 14th March 1592 (Henslowe's diary records
Spanish Tradgedie 1592).

Thomas Kyd's Dramatic Works:
The Spanish Tragedie
The First Part of Jeronimo
The Ur-Hamlet
Soliman and Perseda
Cornelia
The Householder's Philosophie
Verses of Prayse and Joye

An Extract from the Spanish Tragedie by Thomas Kyd - Duke of Devonshire's Quarto (discovered by Frederick S. Boas)

Actus Qvartvs
Fifth passage of Additions, replacing 168-90 but incorporating, in transposed order, 168-78 (...stab him and 190 of original text.)

Hier. But are you sure they are dead?
Cast. I, slave, too sure.
Hier. What, and yours too?
Vice. I, all are dead; not one of them survive.
Hier. Nay, then I care not; come and we shall be friends; Let us lay
our   heades together:
       See, here's a goodly noose will hold them all.
Vice. O damned devill, how secure he is.
Hier. Secure? why doest thou wonder at it?
       I tell thee, Vice-roy, this day I have seene revenge, and in that
sight   am growne a prowder Monarch than ever sate under the
Crowne of   Spaine. Had I as many lives as there be Starres,
       As many heavens to go to, as those lives,
       Ide give them all, I, and my soule to boote,
       But I would see thee ride in this red poole.
etc.
Vice. Be deafe, my senses, I can heare no more.
King. Fall, heaven, and cover us with thy sad ruines.
Cast. Rowle all the world within thy pitchie cloud.
Hier. Now do I applaud what I have acted.
       Nunc iners cadat manus.
Now to express the rupture of my part,
First take my tongue, and afterward my heart.
He bites out his tongue.
King. O monstrous resolution of a wretch.
       See, Vice-roy, he hath bitten foorth his tung
       Rather than reveale what we requirde.
Cast. Yet can he write.

317

King. and if in this he satisfie us not,
    We will devise the 'xtremest kind of death
    That ever was invented for a wretch.
    Then he makes signes for a knife to mend his pen. etc

An Extract of Thomas Kyd's Cornelia

**Thomas Kyd – Cornelia (Julius Caesar and Mark Anthony
ACT IV Scene ii : Caeser. Mar(k) Anthonie.**

Caes. O Rome, that with thy pryde doest over-peare
    The worthiest Citties of the conquered world;
    Whose honor, got by famous victories,
    Hath filed heavens fierie valuts with fright-full horro;
    O lofty towres, O stately battlements,
    O glorious temples, O proude Pallaces,
    And you brave walls, bright heavens masonrie,
    Grac'd with a thousand kingly diadems
    Are yee not styrred with a strange delight,
    To see your Caesars matchles victories?
    And how your Empire and your praise begins
    Through fame, which hee of straunger Nations wins?
    O beautious Tyber, with thine easie streames
    That glide as smoothly as a Parthian shaft;
    Turne not thy crispie tydes, live silver curle,
    Backe to thy grass-greene bancks to welcom us;
    And with a gentle murmure hast to tell
    The foaming Seas the honour of our fight?
    Trudge not thy steames to Trytons Mariners,
    To bruite the prayses of our conquests past?
    And make thyr vaunts to old Oceanus
    That hence-forth Tyber shall salute the seas,
    More fam'd then Tyger or fayre Euphrates?
    Now all the world (wel-nye) doth stoope to Rome:
    The sea, the earth, and all is almost ours.
    Be't where the bright Sun with his neyghbor beames
    Doth early light the pearled Indians,

> Or where his Chariot staies to stop the day,
> Tyll heaven unlock the darknes of the night: etc.

Anth: Come on, brave Caesar
> And crowne thy head, and mount thy Chariot.
> Th'impatient people runne along the street,
> And in a route against thy gates they rushe,
> To see theyr Caesar, after dangers past,
> Made Conqueror and Emperor at last. etc.

Marlowe at about (1591) this time or shortly afterwards, was also engaged in writing his play St. Bartholomew's Massacre.

From the 18th May when Marlowe had been arrested and required to remain in London or elsewhere and until Wednesday 30th May 1593 Christopherus Marlowe had remained under house arrest at the home of his former Patron Sir Thomas Walsingham. At last on the 30th May he had been permitted to leave the confines of Walsingham's home in order to dine with Ingram Frizer, Walsingham's servant, with whom he had then travelled to Deptford. Lord Hunsdon Patron of the Lord Chamberlain's Men having intervened on Marlowe's behalf and Sir Christopherus Hatton having also spoken in Marlowe's favour.

Christopherus Marlowe and Ingram Frizer had arrived together at the main door of the Tavern in Deptford Strande at about 10 o'clock in the morning, having travelled up to London by coach from Scadbury, Chislehurst. The modest Tavern belonged to a Mistress Eleanor Bull, a widow. A smiling Mistress Bull met them at the main door to the house and they requested to be shown immediately to a private dining room upstairs which had been reserved by Ingram Frizer. They climbed the stairs as Mistress Bull led the way, and entered the small dining room sparsely furnished with a table and chairs in the centre of the room and a small bed on the left hand side of the room pushed against the wall.

Marlowe found to his surprise that two other persons were already present when they reached the room, being Robert Poley (who had spied for Sir Francis Walsingham in the height of the Babington conspiracy) and Nicholas Skeres, who was a servant to The Earl of Essex (otherwise known as the Earl of March).

Mistress Bull left the room and quickly returned with a servant who carried their food which had already been prepared, and a large quantity of wine and ale, which was laid on the table before them.

Marlowe felt immediately uneasy as he was shown to his seat at the table and began to twist the topmost pearl button of his black velvet doublet, in his agitation, which eventually worked lose fell to the floor. He retrieved it and placed it in his pocket, not wanting to lose it.

The four proceeded to enjoy their banquet to celebrate Marlowe's release. Much of their conversation centred on the arrest of Thomas Kyd and the play Sir Thomas More which was being attributed to William Shakespeare even though Marlowe had been told by Thomas Kyd that the play had been written by four dramatists, namely: E. Tyllney, Thos. Heywood, Thomas Dekker, Harry Chettle, John Day.

The meal lasted until about 12 noon and they then went for a walk in the garden for some time and then the returned to the room and played cards for the rest of the evening and continued to drink the wine and ale.

When the time came to pay the bill for the food and drinks an argument broke out concerning a matter of pennies.

Christopherus Marlowe who had perhaps drunk too much wine, was lying on the bed near the wall to his left hand side, where the table was placed sat Ingram Frizer. To Frizer's left sat Robert Poley and to his right sat Nicholas Skeres. A fight broke out and it is said that Marlowe took the initiative and wrested Frizer's Ponyard from him and then lunged at Ingram Frizer from behind, inflicting two wounds to the back of Frizer's head. But it would seem more realistic to suppose that Marlowe had drawn his own dagger in order to defend himself when he saw Frizer lunge towards him (otherwise Frizer would surely have been stunned by the blows Marlowe had inflicted upon Frizer's head). As Marlowe was lying on the bed when Frizer came towards him with his dagger (which had been valued at 12d), then Marlowe would have had time to reach for his own dagger as he tried to fight off Frizer, and would probably have had time to stab at him as Frizer's dagger came towards his face. Ingram Frizer then lunged at Marlowe with such force that his ponyard entered Marlowe's right eye and descended to a depth of two inches and the width of one inch. Christopherus Marlowe died instantly and his brains were said to have been spilling out of the wound.

The Works of Christopherus Marlowe

Tamburlaine	1587	
Tamburlaine Part II	1588	
Doctor Faustus	1588/9	Entered for publication January 1601
The Jew of Malta	1588	(23.12.1588 Death of the

Duke of Guise) -Mary Queen of Scots French Uncle

1591 Registered by William Jones on 6th July 1593 in the name of Marlowe

Dido	1591
The Massacre at Paris	1592
Hero and Leander	1593

George Chapman continues after Marlowe's murder

Edward II   1590   Referred to at a supper held on 9th December 1595, attended by Lady Mary Hoby, Lady Scrope, Lord Cobham and The Earl of Essex. The Earl joked to Cobham about a play written by Christopher Marlowe'Richard II' in possession of the Earl of Pembroke's company. [Marlowe wrote for them after 1590]

Lyric Poems
The translation of Ovid's poems

1590 The Earl of Pembroke's Company acted the play Edward II on the 30th January 1593. (It was written by Christopher Marlowe at the end of 1591 or the beginning of 1592) .William Jones registered this play 1 month after Marlowe's death (6th July, 1593).
The Play Sir Thomas More:is linked to Kyd's arrest, 1593
A W POLLARD COMMENTS, 1925:

---

[65] "The Second Earl of Essex, Robert Devereux, was Leicester's stepson, and Burleigh's Ward. His anscestry could be traced back directly to Edward III _: Sir Walter Raleigh - Hugh Ross Williamson

HIC JACET: SIR WALTER RALEIGH

BY THOMAS DEKKER writing for the Admirals Men in 1598
THOMAS KYD
ANTONY MUNDAY author of John a Kent John a Cumber 1593
E Tyllney

Was this ancient play being used by Kyd and Marlowe in 1591 to study the history of King Henry VI (1422-1461) : They were both engaged to work for the Earl of Sussex Players .

Marlowe had already written historical material on the history of france in his Massacre at Paris 1592 [the year before he was murdered.]

A. W. Pollard continues:
"The likeness between the '147 lines and the Jack Cade scenes has become a common-place of criticism. But this is the less conclusive, because the Jack Cade scenes are found in the contention betwixth two famous houses of York and Lancaster, as printed in 1594, and much of the contention is pretty clearly not Shakespeare's work. It might be argued that the 'writer who foisted certain of the Jack Cade scenes into the second part of Henry VI' was also the writer of the 147 lines added to Sir Thomas More, without its being held that such writer was necessarily Shakespeare. Schuckling has argued that the play as a whole is an imitation of Shakespeare, written about 1604-5. He finds parallels between the treatment of the 'play within the play' in Sir Thomas More and in Hamlet. [But the insertion of a play within the play was not the invention of Shakespeare; it was probably in the Hamlet plot which he took over.   ... Nevertheless, there seems a fair certainty of some kind of connection between the '147 lines and Julius Caeser, as well as between these lines and the Jack Cade scenes."
This brings to mind Raleigh's peculiar words spoken on the scaffold:
"Is it not strange for me to make my self Robin Hood, or a Kett, or a

Cade?" and the words he had spoken to Dean Tounson: "Caeser will raise me up I trust."

Mr Pollard also draws comparisons between Sir Thomas More and Triolus and Cressida and Coriolanus.

This would explain why part of the play Sir Thomas More was in Thomas Kyd's neat Italian handwriting and then signed by Thomas Kyd.

On Thursday 5th May between the hours of 11 and 12 at night a rhyme66 was put up against the Dutch churchyard and caused great offence when it was found by the inhabitants and was immediately bought to the attention of the Night Watchman, who referred it directly to the Magistrates, who in turn referred it to the Privy Councillors.

["You, Strangers, that inhabit in this Land,
Note this same Writing, do it understand.
Conceive it well, for Safe-guard of your Lives,
Your Goods, your Children and your dearest Wives".)].

Dekker as an apprentice Dramatist wrote some of part (II) of King Henry VI.

In January 1598 Dekker was arrested for debt by Shakespeare company and ransomed by his new employers.

The first part of King Henry VI (i) was entered in the Stationers Register in March : 1594 as the first part of the contention

---

66
[The rhyme in question appears in the book 'Shakespeare's Hand in the Play of Sir Thomas More - A.W. Pollard 1925] - which was written by [four or five] literary hands in olde English and the undated manuscript which is written in a neat Italian hand, bears the signatures of Thomas Kyd, Thomas Dekker, John Day and Harry Chettle. William Shakespeare appended three pages to the Play Sir Thomas More, after its original completion, and part of it is housed in the British Museum] The dramatists were Anthony Munday and E. Tyllney (Tilney), who were attached to the Lord Admirals Men in 1597. Edwarde Alleyn retired from 1597 to 1600.

Kyd was released in November 1593, but the torture that he had endured and the conditions in which he had lived for those eight months, meant that his health was so poor that he survived for only six months after his release, even though he was still only 36 years old. His dramatic work 'Cornelia' (Julius Caeser) was registered for publication on the 26th January 1594

Thomas Kyd after his release from Newgate Prison registered?

King Henry VI (I)	1592	1594	1623
King Henry VI (II)	1592		1623
King Henry VI (III)	1592	1594	1623
Richard III	1593		1597?

A Chronology of Christopher Marlowe's Life

1564   26 February Christopherus, son of John Marlow, baptized at St. George the Martyr, Canterbury [Register Book].

1579 14 January -December Christopherus Marley, Scholar at King's School Canterbury, receives his grant [Accounts to Treasurer of Canterbury Cathedral].

1580   December. Marlen first appears on the Buttery Book of Corpus Christi College, Cambridge.

1581   17 March. Christopherus Marlen matriculated in convictus secundus, i.e. the middle rank of students [University Register: Matriculation Book].

24 March. Marlin listed among pensionarii, i.e. commoners [Corpus Christi Registrum Parvum].

29 october Merling at class in dialectic [Lansdowne MSS, BritishLibrary] From this year until Lent 1587 Marlin, Marly etc., resident in Corpus Christi, with some absences in 1585 and 1586 [Audit Book, Buttery Book].

1584   Lent. Christopherus Marlin permitted to proceed to B.A. [University Registry: Supplicats, Grace Book].

1585   November. Christopherus Marley witnesses will of Katherine Benchkyn of Canterbury [Canterbury Public Record Office].

1587   31 March. Christopher Marley permitted to proceed to ML.A. [Supplicats Grace Book].

29 June. Privy Council certify that it had been incorrectly rumored that Christopherus Morley had determined to go to Rheims to stay; and that he had on the contrary done the Queen good service, and should be

furthered in his degree at the next commencement i.e. in July [Acts of Privy Council, Public Record Office].

10 November. Election of successor to college scholarship [Registrum Parvum, College Order Book].

16 November. A shooting incident at a playhouse, possibly in performance of Tamberlaine. [See preface to play].

1588   29 March. Robert Greene refers to Tamburlaine. [See preface to play].

1589   28 September. Christoferus Morley, gentleman of London, fights with William Bradley in Hog Lane, Parish of St Giles without Cripplegate; Thomas Watson (the poet) intervenes, is attacked by Bradley and kills him in self defence [Chancery Miscellanea, Public Record Office]. Thomas Watson, gentleman, and Christoferus Marloe, yeoman, both of Norton Folgate, Middlesex, are arrested by the Constable and committed to Newgate by the Lieutenant of the Tower on suspicion of murder [Middlesex Sessions Roll].

19 September. Inquest on Bradley [Chancery Miscellanea].
1 October. Christophorus Marley of London, gentleman, released on bail of £40.00. Richardus Kytchine, gentleman of Clifford's Inn and Hufridus Rowland, horner of East Smithfield, stand surety [Middlesex Sessions Roll].

3 December. Marlowe appears before justices (including Sir Roger Manwood) and is discharged [Middlesex Sessions Roll].

1590   14 August. Tamberlaine published.

1592   [or before] Thomas Kyd dramatist, [author of the Spanish tragedie], writing in one room with Marlowe [Harleian MSS British Library].

1592   9 May. Christopherusus Marle, gentleman of London, bound over in £20 to keep the peace towards Allen Nicholls, Constable of   Holywell Street, Shoreditch, and Nicholause Helliott, Sub-   Constable of the same [Middle Sessions Roll].

3 September. Robert Greene reproves a gifted fellow-Playright for his atheism and Machieavellian self-seeking [Groatsworth of Wit].

10 November. Dedication by C.M. to Thomas Watson's Amintae Guadia.

8 December. Henry Chettle admits to playwrights were offended by Green's posthumous Groatsworth of Wit; One of them he reverences for his learning, but would rather not get to know [Kind Harts Dreame].

[Oxinden Commonplace Book, Folger Library].

1593   12 May. Thomas Kyd arrested and heretical papers which he attributes to Marlowe, discovered in his room [Harleian MSS].

18 May.Privy Council issue warrant for the arrest of Christopher Marlow, at the house of his patron Mr Thomas Walsingham at Scadbury, Chislehurst, in Kent or elsewhere [Acts of Privy Council].

20 May. Christofer Marley, Gentleman of London answers the warrant and is required to remain in daily attendance at the home of Thomas Walsingham in Scadbury [Acts of   Privy Council].

The Privy councillors who examined Marlowe at his Inquest were:

> Archbishop Whitgift
> Sir Christopherus Hatton [one of his servants was executed in Babington plot (a Plot to free Mary Queen of Scots]
> Lord Burghley
> Lord Hunsdon[Queen Elizabeth's cousin]
> Sir James Crofts

30 May. Christopherusus Morley killed in self defence by Ingram Frizer (servant to Mr Thomas Walsingham), in the company of Robert Poley and Nicholas Skeres, at an establishment run by Mistress Eleanor Bull, in Deptford Strand.

1 June. Inquest held on Cristoferus Marlow, slain by Francis Frezer [Chancery Miscellanea]. William Danby Gentleman of Woolwich and Coroner of the Household of Queen Elizabeth I viewed the body of Christopherus Marlowe.

Present at the Inquest of Christopher Marlowe

> Nicholas Draper
> Woolstan Randall of Limehouse
> William Curry of Deptford
> Adrian Walker of Limekills
> John Barber
> Robert Baldwyn
> Giles Ffeld of Upper Deptford
> George Halfpenny from Limehouse
> Hanry Awger
> James Bath jr.
> Thomas Bath sr.
> Henry Bendyn - Limehouse

> John Baldwyne - High Street East
> Alexander Burrage
> Edmund Goodcheepe
> Henry Dabyns (Dobbins), High Street East

Argued over 12d. Marlowe wounded to right eye 2 inches long and to the width of inch which caused his brains to spill out and he met with instant death.

Friday 1 June: Burial of Christopherus Marlowe at St Nicholas Church Deptford, immediately after the Inquest. [Register of St. Nicholas Church, Deptford].

After 1 June Thomas Kyd writes to the Lord Keep Sir John Puckering about Marlowe's monstrous opinions.

2 June A note by Richard Baines about the horrible blasphemies of Christofer Marly or Morly [Harleian mss]. One of Kyd's accusers was Richard Baines, a 'spy' for Sir Francis Walsingham. Whilst Kyd remained in prison, another of Sir Francis Walsingham's men, Robert Poley [who was also employed for the Babington Plot] was present at the murder of Christopherus Marlowe and testified at Marlowe's inquest on the 1st June 1593.67

15 June A Writ of Certiorari issued to summon the case of Ingram Frizer into Chancery [Chancery miscellanea]

Thursday 28 June: Pardon issued to Frizer [Patent Rolls Elizabeth. 35].

---

[67] One of Kyd's accusers was Richard Baines, a 'spy' for Sir Francis Walsingham. Whilst Kyd remained in prison, another of Sir Francis Walsingham's men, Robert Poley [who was also employed for the Babinton Plot] was present at the murder of Christopher Marlowe and testified at Marlowe's inquest on the 1st June 1593.

ILL MAY DAY scenes from] The Booke of Sir Thomas Moore

A.W. Pollard: Edited by W.W. Greg

Scene 1. - A street in the City.]

Enter at one end John Lincolne with [the two Bettses] Fol 3a
together, at the other end enters Fraunces de [Barde, and Doll] a lustie
woman, he haling her by the arme.

Doll.   Whether wilt thou hale me?

Bard.   Whether I please, thou are my prize and I pleade purchase of
thee.

Doll.   Purchase of me? away ye rascall, I am an honest plaine
carpenters wife and thoughe I have no beautie to like a husband yet
whatsoever is mine scornes to stoupe to a straunger: hand off then
when I bid thee.

Bard: Goe with me quietly, or Ile compell thee.

Doll.   Compell me ye dogges face? thou thinkst thou hast the
goldsmithes wife in hand, whom thou enticedst from her husband with
all his plate,and then thou turndst her home to him again, madste him
(like an asse) pay for his wifes boorde.

Bard.   So will I make thy husband too, if please me.

and   Enter Caveler with a paire of dooves, Williamson the carpenter
    Sherwin following him.

Doll   Here comes himselfe, tell him so if thou darste.

Cave.   Follow me no further, I say thou shalt not have them.

Wil.   I bought them in Cheapeside, and paide my monie for them.

Sher.   He did Sir indeed, and you offer him wrong, bothe to take them
from   him, and not restore him his monie neither.

Cave.   If he paid for them, let it suffise that I possesse them, beefe and
brewes may serve such hindes, are piggions meate for a coorse
carpenter?

Lin.   It is hard when Englishmens pacience must be thus jetted on by
straungers and they not dare to revendge their owne wrongs.

Geo.   Lincolne, lets beate them downe, and beare no more of these
abuses.

Lin.   We may not Betts, be pacient and heare more.

Doll.   How now husband? what, one staunger take thy food from
thee, and   another thy wife? bir Lady flesh andblood I thinke can
hardly brooke that.

Lin.   Will this geere never be otherwise? must these wrongs be
endured?

Geo.   Let us step in, and help to revendge their injurie.

Bard.   What art thou that talkest of revendge? my Lord Ambassadour
shall   once more make your Major have a check, if he punishe thee
not for saucie presumption.

Wil.   Indeed my lord Mayor, on the Ambassadours complainte, sent
me to Newgate one day, because (against my will) I tooke the wall of a
straunger. You may doo anything, the goldsmiths wife, and mine now
must be at your commaundment.

Geo.   the more pacient fooles are ye bothe to suffer it.

Bard.   Suffer it? mend it thou or he if ye can or dare, I tell thee fellowe, and she were the Mayor of Londons wife, had I her once in my possession, I would keep her in spite of him that dusrst say nay.

Geo.   I tell thee Lombard, these wordes should cost they best cappe, where I not curbd by dutie and obedience. The Mayor of Londons wife? Oh God, shall it be thus?

Doll.   Why Bettes, am not I as deare to my husband, as my Lord Mayors wife to him, and wilt thou so neglectly suffer thine owne shame? Hands off proude stranger or [by] him that bought me, if mens milkie arts dare not strike a straunger, yet women will beate them downe, ere hey beare these abuses.

Bard.   Mistresse, I say you shall along with me.

Doll.   Touche not Doll Williamson, least she lay thee along on Gods
deare   earthe. (to Caveler.) And you Sir, that allow such coorse cates
to   carpenters, whilste pidgions which they pay for, must serve
your   daintie appetite: deliver them back to my husband again or Ile
call so   many women to myne assistance, as weele not leave one inche
        untorne of thee. If our husbands must be brideled by lawe, and
forced   to beare your wrongs, their wives will be a little lawelesse, and
        soundly beate ye.

Cave.   Come aware de Bard, and let us goe complaine to my Lord
        Ambassadour. Exeunt ambo.

Doll: I, goe, and send him among us, and weele give him his welcome too. I am ashamed that freeborne Englishmen, having beatten straungers within their owne bound[s] should thus be brau'de and abusde by them at home.

333

Sher: It is not our lack of courage in the cause, but the strict obedience that we are bound too: I am the goldsmith whose wrongs you talkte of, but how to redresse yours or mine owne, is a matter beyond all our abilities.

Lin. Not so, not so my good freends, I, though a meane man, a broaker by profession and namd John Lincolne, have long time winckt at these vilde ennormitees with mighty impacience, and, as these two bretheren heere (Betses by name) can witnesse with losse of mind owne liffe would gladly remedie them.

Christopher Marlowe the Dramatist is Murdered 30th May, 1593

1593   12 May. Thomas Kyd arrested and heretical papers which he attributes to Marlowe, discovered in his room [Harleian MSS].

18 May. Privy Council issue warrant for the arrest of Christopherus Marlowe, at the house of his patron Mr. Thomas Walsingham at Scadbury, Chislehurst, in Kent or elsewhere [Acts of Privy Council].

20 May. Christofer Marley, Gentleman of London answers the warrant and is required to remain in daily attendance [Acts of Privy Council].

The Murder of Christopher Marlowe
The Dramatist, 10 am Wednesday 30th May
Midnight 1st June 1593

Christopherus Marlowe had been arrested on the 18th May 1593.
The Privy Councillors who examined Marlowe were:

Archbishop Whitgift
Sir Christopherus Hatton   [one of his servants was executed
in   Babington plot]
Lord Burghley
Lord Hunsdon   [Queen Elizabeth's cousin]
Sir James Crofts

Thomas Kyd had been arrested on the 12th May last and had been
carried off and tortured at Newgate Prison concerning certain text from
the play Sir Thomas More, being a completed play to which William
Shakespeare had tried to append three pages of text, laboriously copied
in a scrivener's hand.

The rhyme in question reads as follows:

Num. CVIII. [From John Strype's Brief Annals of the Church and
State under the reign of Queen Elizabeth,

[("A Rhime set up against the Wall of the Dutch churchyard, on
Thursday May the 5th, between Eleven and Twelve at night. And
there found by some of the Inhabitants of that Place; and brought to
the Constable, and the rest of the Watch. beginning,

"You, Strangers, that inhabit in this Land,
Note this same Writing, do it understand.
Conceive it well, for Safe-guard of your Lives,
Your Goods, your Children and your dearest Wives.)].

The Privy Council decided that immediate action must be taken in
order to prevent riot or insurrection, and appointed Sir Julius Caesar,

Sir Henry Killgrew and Sir Thomas Wilkes to seek out and examine by secret means, all persons suspected as being responsible and they were given leave to search the premises of any writers thought to be involved in the above plots. It was directed that a search be made for any papers or writings which may lead to the guilty persons being identified, after which they should be put to torture until they confessed and revealed all they knew of the matter.

Thomas Kyd had volunteered information to the Privy Councillors during his torture when he admitted to his tormentors that certain heretical papers had been cast in amongst his own and therefore they must have belonged to Christopherus Marlowe, with whom Kyd had once shared a writing chamber in the year 1592.

Thomas Kyd was the author of the Spanish Tragedy pre-1587, a forerunner to Hamlet, and by the year 1591 Kyd had been introduced to Christopherus Marlowe and they had resolved to work together in perfecting the Spanish Tragedie. During this time they shared a writing chamber and were engaged to write for the Earl of Sussex Players. The Spanish Tragedie was not entered for publication until the 14th March 1592 (Henslowe's diary records [68] Spanish Tradgedie 1592). Marlowe at about this time or shortly afterwards, was also engaged in writing his play St. Bartholomew's Massacre.

From the 18th May when Marlowe had been arrested and required to remain in London or elsewhere and until Wednesday 30th May 1593 Christopherus Marlowe had remained under house arrest at the home of his former Patron Sir Thomas Walsingham. At last on the 30th May he had been permitted to leave the confines of Walsingham's home in order to dine with Ingram Frizer, Walsingham's servant, with whom he had then travelled to Deptford. Lord Hunsdon Patron of the Lord

---

[68] Henslowe's Diaries record Spanish Tradgedie 14.3.1592 [registered for publication]

Chamberlain's Men having intervened on Marlowe's behalf and Sir Christopherus Hatton having also spoken in Marlowe's favour.

Christopherus Marlowe and Ingram Frizer had arrived together at the main door of an Eating House in Deptford Strande at about 10 o'clock in the morning, having travelled up to London by coach from Scadbury, Chislehurst. The modest Tavern belonged to a Mistress Eleanor Bull, a widow. A smiling Mistress Bull met them at the main door to the house and they requested to be shown immediately to a private dining room upstairs which had been reserved by Ingram Frizer. They climbed the stairs as Mistress Bull led the way, and entered the small dining room sparsely furnished with a table and chairs in the centre of the room and a small bed on the left hand side of the room pushed against the wall.

Marlowe found to his surprise that two other persons were already present when they reached the room, being Robert Poley (who had spied for Sir Francis Walsingham in the height of the Babington conspiracy) and Nicholas Skeres, who was a servant to The Earl of Essex (otherwise known as the Earl of March).

Mistress Bull left the room and quickly returned with a servant who carried their food which had already been prepared, and a large quantity of wine and ale, which was laid on the table before them.

Marlowe felt immediately uneasy as he was shown to his seat at the table and began to twist the topmost pearl button of his black velvet doublet, in his agitation, which eventually worked lose fell to the floor. He retrieved it and placed it in his pocket, not wanting to lose it.

The four proceeded to enjoy their banquet to celebrate Marlowe's release. Much of their conversation centred on the arrest of Thomas Kyd and the play Sir Thomas More which was being attributed to William Shakespeare even though Marlowe had been told by Thomas Kyd that the play had been written by four dramatists, namely:

The meal lasted until about 12 noon and they then went for a walk in the garden for some time and then the returned to the room and played cards for the rest of the evening and continued to drink the wine and ale.

When the time came to pay the bill for the food and drinks an argument broke out concerning a matter of pennies.

Christopher Marlowe who had perhaps drunk too much wine, was lying on the bed near the wall to his left hand side, where the table was placed sat Ingram Frizer. To Frizer's left sat Robert Poley and to his right sat Nicholas Skeres. A fight broke out and it is said that Marlowe took the initiative and wrested Frizer's Ponyard from him and then lunged at Ingram Frizer from behind, inflicting two wounds to the back of Frizer's head. But it would seem more realistic to suppose that Marlowe had drawn his own dagger in order to defend himself when he saw Frizer lunge towards him (otherwise Frizer would surely have been stunned by the blows Marlowe had inflicted upon Frizer's head). As Marlowe was lying on the bed when Frizer came towards him with his dagger (which had been valued at 12d), then Marlowe would have had time to reach for his own dagger as he tried to fight off Frizer, and would probably have had time to stab at him as Frizer's dagger came towards his face. Ingram Frizer then lunged at Marlowe with such force that his ponyard entered Marlowe's right eye and descended to a depth of two inches and the width of one inch. Christopherus Marlowe died instantly and his brains were said to have been spilling out of the wound.

The Dramatic works of Christopher Marlowe

Tamburlaine	1587	(Written at Cambridge?)
Tamburlaine Part II	1588	
Doctor Faustus	1588/9	
The Jew of Malta	1588 (23.12.1588 Death of the Duke of	
Guise)	Mary Queen of Scots French Uncle	
Edward II	1591	
Dido	1591	(Marlowe/Nash/Kyd?)
the Massacre at Paris	1592	
Hero and Leander	1593	

George Chapman continues after Marlowe's murder

Lyric Poems and translation of Ovids works

A Chronology of Marlowe's Life

1564 26 February Christopfer, son of John Marlow, baptized at St. George the Martyr, Canterbury [Register Book].

1579 14 January - December Christopherus Marley, Scholar at King's School Canterbury, receives his grant [Accounts to Treasurer of Canterbury Cathedral].

1580 December. Marlen first appears on the Buttery Book of Corpus Christi College, Cambridge.

1581 - 17 March. Christopherus Marlen matriculated in convictus secundus, i.e. the middle rank of students [University Register: Matriculation Book].

24 March - Marlin listed among pensionarii, i.e. commoners [Corpus Christi Registrum Parvum].

29 october   - Merling at class in dialectic [Lansdowne MSS, British Library] From this year until Lent 1587 Marlin, Marly etc., resident in Corpus Chisti, with some absences in 1585 and 1586 [Audit Book, Buttery Book].

1584 - Lent. Christopherusus Marlin permitted to proceed to B.A. [University Registry: Supplicats, Grace Book].

1585   November. Christofer Marley witnesses will of Katherine Benchkyn of Canterbury [Canterbury Public Record Office].

1587   31 March. Christopherusus Marley permitted to proceed to ML.A. [Supplicats Grace Book].

29 June. Privy Council certify that it had been incorrectly

rumored that Christopherus Morley had determined to go to Rheims to stay; and that he had on the contrary done the Queen good service, and should be furthered in his degree at the next commencement i.e. in July [Acts of Privy Council, Public Record Office].

10 November. Election of successor to college scholarship [Registrum Parvum, College Order Book].

16 November. A shooting incident at a playhouse, possibly in performance of Tamberlaine. [See preface to play].

1588 29 March. Robert Greene refers to Tamburlaine. [See preface to play].
1589 28 September. Christoferus Morley, gentleman of London, fights with William Bradley in Hog Lane, Parish of St Giles without Cripplegate; Thomas Watson (the poet) intervenes, is attacked by Bradley and kills him in self defence [Chancery Miscellanea, Public Record Office]. Thomas Watson, gentleman, and Christoferus Marloe, yeoman, both of Norton Folgate, Middlesex, are arrested by the Constable and committed to Newgate by the Lieutenant of the Tower on suspicion of murder [Middlesex Sessions Roll].

19 September. Inquest on Bradley [Chancery Miscellanea].
1 October. Christophorus Marley of London, gentleman, released on bail of £40.00. Richardus Kytchine, gentleman of Clifford's Inn and Hufridus Rowland, horner of East Smithfield, stand surety [Middlesex Sessions Roll].
3 December. Marlowe appears before justices (including Sir Roger Manwood) and is discharged [Middlesex Sessions Roll].
1590 14 August. Tamberlaine published.
1592 [or before] Thomas Kyd dramatist, [author of the Spanish tragedie], writing in one room with Marlowe [Harleian MSS British Library].
1592 9 May. Christopherusus Marle, gentleman of London, bound over in £20 to keep the peace towards Allen Nicholls, Constable of Holywell Street, Shoreditch, and Nicholause Helliott, Sub-Constable of the same [Middle Sessions Roll].

3 September. Robert Greene reproves a gifted fellow-playright for his atheism and Machieavellian self-seeking [Groatsworth of Wit].

10 November. Dedication by C.M. to Thomas Watson's Amintae Guadia.

8 December. Henry Chettle admits to playwrights were offended by Green's posthumous Groatsworth of Wit; One of them he reverences for his learning, but would rather not get to know [King Harts Dreame].

14 December. Sir Roger Manwood dies: Christopherus Marlo writes an epitaph. [Oxinden Commonplace Book, Folger Library].

1593 12 May. Thomas Kyd arrested and heretical papers which he attributes to Marlowe, discovered in his room [Harleian MSS].

18 May. Privy Council issue warrant for the arrest of Christopherus Marlow, at the house of his patron Mr Thomas Walsingham at Scadbury, Chislehurst, in Kent or elsewhere [Acts of Privy Council].

20 May. Christofer Marley, Gentleman of London answers the warrant and is required to remain in daily attendance [Acts of Privy Council].

The Privy councillors who examined Marlowe were:

Archbishop Whitgift
Sir Christopherus Hatton [one of his servants was executed in Babington plot]
Lord Burghley
Lord Hunsdon, Lord Chamberlain's Men   [Queen Elizabeth's cousin]
Sir James Crofts

30 May. Christopherusus Morley killed in self defence by Ingram Frizer (servant to Mr Thomas Walsingham), in the company of Robert Poley and Nicholas Skeres, at an establishment run by Mistress

343

Eleanor Bull, in Deptford Strand.

1 June. Inquest held on Cristoferus Marlow, slain by Francis Frezer [Chancery Miscellanea]. William Danby Gentleman of Woolwich and Coroner of the Household of Queen Elizabeth I viewed the body of Christopherus Marlowe.

Present at the Inquest: Nicholas Draper
Woolstan Randall of Limehouse
William Curry of Deptford
Adrian Walker of Limekills
John Barber
Robert Baldwyn
Giles Ffeld of Upper Deptford
George Halfpenny from
Limehouse
Hanry Awger
James Bath jr.
Thomas Bath sr.
Henry Bendyn - Limehouse
John Baldwyne – High Street East
Alexander Burrage
Edmund Goodcheepe
Henry Dabyns (Dobbins), HighStreet East.

Argued over 12d (price of a play?). Marlowe wounded to right eye 2 inches long and to the width of inch which caused his brain to spill out and he met with instant death.

Friday 1 June: Burial of Christopherus Marlowe at St Nicholas Church Deptford, immediately after the Inquest. [Register of St. Nicholas Church, Deptford].

After 1 June Thomas Kyd writes to the Lord Keep Sir John Puckering about Marlowe's monstrous opinions.

2 June A note by Richard Baines about the horrible blasphemies of

Christofer Marly or Morly [Harleian mss]. One of Kyd's accusers was Richard Baines, a 'spy' for Sir Francis Walsingham. Whilst Kyd remained in prison, another of Sir Francis Walsingham's men, Robert Poley [who was also employed for the Babington Plot] was present at the murder of Christopherus Marlowe and testified at Marlowe's inquest on the 1st June 1593.69

15 June A Writ of Certiorari issued to summon the case of Ingram Frizer into Chancery [Chancery miscellanea]

Thursday 28 June: Pardon issued to Frizer [Patent Rolls Elizabeth. 35].

---

69 One of Kyd's accusers was Richard Baines, a 'spy' for Sir Francis Walsingham. Whilst Kyd remained in prison, another of Sir Francis Walsingham's men, Robert Poley [who was also employed for the Babinton Plot] was present at the murder of Christopher Marlowe and testified at Marlowe's inquest on the 1st June 1593.

Henry Percy, Ninth Earl of Northumberland
The Wizard Earl of Syon- 1594

Raleigh woke early for his meeting with the Wizard Earl of Syon and before leaving Durham House he hurriedly ate the fresh bread and cheese that his kitchen man had brought to him on a wooden tray. After dressing in warm clothing for his river journey Raleigh gathered up his papers and placed them in his worn, brown leather case. He then removed his black cloak and his black felt hat from the wardrobe in his study and carried them over his arm as he left his turret. He began to shiver as he walked quickly down the three flights of stairs and out through the double doors at the back of Durham House, where a Wherry and its master waited patiently to convey him along the River Thames. Syon House was a convenient place to reach by river, as it stood very near to the riverbank at Isleworth.

As they proceeded along the River, and Raleigh lit his silver pipe and smoked it leisurely, he observed the early morning scenes around him and thought to himself - 'what a beautiful day this promises to be!' The cloudless sky was pale blue, streaked with pink, and the sun was just beginning to warm the morning air. There was still a light mist upon the surface of the river and a slight chill in the air.

As Raleigh looked up river, he noticed two swans and several small Cygnets which were in their path and they were refusing to change their course. The Wherry master was heading straight towards them and Raleigh, who was concerned that they might be harmed, called out, as he waved his arm 'Swing over to the left hand side man!' but the Wherry master swung too far left across the River, with a sudden jerking movement, and the skiff became entangled in reeds beside the riverbank. After a brief struggle with the oars, they managed to break free of the tall green reeds, but the Wherry master had lost his cap in the struggle, which had fallen into the River and could not be retrieved.

The rest of their journey was uneventful and as they neared the Ninth Earl of Northumberland's Estate they both looked out for the inlet which would lead them into the grounds of Syon House. Raleigh jumped from the wherry and made his way through the dry grass, which crackled underfoot as he proceeded quickly into the beautiful grounds leading to Syon House. He could see the huge sand coloured stone building in the distance which resembled a Castle, and the stone Lion standing proudly on its roof.

As Raleigh walked towards Syon House his mind was flooded with thoughts of the religious conflicts which the people of England had endured since the creation of the Church of England. Syon House had once been a Monastery in the 15th century and Raleigh loved to walk through the lower parts of the house with the Wizard Earl and it was there they would view the priests holes and hiding places which had saved the lives of some of the priests in the reign of Henry VIII, [b.1491] (r.1509-1547)] during the persecution of the Roman Catholics, after King Henry had severed his ties with the Church of Rome and had then created the Church of England and proclaimed himself "of the Church of England on Earth the Supreme Head." and later the burning to death of Archbishop Cranmer and Bishops Latimer and Ridley in the 1550s. Archbishop Cranmer who had declared King Henry VIII's marriage to Catherine of Aragon after the King had married Anne Boleyn. During his time at Oxford University Raleigh had remembered seeing the wooden doors between the outer and inner quadrangles of Balliol, which had scorched by those terrible flames of execution.

The Wizard Earl had told Raleigh that upon King Henry VIII's death his body had lain at Syon House for several days. ++

The Wizard Earl had also told Raleigh that he suspected that there were treasures buried beneath the great stones of those vast floors at Syon House hidden there during the Pilgrimage of Grace. Raleigh had promised to assist the Earl, when together they would endeavour to unearth the hidden wealth, when time presented to them that safety and to discover where the Priests and Monks had buried their golden statuas, ornaments, jewelled chains, their ivory and golden coins and jeweled medallions. They had both considered that these wonderful treasures were probably hidden in a wooden chest or several chests deep below the house and had lain there for since the fifteenth century.

Raleigh brought his mind back to the present time and surroundings and once again heard the birds singing and warbling happily among the branches of the trees, and their leaves were lit up by the sunshine as it filtered through the abundant glossy green leaves, casting delicate blankets of speckled shade across the emerald green grass.

As he walked across the well kept lawns he found the sight breathtaking and he noticed that from a distance the grass resembled a huge green velvet carpet, and noticed that the damp grass had been freshly cut by the scythe-men, probably the day before and the pleasing scent still lingered in the air.

Drawing closer to Syon House he saw Henry Percy the Wizard Earl walking swiftly towards the gardens, followed by his collie dog '"Casca' who ran on a short way ahead of him and kept turning back after running forward a few paces and then stopping to wag his tail in an effort to ensure that the Earl was still following him. The Earl was dressed in his favourite brown woollen cloak, which billowed behind him as he rushed headlong through a small wooden door which led him in to the Rose Gardens.

The Earl was younger than Raleigh by 12 years. Raleigh at that time being 32 and the Earl who had just succeeded at that time was 21 years old. The Earl had many endearing qualities and he was a very kind and considerate man; popular and well loved among his friends. Raleigh had introduced Thomas Harriot the Astronomer to the Earl and through their combined keen interests the [70] School of Night had sprung up and they held regular meetings at Syon House or Durham House, discussing the sciences and writing scientific postulations; and an through their observances of the multitude of aspects of life, they wrote essays and dramatic works.

Henry Percy was alone and Raleigh quickened his pace in an effort to reach him. As Raleigh drew nearer, he could see Henry Percy crouching down observing one of his Bee Hives, and he held a stick in his right hand which was protected by a brown leather glove. He was watching intently as several stray bees, having managed to find their way out of a minute hole near the bottom of the hive, were engaged in the practice of crawling in and out of the tiny hole to join the hundreds of bees within. Percy had been careful to protect himself with his cloak in order to avoid being stung by the bees, and was just attempting to remove the cover of the hive and it brought into Raleigh's mind of the time Henry Percy had once given him an account of Georgics and how Virgil had written of the habits and merits of bees and there he had found discussions page by page on the merits of bees and their wonderful functions and purposes and of the different types of bees in this World, which had persuaded him to keep bees in the first place. Raleigh had never observed the activities of bees in quite the same light again after that.

Henry Percy did not hear Raleigh approaching but he was aware, through a sixth sense that someone stood watching him silently, and assuming that it was one of his servants who observed him, but dared not interrupt the activity in which he was engaged, and without

---

[70] Members of the School of Night were: Sir Walter Raleigh Patron, Thomas Harriot, The Wizard Earl of Syon, Sir Philip Sidney, George Chapman, Christopher Marlowe, Thomas Kyd, Lord Strange the Earl of Derby, Ben Johnson and Edmund Spencer.

allowing himself to be distracted from his present task, he spoke without turning round, and said:

'If you are here to ask about borrowing one of the books from my great Library and there is a gentleman visitor requiring one of those books, then just tell him that I do not mind him borrowing a book (as long as he does not ask to take any of Virgil's works), and provided that the book is returned to me in the same good condition. Every man has the right to read a book and there are precious few to be found worth the reading - except upon the shelves lining the walls of my grand library!" finished the Earl very proudly.

Raleigh who knew how the Earl cherished the books in his library, broke his silence by replying : 'Lest you forget - my own collection of books rival your own.' And then Raleigh laughed as he said 'It is me Henry! Raleigh.'

Henry Percy started in fright as if he had not expected to see Raleigh, and then the stick he had been holding fell from his hand, as he stood up suddenly.

Henry Percy was a tall man of 5'11 with very broad shoulders and a shock of red hair which he said should be allowed to grow just as it pleased. He had deep set, dark brown eyes. He was a wildly eccentric and extremely intelligent man. Very knowledgeable in matters of Science (which had earned him the nickname of 'Wizard Earl' .

The Earl's brown cloak fell loosely about his sturdy body, as he stood up and a large and magnificent gold jeweled pendant was revealed, which was suspended from a thick gold chain, containing four large emeralds, six rubies, and numerous large diamonds which glittered brightly in the sunlight, as it swung to and fro heavily. Beneath his cloak the Earl wore a splendid purple velvet doublet, slashed to reveal crimson silk, which set off the pendant to great advantage and Raleigh thought that the Earl was perhaps a little overdressed for his morning walk.

HIC JACET: SIR WALTER RALEIGH

'Did you receive my message yesterday? I sent Peter Deane here to deliver a letter to you, informing you of my intended visit this morning concerning my planned voyage to Guiana in February. I wish you and Harriot to assist me in the preparations for my forthcoming voyage with the compilation of maps and charts. Harriot has been making some study of the Cross staff for me. Is Harriot here present at Syon House?'

'Harriot has been engaged in some secret work yes, closing himself off from my company like some great artist who would not shew his work until it is finished, but I have not seen him this morning."

'I have received no letter from you." said the Earl as he smiled and shook his head about wildly and his red hair flew about in all directions.

'But it is as good to see you now as it will ever be Raleigh. We shall go into the house immediately and you can tell me of all your important news contained in that letter.'

"I cannot hold the news any longer: Marlowe and Kyd are gone from us now. Sidney is gone. And all three of them murdered."

"And doubtless we shall be too!"

"My letter contained news that Francis Bacon is working off Sir Thomas More and Shakespeare prepares Sir Philip Sidney's Sonnets."

"Then we must ensure that they both have our work also. And perhaps that of Harriot. A little Erasmus mingled amidst the Linacre? to whet their appetites further - Fame Raleigh!"

"It is More than enough for them both to find everlasting fame and yet it will be so well hidden inside a hollow tree that perhaps it will never surface to be read by human eyes."

"Scarce could they comprehend us then for the Gunpowder Plot that will come down upon them."

'But where is Peter Deane? He is normally so reliable and I do not understand what has happened to him! Henry were you at Syon House last night?"

'Oh! Last night? Nooo! I have just returned this morning, not an hour ago. I was invited by the Queen to a Banquet at Hampton Court and I have been away for two days. Do I look wider about the waist?" He asked as he patted the front of his body through his clothing. 'If I do not then it is through no fault of my own. The food was wonderful, oh and the fine wines and ales excellent Raleigh!' You should have joined us. But wait ." said the Earl as he raised a finger to his ear and wagged it about. "Where you not there? I remember searching for you late in the evening."

"Yes, I attended earlier in the day, but my fun was spoiled by Sir Francis Walsingham spying on me and Richard Hakluyt as I lost to him at cards and it marred the day and for my evening's pleasure I took myself back to Durham House and there prepared my papers for this meeting."

"Then your planned voyage to Guiana will coincide with my efforts to join the army in the Netherlands."

Then let us return to the house and seek out Harriot and turn ourselves into spies for his sake.

Once they had returned to Syon House and a serving woman had brought them a silver tray with goblets of fine red wine and they had discussed Raleigh's plans, they hurried up the stairs until they neared a huge room where Harriot had spread out all his charts and papers on a wooden table but instead of entering the room they observed him from a spying place at first in a wooden panel, and the Wizard Earl made a noise like an Owl so that Harriot looked about him but could see no one. Then they both laughed and Raleigh said:

"It is no wonder to me that Harriot spends his time here and not at his study at Durham House, since you afford him a great measure of room and many benefits."

"The man is a genius Raleigh and must not be halted in his studies for the lack of space in which to explore the wonders of his own minde. Here he has all my scientific apparatus at his disposal with which to perform his experiments and I join him so often that it pleases me to have him here with me."

"Then you deprive me of his company and your own."

At this moment Harriot opened the door to his room which led him into the great hallway and there he found his two friends and invited them into his room.

"Come in! Enter! Stay there no longer for there is much to discuss" he cried anxiously as he walked in between the Earl and Raleigh and tugged at their sleeves.

They were hurried to the table in the centre of the room and there Harriot waved his arms about excitedly and said:

"Here I have in my handes [71] "The Doctrine of Nautical triangles Compendious' and the six diagrams or tables for you to examine.

These are instructions to your Sea Captains Raleigh, and I will read to you both, but first I will explain my ideas and findings concerning and surrounding my observations of reconciling the sun and pole star for

---

[71] Thomas Harriot by John Shirley p.88

determining latitude -

:+

'How to know your course to sayle to any place assigned; & in sayling
to keep to [c.o.] make true recconing to find where you are at any time;
& how farre from any place desired.

1. Some Remembrances of taking the altitudes of the Sonne by the
Astrolabe and Sea Ringe.

2. Of taking the altitudes of the Sonne or starres [c.o.] any starre by
the cross staffe with more exactenes then hath ben used heretofore.
[Includes a table of 'Surplus of the Horizon in minutes' to correct for
the 'Hight of the ey above the water in pases'.]

3. How to find the declination of the Sonne for any time of the yeare
& any place by a Speciall table called the Sonnes Regiment newly
made according to late observations.

4. How to find the elevation of the pole, by the Meridian altitude of
the Sonne, & his declination. [Includes a table on 'Elevation of the
pole...']

5. Of taking the altitude or elevation of the North pole by the north
starre & a new rule of the guardes made and calculated according to
praecise & late observations.[72]

6. Of the manner to observe the variation of the compasse, or the wires

---

[72] [These 'late observations' are explained by me as 'these thinges I spake upon conference
with these sortes of men as also upon myne owne experience & triall at sea in sayling to the
Indies, Virginia & homewards.']

of the same, by the Sonnes rising or setting.[73]

---

[73] The Haven-Finding Art, augmented edn., New York, American Elsevier Publishing Co., 1971, p.216.

February, 1603

John Talbot prepares to become apprenticed to
Francis, The Scrivener of 8 Lombard Street

I will begin at the end of my story being the best place to record this history. How many men before me have tried to present this story I cannot say, but I have heard 'that a historian knows everything about a man, and that he might take his bones one morning and arrange them neatly in his pocket by night, only to present them to the World the following morning.

After Raleigh's Trial at Winchester and his imprisonment began in the Bloody Tower, I was among those listed upon the Warrant which read:

Raleigh, having two servants, being myself and Peter Deane, informed me that there was another way in which I could serve him. He went to his chest of papers one day and brought out a bundle of [etc.]

When at last the appointed day arrived, I was very glad of it, since in my great excitement, I had caused myself to mark off each day on the calendar for the months that had passed since Raleigh's imprisonment in the Bloody Tower on 15th December, 1603.

Just as a brave man does not fear the gallows until the final grain of sand falls from the hourglass, I witnessed my own resolve falter and then desert me entirely.

As I prepared to take my leave of Sir Walter, now a prisoner in the Tower of London, I saw a haunted man. As his face turned toward me, reflected in the firelight, I noticed in his hollowed and darkened eyes, a fear I have never seen in him before that time. Knowing that his fate was certain, and that he would remain a prisoner for the rest of his lifetime, I knew that I could do nothing to relieve his misery if I remained with him.

HIC JACET: SIR WALTER RALEIGH

I hung my head very low upon my breast as a feeling of great shame rose up within me and felt as though I were betraying him by leaving. I turned and left the Bloody Tower, I walked away from the very man who had been my master for 18 years. I knew then that his misfortune would haunt me for the remainder of my days.

As I walked from the Tower, I made my way slowly through the City of London. I became aware of how overshadowed my life had become as the servant of an imprisoned man. All about me, people treated me roughly, as they pushed and shoved their way along the streets, or so I thought it was the case, as I hurried through the winding streets. I had been so well used during my employment that I could not reckon on any common treatment whilst away from him. I became increasingly aware of the mention of his name, and it filled the air around me, so that I listened for it with every beat of my heart, as I walked towards Lombard Street, and then, I imagined that I could hear his name on the lips of approaching men just as they had cried out as he left the Tower of London on his way to Winchester in November 1603. They still cried out: "Traitor to the King!" - "Raleigh! - The Queen's fallen favourite has lost his chance with the Privy Council."

With these words ringing in my ears, I found number 8 Lombard Street to be situated in an area where many rich London merchants lived and worked. The streets were busy and the skies did not bode well for a dry afternoon.

I stood for some time outside the "Cardinal's Hat", opposite the home of Francis Kyd, with my hands hidden deep inside my woollen pockets, away from the biting wind, not knowing what to do with them otherwise. As I looked across to the black wooden door, with its large square brass plate, hanging above it, bearing the name "Francis Kyd, Scrivener and Court Letter Writer", I felt an overwhelming need to reflect upon my own fear of being turned away by one of Mr Kyd's servants, without ever being seen or heard by Mr Kyd himself, for a possible position with him as an apprentice scrivener. Even though I had tried, during the months that had recently passed, to reassure myself that my deep desire to learn the Secretary's hand was founded upon my own honourable intention to translate Sir Walter Raleigh's trial papers, and then to show them to the world, my heart sank as I reminded myself once again, that I had received no formal education. I knew that my age was against me in all respects, being at that time still a young man. I imagined that my poor appearance and wretched background, coupled with my Master's misfortune, would do little indeed to recommend me to the learned maw I was about to meet for the first time. I discovered that I h ad the greatest respect building up in my mind for Francis Kyd the Scrivener.

I need not have worried unduly, since in my hand I held a letter of recommendation from Sir Walter Raleigh, written in his own neat script upon a parchment, sealed down with a dark red wax, which he had spared me from his own dwindling supply. Sir Walter had written the letter the evening before my departure, and as he did so, he requested that I remain silent, as I stood beside the door of the Bloody Tower. There were several small logs burning in the grate, to warm us both on that Winter morning. As he walked slowly to his desk, beneath the window and seated himself quietly, the only sound that I can recall as I witnessed that event, was the scratching of his quill upon the parchment, and the snapping and cracking of the logs as they burned in the grate. I stood and watched the flaming red cinders as they escaped into the blackened chimney breast, and the tears welled up in my eyes as I realised that upon my departure, I would be replaced by Peter Deane. I had not been permitted to read the contents of that letter, and still I do not know what news it contained, since it was never shown to me. I could only trust in my heart, that he had given a good account of me therein, since my future depended upon it.

****

All I knew of Francis Kyd, I had learned as a servant to Sir Walter Raleigh. As I carried out my duties, I overheard him talking to his keenest visitors to The Bloody Tower, being Edmund Spencer the Poet, Henry Percy the Wizard Earl and the Widow Morley. They had discussed the tragedies of the great literature of our age, and those discussions had not been entirely upon the merits of that work, but indeed upon the fate of its authors. I saw only one letter from Thomas Kyd addressed to the Countesse of Sussex which I plucked from the chest of Sir Walter Raleigh's papers one day as he was about his experiments in his hen house with the Wizard Earl. Thereafter I was resolved to raise up the memory of Kyd to the World and become a Scrivener myself: It read thus:

Thomas Kyd's Letter to Bridget, the Countess of Sussex
(married Robert Radcliffe aged 16, son of Thomas Radcliffe (1553-1557 – Governor of Ireland)

TO: The Vertuously Noble, and Rightly Honoured Lady,
        The Countess of Sussex (concerning Cornelia)

Having no leysure (most noble Lady) but such as evermore is traveld with th' afflictions of the minde, then which the world affoords no greater misery, it may bee wondred at by some, how I durst undertake a matter of this moment: which both reqireth cuning, rest and oportunity; but chiefely, that I would attempt the dedication of so rough, unpollished a worke to the survey of your so worthy selfe. But beeing well instructed in your noble and heroick dispositions, and perfectly assur'd of your honourable favours past (though neyther making needless glozes of the one, nor spoyling paper with the others Pharisaical embroiderie), I have presum'd upon your true conceit and entertainement of these small endevours, that thus I purposed to make known my memory of you and them to be immortall.
A fitter present for a Patronesse so well accomplished I could not find then this faire president of honour, magnamitie, and love. Wherein, what grace that excellent GARNIER hath lost by my defaulte, I shall

beseech your Honour to repaire with the regarde of those so bitter times and privie broken passions that I endured in the writing it. And so vouchsafing but the passing of a Winters weeks with desolate Cornelia, I will assure your Ladiship my next Sommers better travell with the Tragedy of Portia. And ever spend one howre of the day in some kind service to your Honour, and another of the night in wishing you all happines.

Perpetually thus devoting my poore self

Your Honors in all humbleness
THOMAS KYD

In this letter I heard the name of Rome cry out to me and upon turning to the reverse of it I saw these lines:

Actus secondus: Act II

Cic.   Mourne not for Pompey: Pompey could not die
        A better death then for his Countries weale.
        For oft he search't amongst the firece allarms,
        But (wishing) could not find so faire an end;
        Till, fraught with yeeres and honor both at once,
        He gave his bodie (as Barricade)
        For Romes defence by Tyrants over-laide.
        Bravely he died, and (haplie) takes it ill
        That (envious) we repine at heavens will.

The Widow Morley spoke thus: The history of Mary Queen of Scots is the saddest to relate for all her misery and suffering: From the day of her birth and unto her death she had known little happiness, except at the French Court of King Henri II of France and Catherine d'Medici. Upon her return to England after the death of her husband the Dauphin Francois, she had encountered the rage of Queen Elizabeth I for quartering the arms of the English Court. As a girl of 18 she had been enticed to marry the Earl of Leicester. The Patron of William Shakespeare. [write of Sir Philip Sidney and St Bartholomew's

Massacre)

So it came about that I was sent to Lombard Street to live with Francis Kyd, the heartbroken and elderly father of Thomas Kyd.

****

As I approached the home of Francis Kyd, I carried with me in my head the knowledge I have related to you above, and but for that I would have remained in ignorance and known no more now than I did then about the son of Francis Kyd, being Thomas Kyd the Dramatist, since the great bulk of his dramatic works were destroyed after his arrest on the 12th May 1593.

Francis Kyd was by profession a Court letter writer and a Scrivener, being admitted to the Company of Scriveners in 1557. He was sought out by the Church due to his literary background and offered the position of Church Warden at St. Mary Woolnorth from 1575 to 1576. By 1580, Francis Kyd had risen to the position of Warden of the Company of Scriveners and by this time he also employed several other apprentices, one of them being William Dunce, who later gained admission to the Company in 1591. Since Francis Kyd's profession was well paid, he was able to afford servants. Adjacent to the Kyd family lived a family friend known as Francis Coldocke, who worked as a bookseller and publisher, near the "Cardinal's Hat". I had been told many times that Francis Kyd was an extremely eloquent and kindly gentleman, but that his heart had been broken upon the death of his gifted son Thomas Kyd in [April] 1594.

****

Bringing my mind back to the present, I took off my hat and having gathered up all the courage within me, the words of Sir Walter Raleigh were ringing in my ears:

"If you John Talbot, truly desire to serve me hereafter and desire to raise me up in the eyes of this World, you will devote your time to the study of a Scrivener's hand and all that it entails, henceforth. Only your great determination to succeed, will allow me to bear the loss of you".

Remembering those words, I rapped thrice upon the door. I was relieved to be told by a servant, that Francis Kyd was prepared to meet me without delay, whereupon I was led into a small chamber.

After I had handed the letter of recommendation to Francis Kyd, and he had read its contents silently, he began to speak.

He asked me whether I had any knowledge of the work performed by Noverints or Scriverners, and he wondered whether I could relate to him any examples of their duties and purposes. I found myself uttering by keen reply that the only knowledge I had of their work could be seen recorded upon the precious parchments not yet in my possession. I said that they had been promised to me if I succeeded in my studies. I confessed that I would never be equipped to read them until I had been trained by the greatest Master of this art, (such as he was to me).

Francis Kyd then asked me to explain to him why had approached him, or why I wished to become his apprentice at all - considering the late stage I had reached in my life. He persuaded me to understand that I would not be blessed with many years after my training, to perform my role as a Scriverner. He was at great pains to impress upon me that it would rob me dearly, by way of my time during the course of my studies with him, if I were to emerge therefrom, having achieved my purpose. Even if God saw fit to grant me a longer life than most, (which he prayed I would find to be my case).

When he had finished speaking thus, he prayed that I would not be offended by his words. I felt immediately drawn to impress upon him my own determination to learn the Secretary's hand, and said that my ambition had taken a deep root in me long before my arrival there. I said that he had been recommended to me by learned men (which was not true by the first hand, except that I had heard his name mentioned many times as the greatest master of his art), and that if he refused to teach me to become a master Scrivener then all my future hope was lost.

Having convinced Francis Kyd that I was truly earnest, he told me that it would take me seven years or thereabouts, to perfect my study. More particularly, if I wanted to transcribe from the original hands of the learned masters - who effected many great flourishes within their work, which led the mind away, (as if their own purpose was to confuse all but the learned man), causing a sway in mind and thought, which could present a problem to a novice, such as I was to him. Once again he prayed that I would find no offence or malice in his words, because he spoke truly to me taking great care to explain that a younger man would learn the trade of a Noverint in a clear half of the appointed time he had quoted me.

After listening intently to him, I confess in particular, that I felt myself daunted by the prospect of 7 years of study. I had never caused myself to imagine that it would take such a great interval to bring me to perfection (but I did not confess this thought, thinking that I might squander my cause).

I was concerned to relate to him, that my former role as a Servant had recently been brought to a close, upon the arrest and imprisonment of Sir Walter Raleigh. I told him that my time must be occupied in another manner henceforth, since there had never been room for two servants at the Bloody Tower.

Francis Kyd listened intently, but as I progressed, he became visibly pale and effected a manner of great agitation which he displayed to me by removing himself from his seat in a great hurry. Such fright had been brought down upon him at the mention of the verbatim account of Sir Walter Raleigh's trial being translated from the Secretary's hand.

"The Secretary to King James I of England, will take great affront at its publication whereas it would most surely find its way into the World abroad before it could be stopped. Does it not include the Death Warrant signed by Benjamini Fickborne, Militis?" The King does not look for its publication! Therefore, this work will bring you into the greatest danger, as you work towards it through your aims.

He asked if I might show him the precious parchments I spoke of. I told him that they had been stored in a place where no evil might cause them to be searched out considering the great want of them in the minds of men. Indeed they were sought after, as I knew myself by first hand. And if sufficient cause presented itself to me then I could retrieve the same parchment recording the Death Warrant. As I spoke, I gave him several sidelong glances to indicate my disquiet. Whether he took this to mean that my trust in him had failed at this early period of our association, he did not say. He continued to question me with an unremitting anxiety regarding the content of the remainder of the parchments, and I could only reveal to him what I had been assured, and that was that they contained the true account of the trial of Sir Walter Raleigh. He knew that I could not yet read the Scrivener's hand, but I doubted not the truth contained in them.

I revealed to him that Sir Walter had a great chest of papers and that some were belonging to his friend, Christopherus Marlowe. I had scarcely mentioned the name of that great Dramatist, when he let out a shout which I interpreted as joy mingled in anger, as he raised his hands high above his head as if he had just learned a great secret.

I confess that I became doubtful of his hidden thought after that gesture, because he fell silent, and I resolved to tell him no more at that stage in our first meeting (thinking that I had perhaps revealed too much of my ambition to be considered worthy of my keen resolve to succeed). Again he begged that I might show him the great parchments which I spoke of, since he had an interest in the work of Marlowe. I confess that I could not understand his meaning, and thought it invalid, but urged myself to remember again the words of

Thomas Harriott, who had assured me that this man would not betray me in my work.

He noticed that I had fallen silent and was thereafter at great pains to put my mind at rest concerning my ambition. He spoke no more of the hidden parchments for many months, and only asked me at careful moments, the odd or several question(s) but never again became the questioner of my ambition. Nor did he ever ask me to speak out my private thought concerning them, which brought me some comfort where my study brought me little hope of success, at least not within the first two years.

With the passing of time, I admitted that I had encouraged a great secrecy to develop in my mind concerning them, but remembered Thomas Harriott's warning, and my first tuition in the art of secrecy: which had been - never to reveal the results of my prize to any living soul, until I could read and understand them myself. He told me that armed with firsthand knowledge, I would fell my opposition before they could think on the content of my future publication.

I shared the home of Francis Kyd and his wife Anna, for 7 years. I worked harder under the tuition of Kyd and his apprentices than I had ever worked in my life, but never once did I shirk my appointed tasks even though I often translated the work of others, that I had no knowledge of. I was by the end of my apprenticeship, able to produce a proficient Secretary's Hand.

At least two years of my apprenticeship had passed without a thought for the dramatic works of [74]William Shakespeare. He had entered

---

[74] Dr G B Harrison says: In the words of Walter Bagehot, one of the sanest of Victorian critics: "First of all, it may be said that Shakespeare's works could only be produced by a first-rate imagination working on a first-rate experience. It is often difficult to make out whether the author of a poetic creation is drawing from fancy or drawing from experience; but for art on a certain scale, the two must concur. Out of nothing, nothing can be created. Some plastic power is required, however great may be the material. And when such works as Hamlet and othello,

London at the age of 16 and worked upon the stage as an actor, having left off his education at the age of 15 turning his mind to writing and becoming famous in the year.

That morning, I worked on a translation from Latin which presented itself to me as Robert Greene's letter dated Autumn 1592: which he wrote bitterly as he lay dying of hunger, being the best known writer of his age:

"Base minded men, all three of you, if by my misery you be not warned; for unto none of you, like me, sought those burrs to cleave; those puppets, I mean, that spake from our moths, those antics garnished in our colours. is it not strange that I, to whom they all have been beholding, is it not like that you to whom they all have been beholding, shall, were ye in that case as I now am, be both at once of them forsaken? Yes, trust them not; for there is an upstart crow, beautified with our feathers, that with his [75]Tiger's heart wrap'd in a player's hide, supposes he is as well able to bombast out a blank verse as the best of you: and being an absolute Johannes Factotum, is in his own conceit the only Shake-scene in a country. O that I might entreat your rare wits to be employed in more profitable courses, and let those apes imitate your past excellence, and never more acquaint them with your admired inventions!"

---

still more, when both they and others not unequal, have been created by a single mind, it may be fairly said, that not only a great imagination but a full conversancy with the world was necessary to their production. The whole powers of man under the most favourable circumstances are not too great for such an effort. We may assume that Shakespeare had a great experience."

[75] Dr J B Harrison says: "The 'tiger's heart wrap'd in a player's hide" is a parody of a line from King Henry VI, Part 3, Act I, Scene IV, and it seems fairly obvious that the reference is to Shakespeare. The letter was printed soon after in a collection of Greene's scraps, which were put together under the title of A Groatsworth of Wit bought with a Million of Repentance. From 1592 and onwards it is possible to trace Shakespeare's life with more certainty and in greater detail. In March, 1592, Lord Strange's Players, who were then acting at the Rose Theatre in Southwar, produced a new play called Harry the Sixth. It was a great success, and according to a contemporary no less than 10,000 people went to see it in the first six months of its appearance. This has been generally taken to be Shakespeare's First Part of King Henry VI which history was written by Sir Thomas More for Sir Francis Bacon.

I began to grow uneasy one day, as I came to realize that Francis Kyd had repeatedly given me the words of his deceased son, to faithfully copy; even though I had no hope of ever reading or understanding their content at such an early stage of my study.

One day, whilst deeply engrossed in the translation of a short passage from a Scrivener's hand into English, which Francis Kyd had asked me to translate for him. I may readily own that I was so completely taken up in my own mind with my work, that it did not occur to me, the passage was from a play entitled 'St. Thomas More'.

I transcribed it thus:

"Libels set out against the Strangers

As I continued to trace the words upon the parchment with my quill, leaving trails of black ink behind me, being proud of my extraordinary progress, which showed itself to me suddenly, after many years of labour, I found that I could now read and understand the words I had begun to pirate:

Ill May Day Scenes from the Book of Sir Thomas Moore [76]
Scene 1. - A street in the City.]

Enter at one end John Lincolne with [the two Bettses] [77]

together, at the other end enters Fraunces de [Barde, and Doll] a lustie woman, he ha[u]ling her by the arme.

---

[76] A.W. Pollard: Edited by W.W. Greg

[77] Fol3a********check

Doll.   Whether wilt thou hale me?

Bard.   Whether I please, thou are my prize and I pleade purchase of thee.

Doll.   Purchase of me? away ye rascall, I am an honest plaine carpenters   wife and thoughe I have no beautie to like a husband yet whatsoever   is mine scornes to stoupe to a straunger: hand off then when I bid   thee.

Bard: Goe with me quietly, or Ile compell thee.

Doll.   Compell me ye dogges face? thou thinkst thou hast the goldsmithes   wife in hand, whom thou enticedst from her husband with all his plate,   and then thou turndst her home to him again, madste him (like an   asse) pay for his wifes boorde.

Bard. So will I make thy husband too, if please me.

Enter Caveler with a paire of dooves, Williamson the carpenter and Sherwin
         following him.

Doll   Here comes himselfe, tell him so if thou darste.

Cave.   Follow me no further, I say thou shalt not have them.

Wil.   I bought them in Cheapeside, and paide my monie for them.

Sher.   He did Sir indeed, and you offer him wrong, bothe to take them
from   him, and not restore him his monie neither.

Cave.   If he paid for them, let it suffise that I possesse them, beefe and
          brewes may serve such hindes, are piggions meate for a coorse
          carpenter?

Lin.   It is hard when Englishmens pacience must be thus jetted on by straungers and they not dare to revendge their owne wrongs.

Geo.   Lincolne, lets beate them downe, and beare no more of these abuses.

Lin.   We may not Betts, be pacient and heare more.

Doll.   How now husband? what, one staunger take thy food from thee, and another thy wife? bir Lady flesh andblood I thinke can hardly brooke that.

Lin.   Will this geere never be otherwise? must these wrongs be endured?

Geo.   Let us step in, and help to revendge their injurie.

Bard.   What art thou that talkest of revendge? my Lord Ambassadour shall   once more make your Major have a check, if he punishe thee not for saucie presumption.

Wil.   Indeed my lord Mayor, on the Ambassadours complainte, sent me to Newgate one day, because (against my will) [78] I tooke the wall of a straunger. You may doo anything, the goldsmiths wife, and mine now must be at your commandment.

Geo.   the more pacient fooles are ye bothe to suffer it.

Bard.   Suffer it? mend it thou or he if ye can or dare, I tell thee fellowe, and   she were the Mayor of Londons wife, had I her once in

---

[78] I tooke the wall of a straunger. - Thomas Kyd refers to his arrest for the Ill May Day Scene and he was accused of inciting hatred against the Straungers of London (the immigrants).

my possession, I would keep her in spite of him that dusrst say nay.

Geo.   I tell thee Lombard, these wordes should cost they best cappe, where I not curbd by dutie and obedience. The Mayor of Londons wife? Oh God, shall it be thus?

Doll.   Why Bettes, am not I as deare to my husband, as my Lord Mayors wife to him, and wilt thou so neglectly suffer thine owne shame? Hands off proude stranger or [by] him that bought me, if mens milkie harts dare not strike a straunger, yet women will beate them downe, ere they beare these abuses.

Bard.   Mistresse, I say you shall along with me.

Doll.   Touche not Doll Williamson, least she lay thee along on Gods deare earthe. (to Caveler.) And you Sir, that allow such coorse cates to carpenters, whilste pidgions which they pay for, must serve your daintie appetite: deliver them back to my husband again or Ile call so many women to myne assistance, as weele not leave one inche untorne of thee. If our husbands must be brideled by lawe, and forced to beare your wrongs, their wives will be a little lawelesse, and soundly beate ye.

Cave.   Come aware de Bard, and let us goe complaine to my Lord
            Ambassadour. Exeunt ambo.

Doll: I, goe, and send him among us, and weele give him his welcome too. I am ashamed that freeborne Englishmen, having beatten straungers within their owne bound[s] should thus be brau'de and abusde by them at home.

Sher: It is not our lack of courage in the cause, but the strict obedience that we are bound too: I am the goldsmith whose wrongs you talkte of, but how to redresse yours or mine owne, is a matter beyond all our abilities.

Lin.   Not so, not so my good freends, I, though a meane man, a broaker by profession and namd John Lincolne, have long time winckt at these vilde ennormitees with mighty impacience, and, as these two bretheren heere (Betses by name) can witnesse with losse of mind owne liffe would gladly remedie them. "

A cold chill fell upon me as I worked, yet for the thought in my mind I came to no understanding of it, save for the name William Shakespeare, which kept weaving its way forward in my mind. So swiftly did these thoughts come forward to me, and with no uncertain cause for my own safety, did I banish them to the back of my mind. Working in this way I had caused my mind to become a circle of questions, and so I found that as they came forward again, I was apart from myself in the diligence I would show to my work and to the work of William Shakespeare, since I knew these to be his words. [79]

I disregarded my quill in favour of my own conscience and departed from 8 Lombard Street in order to seek out my good friend and companion Peter Deane. [insert here the passage relating to the hidden papers in the great Barn at Syon House - the chest containing the papers which are later conveyed to the basement of 5 Bell Yard]

When I had finished translating the complete passage, I found out completely, the reason for Shakespeare's name coming so readily forward:

The burning down of the [80] Globe Theatre during the performance of

---

[79] The Play Sir Thomas More in the British Museum - [three pages copied out and appended to the play after the arrest, torture and death of Francis Kyd in 1594] found to be in the handwriting of William Shakespeare. William Shakespeare did not write in the hand of a Scrivener, nor did he translate from Italian as Francis Kyd had done. - Did William Shakespeare suffer from writer's cramp? asked Pollard 1923.

[80] Richard Burbage was the most popular actor of his day. He built the Globe Theatre and produced most of William Shakespeare's plays there. William Jaggard published

the play King Henry VIIII: I began to wonder at the connection between that play and the passage from the play Sir Thomas More wherein I had just occupied my own hand in translating it.

I reckoned that the play King Henry VIII written by William Shakespeare in 1613.[81] had some connection with the play 'St Thomas More' who had been King Henry VIII's wretched advisor, beheaded for Treason in 1535 and his head was set up on Tower Bridge.

Shakespeare's plays, together with poetry by Sir Walter Raleigh and Christopher Marlowe and Thomas Nash in the name of William Shakespeare, considering that name to sell more than the rest. At the time of William Shakespeare's death 12 plays were published in his name

[81] King Henry VIII - written late in Shakespeare's career 1613: Act i sc. i: "This holy fox, Or Wolf, or both, (for he is equal ravenous As he is subtle" (and Subtle The Alchemist) a character in Ben Johnson's play - published in 1612 by Walter Burre by Thomas Burre. - Sold at the west-end of Paules. Walter Burre - Sir Walter Raleigh's publisher - History of the World Part I.

[82]Sir Thomas More – Arthur B Allen

His head was set upon Tower Bridge in 1535

Thomas More was born in Milk Street within the City of London in 1478. He was educated at St. Anthony's School, Threadneedle Street, London and was then placed in the household of Cardinal Morton, Archbishop of Canterbury. His father, Sir Thomas More, was a barrister and afterwards became a justice of the Court of King's Bench. Young Thomas went up to Oxford where [83]Linacre taught him Greek. It is an interesting point, this learning of Greek, for the language was not then accepted by the University. It was a novelty, and those who learned it did so voluntarily and were frowned upon by the authorities. So much so that his father removed Thomas from Oxford before he had taken his degree, and entered him at New Inn to begin a study of the Law. When More was twenty years of age he submitted himself to severe training. He grew disgusted with the World, so he took rooms near the Charterhouse, and began to live the life of a [84]Carthusian monk. He wore a hair shirt next his skin, scourged himself every Friday and every fast day. When he slept he lay upon bare boards with a log of wood for his pillow. He allowed himself no more than four to five hours of sleep. But, although he had given himself this type of training, the time came when he was to leave it all, again from choice; but he remained always a devout and a God-fearing man.

---

[82]Source Arthur B. Allen, Rockcliffe, The Oxford Guide Book, St Swithins, Prayer Book, Talbot & Co., 30 Brooke Stree, Holborn, EC1.

[83]Thomas Linacre founded the College of Physicians in 1518 and attended All Souls College Oxford University. All Souls was founded in 1438 by King Henry VI and Henry Chichele, Archbishop of Canterbury.

[84]From the Pitkin Guide: O.S.B. is the Order of St Benedictine Monks.

When More and [85]Erasmus met they became firm friends, and one great result of their meeting was to send More back again to his Greek studies. So the scholarship of More grew and flourished; yet he never forgot that he was by profession a lawyer. More was also a friend of [86]Colet.

In 1502 he was made Under-Sheriff of the City of London, and in 1504 he had the courage to oppose Henry VII's demand for money in the House of Commons. When Henry VII died More was safe again,

---

[85]Desiderius Erasmus. His name was original Gerhard Gerhards, or Geert Geerts. He was born in or about the year 1466 in Rotterdam, and died in 1536. Erasmus travelled widely, became the foremost scholar in Europe, and in the end was recognised as the leader of the Renaissance in Nothern Europe. During his first visit to England he met Sir Thomas More, with whom he became fast friends. he returned to England in 1510 and stayed until 1514, during which time he taught Greek at Cambridge.

[86]Dean John Colet was born in London in 1466. He was educated at St. Anthony's School, London, and then in 1483 went up to Magdalen College, Oxford, where he studied for seven years. In 1493 he visited Paris and Italy to improve his knowledge of both Greek and Latin. It was while on the Continent that Colet met Erasmus. when he returned home in 1497 he entered the Church, settled in Oxford where he lectured upon The Epistles of St. Paul without fee. Actually he held office as rector of Dennington in Suffolk. Later he became prebendary of York and canon of St. Martin's-le-Grand, London. In 1502 he was appointed prebendary of Sarum and 1505 prebendary of St. Paul's. Then, having taken his degree of Doctor of Divinity, Colet was appointed Dean of St. Paul's.

Between the years 1508-1512 he worked on his plans for founding St. Paul's School. They were completed in 1512, and William Lilly the famous grammarian became the first master. The Company of Mercers were appointed as Trustees.

Colet was a fearless and a tireless preacher, and, being much in advance of his times, he made many enemies. He died suddenly in 1519 and was buried in St. Paul's. During his lifetime he served as chaplain to Henry VIII.

and he soon attracted the attention of Henry VIII, and of [87] Wolsey. He was knighted in 1514 and sworn in as a member of the Privy Council. In 1523 he was elected Speaker of the House of Commons. When Wolsey fell into disgrace More became Chancellor. High office did not, however, alter More. When he saw that Henry VIII was determined to divorce [88] Catherine of Aragon in order to marry Anne Boleyn, he resigned. Henry never forgave or forgot. In the end More was executed for his religious opinions together with Bishop Fisher in the year 1535. His head was set upon Tower Bridge. Sir Francis Bacon in a later age took full advantage of the literary works produced by the Martyr Sir Thomas More which is still exploited by the British Government even today, mingled as it has been with the work of Sir Walter Raleigh who was beheaded on the 29th October 1618 and lived at the Court of Queen Elizabeth I being of Bacon's own Elizabethan age and time.

As from Professor Mumby:
Sir Francis Bacon drew material from Sir Thomas More's great work the 'History of the Life and death of King Edward V, and of the

---

[87] Cardinal Wolsey in the 1520s closed 29 assorted religious houses in order to endow a grammar school at his birthplace, Ipswich, and another new college Christ Church at Oxford but none of these actions were an attack on monasticism itself. They simply involved the redeployment for educational purposes of some of the surplus wealth of the religious orders.

[88] Thomas Cranmer: who was born in 1489 and died in 1556 was the famous English reformer, Archbishop of Canterbury in 1533. He Declared Henry VIII's marriage with Catherine of Aragon null and void. He married Henry and Anne Boleyn. Crowned Anne and stood as godfather to the future Queen Elizabeth. He played a foremost part in annulling the marriage with Anne Boleyn, and divorcing Anne of Cleves. Encouraged the translation of the Bible, and ordered a copy to be placed in every Church. Gave to the Book of Common Prayer its beautiful and rhythmical language. He was burned at the stake in 1556 in Oxford and between the outer and inner doors of the Baliol College Quadrangles (whose proper name is 'The King's Hall and College of Brasenose') where the wooden doors can be seen scorched by the flames which burned to death Archbishop Cranmer and Bishops Latimer and Ridley when they were executed in Broad Street in the 1550s for their Protestant beliefs.

usurpation of Richard III.' Sir Francis Bacon must also have made some use of the manuscript treasures of Sir Robert Cotton, even though under the sentence which was imposed upon him he was excluded from London.

More's great work was Utopia, wherein he expressed ideas very much in advance of his times. Sir Thomas More's Utopia. With Notes by the Rev. Professor Lumby, D.D. 1876. London: Cambridge Warehouse, 17 Paternoster Row.

The Order of St Benedictine – from the days of St Thomas More, before King Henry VIII destroyed all the Monasteries, having broken with the Church of Rome, in order to divorce Katherine of Aragon, who had formerly been married to King Henry's brother, Arthur, and marry Anne Boleyn – From The Pitkin Guide

This is how the Monks lived

From the Prologue to the Rule of St Benedict
"In living our life . the path of God's commandments is run with unspeakable loving sweetness; so that never leaving His school, but persevering in the monastery until death in His teaching, we share by our patience the sufferings of Christ and so merit to be partakers of his kingdom."

In medieval England, as elsewhere in Europe, there were many communities of monks and nuns. Although their rules differed in detail, each monastic foundation and house had certain features in common. These derived from the original monastic ideal and Rule of St Benedict (c.480-547). They all lived as communities, bound in obedience to the orders of an acknowledged head; an abbot, abbess, prior or prioress. They all took vows of celibacy and wore distinctive habits. In theory, they all lived in poverty, although in practice this usually meant that as individuals they possessed very little personal property. As members of communities some of them were collectively very wealthy indeed.

A Monk's Summer Timetable

Midnight	**Matins in the church**
1 a.m.	**Return to bed**
6.0 a.m.	**Prime in the church**
6.30 a.m.	**Breakfast**
	Work on reading

9a.m.	**Chapter Mass in the church**
10a.m.	**Chapter meeting in the Chapter House**
11a.m.	**High Mass in the church**
12 noon	**Dinner**
	Siesta
2p.m.	**Nones in the church**
2.30p.m.	**Work**
4p.m.	**Vespers in the church**
4.30p.m.	**Work**
6p.m.	**Supper**
7p.m.	**Compline (evening prayer) in the church, then to bed**

Vespers of the Dead:
Priest: I will walk before the Lord in the land of the living.
Psalm 116
1.   I am well pleased: that the Lord hath heard the voice of my prayer;
2.   That he hath inclined his ear unto me: therefore will I call upon Him as long as I live.
3.   The snares of death compassed me round about: and the pains of hell gat hold upon me.
4.   I shall find trouble and heaviness, and I will call upon the Name of the Lord: O Lord, I beseech Thee, deliver my soul.
5.   Gracious is the Lord, and righteous: yea, our God is merciful.
6.   The Lord preserveth the simple: I was in misery, and He helped me.
7.   Turn again then unto thy rest, O my soul: for the Lord hath rewarded thee.
8.   And why: Thou hast delivered my soul from death: mine eyes from tears, and my feet from falling.
Rest eternal: grant to them, O Lord. And let light perpetual: shine upon them.
All Say: I will walk before the Lord in the land of the living.
Priest: Woe is me, O Lord, that I am constrained to dwell with Mesech.

Psalm 120

1.   When I was in trouble I called upon the Lord: and he heard me.
2.   Deliver my soul, O Lord, from lying lips: and from a deceitful tongue.
3.   What reward shall be given or done unto thee, thou false tongue: even mighty   and sharp arrows, with hot burning coals.
4.   Woe is me, that I am constrained to dwell with Mesech: and to have my habitation among the tents of Kedar.
5.   My soul hath long dwelt among them: that are enemies unto peace.
6.   I labour for peace, but when I speak unto them thereof: they make them ready to battle.

All say: Woe is me, O Lord, that I am constrained to dwell with Mesech.

Priest: The Lord shall preserve thee from all evil: yea, it is even He that shall keep thy soul.

Psalm 121.

1.   I will lift up mine eyes unto the hills: from whence cometh my help.
2.   My help cometh even from the Lord: Who hath made heaven and earth.
3.   He will not suffer thy foot to be moved: and He that keepeth thee will not   sleep.
4.   Behold, He that keepeth Israel: shall neither slumber nor sleep.
5.   The Lord himself is thy keeper: the Lord is thy defence upon thy right hand;
6.   So that the sun shall not burn thee by day: neither the moon by night.
7.   The Lord shall preserve thee from all evil; yea, it is even He that shall keep thy   soul.
8.   The Lord shall preserve thy going out, and thy coming in: from this time forth for evermore.

Rest eternal: grant to them, O Lord.

And let light perpetual: shine upon them.

All say: The Lord shall preserve thee from all evil: yea, it is even He that shall keep thy soul.

Priest: If what is done amiss Thou wilt be extreme to mark, O Lord: O Lord, who may abide it.

Psalm 130.

1. Out of the deep have I called unto Thee, O Lord: Lord, hear my voice.
2. O let Thine ears consider well: the voice of my complaint.
3. If Thou, Lord, wilt be extreme to mark what is done amiss: O Lord, who may abide it?
4. For there is mercy with Thee: therefore shalt Thou be feared.
5. I look for the Lord; my soul doth wait for Him: in his word is my trust.
6. My soul fleeth unto the Lord: before the morning watch, I say, before the morning watch.
7. O Israel, trust in the Lord, for with the Lord there is mercy: and with Him is plenteous redemption.
8. And He shall redeem Israel: from all his sins.

Rest eternal: grant to them, O Lord.

And let light perpetual shine upon them.

All say: If what is done amiss Thou wilt be extreme to mark, O Lord: O Lord, who may abide it?

Priest: Despise not, O Lord, the works of Thine own Hands.

Psalm 138.

1. I will give thanks unto Thee, O Lord, with my whole heart: even before the gods will I sing praise unto Thee.
2. I will worship toward Thy holy temple, and praise Thy Name, because of Thy loving-kindness and truth: for Thou hast magnified Thy Name and Thy Word above all things.
3. All the kings of the earth shall praise thee O Lord: for they have heard the words of Thy Mouth.
5. Yea, they shall sing in the ways of the Lord: that great is the glory of the Lord.
6. For though the Lord be high, yet hath He respect unto the lowly: as for the proud, He beholdeth them afar off.
7. Though I walk in the midst of trouble, yet shalt Thou

refresh me: Thou shalt stretch forth Thy hand upon the furiousness of mine enemies, and Thy Right Hand shall save me.

8.   The Lord shall make good His Lovingkindness toward me: yea, Thy mercy, O Lord, endureth for ever; despise not then the works of Thine own Hands.

All say: Despise not, O Lord, the works of Thine own Hands.

V.   I heard a voice from Heaven saying unto me,

R.   Blessed are the dead which die in the Lord.

Priest: All that the Father hath given Me shall come to Me: and him that cometh unto Me, I will in no wise cast out.

Magnificat.

1.   My Soul doth magnify the Lord: and my spirit hath rejoiced in God my Saviour.

2.   For He hath regarded: the lowliness of His handmaiden.

3.   For behold from henceforth: all generations shall call me blessed.

4.   For He that is mighty hath magnified me: and Holy is His Name.

5.   And His mercy is on them that fear Him: throughout all generations.

6.   He hath shewed strength with His arm: He hath scattered the proud in the   imagination of their hearts.

7.   He hath put down the mighty from their seat: and hath exalted the humble and meek.

8.   He hath filled the hungry with good things: and the rich He hath sent empty away.

9.   He remembering His mercy hath holpen His servant Israel: as He promised to our forefathers, Abraham and his seed, for ever.

Rest eternal: grant to them, O Lord.

And let light perpetual: shine upon them.

All say:All that the Father hath given Me shall come to Me: and him that cometh unto Me I will in no wise cast out.

All kneel:Our Father (secretly).
V.   And lead us not into temptation.
R.   But deliver us from evil.

Principal Monastic Orders: Ancient Mystical Order Rosae Crucis Raleigh's School of Night continued their literary work.

Monks	Canons	Friars
Benedictine	Augustinian	Augustinian
Cistercian	Premonstratensian	Dominican (Black friars)
Carthusian		Franciscan (Grey friars)
Cluniac		Carmelite (White friars)

English monasticism is as old as English Christianity. Augustine and his companions who came to Canterbury in 597 all lived by the Benedictine rule. Aidan and his companions who evangelized the north were monks of a Celtic style characterized by its reclusive, extremely ascetic way of life.

By the time of the Black Death (1348-9) there were nearly 1,000 houses of which 200 were friaries and 150 were nunneries in the United Kingdom. It is estimated that 14,000 men and 3,000 women lived the religious life. In April 1536, in the 27th year of the reign of King Henry VIII, there were scattered throughout England and Wales more than 800 monasteries, nunneries and friaries and within them 10,000 monks, canons, nuns and friars. By April 1540 there were none. Their work became Shakespeare's work. Their work became Sir Francis Bacon's work.

In the 1520s Cardinal Wolsey closed 29 assorted religious houses. When the Dissolution proper began in 1536 with the Act for the Suppression of the Lesser Monasteries, it was also at first presented as a reform. In the introduction of the Act, considerable stress was laid upon the worthiness of the 'great and honourable monasteries' where religion was 'right well kept'. They were contrasted with the smaller houses which, it claimed, were 'sunk irredeemably in iniquity', had 'resisted all attempts at reform for 200 years or more', and should therefore be closed down. It further suggested 'The idle and dissolute monks and nuns who live in these little dens of vice should be dispersed amongst the greater abbeys where they will, by discipline and example, be brought to mend their ways. The properties and endowments thus vacated can then be transferred to the king, to put such better uses as he may think fit.'

In 1536 three out of every 10 religious houses were suppressed by the 1536 Act and these the smallest and least significant, there was still considerable hostility towards the government, especially in the north. In October 1536, a rebellion, known as the 'Pilgrimage of Grace', took place. It was not solely about the Dissolution, but rather an accumulation of grievances of which the Dissolution proved the final spur to action. Dispossessed monks and nuns were encouraged to re-enter their former homes and to resume their former way of life. The permanent restoration of suppressed abbeys was high on the rebels' list of demands and the greater religious houses were pressed very hard to contribute men and money to the cause.

But the rebellion failed. The King played for time, and when the rebels fell out among themselves he crushed them without mercy. Those larger abbeys which had helped the rebels were immediately in danger. Often on very flimsy pretexts, abbots were executed, monks turned out and abbey properties forfeited. These were the first of the greater abbeys to fall.

By 1540 the Dissolution was complete. The buildings and properties of all religious houses up and down the country had passed, by suppression or surrender, into the hands of the Crown. The religious had been pensioned off and dispersed. Their altar plate and vestments had been gathered into the king's jewel house. Their bells had been recast as cannon in the Tower foundry. The lead had been stripped from the abbey roofs for use as shot. To reshape it ready for transport, local pit furnaces were dug at many abbeys, and the roofing timbers used as fuel.

Oxford University: by Arthur B. Allen

1510   Henry VIII granted its charter.

1570   The University was incorporated by Queen Elizabeth.

1602   [89]The Bodleian Library was opened . Sir Thomas Bodley the founder of the famous Library, was born in 1544. His father John Bodley had to leave England when Thomas was about twelve years of age because of his Protestant views. Thomas accompanied his father and studied in Geneva University. But when Queen Elizabeth ascended the throne of England the Bodleys returned, and Thomas entered Magdalen College, Oxford. In 1563 he took his degree as Bachelor of Arts and in 1564 was admitted a Fellow of Merton College. In 1566 he took his degree as Master of Arts and left Oxford ten years later to make a tour of Europe. Bodley spent four years travelling and then returned again to Oxford. He became Gentleman Usher to Queen Elizabethan. We next hear of Thomas Bodley as Ambassador to Denmark, and then as Ambassador to several of the German princes. After being sent on a secret mission to France he went as Ambassador to the United Provinces. He retired from the Court in 1597 and began the foundation of his library. He was knighted by James I. Sir Thomas died in 1612.

In 1602 when he opened it, his library contained some 2,000 volumes, many of which he gave himself. In 1610 he obtained a grant from the Stationers' Company of a copy of every work printed in the country.

Let us turn now to the history of the Colleges themselves and discover

---

[89] The Bodleian Library, the main library of the University of Oxford, is one of the largest, richest and oldest in the world. In 1610 the Library secured the right to a copy of every book published in this country, and so became the first copyright library; there are now five others in the British Isles. The Bodleian has over four million books, countless papers and pamphlets, priceless manuscripts and many works of art.

which were founded during the same period:

Brasenose was founded by William Smythe, Bishop of Lincoln, and Sir Richard Sutton, in 1509.

Corpus Christi was founded by Richard Fox, Bishop of Winchester in 1516.

Christ Church, originally founded by Wolsey and called Cardinal College in 1525, was re-founded by Henry VIII as Christ Church in 1532.

Trinity was founded by Sir Thomas Pope in 1554.

St. John's was founded by Sir Thomas Whyte, Lord Mayor of London, in 1555.

Jesus College was founded by Dr. Hugh Price and Queen Elizabeth in 1571.

HIC JACET: SIR WALTER RALEIGH

Thomas Kyd and Christopherus Marlowe shared a writing chamber in 1591/2 but an evil and wicked double tragedy had fallen down upon them and when this hint was given to me that it was in some way connected to William Shakespeare in a sinister way, it was enough to chill my bones and this news caused my mind to be so overtaken with thought that I could not sleep for the heavy reckoning of it.

The Globe Theatre is burned to the grounde in Londone

Letter by Wootton recording the burning down of the Globe Theatre - a performance of King Henry VIII - recorded thus [90] - 2nd July 1613

'["Now let matters of state sleep, I will entertain you at the present with what hath happened this week at the Bank's side. The King's Players had a new play, called 'All is True', representing some pieces of the reign of Henry the 8th, which was set forth with many extraordinary circumstances of pomp and majesty, even to the matting of the stage, the Knights of the Order with their Georges and Garter, the Guards with their embroidered coats, and the like : sufficient in truth within a while to make greatness very familiar, if not ridiculous. Now, King Henry, making a masque at the Cardinal Wolsey's house, and certain cannons being shot off at his entry, some of the paper, or other stuff, wherewith one of them was stopped, did light on the thatch, where being thought at first but an idle smoke, and their eyes more attentive to the show, it kindled inwardly, and ran round like a train, consuming within less than an hour the whole house to the very ground. This was the fatal period of that virtuous fabric; wherein yet nothing did perish, but wood and straw, and a few forsaken cloaks; only one man had his breeches set on fire, that would perhaps have broiled him, if he had not by the aid of a provident wit put it out with bottle-ale."]'

[seek out Peter Deane - to find evidence] - depart and return.

As the darkness of that evening approached on slow wings, I witnessed my own desire to seek out Francis Kyd. With deep feelings of my master's great honour (now raised up) in my mind, and with a respect for my future profession in my heart, (feeling that I had caused my mind to stoop very low in the future estimation of my kind employer

---

[90] Sir Henry Wotton wrote of the burning down of the Globe Theatre on July 2nd, 1613.

for my earlier deeds that day) I made my way to his chamber and had caused myself to be worked into an angry passion through my own misunderstanding. I rushed angrily from my desk and hurried through all the likely places in the house in search of Francis Kyd. I found myself exhausted and yet how easily I might have found him occupied in another part of the house, being already prepared for me in his study chamber, and as it was the very same chamber that I had been invited into to take my first interview with him upon my arrival at that place years before, the spirit within me seemed to darken and almost fled entirely, as I found I had cause to enter the room so justly defined for his purpose (as I saw it then).

I was so confused in my mind that I felt I must drive myself forward in my resolve to speak to Francis Kyd, and to enquire why he had caused me to work as a Pirate in translating the already known work of William Shakespeare, when Shakespeare would do as well to attend to those tasks himself.

My purpose momentarily left me, as I searched my mind again for the cause to enter his private chamber. I found him seated at his desk and a great gall broke out in my throat so that I could not speak for fear of my own memory failing me. There he sat behind his desk, taking sips of his preferred red wine from a silver goblet, in a very slow and exaggerated manner, as if to show some contentment to me, which enticed me into a great anger at his demeanour. He smiled very kindly towards me, as if to put me at ease with him, and showed a great understanding through his manner, as I approached him. It were to me as if he expected me to appear at any given moment. He spoke out to me, quite readily at first, saying : "I have waited for you to appear, John Talbot, and I have much to reveal to you within this Chamber".

Feeling that I would be questioned upon my knowledge of William Shakespeare and his work, (just as I in turn had caused myself to stand before my tutor in order to question his own knowledge) my eyes darkened as I looked into his face. The room, which had been bright with the glow of eight half burned candles (indicating to me that he had been seated there for several hours), seemed to dim as I entered at that moment and suddenly there was no light offered to me. I turned my face toward the warm, bright glow of his comfortable fireside and yet no light came into my eyes save a few glowing red embers.

I could sense that there was some dark secret hidden deep in his mind, concerning his deceased son, Thomas Kyd and although I had been acquainted with a little of his history, (since The Spanish Tradgedie was the most popular Elizabethan play after Thomas Kyd's death)[91].

Remembering my earlier torments concerning William Shakespeare and the work I had copied, I meant to speak out on the play Sir Thomas More and yet

Raleigh's Headless Warriors[92] came foremost into my mind.

Francis Kyd stood and leaning forward, he reached out his warm hand to me, and as he did so, he clutched at my right arm where his fingers grew spiteful and angry all at once, and my arm grew cold as he spoke:

*[My son, was the original author of Hamlet[93], who died for his work

---

[91] registered at Stationers Hall in 1594

[92] Sir Walter Raleigh, The Great Rich and Beautiful Empire of Guiana (1596; UK: The Trustees of the British Library, 1596/19[ ]) Pages. "whose heads appear not above their shoulders they are called Ewaipanoma; they are reported to have their eyes in their shoulders and their mouths in the middle of their breasts, and that long train of hair growing backward between their shoulders".

[93] F S Boas - The Works of Thomas Kyd 1922 referring to the Spanish Tradgedie ... ["Er...Hamlet"].

William Shakespeare - Hamlet - 1601

and through his great courage, and even throughout his torture at Newgate in 1593[94], he did not falter or reveal where it was hidden. I have his manuscripts here, some secreted away in the very wall of this house, and others deep below the floor. I have resolved never search them out while my own fear remains greater than his.

He wrote in Latin, he wrote in a Scrivener's hand and if that were not enough, he translated the great tradgedies from Italian and German into English for [Henry the Fourth Earl of Sussex]; but show me the hand of William Shakespeare and his translation of the original story of Hamlet which was written in the Autumn of 1601?

The story of Hamlet was taken from a translation first found in Historia Danica of Saxo Grammaticus written in the 13th century (printed in Paris in 1514). It was re-told by Belleforest in Histoires Tragiques 1570 and dramatised into the English by Thomas Kyd pre-1589.

It is not for me to prove him the author of that play and yet in memory of his achievements in life and for his death at the age of 34[2], I ask you to search your mind and conscience, John Talbot. I stand here and beg you to reveal the manuscripts that will prove his innocence and that of Marlowe, and bring them peace in the World where I will soon join them.

Or Is it to Othello that you wish me to refer for the Headless men? I will bring you to understand that as Sir Walter Raleigh was taken to be

---

[94] On leaving the Merchant Taylors School, founded in 1561, Thomas Kyd served his father as an apprentice Scrivener or Noverint, under whose tuition he learned to produce a perfect Secretary's hand. By 1589 Kyd had changed his career and worked as a translator from Italian into English and translated the 'Householder's Philosophie'.

tried at Winchester Castle in November 1603, the King called his Players to Wilton in Salisbury in December 1603 in time to see the Judgment passed upon Sir Walter Raleigh on the 13th December. The King's Men, formerly the Lord Chamberlain's Men after March 1603. The King paid his Players £40 each and made them a gift of £30 each for loss caused by the Plague which raged in London.

I became so enraged to hear that Raleigh's "Headless Warriors" were contained in William Shakespeare's Tempest making a parody of his great work contained in the account of his first voyage to Guiana that I knocked the cup from Francis Kyd's hand and bid him release me from this solemn and unenviable work in order that I might seek out my rest in my own way and I further requested him to understand that my aim had been to study the Scrivener's hand so that I might hereafter write the history of Sir Walter Raleigh peacefully and diligently.

But he said to me, as he caused his wretched and suddenly uncaring face to be drawn into the light of the glowing candle, "I have no fear for my safety when I speak truthfully and yea, with the hope in your heart that has been put there by the great Lord of Heaven, I should cause you no fear for your own. Nor will God allow fear into your heart for the work I speak of has been created by great Noblemen and Gentlemen and each man has caused me to be patient and I have worked towards this purpose for many years in order to bring these works into the light of common knowledge, so that ignorant men can share in their glorious memory. Shakespeare will not steal their memory nor the glorious memory of their words from them after their death as he did before it."

Trust not any knowledge that is weak in your mind concerning this work, since I have preserved it and now I will cause it to be brought into the open in order that I might show the work relating to the ancient Kings of England to be the work of Marlowe (Edward II), and Henry Greene (Henry IV?)[95] and Heywood.

---

[95] In 1599 John Hayward issued a proser version of Henry IV with a dedication to the Earl of Essex and Hayward was imprisoned in the Tower of London.

"If you have cause to scorn my thought, think on it plainly: It took a learned man (such as you call me) an entire lifetime to learn my art, and to present it to you with great perfection, but I could not have written the history of Henry the IV, or the V or the VI without some tutor to guide me. Where was William Shakespeare's tutor after he left off his education at 15, fled Stratford upon Avon in at the age of 17 and I will reveal that he first acted upon the stage before he honed his feather quill.

Here Thomas Kyd stood and waved a great sheath of parchments at me with such passion that I had cause to believe at that moment that he was ready to hand them to me for translation.

William Shakespeare was busy writing Othello and drew upon the Headless Warriors and Ewapanaima(sp) recorded in Sir Walter Raleigh's book the Great Rich and Beautiful Empire of Guiana and performed his play before the King and Court at Whitehall Palace on November 1st 1604.

Find original version of John Talbot's meeting with Francis Kyd in this room - he goes to the cupboard and brings out a scroll of papers, two silver goblets and a bottle of red wine in a toast to [Robert Greene:] and proceeds to read
to John Talbot to enlighten his mind to the true events:

To "gentlemen his quondam acquaintances that spent their wits in making plays", HE WARNS THREE OF THEM (who are probably Marlowe, [Nashe], Peele and Kyd, against a new writer:

"Base minded men, all three of you, if by my misery you be not warned; for unto none of you , like me, sought those burrs to cleave;

those puppets, I mean, that spake from our moths, those antics garnished in our colours. it is not strange that I, to whom they all have been beholding, is it not like that you to whom they all have been beholding, shall, were ye in that case as I now am, be both at once of them forsaken? Yes, trust them not; for there is an upstart crow, beautified with our feathers, that with his Tiger's heart wrap'd in a player's hide, supposes he is as well able to bombast out a blank verse as the best of you: and being an absolute Johannes Factotum, is in his own conceit the only Shake-scene in a country. O that I might entreat your rare wits to be employed in more profitable courses, and let those apes imitate your past excellence, and never more acquaint them with your admired inventions!"[96]
Robert Greene 1592

The murder of Chistopher Marlowe in 1593, and the arrest and torture of Thomas Kyd in 1593, who died in 1594.

---

[96] "The letter was printed soon after in a collection of Greene's scraps, which were put together under the title of A Groatsworth of Wit bought with a Million of Repentance.

The Explanation for Thomas Kyd's Arrest

Christopher Marlowe is Murdered

1593   12 May. Thomas Kyd arrested and heretical papers which he attributes to Marlowe, discovered in his room [Harleian MSS].

18 May. Privy Council issue warrant for the arrest of Christopherus Marlowe, at the house of his patron Mr Thomas Walsingham at Scadbury, Chislehurst, in Kent or elsewhere [Acts of Privy Council].

20 May. Christofer Marley, Gentleman of London answers the warrant and is required to remain in daily attendance [Acts of Privy Council].

Slain by Ingram Frizer in the company of Robert Poley and Nicholas Skeres at a house in Deptford Strande, which was a few hundred yards from Deptford Bridge.

Famous Classical Schools founded between 1485 – 1603 in England

From the Background Book, The Spacious Days of Queen Elizabeth I

[97]

Aldenham 1597
Felsted 1564
Allhallows, Rousdon 1515
Giggleswick 1512
Bedford 1552
Gresham 1555
Bedford Modern 1566
Harrow 1571
Berkhamstead 1542
Haverfordwest Grammar School 1488
Brentwood, Essex 1557
Bristol Grammar School 1532
Highgate 1562
Bromsgrove 1527
King Edward's, Birmingham 1552
Christ College, Brecon 1541
[98] King Edward VI, Stourbridge 1552
Christ Hospital 1552
The Cooper's Company's School 1536
King Henry VIII, Coventry 1545

---

[97] Tthe Spacious Days of Queen Elizabeth – Arthur B Allen

[98] Edward Seymour the Earl of Hertford, the Uncle to Edward VI became protector during Edward's minority

HIC JACET: SIR WALTER RALEIGH

King's College, Taunton 1522
Coventry, Bablake School 1560
King's School, Bruton 1519
Cranbrook 1520
King's School, Canterbury 1600
The Crypt, Gloucester 1539
King's School, Chester 1541
Dauntsey's School, Devizes 1543
King's School, Ely 1543
Dorchester Grammar School 1569
King School, Macclesfield 1502
Elizabeth College, Guernsey 1563
King's School, Rochester 1542
Emanuel School, London 1694
King's School, Worcester 1541
Leeds Grammar School, 1552
St. Bees', Cumberland 1587
Maidstone Grammar School 1549
St. Olave's, London 1572
Manchester Grammar School 1515
St. Paul's 1509
Mercers' School 1542
Sherborne 1550
Sedburgh 1525
Merchant Taylors' 1561
Thomas Kyd, Dramatist attended this school
Royal Grammar School, Newcastle-on Tyne 1545
Shrewsbury 1552
Stamford, Lincolnshire 1532
Nottingham High School 1513
Stockport Grammar School 1487
Oakham 1584
Stonyhurst 1592
Oundle 1556
Sutton Valence 1576

Pocklington School, East Yorkshire Tonbridge 1553
Uppingham 1584
Whitgift 1596
Wakefield 1591
Wolverhampton Grammar
School 1512
Queen Mary's Walsall 1554
Repton 1557
York, Archbishop Holgate's School 1546
Rugby 1567
Wellingborough 1595

******

[99] The Dramatist, Thomas Kyd was born to Anna and Francis Kyd and baptised at St. Mary Woolnorth in the Ward of Langborn, on the 6th November 1558. Thomas had a younger sister Ann, who was born on the 24th September 1561 and a brother named William, who outlived Thomas and died in 1602. His mother died towards the end of 1605.

Thomas Kyd, Dramatist

---

[99] By the time Thomas Kyd had reached the age of 32 his life was over. He was arrested and then tortured in Newgate Prison and died soon afterwards. He had been Christopher Marlowe's co-writer. Very few people of today have ever heard of Thomas Kyd. That is because he wrote ER... Hamlet, among other great Elizabethan tragedies. He also used to translate from Italian into English. Kyd had received a brilliant education, just as Christopher Marlowe had. Kyd was educated at the Merchant Taylors' School, founded in 1561, where he received a classical education and could write in English, Italian, French and Latin.

In this story, I have tried to create a scene so that you can imagine what Thomas Kyd's life was like as a child and how he came to be such a great writer, and then his arrest and torture at Newgate Prison. Only fragments of his work have survived. This is because the Privy Councillors stole all his work when they searched his writing chamber after his arrest. Among Kyd's papers were works he had written with Christopher Marlowe.

Francis Kyd was by profession a court letter writer or Scrivener, and he became a member of the Company of Scriveners in 1557. Due to his literary background Francis Kyd, was sought after by the Church and offered the position of Church Warden at St Mary Woolnorth, which he held from 1575 to 1576.

The Kyd family were fairly wealthy and because Francis Kyd's occupation was well paid, they were able to employ servants at their house in Lombard Street, a well to do area in the City of London, where many rich London merchants lived. Adjacent to them lived a family friend, Francis Coldocke, who worked as a bookseller and publisher near the "Cardinal's Hat".

By 1565, when Thomas Kyd had reached the age of seven, he was already able to read and write in Latin and in English, which was unusual at this time, since children were rarely taught English, even in Grammar schools.

Thomas was very quick to learn and he was a quiet, but strong willed child. He had several friends of his own age in Lombard Street but he rarely found time to play the games that other boys of his own age played, being the outdoor games for younger children, Leapfrog, Battledore and Shuttlecock, Seesaw and Bowling the Hoop, because he was always so eager to learn, and was rarely without his books. One of his friends, William Coldocke, the son of Francis Coldocke the bookseller, shared his love of learning, and had at the age of six taught him to play chess, on a circular chess board, with four circles of sixteen spaces, each space being black and then white. It was a game that pleased Thomas and he spent many hours playing: The chessmen were laid on opposite sides of the board, thus:

6, 1, 2, 6
6, 4, 4, 6
6, 5, 5, 6
6, 3, 3, 6

The King: 1. The Queen of Fevee: 2, The Castle, Rook, or Rock 3, The Knight 4, The Bishop or Alfin 5, and The Pawns 6.

William Coldocke also used to visit the Kyd's house for daily lessons in reading and writing, which were provided by Francis Kyd who employed a Tutor for Thomas, and firmly believed that Thomas would learn more quickly if he had a companion in the classroom, which was a little office at the back of the house. William Coldocke would often bring books with him from his father's bookshop and they would use them to copy from, and this gave Thomas an early love of books and literature. Thomas was also taught music and the instrument he played was a tenor Viol, the ancestor to the Violin and his mother Ann, an accomplished musician, played the Spinet, an oblong harpsichord, which was also known as the Virginal, a name given to it since it was mainly played by women, but others said it gained the name Virginal because it was used to accompany the Angelus ad Virginem.

When Francis Kyd was satisfied that his son had the necessary aptitude for learning, and that his quick wit could secure him in a career as a Noverint, he decided that it was time for his son to receive a classical education.

Francis Kyd made preparations for Thomas to be entered at the Merchant Taylor's School, in London, which had been founded in 1561, and having visited the school to satisfy himself that it was the right place to send Thomas, he had not been disappointed with what he saw and heard about that School. He then wasted no further time and entered Thomas for his first examination.

On the morning that Thomas was due to take his entrance examination, he found himself being woken earlier than usual and had been dressed in his best clothes. He stood before his mother, Anna, and he was wearing his dark grey tunic with a white round necked shirt underneath, which buttoned up to his neck, black leggings and black leather shoes. His mother was fussing over him in order to arrange his light brown hair to best effect, whilst telling him that his appearance was very important to her, and that he must be neat at all times so that she would be very proud of him.

Thomas twisted and turned anxiously as he reached out in order to retrieve his ABC book, from the middle of the table, where he had left it the night before. It contained the catechism in Latin and English, which he had been memorizing. He could see that his four year old sister Ann was trying to reach it, so that she could practice her alphabet, and she was holding a pencil in her hand and looking very mischievous.

"No Ann, it is my book! Leave it there! I need it to practice from in a minute when Father tests me, and I don't want you scribbling all over it! You can use the Horn Book instead, because you are still too young for the ABC book".

A Horn Book was the first book an Elizabethan child would use, to learn to read and write before he went to School. The Horn Book contained the Alphabet, with the vowels picked out, and a child would be taught to read by his mother. It also contained a collection of monosyllables, an Invocation and the Lord's Prayer. The other side was blank for the child to learn to write.

The Horn Book looked like a flat piece of wood with a handle at the bottom of it and a piece of parchment was pinned to it containing the following:

~~~~~~

First the sign of the cross: + Abcdefghijklmnopqrstuvwxyz & ... aeiou

The next line was called the Christ Cross row:

ABCDEFGHIJKLMNOPQRSTUVWXYZ.

AEIOU   **AEIOU**

AB EB IB OB UB   BA BE BI BO BU
AC EC IC OC UC   CA CE CI CO CU
AD ED ID OD UD   DA DE DI DO DU

In the name of the Father, and of the Son, and of the Holy Ghost
                                                        Amen

Our Father, which art in Heaven,
Hallowed be thy name; thy ....
Kingdom come thy Will be done on
Earth, as it is in Heaven. Give us
this Day our daily Bread; and ...
forgive us our trespasses, as we forgive them that trespass against us -
And lead us not into Temptation, but
deliver us from Evil, Amen.

~~~~~~

"Look Ann! the Horn Book is over there on the bookshelf". said
Thomas, as he pointed to the other side of the room. At which news
his younger sister sat down on the floor and started to cry in an effort
to win some attention.

His mother, Anna, had finished combing Thomas's hair and said "You
won't be needing the ABC book any more now Thomas. We will give
the Horn Book and the ABC book to Ann shall we? And then she can
learn her alphabet and catechism whilst you are out at school all day,
just like you used to do when William was at School. Remember?
You are growing up now and you will be using paper and books from
now on. Now go and see your father, he needs to talk to you."

One of the servants was busy mopping up the milk that little Ann had
just spilt all over the table, and clearing away the cups and plates on to

a tray as the family had just finished their breakfast.

His father, Francis, was watching everyone impatiently as he sat at the head of the table, which was placed near the warmth of the hearth, and he was most anxious to ensure that Thomas would pass his entrance examination. He drummed his fingers on the table top in anticipation, as he waited to speak to his youngest son, and as his impatience grew he called across the room to Thomas who was looking for the Horn Book to give to his sister.

"Now Thomas! Listen carefully to me" We will leave for the School in one hour. Have you prepared yourself and learned your catechism?" asked his father firmly. "I would not want you to fail, because the School to which I am about to send you is the very best that I can afford. You will receive a much better education than I did and that is very fortunate for you! Why, in my day, a boy must never be educated to a higher standard than that of his father before him, since it was a commonly held belief that if a child were educated to a higher standard, then he would become an upstart through his learning, and the result would be that his father would not be able to rule him by any measure!"

"Yes Sir!" replied Thomas - "I have learned my catechism thoroughly just as you said I should. I have practised it over and over, and written it out in a fair hand in the ABC book, both in English and in again in Latin. Shall I read it to you first in Latin or in English, Father? said Thomas eagerly, as he held his ABC book up proudly for his father to inspect. He had been looking forward to his day of enrollment at the Merchant Taylor's School for a long time now and had been well prepared in advance.

"Well first of all, I will hear it in Latin, because perhaps that will be the more difficult for you, but give the 'ABC' book to your Mother! You will not be permitted to take that with you to the examination and the Headmaster will expect you to recite from memory and write from memory. Can you do that for me?"

"Yes, I know I can!" said Thomas confidently as he walked towards his father and stood before him. Once he had recited his catechism in both English and in Latin without any errors, his father was most satisfied.

Then it was time for Thomas and his Father to set off for the School, wishing to allow themselves plenty of time for the ten minute walk, so that they would not have to rush, nor would they be late for Mr Mulcaster, since Francis Kyd always said that it was the height of bad manners to be late for an appointment and showed disrespect.

They left their house, and made their way down Lombard Street. As they passed the Parish Church, Thomas looked across at the graveyard, and the graves all covered with grass, which he could just manage to see, over the old red brick wall, and he could not help thinking about their former servant, Prudence Cook. She had been buried in that graveyard, having died two years before. Prudence, it seemed to Thomas, was not so old that she should have died, and he still missed her very much. She had been so kind to him and his brother and little sister. Sometimes, on a Sunday after Church Service, he would accompany his Mother to the little graveyard behind the Church, in order that they could take flowers for Prudence, and there, his Mother would let him lay the flowers out on their former servant's grave in order to show her spirit that they all still remembered her.

Thomas found himself feeling very sad now, and his father often told him that he had an overactive mind and that he should not think so much about the spirit world, whenever he asked questions about the dead, which he often did. Thomas wanted to know whether the spirits of the dead could still see and hear living people, and he wanted to know if Prudence still lived at their house in the form of a ghost or spirit. His mother said she thought that the spirit of Prudence was still with them at their house and sometimes Thomas imagined that he saw her there in his room late at night, standing beside his bed and it gave him a comforting feeling. When he grew up, he thought to himself, he would write about ghosts and spirits and explain to his reader, the effects they had on living men.

Thomas was just about to ask his father about this, when his attention was quickly diverted as he heard his father speaking to him in a raised voice.

"Pay attention Thomas! I want you to remember very carefully, the route we are taking to your School, so that you don't get lost when you have to walk to and from the School on your own. Do you think you can do that for me?

Now here we are in St. Swithin's Lane. We will shortly be turning left into Candlewick Street and on towards the River Thames, but we won't be going that far up, because from there, we are going to turn into Bush Lane, and then we will find the little passageway which leads us into Suffolk Lane. Once we have reached Suffolk Lane, we will know that we have found your new School. Now! As we reach each street, I will tell you the name of it, and then on the way home, I will test your memory, to see how much you have remembered. Then, on our way back, let us see if you can lead me home. It is always a good idea to look for things to use as landmarks. And Francis Kyd peered around himself in order to give a good example of a landmark. Yes! Such as that green door there, and this white building here, which we are just passing!" his father continued, as he waved his right arm in various directions. We are now in the Parish of Lawrence Poultney in the Ward of Downgate.

Thomas took great care to remember the way, by looking intently at each building they were passing, and then committing to his memory the names of the streets, (St. Swithin's, Candlewick, Bush and then Suffolk), and the colours of the buildings in order to impress his Father, which he was always very anxious to do.

As they approached the Merchant Taylor's School, Thomas gasped at the sight of the huge and beautiful building which his father told him had once been a mansion belonging to the wealthy Radcliffe family. Now the School was one of the largest and most distinguished in England, and held 250 pupils. One of those pupils was the poet, Edmund Spenser.

Once inside the School, Francis Kyd was asked to take a seat and wait in a small chamber while his son was led away to a classroom in order that he could be examined. In the classroom Thomas was met by the Headmaster, Richard Mulcaster and Thomas was required to transcribe a passage from the Bible in a neat hand in English, and then to recite his catechism in Latin and in English.

Once the tests were completed and the Headmaster was satisfied with the aptitude which Thomas had displayed he said "Well done Boy! We will now proceed to the room where your father is waiting and we will have you entered in the School Registration Book for all new boys."

As the tall thin Headmaster rushed down the long school corridor, with his long black cloak flying wildly behind him, Thomas decided that it gave him a look of great importance and already he found himself in awe of his surroundings, and he had to break into a run to keep up with Mr Mulcaster.

Mulcaster spoke as rapidly as he walked and did not bother to turn around as he addressed Thomas, but this voice echoed down the corridor and seemed to bounce off the walls: "I hope you are in good health boy, for we believe in this school, that it is as important to exercise the body as well as the mind, and therefore it will not do for you to dawdle. So come along now! Keep up, Keep up!. At this school you will be expected to participate in all the indoor and outdoor games that the other boys play. For indoor sports we recommend dancing, wrestling, fencing, top-and-scourge, and for outdoor games we encourage walking, running, leaping, swimming, riding, hunting, shooting, handball, tennis, football and armball, " And so they continued down the long school corridor, and Thomas realised that at last he would have to leave his books sometimes and finally join in and play the games he had never really enjoyed playing.

As they re-entered the small chamber. Thomas could see that his Father displayed his anxiousness by tapping his foot on the floor, and in an effort to calm him, Thomas peered out at his Father from behind Mr Mulcaster's cloak and smiled, and nodded to indicate that everything had gone well, but as he listened for Mr Mulcaster to announce that he had passed his tests with credit, he found himself disappointed, because the headmaster merely said:

"Follow me Mr Kyd. We now have to go through the formal process of registering young Thomas at the School and you will be required to pay the fee of 12d to have his name entered in the School's book, and you will also need to pay a further sum of 5s for the Term ahead. If you wish to pay his fees for the year in advance, then you may do so."

Thomas had to attend the school every day from 7 o'clock in the morning until 11 o'clock and after a two hour break, returned to the classroom at 1 o'clock until 5 o'clock. Thomas was educated at the School for nine years until 1574.

Upon leaving school at the age of sixteen, Thomas served his father as an apprentice Scrivener or Noverint, for a future career as a court letter writer. During his apprenticeship he learned to produce a perfect Secretary's hand.

It must be said that a Secretary's hand is not an easy one to learn to read or write, and had it not been for his father who taught him so patiently, Thomas had to admit that he would never have mastered it, and he still remembered his early lessons, and the peculiar scribble that he used to watch his father write so carefully.

[100]The Elizabethan Secretary's Hand

"The Secretary's Hand has an alphabet of its own which must first be learned" said Francis Kyd to his son, "and if you will take a seat at this desk I will go through the alphabet with you first and you may practice the ligatures thoroughly.

[One thing I would like to mention to you, is that when Queen Elizabeth signed the Death Warrant of Mary Queen of Scots on the 1st February, 1587, it was written in a Secretary's Hand. Now Queen Elizabeth did not know how to read a Secretary's Hand and her claim that she did not know what she was signing, was perfectly true. And the Queen claims that the Death Warrant was cast in amongst her other papers for her signature, and she did not know that she had signed it]."

"How long do you think it will take me to learn this new alphabet, Sir?" asked Thomas of his Father, as he made himself comfortable at his desk.

"To master the alphabet of the Secretary's hand is the most difficult, and your progress will of course be a matter for yourself to determine, since it depends on your own diligence and hard work. All I can do Thomas, is teach you in the same way that I was taught. It took me several months to learn the Secretary's Hand Alphabet, but you have already mastered the English language, and that is in itself of great assistance to you, since you are in the minority in that respect. As you know, most school boys in England are not taught English. They must rely on their good Latin or French to get them through their everyday lives".

"And so! Now we will look at the Secretary's Hand in great detail:

---

[100] The Secretary's Hand or the hand of an Elizabethan Scrivener can be found in Lionel Munby's publication entitled "Reading Tudor and Stuart Handwriting published by the British Association for Local History 01243 787639.

A   The 'a' is often written like a modern 'a', but sometimes the two parts of the letter are separated so that it looks like a modern 'oi' without a dot. Occasionally small 'a' is written like a curved capital 'A' but without its crosspiece.

B   'b' is like a modern 'b'.

C   'c' is the most confusing letter, because it is written like a modern 'r' and is often misread as 'r'. So pay particular attention to 'c'. I always say to myself when I see this ligature: "R not C when I view C."

D   'd' when carefully written, looks like a printed 'd' tipped to the left. When running hand is written, the stroke is looped to save time, and can also lean markedly to the left.

E   'e' is another difficult letter to learn. It looks like a squashed version of a running 'd' or 'b' - the letters can be confused. What appears to be quite a different way of writing 'e', one shallow saucer on top of another, is produced by emphasizing the down strokes of the pen and omitting the up and over strokes.

F   'f' is written like a modern printed 'f' but with the tail below the line; this is how it can be distinguished from a 't'.

G   'g' needs to be looked at carefully, for it can easily be taken for a 'y'. It is written with a curved 'u' base on top of which a straight line was drawn from left to right, usually sticking out to the right. The tail is usually, but not always, drawn straight down and then curved to the left.

'h' is most easily identifiable by the enormous flourish given to its tail below the line. This is not omitted, even when the writer in a hurry draws only one loop, instead of two, above the line. The result looks nothing like a modern 'h', and its shape should be looked at carefully.

I & J   'i' and 'j' are interchangeable. The small letter is written like a
         modern 'i'; the form of the capital is between a modern capital
'I' and 'J'.

It would seem sensible, when transcribing, to write the modern letters,
but many scholars always transcribe the lower case 'i' while
differentiating the capitals.

K   'k' looks like something between a 'b' and a modern 'k' with its
kick   horizontal.

L   'l' is like modern 'l'.

M & N 'm' and 'n' retain something from the medieval form: the strokes
are joined not at the top by a curve but from the bottom left to top right
by a straight line. Such letters are called minims, since the word
'minim' in a medieval hand would have consisted of 10 identical
downward strokes joined by nine diagonal upward strokes.

O   'o' is 'o'. Two Os together often share a side, and look rather
like a 'w'.

P   'p' requires concentration; it is more like a printed than a
modern handwritten 'p', but the part of the letter above the line could
be divided, as the Secretary Hand 'a' sometimes is.

Q   'q' is reasonably like a modern 'q'.

R   'r' has its downward and upward strokes separated; it
sometimes looks like a modern 'w', but it could be written like an old-
fashioned 'e', or like a 'z', especially when used as a superscript letter
and in contractions.

S   's' is written in several ways. At the beginning and in the
middle of words it is written in a long form exactly like a Secretary
Hand 'f' but not crossed. Final 's' was usually written like a '6' leaning

to the right. A great many words ended with a silent 'e' as in modern French, so plurals in 'es' are common. There is a separate symbol for final 'es' or 'is'; it looks like modern 'e' with its tail lengthened and sprawling below the line.

T   't' is like a modern printed 't'; it can be confused with Secretary 'c' or with 'f'.

U & V 'u' and 'v' were used interchangeably, like 'i' and 'j', but there are different forms for both capital and small letters. Unmoved might be written 'unmoued' or 'unmoved' or in any mixture, but it would seen rather pedantic to transcribe this in anything but the correct modern form.

U   'u' is written like a modern 'u', but is easily confused with 'n'.

V   'v' is written differently. In the most common form the pen travels up to the right hand side of the 'v' and turns to the left across the top in a straight or curved line.

W   'w' (double 'u/v') consists of a Secretary Hand 'v' to the left of which part of another 'v' is added. Unlike the modern 'w' the left hand half of the letter is joined at the top instead of the bottom. Both 'w' and 'v' can often be identified because they frequently begin with a great flourish from above, which makes them look like the first letter of a 'w' and can easily be misread as two letters.

X   'x' when written in running hand has a tail below the line from the bottom of the left hand cross; this can sometimes be confused with a hurried 'h' or 'p'.

Y   'y' is written like a Secretary Hand 'v' with a tail which bent first to the left and then curved to the right. It can most easily be distinguished 'f' from 'g' by the straight line across its top; in a 'y' this never has a projection to the right as it had in a 'g', and it is usually less horizontal than in a 'g'.

Z   'z' is not too different from a modern handwritten 'z'.

Once your have mastered the Alphabet of the Secretary's Hand Thomas, I will go on to teach you the Ligatures and Contractions, but I will mention them to you now, since they are just as important.

Take for instance , ch, ss, sh, th, st, ff:

The most frequent form of contraction consists of omitting letters and drawing a line above the word: 'tenements' is written 'tents' with a line above it. Writers are often too lazy to lift their pen to make this line, and so continue in an upward curve from the end of the last letter. Something like a French circumflex accent can indicate omitted letters.

The letter with which contractions are most often associated is 'p', 'p' followed by a vowel and 'r' shown by a horizontal line through the stem of the 'p', or by an upward curve from the tail of the 'p', to the left, which turned back across the tail just below the line.

'p' followed by 'r' and then by a vowel is shown in different ways:"

And then Francis Kyd took his up his quill again, and went on to indicate the correct ways in which to write these words, and Thomas copied them out diligently.

"The other important form of contraction is the superscript letter, written above the line, which tells the reader that some letters before it have been omitted. It survives when we write 9th for ninth; we ought, incidentally, to write Mr. as Mr with a raised superscript 'r'.

A superscript 'r' commonly indicates an omitted 'u', as in Savoy which should be transcribed as Savio[u]r.

The most common superscript in familiar short words like w with a superscript t, or w with a superscript 'th' = w[i]th, or 'w' with a superscript 'ch' = w[hi]ch.

When 'that' or 'the' or 'them' is abbreviated, an old Anglo-Saxon letter called the 'thorn', written at first more like a modern 'y', is used for 'th'; but soon 'thorn' will be written like the Secretary Hand 'y'. The best practice is to transcribe 'thorn' as 'th' not as 'y' which was the habit in my own day. So 'y' with a raised 't' is th[a]t and 'ye' is 'the', not 'ye'. But remember that there is a word 'ye', meaning 'you' in the plural, spelt with a real 'y'! Incidentally, 'y' was is often written instead of 'i', particularly in words like 'if' and 'it' which should be transcribed as 'yf', 'yt'.

You must remember when you are ready to transcribe documents from originals Thomas, that the comma is fairly new to us in the sixteenth century. Round brackets are used for parentheses and often as inverted commas. A transcript should be faithful to the original.

And now finally, I will tell you about the Numerals of a Secretary's Hand:

1 = j   2 = ij   3 = iij   4 = iiij   5 = v

'i' and 'j' both represent '1'; the last '1' is always represented by 'j'.

6 = vj   7 = vij   9 = ix   10 = x 11 = xj and so on.

15 = xv   20 = xx   40 = xl 50 = l 100 = C

500 = D   1000 = M

"As a man of the Church father, and so learned, you must teach me the Roman names for basic days to record in my own work when I am grown"

"You try to run before you walk Thomas, but here they are:"

[101]The Roman Calendar

Kalends   1st day
Nones   5th day
Ides   13th day

The word calender is taken from Kalends. All other days were reckoned in relation to these three as:

a(nte)   d(iem)   iii   Nones - = 5th day   Ides =
13th day

a(nte) d(iem) iii nonas = 3 days before nones = the 3rd, not the 2nd, because you count the days at either end.

There were long months when two of theh three basic days changed. Remember it as:

In March, July, October, May
Nones on the 7th Ides on the 15th day.

Saints Days
die natalis Domini (dni)
Christi Redemptoris mundi = on the birth day of our lord Christ, saviour of the world (= December 25)
die feste Santae Virginis Mariae = on the feast day of the Blessed Virgin Mary (= March 25, the beginning of the church year)
die feste SS Philippi et Jacobi = the feast day of st Philip and St James (=May 1, often the first day of the Easter Quarter Sessions)
feste Sancti Johannis = feast of St John (Baptist) = June 24 (Midsummer Sessions)
feste Santi Micaelis = feast of St Michael (=eptember 25, Michaelmas sessions).

---

[101]From "A McLaughlin Guide : Simple Latin for Family Historians by Eve McLaughlin: Public Record Office Kew Richmond Surrey.

Pounds, shillings and pence are indicated by superscript letters. The £ sign 'li' is short for libra, the Latin word for pound. Written with a Capital L with a contraction line, to show 'ibra' omitted, drawn above the bottom loop.

The shilling sign is the final 's' symbol for 'solidus';

The pence sign is 'd' for 'denarius' they were two Roman coins.

Since counting is done in scores of twenty (20), a large number might be put into numerals as a number of scores. The sum total of an inventory might be written as 'vjxxvjli (the xx and li being in superscript) vs iiijd, which is spoken as six score and six pounds (i.e. £126), five shillings and four pence.

Our four pence coin called the 'Groat' is useful because so many calculations are done in marks or parts of marks. Although there was never a coin worth a mark, but people made gifts and valued objects in that unit which was two-thirds of a £, that is 13s 4d; half a mark is 6s 8d.

'Di', short for the Latin 'dimidium, is a half,

but

'ob', short for the Latin obulus from the Green coin, was 1/2d,

'qu', short for quarteria, was 1/4d.

The square measurements are in acres, roods and perches and are abbreviated a, r, p.

40 perches = 1 rood
4 roods   = 1 acre

Confusion can arise because a perch is also a measure of length: rod, pole and perch were different names for the same distance, which became standardised at 5 1/2 yards.

"Calendar Dates:

In 1582 Pope Gregory XIII replaced the Julian calendar, introduced by Julius Caesar in 45 B.C., with the Gregorian calendar. This was intended to remedy the growing divergence between the calendar year and the solar year by reducing slightly the number of leap years; in only one in four future centuries was the first year to be a leap year. But a discrepancy already existed and to remove this the calendar had to catch up with the solar year."

It must be remembered that a monarch's reign does not correspond with a calendar year, but runs from the date of accession to the date of death.

IE: Mary Tudor died and Elizabeth Tudor came to the throne on 17th November 1558. So the first year of Elizabeth's reign extended from 17th November 1558 to 16 November 1559 inclusive.

Therefore:

1 December 1 Elizabeth was 1 December 1558, while 1 March 1 Elizabeth was 1 March 1559.

A Saints day can be used instead of the day of the month; using the Monarch's reign for the calendar year.

1st	=	1 superscript o, for primo
2nd	=	2 superscript do, for secundo
3rd	=	3 superscript o, for tertio
4th	=	4 superscript to, for quarto
5th	=	5 superscript to, for quinto
6th	=	6 superscript to, for sexto

HIC JACET: SIR WALTER RALEIGH

7th	=	7 superscript mo, for septimo
8th	=	8 superscript o, for octavo
9th	=	9 superscript o, for nono
10th	=	10 superscript o, for decimo

Time

ante   = before ante meridiem = a.m. before mid-day

post   = after post meridiem   = p.m. after mid-day

antea   = previously   postea = afterwards

nunc   = now

primus = first

ultimus = last

proximus = next

hora = hour

dies = day

mensis = month

annus = year

usually met with expressions like:

eidem die = on the same day

eadem hora = in the same hour

eodem mense/anno = in the same month, year

proximo die/mense/anno on the next day, in the next month/year

ultimo die Octobris = on the last day of October

primo die mensis (Aprilis) = on the first day of the month (of April)

Anno Domini, Ao Dni - AD, in the year of our Lord

anno(que) praedicto/p'dicto = and in the aforesaid year

prima luce = at first light, dawn

nocte, noctu = a night

hodie = today

pridie = yesterday

cras = tomorrow

And that concludes my tuition regarding the Secretary's Hand Thomas, now you must set to work and learn all I have taught you."

Thomas set about learning the Secretary's Hand from the notes his father had given him and made simple translations to begin with, but after a period of time be was able to transcribe more difficult documents.

For the next fifteen years Thomas Kyd worked as his father's apprentice, but during this time he was also busy in his spare time writing his dramatic works.

In 1580 Francis Kyd had risen to the position of Warden of the Company of Scriveners and by this time he also employed several other apprentices, one of them, William Dunce who later gained admission to the Company in 1591.

By 1589 Kyd had changed his career from Noverint and thereafter worked as a translator from Italian into English and at about this time he translated the 'Householder's Philosophie'.

Thomas Kyd wrote the Spanish Tragedy pre-1587, a forerunner to Hamlet, and by 1591 Kyd had been introduced to Christopherus Marlowe and they resolved to work together on [Hamlet or in perfecting the Spanish Tragedie], and during this time they shared a writing chamber as they were engaged to write for the Earl of Sussex Players. The Spanish Tragedie was not entered for publication until the 14th March 1592 (Henslowe's diary records Spanish Tradgedie 1592). Marlowe at about this time or shortly after, was also engaged in writing St. Bartholomew's Massacre.

Thomas Kyd started to produce great dramatic works and one of his first to be published was the Murder of John Brewen Goldsmith of London, printed for John Kid and sold by Edward White, dwelling at the north door of Pauls Churchyard, at the sign of the Gun in 1593.

At the beginning of 1593 there was a further outbreak of the Plague. Since there was great unemployment in London, the restless community sought to drive out the French, Dutch and Belgians, who were termed 'Strangers'. These were known as the anti alien disturbances. Since these strangers were dwelling in the City and employed in trades and professions, they were subjected to bitter attacks upon their premises by the unemployed youths of the City of London who resented them.

[("Num CVIII.

Strangers, Flemings and French in the City of London. And complaints of them and Libels against them; Anno 1593. Mss. Car. D. Hallifax. They contented not themselves with Manufactures, and Ware-Houses, but would keep Shops, and retail all manner of goods. The English Shopkeepers made several Complaints and Remonstrances against them. Whereupon a strict Account was taken in every Ward of all Strangers inhabiting within London, with their Servants and Children. And Certificates were returned the 4th May. When the Total of all the Strangers, with their Children and Servants, born out of the Realm, were 4300. Of which 267 were Denizons.

Another Scrutiny was made the same Year, 1593, by Order of the Chief Magistrates. Which was done by the Ministers and chief Officers of the Foreign Churches in London, and in the same Month of May. By which the |Number of the Strangers of the French, Dutch and Italian Churches, did amount to 3325. Whereof 212 were found to be English born.

Complaint of them.

The Artificers Freemen with the City and Suburbs in London, made Complaint, by several Petitions, against the Trades and occupations exercised by Strangers. And upon due Information the Households appeared to be only 698.

Libels set out against the Strangers.

While these Enquiries were making, to incense the People against them, there were these Lines in one of their Libels.

[102] 'Doth not the World see, that you, beastly Brutes, the Belgians, or rather Drunken Drones, and faint-hearted Flemings; and you, fraudulent Father, Frenchmen, by your cowardly Flight for your own natural Countries, have abandoned the same into the Hands of your proud, cowardly Enemies, and have by a feigned Hypocrisy, and counterfeit shew of Religion, placed yourselves in a most fertile Soil, under a most gracious and merciful Prince. Who hath been conttented, to the great Prejudice of her own natural Subjects, to suffer you to live here in better Case and more Freedom, than her own People. - Be it known to all Flemings and Frenchmen, that it is best for them to depart out of the Realm of England, between this and the 9th of July next. If not, then to take that which follows. For that there shall be many a sor Stripe. Apprentices will rise, to the number of 2336 and all the Apprenctices and Journeymen will down with the Flemings and Strangers.'

Various threats and libels were pasted on the walls and doors of their houses, in order to incite public hatred against the 'strangers' and by the 22nd April 1593 the Privy Council had decided that it was time to seek out the factious persons.

As a direct result of this the Chief Magistrates had directed that a count of all 'strangers' of the French, Dutch and Italian churches should be carried out immediately and they were informed that their count amounted to 3,325 of which 212 were shown to be of English birth and their households amounted to a total of 698.

On Thursday 5th May between the hours of 11 and 12 at night a rhyme103 was put up against the Dutch churchyard and caused great

---

[102] Sir Thomas More: Shakespeare's Hand in the Play: A.W. Pollard

[103] [The rhyme in question appears in the book 'Shakespeare's Hand in the Play of Sir Thomas More - A.W. Pollard 1925] - which was written by [four or five] literary hands in olde English

offence when it was found by the inhabitants and was immediately bought to the attention of the Night Watchman, who referred it directly to the Magistrates, who in turn referred it to the Privy Councillors.

[104] The rhyme in question reads as follows: Num CVIII - From John Strype's Brief Annals of the Church and State under the reign of queen Elizabeth, being a continuation of the Annals of the Church of England Vol IV London 1731.

[("A Rhime set up against the Wall of the Dutch churchyard, on Thursday May the 5th, between Eleven and Twelve at night. And there found by some of the Inhabitants of that Place; and brought to the Constable, and the rest of the Watch. beginning,

[105] "You, Strangers, that inhabit in this Land,
Note this same Writing, do it understand.
Conceive it well, for Safe-guard of your Lives,
Your Goods, your Children and your dearest Wives.")].

---

and the undated manuscript which is written in a neat Italian hand, bears the signatures of Thomas Kyd, Thomas Dekker, John Day and Harry Chettle. William Shakespeare appended three pages to the Play Sir Thomas More, after its original completion, and part of it is housed in the British Museum] The dramatists were Anthony Munday and E. Tyllney (Tilney), who were attached to the Lord Admirals Men in 1597. Edwarde Alleyn retired from 1597 to 1600.

[104] Num. CVIII. [From John Strype's Brief Annals of the Church and State under the reign of Queen Elizabeth,

[105] This is the ryhme which appears in the play Sir Thomas More and led to the arrest and torture at Newgate Prison of Thomas Kyd (Christopher Marlowe's co-writer) on the 12th May 1593. Christopher Marlowe was arrested on the 18th May 1593 and murdered on the 30th May 1593. William Shakespeare had appended three pages to this play and claimed it as his own play, although those three pages are now in the British Museum.

The Privy Council decided that immediate action must be taken in order to prevent riot or insurrection, and appointed Sir Julius Caesar, Sir Henry Killgrew and Sir Thomas Wilkes to seek out and examine by secret means, all persons suspected as being responsible and they were given leave to search the premises of any writers thought to be involved in the above plots. It was directed that a search be made for any papers or writings which may lead to the guilty persons being identified, after which they should be put to torture until they confessed and revealed all they knew of the matter.

Some of the rioters were apprehended and found to be apprentices to trades. They were put into the stocks or carted and whipped and this was done in order to serve as a warning to other apprentices.

[("The Court, upon these seditious Motions, took the most prudent Measures to protect the poor Strangers and to prevent any Riot or Insurrection: Sending for the Lord Mayor and Aldermen; resolving that no open Notification should be given, but a private Admonition only, to the Mayor and discreetest Aldermen. And they not to know the Cause of their sending for. Orders to be given to them to appoint a strong Watch of Merchants and others, and like handicrafted Masters, to answer for their Apprentices and Servants Misdoing. The Subsidy-Books for London and the Suburbs, to be seen: how many Masters, and how may Men, and to what Trades, and if they use double Trades. The Preachers of their Churches to forewarn them of double Trades. And such as be of no Church to be avoided hence. And a Proclamation of these Things to be made publickly in Guild-Hall.

After these Orders from the Council Boards, several young Men were taken up, and examined about the Confederacy to rise, and drive out the Strangers - Some of these Rioters were put in to the Stock, carted and whipt; for a Terro to other Apprentices and Servants. Mss. Car. D. Hallifax").].

One of the first victims to be arrested upon suspicion of the above offences was Thomas Kyd, when on the 12th May 1593 his writing chamber had been searched and papers were found which were considered to be written from a heretical viewpoint and were found to be blasphemous.106

Poor Thomas Kyd who had always lived such a peaceful life and was only ever concerned with his books and his love of learning, was immediately seized and carried off to Newgate Prison, where he was to spend eight terrible months and his health deteriorated rapidly. He was not allowed to know any of the evidence held against him until he came to trial when he would hear it at Court. He was allowed no Counsel to defend him. He had no chance of cross-examination of the witnesses, and all this was commonplace during Elizabethan trials.

All around him, Thomas Kyd could see the human misery and the destruction of the lives of these wretched people. He felt that his own life would never be the same again after his experiences in this dreadful place. No human being, he thought, should ever be subjected to such mental and physical torture as this place had wrought upon them all. His own ordeal was still to come, but he could see the results all around him, of the treatment he might expect from the Privy Councillors against himself.

There were young men lying on the prison floor in their filthy rags, crying out in agony having been tortured and then brought back here, to be left to die in the Prison, or to await hanging, which he thought would be a mercy to relieve their pain and suffering. Some men could barely walk a few steps before falling to the ground. All the inhabitants were powerless to help them or offer them any aid, and this only served to heighten their misery.

One of Kyd's accusers was Richard Baines, a 'spy' for Sir Francis

---

106

Walsingham, who was known as the 'Spymaster' of the Catholics. Whilst Kyd remained in prison, another of Sir Francis Walsingham's men, Robert Poley [who was also employed for the Babington Plot, to free Mary Queen of Scots,] was present as a witness at the murder of Christopherus Marlowe and testified at Marlowe's inquest held on the 1st June 1593.

Kyd had also written to his former patron, Henry, Fourth Earl of Sussex for whom he and Marlowe had been engaged to write in 1591, for the Earl of Sussex Players, in the hope that the Earl could use his influence to have him released.

Newgate prison dated back to 1218, and stood opposite the Old Bailey, down to the western end of Newgate Street. In 1423 the prison had been enlarged and improved by the Lord Mayor, Richard Whittington, but no improvements had been made since that time.

There was no ventilation or sanitation inside the huge prison, where all classes of prisoner were thrown in together: the depraved, the desperate and the innocent were all flung among the filth, where rats and mice roamed freely among the prisoners. The infested prison walls were covered with mould and running with dampness. The prisoners some of them homeless children, or pregnant women who gave birth in the prison, ranged from murderers, thieves, debtors, highwaymen, foreign pirates, or prostitutes, and they could all expect to wait months before they were called for trial. The prisoners themselves who had to sleep on the stone floor, became infested with lice, fleas and mites, brought about by the lack of sanitation; coupled with their poor diet (their food being cooked over huge fires and served up from filthy posnets or pans, into unwashed porringers or bowls), within the confines of that prison of hell. This meant that many of the weaker prisoners could not survive these conditions and so they died there in the prison, some of them never knowing what their crime had been.

At Newgate Prison, Thomas Kyd underwent interrogation and rigorous torture by the pressing and crushing of his fingertips under the instructions of William Deyos, one of the Keepers of Newgate. Eight months later Kyd was called before the Sessions Hall near Newgate Prison and there he was examined concerning the heretical papers which had been found. The keepers were concerned that Thomas Kyd should not be identified as the author of Hamlet. During his eight month imprisonment, Kyd had voluntarily written letters of apology to the Lord Keeper of the Great Seal, Sir John Puckering claiming that the papers discovered in his writing chamber were the property of Christopherus Marlowe and he said that the papers must have been cast in whilst they had shared a writing chamber in 1591. Kyd was released in November 1593, but the torture that he had endured and the conditions in which he had lived for those eight months, meant that his health was so poor that he survived for only six months after his release, even though he was still only 36 years old. His dramatic work 'Cornelia' was registered for publication on the 26th January 1594.

The Babington Plot : August 1586

One of Kyd's accusers had been Richard Baines, another spy for Walsingham in the Babington Plot August 1586. Sir Anthony Babington was the former page to Lord Shrewsbury, Mary Queen of Scots Jailor. Mary Queen of Scots was convicted under the 1585 Act for the Queen's Safety and Sir Francis Walsingham swore a pledge of Allegiance and a Bond of Association to the Queen to protect and defend her. Parliament made the Association statutory, bearing thousands of signatures. Raleigh's brother in law, Arthur Throckmorton was arrested at his lodgings near the Docks and racked twice by Walsingham for his part in the Babington Plot.

About fifteen months after Christopherus Marlowe's murder, Thomas Kyd was buried on the 15th August 1594 at the age of thirty six. Kyd's grave was destroyed during the Great Fire of London in 1666 and no trace of it remains. His premature death being attributed to his earlier torture and incarceration at Newgate Prison and he never regained his former healthy constitution.

Kyd's Spanish Tragedy remained one of the most popular of Elizabethan dramas, and some of his other dramatic works were published after his death.

HIC JACET: SIR WALTER RALEIGH

Preparations for the Battle of Cadiz - 1596

In the Spring of 1596 it would have appeared to any man, woman or child living in the midst of London that God had foresaken all who lived in that City
and had withdrawn from them his promise of mercy for their future happiness and salvation. Men who had lost their sons and daughters and women who had lost their beloved husbands through the terrible tragedies that the plague had brought into the confines of their homes, shook their heads with dread and fear as they displayed their grief to any who would listen. They went in search of the priests of St Paul's and the Nuns in Convent Garden and prayed for mercy as they sought out the reasons why their own lives should have been afflicted with such terrible injustice. Others lived in continual fear that the Plague would send them into early graves in pits of Moorfields or beyond.

The dark sky was filled with heavy clouds and the torrential rain fell without mercy upon the bleak and deserted streets of plague infested London where the streets were already laden with mud.

The seemingly endless war with Spain had plunged the entire country into the depths of financial ruin. The Farmers crops were ruined for the second year, with the of further floods. The result was a disaster for the entire country causing widespread famine.

People were dying of hunger in the streets. Morale was ebbing and the town and village folk became desperate. [107] Ragged and starving beggards roamed from one village to another, sometimes walking for days at a time in their desperate search for food. Only to find themselves driven away by the Justices in the very towns where they sought refuge. In their turn, the despairing Justices had resolved to

---

[107] The England of Elizabeth - A.L. Rowse

take a firm stand and could therefore offer no alms to starving strangers who wandered into their villages. The Justices turned them away for the very same reasons that these poor abandoned folk sought out new homes, and those reasons were the spreading plauge. All remaining supplies of food must be preserved for their own townsfolk cried the Justices.

Thus, the unfortunate wandering beggars and vagabonds were either flogged or threatened with flogging, fixed into the Village Stocks, whilst persistent offenders faced arrest and imprisonment if they did not return to their own homes in the towns or villages they had left behind them. These pitiful beggars who were crying out for food, were often homeless and therefore had nowhere to go and they were invariably found the next morning, lying dead by the roadside, because they did not have the strength or wherewithall to proceed step further.

Queen Elizabeth was herself in the depths of despair and she had called an emergency meeting of her Court Advisers at Somerset House, where they discussed the question of King Philip of Spain and his renewed efforts to invade England with another Armada, and it was agreed that England would have no choice but to declare War upon Spain.

The queen hastily summoned the [108] Howards, Essex and Vere to this meeting and there it was ordered that a fleet consisting of 96 ships, should set sail for Spain without delay - their objective was to sink and destroy as many of King philip's war ships as they could, in order that the spanish fleet should pose no further threat to the Realms of England or to Ireland.

Sir Walter Raleigh, who was still out of favour with Queen Elizabeth at this time, had also been summoned to the meeting. There, during bitter discussions, the Queen had ordered Raleigh to co-operate with

---

[108] Sir Walter Raleigh by Hugh Ross Williamson

two of her cousins, the Second Earl of Essex, Robert Devereux and the elderly Lord Howard, Baron of Effingham, who were to be in joint command of the Third Squadron as it was deemed by the Queen to be named.

The Queen had smiled wistfully across the table as she looked at Raleigh and condescendingly proceeded to explain to him that her dear Lord of Essex would sail on the "Repulse" and her 'good Thomas' - Lord Howard was thenceforth appointed as Admiral on the "Ark Royal", whilst his nephew, Thomas Howard was destined to sail as Vice Admiral on the "Nonpareil".

Raleigh had commissioned the "Ark Raleigh" to be built in 1587, being a ship of 800 tons, which could carry 270 mariners, 34 Gunners, 126 soldiers and carried 55 guns. Raleigh had hoped to command that ship at the forthcoming Battle of Cadiz, but since he had sold it to the Queen and she had re-named it the "Ark Royal", the Queen exercised her power and was in no mood for ill will on this morning.

Raleigh was convincingly informed that he would serve as Rear Admiral on the "Warspite". His mood lightened at this particular news because he knew it would be a ship of greater maneuverability.

Press gangs had been scouring the country in search of crews to man the ships and the majority of the ships in the English Fleet had been made ready to sail. Essex and Howard had readily volunteered to inform the Queen that Raleigh still needed some 200 men before his ship could be made ready to sail and no time was lost in squaring all the blame on Raleigh for their delayed departure.

The Queen pointedly told Raleigh that he must gather his men without any further delay.

Raleigh returned to Durham House and hastily made preparation. He left London accompanied by 40 soldiers on horseback and they promptly set off for Gravesend. They soon found themselves dragging through the heavy mud as they proceeded on their journey. It had been necessary for them to ride through the night because of their lack of time. The extreme weather conditions made their journey particularly slow and difficult and Raleigh's temper was becoming increasingly overworked.

By the time they reached the outposts of Gravesend, their Wagons were half filled with men. Some of them were the very ragged and starving beggars who had been pressed at the towns and villages on their own journey towards Gravesend. Most of the men were eager to accompany Raleigh to Cadiz and fight the Spaniards, but just as many others were anxious to change their minds without a moments notice. They displayed their doubts by deserting as soon as the wagons came to a halt, where they sprang out and ran off in every direction. Raleigh and his soldiers had to chase after them, dragging them out of the alehouses and Taverns where they sought refuge and complained bitterly to all who would listen. They were put forcibly back into the wagons.

Raleigh shivered as he pulled his soaking black cloak tightly around his shoulders and reached to wipe the splashes of rain from his face because his black felt hat was dripping and he had therefore to remove it from his head. He was very angry and uncomfortable but had no choice except to continue in his pursuit of the runaway mariners.

This was the fifth alehouse he and his men had searched, but no sooner had he pressed these men, than they ran away saying they would not serve him. He was at his wits end. He needed at least thirty more men and he would have to take them all by force.

News was fast spreading throughout the countryside that Sir Francis Drake and Sir John Hawkins had died of Dysentery and had been buried at Sea. This sad fact did nothing to raise the morale of the enlisting men, even though some of them had sailed with Raleigh before and were singing merrily in the wagons in an effort to cheer the rest. It seemed to please most of them but the rest feared they would never see England again.

As the last of the men were rounded up and put into the Wagons, Raleigh who had spoken kindly but firmly to his men, told them that they would all receive fair pay and have a share of the treasures which were to be looted from Cadiz after they had destroyed King Philip II of Spain's warships. The men cheered by this news,broke into song intermittently as they continued on their journey towards Plymouth as they dragged back through the cold wind and rain. It was a good prospect to know that they would have food and drink and somewhere dry to sleep on board Raleigh's ship and they might waylay a Spanish Silver fleet on their way there or back and sail home with its holds laden with treasure and take a share of it home with them.

At last Raleigh and his soldiers and his full crew of mariners arrived in Plymouth to join the Lords, and Knights who waited kicked their heels as they waited impatiently for them. They complained bitterly to Raleigh about the delays they were encountering. At last the rain and storms had ceased and they were ready to set sail.

Their fleet of ships had been loaded with food and equipment in readiness for their voyage together with spare sails, rigging and yards, artillery, weaponry, hospital stores, cordage, chandlery, oil and animal feed.

2,500 soldiers were armed with their muskets, long-bows and pikes and the Musketeers were each armed with a wheel-lock arquebus together with a U-topped crock on which to rest his musket barrel for land combat.

A total of 11,500 sailors marched forward to their ships - walking proudly up the gangplanks dressed in the uniforms provided to them. As the men boarded their ships they were smiling and waving to those still on shore and others were singing or cheering amidst feelings of great happines and optimism at the prospect of returning home with treasure and food.

There were 96 ships and 14,000 men ready to depart and it was a magnificent sight to behold. With colourful banners flying from the ships flagstaffs and masts; 6,500 of the men were soldiers serving under Sir Francis Vere who was in command of the "Rainbow", a ship built in 1596 of 500 tons, carrying 150 mariners, 24 gunners, 76 soldiers and 54 guns.

The English Fleet were to be accompanied by a contingent of 24 Dutch ships, their sides pierced with gunports, carrying 2,500 men who were already prepared and standing out to sea.

The Fleet set sail at 5 p.m. on the 1st June 1596 led by Lord Howard, the veteran of the Spanish Armada on the "Ark Royal", The Earl of Essex (otherwise known as the Earl of March) on the "Repulse", the younger Howard on the 500 ton ship "Nonpareil" and Lord Thomas Howard as Vice Admiral on the "Merhonour". The ships were carried out to sea on a high tide.

In the midst of the exciting prospect of War with Spain, people rushed from their huge houses or humble cottages alike, in the surrounding towns and villages, using whatever mode of conveyance they could procure - travelling to Plymouth on carts, wagons, on horseback, by mule. Those without means of transport travelled on foot promising themselves never to miss this day and all with one aim in mind - to watch with their own eyes, this great fleet of ships leaving England. They waved good-bye to their loved ones, as they wished them a great victory over Spain and prayed for their safe return to the shores of England.

Sir Walter Raleigh stood proudly on the deck of the "Warspite" as he gave the order to set sail, and the ship moved off, accompanied by the sound of bugles mingled with great cheers of joy both on board and onshore.

Raleigh spoke to his Officers and Crew and informed them of the following news:

"It is with great sadness that I must now inform all men on board the "Warspite", who have not already heard the terrible news - that my dear kinsman, [109] Sir Francis Drake is dead! The remainder of Drake's crew and the rest of the fleet returned to England at the end of May.

That great and illustrious Master of the Sea, took ill as the fleet lay at anchor for 12 days off Escudo de Veragua. Drake perished of Dysentery on or about the 28th January 1596 and was buried at sea in a lead coffin as the fleet lay at anchor at Puerto Bello, off the Isthmus of Panama. Just before he died, and as he lay in the Sick Bay just above the Ballast line of his Flagship "The Defiance" - he called to Whitlocke for his suit of armour to be put on him "so that he might die like a soldier".

Sir John Hawkins is also dead! The cause of his death was by Dysentery and he died before Drake, also being buried at Sea."

Raleigh went on to inform his men of their expected duties during the forthcoming voyage, but curtailed his speech due to the great sadness rising up in his mind with the renewal of his thoughts concerning Drake's death. He hurried towards his cabin on the first deck to seek some relief for his own feelings, not wishing others to witness them. As he entered his cabin he was surprised to find himself surrounded by the familiar faces of his friends: As he looked around him he noted, George Chapman the Poet and dramatist who accompanied Raleigh on many of his voyages, Lawrence Kemys and The Wizard Earl" of Syon Henry Percy, being the Ninth Earl of Northumberland who had complained bitterly at the last moment, that he was being left behind, and had caused himself to be rushed by coach from Syon House down

---

[109] Sir Francis Drake by George Malcolm thomson - Raleigh is related to Sir Francis Drake through his father's first wife.

to Plymouth, so determined was he to join Raleigh. Finally, and inconspicuously in a corner, there stood the very thoughtful Thomas Harriot, the astronomer and mathematician who always wore a countenance filled with unanswered questions, so great was his pursuit of knowledge. Harriot was present because he wanted to observe and record the positions of the stars at different latitudes.

They all gathered around a large map table in the centre of the cabin and Raleigh handed a goblet of sweet red wine to each man and proposed a toast: Saying:

"I am resolved to be revenged for the "Revenge" or to second her with mine own life" - they were all committed to avenge Spain for the death of Sir Walter Raleigh's cousin, Sir Richard Grenville who had died on board the "St Philip" in the wake of the Battle of the [110] Azores in 1591.

Raleigh then removed a letter from his worn leather case and proceeded to recite loudly the words that Sir Richard Grenville had written upon his death bed:

"Here I die, Richard Grenville, with a joyful and quiet mind, for that I have ended my life as a true soldier ought to do that hath fought for his country, queen, religion and honour, whereby my soul departeth most joyfully out of this body - and shall always leave behind it an everlasting fame as a valiant and true soldier that hath done his duty as he was bound to do."

To which each man raised his goblet of wine and drank in silence as a mark of deepest respect of Sir Richard Grenville.

As these events were taking place in Raleigh's cabin, each mariner on board the "Warspite" was put to work on his own particular duties.

---

[110] See Sir Walter Raleigh's own manuscript entitled "The Truth about the Battle of the Azores contained in his booke The Great Rich and Beautiful Empire of Guiana 1596.

HIC JACET: SIR WALTER RALEIGH

The decks were scrubbed, the guns and cannon were cleaned, and oiled and the cabins were made orderly as the men settled in for the long journey ahead.

In Raleigh's cabin, Thomas Harriot and Henry Percy stood around the map table and consulted the Mariner's Mirrour, which had been published in 1588 and consisted of maps and charts compiled by the Dutch seaman and cartographer, Lucas Janszoon Wagenaer.

Tears blurred Raleigh's eyes as he once again unwrapped and looked at the magnificent object that had once belonged to Sir Francis Drake and had been left to Raleigh in Drake's Will. He held it tightly in his hand and looked up a circular gilt and brass astrological conmpendium, measuring three and a half inches in diameter. He turned it over in his hand and opened up the highly polished case; one of the inner disks was engraved with the name "Humfray Colle - 1596" and in total the compendium comprised of 7 layers of navigational information. One layer contained a latitude of European ports, another depicted tide tables; another a calculator to define the ship's position by observing the point of the sun in the sky at noon; a sight indicator for the time of day by shadow. There was also a perpetual calendar to indicate religious days and saints' days. It had been a gift from his relative to Sir Francis Drake who, just before his death in the Caribbean, had made it known that he wished Raleigh to inherit the compendium and it was brought back to England and delivered by messenger to Raleigh at Sherborne Castle, together with a letter.

Thomas Harriot had promised Raleigh that he would improve upon the astrological information contained in the compendium by enlarging its circumference and he was already busy compiling his own charts and calculations:

[111] **"Of Shotinge in ordinaunce"** by Thomas Harriott

"Considerations

Of one bullet out of one peece, shot at sundry times vpon severall angles of Random; the temper of the peece supposed to be one & the same quantity of powder and all other considerations alike.
Extra medium materiale.

1.   In the motion of the bullet we are to consider it in the pece & also what it is out of the same.

2.   In the pece it is vnequall & this poynte of swiftest motion is at the   mouth of the pece in all angles.

3.   This inequality riseth from two causes: if the force of the powder did continue to be one in the whole length of the pece; yet the motion of the bullet wold be vnequall, but the force of the powder being [c.o.] growinge greater & greater as it repeateth more [c.o.] accordinge as it taketh fire, not beinge all fired vntill it cometh to the mouth of the pece, then also is the lesse resistance of the medium whereby the 2 is manifest, the force of the last powder fired is greater because it is fired in motion.

4.   In all angles of Random betwene the horizon & Zenith, the motion of the bullet is swiftest [c.o.] swifter the nerer the peece inclineth to the horizon; so that in the levell situation of the pece, the bullet emergeth the length of the sayd pece in the shortest time; & in the Zenith line to the longest. but the shortest time; absolutely is in this perpendicular situation downeward & so of the rest accordingly.

The carriages recoyle vnequally according to the angle of Random.
The Asperity of the bullet somewhat hindreth.

---

[111] Thomas Harriot by John Shirley

The vnequall wayt of the powder in severall charges. Ramminges. Ayre more dense &.
Wind. etc."

Raleigh and Henry Percy had pledged to work together in quieter moments to improve the navigational information.

Above Raleigh's cabin, the Ship's Master summoned all men to the deck and rad out to the crew of the "Warspite" what they could expect to eat during the voyage:

"It is my duty to provide every man who serves Sir Walter Raleigh aboard this ship with the this list of a man's daily fare: And each man among you will receive the following generous quantities of food and drink:

[112]**Ship's Menu**
One Gallon of Beer per day
1lb Biscuit per day
1lb of Salt beef on Sunday, Tuesday and Thursday
1/4 of a Stockfish or part of a Ling on Wednesday, Friday and Saturday, plus
Cheese and Butter
1lb of Salt Pork with peas on Monday

this giving each man the following quantities of food per week:

Ship's Menu continued,

8lb of Beef

---

[112]From the Illustrated Armada handbook - David A. Thomas

7lb of Biscuit
9lb of Salted Fish
3/4lb of Cheese
3/4lb of Butter
and 7 Gallons of Beer

And now I will relate to each man among you the rate of his expected earnings for this memorable voyage:

I will give out the annual figure, although we will not be at sea for a year, nothing like a year, but you can expect your pay to be calculated at the end of the voyage - that is, when we return to England, where you will receive your pay.

Each Mariner will receive Pounds 6.10.0d a year
Each Gunner will receive Pounds 9.15.6d a year
The Carpenters among you will receive Pounds 10.8.7d a year
The Boatswains Pounds 10.17.3d a year
Each Cook will receive Pounds 7.12.1d a year
and the Purser Pounds 8.13.9d a year"

These figures take account of the increased rates of pay for seamen which were raised by the late John Hawkins and I trust that none will find cause for complaint of his expected earnings.

Finally, I must tell you that no blasphemy or idleness will be tolerated aboard this ship"

****

On the 14th May 1596, a messenger bearing important news, had reached King Philip II of Spain who waited anxiously at the Escorial Palace near Madrid, and the aid in his role as messenger informed the King that Sir Francis Drake and John Hawkings had perished off the Island of Escudo de Veraguas in the Caribbean, both men having been buried at sea.

King Philip, upon being informed of the events which had taken place, had rejoiced at this provident news and it was noted to be in a fashion most unbecoming to a King, after which he said that this news would help him to get better. The King of Spain's happiness was to be short-lived however, as the dreadful news reached him, which confirmed that his second Armada which had sailed from Spain to invade Ireland and then England, had failed once more - this time, having been driven back by a Hurricane.

On the morning of the 20th June King Phlip II of Spain, found himself engulfed in a paroxysm of rage which fell upon him as he received a further message whilst sitting at his desk, writing letters in his study at the Escorial Palace. The message informed him that Queen Elizabeth I had given orders that a Fleet be sent to Cadiz in direct retaliation for his second Amada sailing towards England and that she would suffer no more of his threats of invasion upon her Empire.

The furious King had to make rapid preparations in an effort to curtail the threatened invasion of Cadiz, and many of the Spanish ships bearing treasures, spices and ammunition had recently been attacked and seized by that English Pirate and Sea Dog Sir Francis Drake - and now this! How much more could he bear?

It appeared that every time the Spanish Silver Fleets, on their way from King Philip's Portuguese mines had set a direct course for Spain and taken to the high Seas, there were English Pirates lying in wait to loot all his wealth. He the King of Spain! And thereafter to carry it back effortlessly to the laughing Queen of England.

King Philip of Spain remembered the young and bright eyed, dancing Princess when he had been married to Elizabeth's sister, Mary Tudor and he had been ridiculed and scorned in England by all her Englishmen - the Lords, the Ladies (laughing behind their waving fans), and the Knights who had snubbed him or scoffed at his accent and mannerisms. Oh, he could not bear to live there a moment longer and he had proclaimed that he could stand no more. He advised Queen Mary Tudor that he would reside at his Escorial Palace and thus he left poor Queen Mary to her throne, her prospects and her vicious people! It was no fault of his own that she had refused to renounce her dominions and throne for him, never to accompany him back to Spain. But British Monarchs were renowned to be staunch in their beliefs, and as a daughter of Henry VIII he could not help but wonder what impending disasters would manifest themselves upon Spain next.

A portrait of Sir Walter Raleigh at about the time he was preparing for The Battle of Cadiz in 1596. Raleigh was accompanied by Robert Devereux, Second Earl of Essex to fight the Spaniards

A portrait of Robert Devereux, Second Earl of Essex

The Story of the Battle of Cadiz, 1596
'Guateral' Raleigh and Robert Devereux the Second Earl of Essex

[113]Cadiz and the Sea Dogs

Fear hung in the air as the English Fleet, the Third Squadron, consisting of 96 ships accompanied by a Dutch contingent of 24 ships approached Cadiz on the morning of the 22nd June 1596.

---

[113] see accounts of ships, menus, ordinances in The illustrated Armada Handbook by David A. Thomas.

The sea swirled around the huge and beautiful English Carracks as the sun shone down on their freshly scrubbed triple decks, overhanging bows and stern castles. Colourful flags and banners fluttered from the flagstaffs depicting the coats of arms of the Lords and Knights aboard these vessels.

The ships were armed mainly with guns of the culverin and demi-culverin class; the medium to long range cannon with weak shot but strong range, and the culverin which fired 17lb shot up to a distance of 330 yards or 2,400 paces.

The Carracks were followed by the Great Ships of 300 tons which carried demi-culverin guns capable of firing 9lb shot within a range of 2,500 paces, and then the smaller ships - the Galleasses which were worth their weight in gold in sea battle,as one Galleasse was equal to five Galleys, with the advantage of the speed of a galley and the firepower of a Galleon. The English had captured many of these Spanish ships when the 'Invincible' Spanish were defeated effortlessly at the Armada on the 21st July, 1588 and they were being employed in this Battle, which to the King of Spain had heaped insult upon his injured pride.

The smaller frigates carried a maximum of 30 guns, being the size of the robinet, which fired shot of 8 ounces to 1lb and the Falcon, capable of firing shot of 2-3lb, or the Falconet which fired shot of 1-2 lb.

The Spanish Galleons were armed with the Cannon-Perier which fired stone balls weighing up to 24lb - these were the unwieldy and ship-smashing cannon, preferred by the Spaniards.

The English Officers and crews of the Fleet, knew that they held the chief advantage by standing out to sea and firing their long range guns upon the Spaniards who had no matching fire power.

The massive double and triple deck Spanish Galleons were already lined up in formation under the walls of the City and the Spanish gunners amidst the sandy dunes in readiness, but the Spanish Captains and Generals could only look out to Sea in complete awe of the approaching English ships.

The Spanish crews had no alternative but to wait for battle at close range and as they fired their guns and cannon in vain to entice the English fleet to move closer into the bottle neck which formed Cadiz harbour, they knew in their hearts that they faced defeat once more.

Heavy smoke billowed up through the morning air, causing a dense screen to build up all along the harbour wall, which could only hinder the Spanish further, and as their targets were obscured, they found that they could do little except wait and spend their time praying to God.

Sir Walter Raleigh had been ordered to make a reconnaissance of the coastline for fugitive Spanish Galleons and other craft such as Spanish fire ships, which might be lying in wait for them and in his absence, Admiral Howard had called a Council of War.

When Raleigh returned to his position among the Fleet, he was angered as he found that the Howards, Essex and Vere had ordered the crews to prepare for a military attack on the City of Cadiz, and he watched in disbelief as the musketeers and soldiers prepared for attack, and were already disembarking from their ships for land combat. Just as quickly as they were lowered into their flyboats, they sank, as they endeavoured to negotiate the sea which was becoming more ferocious with each passing hour and a fierce storm was promised.

Raleigh was strongly in favour of a naval attack on the Spanish Galleons and went straight to Essex, complaining bitterly that the tactics being employed would bring "our general ruin, to the utter overthrow of the whole army, their own lives and Her Majesty's future safety". Essex said Lord Howard "would not consent to enter with the fleet 'till the Town were first possessed" and Raleigh pointed out that the "twenty men in so desperate a descent would have defeated them all". Essex implored Raleigh to speak to the good Admiral Howard to see if he could persuade him to abandon his tactics for land combat.

Immediatley Raleigh had finished speaking to Essex, he took a flyboat and proceeded directly to the elderly Lord to whom he pointed out the sheer folly of such an action which would bring absolute defeat to the entire Fleet. Howard, listened intently and upon finding himself convinced of Raleigh's sound judgement, he saw fit to cancel his former orders and recalled the rejoicing soldiers to their ships.

A very serious Lord Admiral Howard then proceeded to ask Raleigh (who knew better of his own naval tactics having the benefit of experience in these matters), to put pen to paper immediately and was asked to set out his own strategy for an attack on the City of Cadiz which must take place the following morning.

Raleigh made his way back to the 'Warspite', smiling triumphantly. As he passed the 'Repulse' he noticed that the Earl of Essex stood on its deck, looking down upon him, together with all his officers and crew, who were crowded about him. They peered over the sides of the ship (and through the portholes) as they observed Raleigh passing by. The Earl of Essex (otherwise known as the Earl of March) waved his arms furiously in the air in a criss cross motion and begged Raleigh to give him news of Lord Howard's decision. Raleigh used just one word to convey his victory as he cried in a loud voice "ENTRAMOS", to which Essex, with even louder shouts of joy, lifted his right arm and removed his blue velvet cap with its ornamental yellow feather and flung it directly into Sea.

By the time Raleigh had returned to his cabin it was 10 o'clock before midnight. He sat down and wrote a message accompanied by diagrams depicting the envisaged battle scenes, to the Lord Howard and he set out his out strategic plans for the forthcoming battle. This information was immediately relayed to Lord Howard via a Messenger and Raleigh settled back for a restful evening with The Earl of Essex and the Lords, and they spoke of their future victory.

All that day, the Spanish army had prepared themselves for a land attack by the English soldiers. The civilians had taken the precaution of fleeing inland to safety, carrying their precious belongings with them, taking refuge wherever they could find it among the sandy and grass covered hills. Some of them hid in the long grass only daring to raise their heads on occasion, in order to peer out at their surroundings in bewilderment. As often as they dared to do this, in an effort to observe what was happening around them, an even greater fear built up and surrounded them all. Spanish voices everywhere were crying out that "GUATERAL" would approach in the morning. The Priests walked among the people and spoke to them saying 'Have faith in God'.

The English crews were up at daybreak and by 7 a.m. while it was assumed the Spanish were still sleeping, Lord Howard hoisted the Royal Standard of the "Ark Raleigh", signaling to all ships to move forward and to engage in battle.

Lord Howard had given Sir Walter Raleigh the place of honour and he was permitted to lead the ships of London into Battle As the ships moved forward, they fired their cannonade in unison - so that the King of Spain would be woken and frightened from his bed in the Escorial Palace in Madrid.

The colourful flags which depicted the coats of arms of the Knights and Lords abroad these shipping were waving furiously as the 'Warspite' led the 'Rainbow' followed by the 'Lion', the 'Mary Rose' and then the 'Swiftsure. Behind them the 'Dreadnought' led the 'Nonpareil'.

The blasting cannonade reverberated around the Spanish ships and surprised their crews into the prospective onslaught of battle, with the pitiful realization that they were not equipped to retaliate sufficiently.

HIC JACET: SIR WALTER RALEIGH

The decks were surrounded by thick black smoke and the barefooted gunners coughed and spluttered as they re-loaded the cannon and tried in vain to avoid breathing the fumes of the stinging smoke into their lungs.

Raleigh waved his arms high in the air and ordered that all the ships guns be silenced.

The Bugles were taken up and blown loudly in defiance of the Spanish gunfire from their Galleons, and Raleigh looked to the Sea below and watched the Spanish Zabras, fregatas and Patches of 60 to 70 tons weaving and bobbing on their way towards the English fleet. The Spanish craft were to be picked off by the gunners mercilessly, and as one by one they sank, their sailors leaping into the sea for comfort, they were rescued by the Spanish, only to be plunged into the sea once more as the rescuing ship also sank.

Six English fireships of 130 to 150 tons were sent ahead of the Fleet (to be sacrificed in battle with the due permission of the Captain) and each with a specified target in order to inflict as much damage as possible on the Spanish ships.

If the Captain of a fireship were to be successful in destroying his target he would be rewarded with the sum of £100 (or a gold chain and medal of equal value) 'to remain as a Token of Honour to him and Posterity'. Each crew member was paid £10.00 for serving aboard a fireship, but if the target was the enemy flagship then the potential rewards were to be doubled.

The fireships were loaded with old scrap sails and rotting cordage; discarded timber, pitch normally used for caulking and the remains of old wooden decks; together with tar, oil and rotten or nearly rotten sacking; complimented with discarded spars, scrap sails and finally, barrel staves and more pitch. Tar and oil had been carefully smothered over the decks, masts and yards. There were up to eight small guns on board each ship which were loaded with shot and made ready to fire as their helms were carefully lashed to keep the ships on course and toward a Spanish target.

The skeleton crews aboard each fire ship were armed with grappling irons
ready to pull the Spanish ships broadside to broadside while their crew members waited for the right moment to ignite the carefully laid powder trains and once they had watched the Spanish ships ignite and they were sure their work was successful, the English crew members then made a hasty escape from the flaming ships by lowering themselves down ropes and safely into their small boats which were towed alongside them. Having completed their destructive work, the Captains and crews hurried back to the rejoin the main Fleet.

Raleigh's extreme objective was to capture the "St Philip" and to avenge Spain for the death of his cousin, Sir Richard Grenville, who died after writhing in agony for three days on board the St. Philip from the effects of crushing and eating glass rather than suffer defeat and offer himself as a prisoner to the Spanish officers at the Battle of the Azores in 1591.

The 'Rainbow' and the younger Howard on the 'Nonpareil' took the lead and sailed ahead of Raleigh who had gone to The Earl of Essex (otherwise known as the Earl of March) to ask for additional flyboats.

Raleigh was determined not to be outdone by the Lords and nosed forward in the 'Warspite' and he swung it athwart so effectively that it blocked the way of all other ships in his path in order to ensure that not even a single flyboat should pass him and he cried out - 'I did that so I was sure that none should outsmart me again for that day!'.

The Spanish officers conferred and then despaired of their prospects, as their ships were offered up to the English Fleet like helpless pawns in their own seas and as the English nudged towards the Spanish Galleons, the murderous Spanish crews sat below the wooden decks of their Galleons with hatred flashing in their dark eyes and they waited as patiently as spiders for the English ships to reach them - broadside to broadside. Only then would they engage in battle, man against man, sword against sword.

As Raleigh moved forward he 'laid out a warp by the side of the 'St. Philip' to 'shake hands with her' but the Spaniards, seeing Guateral approaching, decided to run their ships aground and they prepared to abandon ship as their decks were peppered and raked with shot and they were suffering under heavy cannon fire. The decks of the 'St Philip' ran with the blood of the Spanish crew and its officers. The remaining screaming Spanish sailors either jumped or tumbled into the vicious sea and heavy black mud, some drowning or sinking; others horribly burned and disfigured.

The 'St. Philip' was afire like a ship from Hell and Raleigh did not know whether the Spanish officers had fire her or whether it had been achieved by cannon fire from the 'Warspite'.

Raleigh and his crew watched in awe of the relentless red, leaping flames that sprang up furiously and ate away at the ship's ordnance, as the fire licked the decks of the St Philip and rolled and danced up and down its masts. The red sparks flew high into the air, igniting the wood and charred cinders which were dripping deep beneath her decks and devouring every part of that great ship.

Sir Richard Grenville had been avenged and Sir Walter Raleigh was a happy man that day. As the guns fell silent and the billowing black smoke abated, the Spanish crews who lay dead could not be counted.

But Raleigh had been injured in the midst of battle. A blast from the 'St Philip' had sent splinters of wood flying through the air and in all directions, some of which had penetrated and gouged his left leg.

As the English Lords, Captain and their crews took their flyboats and headed for the City of Cadiz, rushing headlong into armed combat

449

with the Spaniards they sought to defeat the few who still stood and were able to fight and offer resistance against the superior English weaponry and leaving a trail of devastation behind them as they continued to sack Cadiz.

Raleigh, who was in great pain from his leg wound, had insisted upon being taken ashore. He was therefore borne upon the shoulders of his men, but his attempts to mount a horse had failed due to his terrible wound and the blood soaked through his hose and be would have a bandage to stem the flow from it.

Sir Walter Raleigh had been lamed for life. He neither claimed nor received recognition for the victory of battle through his own strategic planning, and yet he drew comfort from the fact that the great and mighty Galleon the 'St. Philip' which had been used as a prison to confine his cousin, Sir Richard Grenville beneath its decks in 1591, now lay at rest on the bottom of the Spanish ocean, reduced to a pitiful and charred black ruin.

Onshore and amidst the excitement of supreme victory, The Earl of Essex (otherwise known as the Earl of March) and Lord Howard ran wild with delight and rejoiced in their own victory. A Banquet was held in the sacked city of Cadiz and taking up their swords they proceeded to knight sixty six men to commemorate the Battle of Cadiz.

The Earl of Essex (otherwise known as the Earl of March) wished to remain in Cadiz and to hold it as a fortress to compensate the Queen for the loss of Calais, which had been recaptured by the Duc of Guise on the 8th January 1558, having been lost to France for 211 years, (and thereby destroying the English stronghold and domination of that town), but the Queen would not hear of her Court favourite staying behind in Spain and putting himself in such terrible danger. The Queen's favourite Earl was summoned forth to re-join her at the English court.

The Queen had not yet been told that King Philip had ordered his treasure ships to be sunk during the battle and that there would be no treasure taken back to England for her unless they could waylay a Silver fleet on their way home.

Elizabenthan Theatres and Dramatic Companies

William Jaggard published Shakespeare's plays

The Fortune Theatre was built in 1599
The Swan Theatre was built in 1595.
Dulwich College documents of Rose & Fortune Theaters - Edward Alleyne and his stepfather, Philip Henslowe

[Entertained the Earl of Worcester's Company of Players on 5th September 1571 to September 30 1572]

Queen Elizabeth's Men

Were not confined to court performances and they toured the provinces. The Lord Mayor of London leased them a playhouse.

The Queen's Players
The Earl of Sussex Players - Christopherus Marlowe and Thomas Kyd shared a writing chamber and wrote for this dramatic company in 1591/2.

John Shakespeare - Constable of the court of Leet [1568 Baillif]:
The Earl of Leicester : The Earl of Leicester's Company
The Earl of Essex (otherwise known as the Earl of March) went to Stratford in 1587

Richard Burbage was the most popular actor of his day. He was responsible for building the Globe Theatre and produced most of Shakespeare's plays there.
Hemminge [114] Robert Greene [Biographies 1592]

---

[114] see Robert Green's Biographies

William Drummond of Hawthorn: Entertained Ben Johnson and their conversations were recorded.

Shakespeare's Law Suite: Prof. C.W. Wallace 1910
Bishop of Worcester Ecclesiastical Records 1564/5

Sir Thomas Lucy of Charlcote nr. Stratford accused William Shakespeare of Deer Stealing and Shakespeare fled to London.

He was the Commissioner of the Trial of Mary Queen of Scots in 1585 (the Trial of Robert Devereux, the second Earl of Essex 1601); the Union of Scotland 1604; the Gunpowder Conspiracy 1606.

They recruited a dozen leading actors from existing troupes, headed by Richard Tarleton, [a jester who used to make the Queen laugh and told her to remove the paint from her face].

"

Dramatists:
E. Tilney (Tyllney
Thomas Dekker
Harry Chettle
John Day
The Chamberlain's Company:
Edward Alleyn the most famous of Players, retired in 1597 to 1600.

John Hemminge and Henry Condell were also featured players. They later edited plays.

The companies all chose Protectors at Court.

William Vaughan wrote an account of Marlowe in Golden Grove [1600].

Henslowe's Diary records: "£3.10s recorded on 30 January 1598/9 discharging Dekker from the Arrest of the Chamberlain's Men (Henslowe's Diary Folio 53).

The authors rights were purchased for between £10 and £12 and became the property of the actors.

1583 : [Charles Howard b.1536 d.1624; Ambassador to France 1559 appointed to congratulate Francis II on his accession. Lord Chamberlain 1574 to 1585 and Lord High Admiral 1585 to 1618] He was known as the Lord Howard of Effingham. (The Commander of the English fleet against the Armada).

1585   Kyd was writing for the Queen's company

1587/8   Kyd was in service as a tutor or secretary to Henry Fourth Earl of Sussex and Bridget Countess of Sussex aged 19 married Robert Radcliffe. She was Kyd's patron.

1587   William Shakespeare came to London 1587-1587
1588   Known as "The Lord Admiral's Players" or "Queen Elizabeth's Men" directed by Edward Alleyn and Philip Henslowe. For this company, Christopherus Marlowe was given his first opportunity to display his genius in 1588.

1590   The Earl of Pembroke's Company [1590] acted the play Edward II on the 30th January 1593. (It was written by Christopherus Marlowe at the end of 1591 or the beginning of 1592), William Jones registered this play 1 month after Marlowe's death (6th July, 1593).

1591   Thomas Kyd Dramatist and Christopherus Marlowe
were   engaged to write for the Earl of Sussex Company of Players.

1592   March: Lord Strange's Players produced a play at the Rose Theatre: entitled 'Harry' [Henry VI]. 10,000 people went to see the play in the first six months of its opening. The well known writer, Robert Greene died penniless, in the Autumn of that year.

1594   [115] A rival troupe "The Lord Chamberlain's Men" were formed in 1594. Lord Hunsdon, Henry Carey see Marlowe's Inquest, [Queen Elizabeth's cousin through his mother Mary Boleyn, Anne Boleyn's sister] reorganized the Company and it became linked with William Shakespeare. [See dark lady Sonnetts - XXXIII - XLIII].

1594   January 26: Cornelia written by Thomas Kyd
registered

1594   Lord Strange Ferdinando Stanley, The Earl of Derby died on 16 April 1594. Poisoned

---

[115] see Marlowe's Inquest

The Dramatic Works of Christopherus Marlowe

1587	Tamburlaine (written at Cambridge)
1587	Tamburlaine Part II
1588	[116]The Jew of Malta [Death of Duke of Guise
23.12.1588][117]	
1588/9	Doctor Faustus
1591	[118]Edward II
1591	Dido
1592	The Massacre at Paris
1593	Hero and Leander
	Lyric Poems

George Chapman's continuation of Hero & Leander after Marlowe's murder.

---

[116] Marlowe writes the Jew of Malta during his absence from Corpus Christi College from February to July 1587

[117] Mary Queen of Scot's Uncle

[118] The Earl of Pembroke's Company [1590] acted the play Edward II on the 30th January 1593. (It was written by Christopher Marlowe at the end of 1591 or the beginning of 1592), . William Jones registered this play 1 month after Marlowe's death (6th July, 1593).

The Dramatic works of Thomas Kyd

The Spanish Tragedie
Cornelia
Soliman and Perseda
The Householders Philosophie
The Murder of John Brewen Goldsmith of London
Fragments of Kyd's lost works
The First Part of Jeronimo
St. Thomas More

The Elizabethan London Theaters
Each rival Company had a Protector at Court
Elizabethan plays were registered in the Register of the Stationer's
Company. the Censure of plays was the Master of Revels who
charged a fee for his services.

A quarto: Four leaves of eight pages. 14 of Shakespeare's plays were
published in quartos: four in pirated versions.

Francis Meres records 12 of Shakespeare's plays written by the
Autumn of 1598, when Mere's book Palladis Tamia was sent for
publication. Meres lists the best dramatists in Palladis Tamia or Wits
Treasury:

Tragedy:
Lord Buckhurst
Dr. Leg of Cambridge
Doctor Edes of Oxford
Master Edward Ferys
Christopherus Marlowe
Peele
Watson
Kyd
Shakespeare
Drayton
Chapman
Dekker
Benjamin Johnson

The William Shakespeare became famous in the year 1594 after the
death of Greene [119] the best known writer of his time, who died in
poverty in 1592, left a letter behind him for all to read:

---

[119] In his letter of 1592, Greene refers to King Heny VI, Part 3, Act I Scene IV - which was
taken from a play acted by Lord Strange's Players in March 1592 at the Rose Theatre. 10,000
people went to see it in the first six months of its appearance - [The Life and Writings of
William Shakespeare - Dr. G.B. Harrison].

[To "gentlemen his quondam acquaintances that spent their wits in making plays", HE WARNS THREE OF THEM (who are probably Marlowe, [Nashe], Peele and Kyd, against a new writer:

"Base minded men, all three of you, if by my misery you be not warned; for unto none of you , like me, sought those burrs to cleave; those puppets, I mean, that spake from our mouths, those antics garnished in our colours. It is not strange that I, to whom they all have been beholding, is it not like that you to whom they all have been beholding, shall, were ye in that case as I now am, be both at once of them forsaken? Yes, trust them not; for there is an upstart crow, beautified with our feathers, that with his Tiger's heart wrap'd in a player's hide, suposeshe is as well able to bombast out a blank verse as the best of you: and beig an absolute Johannes Factotum, is in his own conceit the only Shake-scene in a country. O that I might entreat your rare wits to be employed in more profitable courses, and let those apes imitate your past excellence, and never more acquaint them with your admired inventions!"[120]

The murder of Chistopher Marlowe in 1593, and the arrest and torture of Thomas Kyd in 1593, who died in 1594.

Shakespeare published Romeo and Juliet, Midsummer Nights Dream, King Richard II (Summer 1597), King John, The Merchant of Venice.

In 1597 King Henry IV Part I: Sir John Falstaff was then known as Sir John Oldcastle. Lord Cobham[121]

---

[120] "The letter was printed soon after in a collection of Greene's scraps, which were put together under the title of A Groatsworth of Wit bought with a Million of Repentance.

[121] The Nephew of William Cecil, who was implicated in the Spanish Bye and Main Plot through his letters to Sir Walter Raleigh, objected to the portrayal of Sir John Oldcastle who was a deceased relative of Cobham's. Cobham objected to this libel against his ancestor and Shakespeare altered the name to Falstaff.

The Companies of Actors were governed by their Protectors at Court. Once the plays had been written, often by as many as 8 Dramatists, they were sold to the acting company and were no longer the property of the Dramatist. If a Dramatist ceased to be employed by a Dramatic company, he was often pursued for debt to his former employer, [the company] if they had bought his work previously : This is interesting, since if a Dramatist refused to sell his portion of the play which he had penned, and the play had been sold wholesale, then it would cease to be his property and he had lost his rights to his work.

See William Dekker and the Lord Chamberlains Men - [diary Henslowe - Folio 52] - £3.10s recorded 30 Jan 1598/9 discharging Dekker from the Arrest of the Lord Chamberlain's Men ref. the play, St. Thomas More - See signatures to this play:

The Patron of William Shakespeare was the Earl of Leicester - [find out date of Leicester's death: Leicester was urged to marry Mary Queen of Scots in - after the death of Sidney at Zutphen, murder of Marlowe, and death of Kyd Shakespeare publishes Sonnets: [Was Leicester present at the Battle of Zutphen? Was Leicester a friend of The Earl of Essex (otherwise known as the Earl of March) - same faction?

Anthony Munday : wrote for Admirals Men 1597:

Edward Allyn an Actor : Retired from 1597 until 1600. Wrote for Lord Admirals Men as a servant 1594 - until 8 Jan. 1597/8. [Retired for a short time :Why? copyright?]

Marlowe worked with Lord Admirals Company - 1588-?

William Vaughan wrote an account of Marlowe in Golden Grove 1600.

The Globe Theatre

The destruction of the Globe Theatre is described in a letter by Sir Henry Wootton 2nd July 1613.

The Queen's Players:
Members were:

John Shakespeare - Constable of the Court of Leet [1568 Baillif]
JS. Entertained the Earl of Worcester's Company of Players September 5th 1571 to September 30th 1572. as John, Chief alderman.

The Earl of Leicester
The of Essex [Stratford 1587]
William Shakespeare to London 1585-1587
[   ] Burbage
Heminge
Greene [see Robert Greene's Memoirs]

The Lord Chamberlain's Men - "Kings Men"

Patron Lord Henry Hunsdon - Queen Elizabeth I's cousin and court chamberlain.

The Authors rights were the property of the actors, which they purchased for between £10 to £12.00. There was no law of copyright in Elizabethan times.

Edward II : Acted by the Earl of Pembroke's Men on 30th January 1593:
[Marlowe]

Henslowe's Diary: "2 lost plays" March 1588/9" £6.00 to Dramatists Chettle and Porter] for a play called the "Spencers".

461

William Shakespeare

Wrote Love's Labour's Lost in 1593 and depicts Raleigh as Dom Armado the Spaniard.

Raleigh's School of Night replied with Willobie His Avisa.

Shakespeare's Othello (1604) - acted before the King at Whitehall Palace on November 1st 1604.

In Act 1, scene iii refers to the "Anthropophagi, and men whose heads do grow beneath their shoulders"

making reference to the "Headless Warriors" mentioned in a book written by Sir Walter Raleigh in 1595 and which became a bestseller in 1596. It contains the following passage for comparison:

"whose heads appear not above their shoulders they are called Ewaipanoma; they are reported to have their eyes in their shoulders and their mouths in the middle of their breasts, and that long train of hair growing backward between their shoulders".

and again in the Tempest (1611) Performed at Court November 1st 1611.

Gon: "Gaith Sir, you need not fear: when we were boys, who believe that there were mountaineers dew-lapped like bulls, whose throats had hanging at them wallets of flesh? ... or that there were such men whose heads stood in their breasts which we now find, each putter out of five for one will bring us good warrant."

[122]New Atlantis

"This fable my Lord devised, to the end that he might exhibit therein a model or description of a college instituted for the interpreting of nature and the producing of great and marvelous works for the benefit of men, under the name of Salomon's House, or the College of the Six Days' Works. And even so far his Lordship hath proceeded, as to finish that part. Certainly the model is more vast and high that than can possibly be imitated in all things; notwithstanding most things therein are within men's power to effect. His Lordship thought also in this present fable to have composed a frame of Laws, or of the best state or mould of a commonwealth; but foreseeing it would be a long work, his desire of collecting the Natural History diverted him, which he preferred many degrees before it.

This work of the New Atlantis (as much as concerneth the English edition) his Lordship designed for this place, in regard it hath so near affinity (in one part of it) with the preceding Natural History.

[The work ends with the sad words ...

"And when he had said this, he stood up; and I, as I had been taught, kneeled down; and he laid his right hand upon my head, and said: 'God bless thee, my son, and God bless this relation which I have made. I give thee leave to publish it for the good of other nations; for we here are in God's bosom, a land unknown.' And so he left me; having assigned a value of about two thousand ducats, for a bounty to me and my fellows. For they give great largesses where they come upon all occasions. [The rest was not perfected]."

---

[122] Permission given to the author to include the New Atlantis given by The British Library by letter dated [   ]

Walter Rawley"

{[" ... 'We sailed from Peru, (where we had continued by the space of one whole year,) for China and Japan, by the South Sea; taking with us victuals for twelve months; and had good winds from the east, thought soft and weak, for five months' space and more. But then the wind came about, and settled in the west for many days, so as we could make little or no way, and were sometimes in purpose to turn back. But then again there arose strong and great winds from the south, with a point east; which carried us up (for all that we could do) towards the north: by which time our victuals failed us, though we had made good spare of them. So that finding ourselves in the midst of the greatest wilderness of waters in the world, without victual, we gave ourselves for lost men, and prepared for death. Yet we did lift up our hearts and voices to God above, who 'showeth his wonders in the deep'; beseeching him of his mercy, that as in the beginning he discovered the face of the deep, and brought forth dry land, so he would now discover land to us, that we might not perish. And it came to pass that the next day about evening, we saw within a kenning before us, towards the north, as it were thick clouds, which did put us in some hope of land; knowing how that part of the South Sea was utterly unknown; and might have islands or continents, that hitherto were not come to light. Wherefore we bent our course thither, where we saw the appearance of land, all that night; and in the dawning of the next day, we might plainly discern that it was a land; flat to our sight, and full of boscage; which made it shew the more dark. And after an hour and a half's sailing, we entered into a good haven, being the port of a fair city; not great indeed, but well built, and that gave a pleasant view from the sea: and we thinking every minute long till we were on land, came close to the shore, and offered to land. But straightways we saw divers of the people, with bastons in their hands, as it were forbidding us to land; yet without any cries or fierceness, but only as a warning us off by signs that they made. Whereupon being not a little discomforted, we were advising with ourselves what we should do. During which time there made forth to us a small boat, with about either persons in it; whereof one of them had in his hand a tipstaff of a yellow cane, tipped at both ends with blue who came aboard our ship, without any show of distrust at all. And when we saw one of our number present himself somewhat afore the rest, he drew forth a little scroll of parchment, (somewhat yellower than our parchment, and shining live the leaves of writing tables, but otherwise soft and flexible,) and delivered it to our foremost man. In which scroll were written in ancient Hebrew, and in ancient Greek, and in good Latin of the School, and in Spanish, these words; 'Land ye not, none of you; and provide to be gone from this coast within sixteen days, except you have further time given you. Meanwhile, if you want fresh water, or victual, or help for your sick, or that your ship needeth repair, write down your wants, and you shall have that which belongeth to mercy. This scroll was signed with a stamp of cherubins' wings, not spread not spread but hanging downwards, and by them a cross. This being delivered, the officer returned, and left only a servant with us to receive our answer. Consulting hereupon a[monk]amongst ourselves we were much perplexed. the denial of landing and hasty warning us away troubled us much; on the other side, to find that the people had languages and were so full of humanity, did comfort us not a little. And above all, the sign of the cross to that instrument was to us a great rejoicing, and as it were a certain presage of good. Our answer was in the Spanish tongue; 'That for our ship, it was well; for we had rather met with calms and contrary winds than any tempests. For our sick, they were many, and in very ill case; so that if they were not permitted to land, they ran danger of their lives. Our wants we set down in particular; adding, 'that we had d some little store of merchandise, which if it pleased them to deal for, it might supply our wants without being chargeable unto them'. We offered some reward in pistolets unto the servant, and a piece of crimson velvet to be presented to the officer; but the servant took them not, nor would scare look upon them; and so left us, and went back in another little boat which was sent for him.

About three hours after we had dispatched our answer, there came towards us a person (as it seemed) of place. He had on him a gown with wide sleeves, of a kind of water chamolet, of an excellent azure colour, far more glossy than ours; his under apparel was green; and so was his hat, being in the form of a turban, daintily made, and not so huge as the Turkish turbans; and the locks of his hair came down below the brims of it. A reverend man was he to behold. He came in a boat, gilt in some part of it, with four persons more only in that boat; and was followed by another boat, wherein were some twenty. When he was come within a flight-shot of our ship, signs were made to us that we should send forth come to meet him upon the water; which we presently did in our ship-boat, sending the principal man amongst us save one, and four of our number with him. When we were come within six yards of their boat, they called to us to stay, and not to approach father; which we did. And thereupon the man whom I before described stood up, and with a loud voice in Spanish asked, 'Are ye Christians? [nota: Did Sir Francis Bacon speak Spanish?]; We answered, 'We were'; fearing the less, because of the cross we had seen in the subscription. At which answer the said person lifted up his right hand towards heaven, and drew it softly to his mouth, (which is the gesture they use when they thank God,) and then said: 'If ye will swear (all of you) by the merits of the Saviour that ye are no pirates, nor have shed blood lawfully nor unlawfully within forty days past, you may have licence to come on land. 'We said, 'we were all ready to take that oath.' Whereupon one of those that were with him, being (at it seemed) a notary, made an entry of this act. Which done, another of the attendants of the great person, which was with him in the same boat, after his lord had spoken a little to him, said aloud: 'My lord would have you know, that it is not of pride or greatness that he cometh not aboard your ship; but for that in your answer you declare that you have many sick amongst you, he was warned by the conservator of Health of the city that he should keep a distance.' [Note how well advanced they were in matters of health, being not as it today in 1996 in Great Britain in November 1996]; We bowed ourselves towards him, and answered, 'We were his humble servants; and accounted for great honour and singular humanity towards us that which was already done; but hoped well that the nature of the sickness of our men was not infectious.' So he returned; and a while after came the notary to us aboard our ship; holding in his hand a fruit of that country, like an orange, but of colour between orange-tawney and scarlet, which case a most excellent odour. He used it (as it seemeth) for a preservative against infection. He gave us our oath; 'But the name of Jesus and his merits': and after told us that the next day by six of the clock in the morning we should be sent to, and brought to the Strangers' House, (so he called it,) where we should be accommodated of things both for our whole and for our sick. So he left us; and when we offered him some Pistolets, he smiling said, He must not be paid twice for one labour': meaning (as I take it) that he had salary sufficient of the state for his service. For (as I after learned) they call an officer that taketh rewards, twice paid. [As an MP would today I imagine].

The next morning early, there came to us the same officer that came to us at first with his cane, and told us, 'He came to conduct us to the Strangers' House; and that he had prevented the hour, because we might have the whole day before us for our business. 'For,' said he, 'if you will follow my advice, there shall first go with me some few of you, and see the place, and how it may be made convenience for you; and then you may send for your sick, and the rest of your number which ye will bring on land.' We thanked him, and said 'That this care which he took of desolate strangers God would reward.' And so six of us went on land with him: and when we were on land, he went before us, and turned to us, and said, 'He was but our servant, and our guide.' He led us through three fair streets; and all the way we went there were gathered some people on both sides standing in a row; but in so civil a fashion, as if it had been not to wonder at us but to welcome us; and divers of them, as we passed by them, put their arms a little abroad; which is their gesture when they bid any welcome. The Strangers' House is a fair and spacious house, built of brick, of somewhat a bluer colour than our brick; and with handsome windows, some of glass, some of a kind of cambric oiled. He brought us first into a fair parlor above stairs, and then asked us, 'What number of persons we were? And how many sick?' We answered 'We were in all (sick and whole) one and fifty persons, whereof our sick were seventeen. He desired us to have patience a little, and to stay till he came back to us; which was about an hour after; and then he led us to see the chambers which were provided for us, being in number nineteen: they having better than the rest, might receive four of the principal men of our company, and lodge them alone by themselves; and the other fifteen chambers were to lodge us two and two together. The chambers were handsome and cheerful chambers, and furnished civilly. Then he led us to a long gallery, like a dorture, where he showed us all along the one side (for the other side was but wall; and window) seventeen cells, very neat ones, having partitions of cedar wood. [quarantine chambers]. Which gallery and cells, being in all forty, (many more than we needed,) were instituted as an infirmary for sick persons. And he told us withal, that as any of our sick waxed well, he might be removed from his cell to a chamber; for which purpose there were set forth ten spare chambers, besides the number we spake of before. This done, he brought us back to the parlor, and lifting up his cane a little, (as they do when they give any charge or command,) said to us, 'Ye are to know that the custom of the land requireth, that after this day and to-morrow, (which we give you for removing of your people from your ship,) you are to keep within doors for three days. But let it not trouble you, nor do not think yourselves restrained, but rather left to your rest and ease. You shall want nothing, and there are six of our people appointed to attend you, for any business you may have abroad.' We gave him thanks with all affection and respect, and said, 'God surely is manifested in this land.' we offered him also twenty pistolets; but he smiled, and only said; 'What? twice paid!' And so he left us. Soon after our dinner was served in; which was right good viands, both for bread and meat: better than any collegiate diet that I have known in Europe. We had also drink of three sorts, all wholesome and good; wine of the grape; a drink of grain, such as it with us our ale, but more clear; and a kind of cider made of a fruit of that country; a wonderful pleasing and refreshing drink. Besides, there were brought in to us great store of those scarlet oranges for our sick; which (they said) were an assured remedy for sickness taken at sea. There was given us a also a box of small grey or whitish pills, which they wished our sick should take, one of the pilles every night before sleep; which (they said) would hasten their recovery. The next day, after that our trouble of carriage and removing of our men and goods out of our ship was somewhat settled and quiet, I thought good to call our company together; and when they were assembled said unto them; 'My dear friends, let us know ourselves, and how it standeth with us. We are men cast on land, as Jonas was out of the whale's belly, when we were as buried in the deep: and now we are on land, we are but between death and life; for we are beyond both the old world and the new; and whether ever we shall see Europe, God only knoweth. It is a kind of miracle hath brought us hither: and it must be little less that shall bring us hence. Therefore in regard of our deliverance past, and our danger present and to come, let us look up to God, and every man reform his own ways. besides we are come here amongst a Christian people, full of piety and humanity: let us not bring that confusion of face upon ourselves, as to show our vices or unworthiness before them. Yet there is more. For they have by commandment (though in form of courtesy) cloistered us within these walls for three days: who knoweth whether it be not to take some taste of our manners and conditions? and if they find them bad, to banish us straightways, if good, to give us further time. For these men that they have given us for attendance may withal have an eye upon us. Therefore for God's love, and as we love the weal of our souls and bodies, let us so behave ourselves as we may be at peace with God, and may find grace in the eyes of this people.' Our company with one voice thanked me for my good admonition, and promised me to live soberly and civilly, and without giving any the least occasion of offence. So we spent our three days joyfully and without care, in expectation what would be done with us when they were expired. During which time, we had every hour joy of the amendment of our sick; who thought themselves cast into some divine pool of healing, they mended so kindly and so fast.

The morrow after our three days were past, there came to us a new man that we had not seen before, clothed in blue as the former was, save that his turban was white, with a small red cross on the top. He had also a tippet of fine linen. At his coming in, he did bend to us a little, and put his arms abroad. We of our parts saluted him in a very lowly and submissive manner; as looking that from him we should

469

receive sentence of life or death. He desired to speak with some few of us: whereupon six of us only stayed, and the rest avoided the room He said: 'I am by office governor of this House of Strangers, and by vocation I am a Christian priest; and therefore am come to you to offer you my service, both as strangers and chiefly as Christians. Some things I may tell you, which I think you will not be unwilling to hear. The state hath given you licence to stay on land for the space of six weeks: and let it not trouble you if your occasions ask further time, for the law in this point is not precise; and I do not doubt but myself shall be able to obtain for you such further time as may be convenient. Ye shall also understand, that the Strangers' House is at this time rich, and much aforehand; for it hath laid up revenue these thirty-seven years; for so long it is since any stranger arrived in this part: and therefore take ye no care; the state will defray you all the time you stay; neither shall you stay one day the less for that. As for any merchandise ye have brought, ye shall be well used, and have your return either in merchandise or in gold and silver: for to us it is all one.. And if you have any other request to make, hide it not. For ye shall find we will not make your countenance to fall by the answer ye shall receive. Only this I must tell you, that none of you must go above the Karam' (that is with them a mile and a half) 'from the walls of the city, without especial leave.' We answered, after we had looked awhile one upon another admiring this gracious parent-like usage: 'That we could not tell what to say: for we wanted words to express our thanks; and his noble free offers left us nothing to ask. It seemed to us that we had before us a picture of our salvation in heaven; for we that were while since in the jaws of death, were now brought into a place where we found nothing but consolations. For the commandment laid upon us, we would not fail to obey it, thought it was impossible but our hearts should be inflamed to tread further upon this happy and holy ground. We added; 'that our tongues should first cleave to the roofs of our moths, ere we should forget either his reverend person or this whole nation in our prayers.' We also most humbly besought him to accept of us as his true servants, by as just a right as ever men on earth were bounden; laying and presenting both our persons and all we had at his feet. He said; 'He was a priest, and looked for a priest's reward: which was our brotherly love and the good of our souls and bodies.' So he went from us, not without tears of tenderness in his eyes; and left us also confused with joy and kindness, saying amongst ourselves, 'That we were come into a land of angels, which did appear to us daily and prevent us with comforts, which we thought not of, much less expected.'

The next day, about ten of the clock, the governor came to us again, and after salutations said familiarly, 'That he was come to visit us': and called for a chair, and sat him down: and we, being some ten of us, (the rest were of the meaner sort, or else gone abroad,) sat down with him. and when we were set, he began thus: 'We of this Island of Bensalem,' (for so they call it in their language,) 'have this; that by means of our solitary situation, and of the laws of secrecy which we have for our travelers, and our rare admission of strangers, we know well most part of the habitable world, and are ourselves unknown. Therefore because he that knowetheth least is fittest to ask questions, it is more reason, for the entertainment of the time, that ye ask me questions, than that I ask you.' We answered; That we humbly thanked him that he would give us leave so to do: and that we conceived by the taste we had already, that there was no worldly thing on earth more worthy to be known than the state of that happy land. But above all,' (we said,) 'since that we were met from the several ends of the world, and hoped assuredly that we should meet one day in the kingdom of heaven, (for that we were both parts Christians,) we desired to know (in respect that land was so remote, and so divided by vast and unknown seas, from the land where our Saviour walked on earth,) who was the apostle of that nation, and how it was converted to the faith?' It appeared in his face that he took great contentment in this our question: he said, 'Ye knit my heart to you, by asking this question in the first place; for it sheweth that you 'first seek the kingdom of heaven'; and I shall gladly and briefly satisfy your demand.

'About twenty years after the ascension of our Saviour, it came to pass that there was seen by the people of Renfusa, (a city upon the eastern coast of our island,) within night, (the night was cloudy and calm,) as it might be some mile into the sea, a great pillar of light; not sharp, but in form of a column or cylinder, rising from the sea a great way up towards heaven: and on the top of it was seen a large cross of light, more bright and resplendent than the body of the pillar. Upon which so strange a spectacle, the people of the city gathered apace together upon the sands, to wonder; and so after put themselves into a number of small boats, to go nearer to this marvellous sight. But when the boats were come within about sixty yards of the pillar, they found themselves all bound, and could go no further; yet so as they might move to go about, but might not approach nearer: so as the boats stood all as in a theatre, beholding this light as an heavenly sign. It so fell out, that there was in one of the boats one of the wise men of the society of Salomon's House; which house or college (my good brethren) is the very eye of this kingdom; who having awhile attentively and devoutly viewed and contemplated this pillar and cross, fell down upon his face; and then raised himself upon his knees, and lifting up his hands to heaven, made his prayers in this manner:

' "Lord God of heaven and earth, thou hast vouchsafed of thy grace to those of our order, to know thy works of creation, and the secrets of them; and to discern (as far as appertaineth to the generations of men) between divine miracles, works of nature, works of art, and impostures and illusions of all sorts. I do here acknowledge and testify before this people, that the thing which we now see before our eyes is thy Finger and a true Miracle; and forasmuch as we learn in our books that thou never workest miracles but to a divine and excellent end, (for the laws of nature are thine own laws, and thou exceedest them not but upon great cause,) we most humbly beseech thee to prosper this great sign, and to give us the interpretation and use of it in mercy; which thou dost in some part secretly promise by sending it unto us."

'When he had made his prayer, he presently found the boat he was in moveable and unbound; whereas all the rest remained still fast; and taking that for an assurance of leave to approach, he caused the boat to be softly and with silence rowed towards the pillar. But ere he came near it, the pillar and cross of light brake up, and cast itself abroad, as it were, into a firmament of many stars; which also vanished soon after, and there was nothing left to be seen but a small ark or chest of cedar, dry, and not wet at all with water, though it swam. And in the fore-end of it, which was towards him, grew a small green branch of palm; and when the wise man had taken it with all reverence into his boat, it opened of itself, and there were found in it a Book and a Letter; both written in fine parchment, and wrapped in sindons of linen. The Book contained all the cononical books of the Old and New Testament, according as you have them, (for we know well what the churches with you receive); and the Apocalypse itself, and some other books of the New Testament which were not at that time written, were nevertheless in the Book. And for the Letter, it was in these words:

' "I Bartholomew, a servant of the Highest, and Apostle of Jesus Christ, was warned by an age that appeared to me in a vision of glory, that I should commit this ark to the floods of the sea. Therefore I do testify and declare unto that people where God shall ordain this ark to come to land, that in the same day is come unto them salvation and peace and goodwill from the Father, and from the Lord Jesus."

'There was also in both these writings, as well the Book as the Letter, wrought a great miracle, conform to that of the Apostles in the original Gift of Tongues. For there being at this time in this land Hebrews, Persians, and Indians, besides the natives, every one read upon the Book and Letter, as if they had been written in his own language. And thus was this land saved from infidelity (as remain of the old world was from water) by an ark, through the apostolical and miraculous evangelism of St. Bartholomew.' And here he paused, and a messenger came, and called him from us. So this was all that passed in that conference.

the next day, the governor came again to us immediately after dinner, and excused himself, saying, 'That the day before he was called from us somewhat abruptly, but now he would make us amends, and spend time with us, if we held his company and conference agreeable.' We answered, 'That we held it so agreeable and pleasing to us, as we forgot both dangers past and fears to come, for the time we heard him speak: and that we thought an hour spent with him, was worth years of our former life.' He bowed himself a little to us, and after we were set again, he said; 'Well, the questions are on your part.' One of our number said, after a little pause; 'That there was a matter we were no less desirous to know, than fearful to ask, lest we might presume too far. But encouraged by his rare humanity towards us, (that could scarce think ourselves strangers, being his vowed and professed servants,) we would take the hardiness to propound it: humbly beseeching him, if he thought it not fit to be answered, that he would pardon it, though he rejected it.' We said; 'we well observed those his words, which he formerly spake, that this happy island where we now stood was known to few, and yet knew most of the nations of the world; which we found to be true, considering they had the languages of Europe, and knew much of our state and business; and yet we in Europe (notwithstanding all the remote discoveries and navigations of this last age,) never heard any of the least inkling or glimpse of this island. This we found wonderful strange; for that all nations have inter-knowledge one of another either by voyage into foreign parts, or by strangers that come to them: and though the traveller into a foreign country doth commonly know more by the eye than he that stayeth at home can by relation of the traveller; yet both ways suffice to make a mutual knowledge, in some degree, on both parts. But for this island, we never heard tell of any ship of theirs that had been seen to arrive upon any shore of Europe; no, nor of either the East or West Indies; nor yet of any ship of any other part of the world that had made return from them. And yet the marvel rested not in this. For the situation of it (as his lordship said) in the secret conclave of such a vast sea might cause it. But then that they should have knowledge of the languages, books, affairs, of those that lie such a distance from them, it was a thing we could not tell what to make of; for that it seemed to us a condition and propriety of divine powers and beings, to be hidden and unseen to others, and yet to have others open and as in a light to them.' At this speech the governor gave a gracious smile, and said; 'That we did well to ask pardon for this question we now asked; for that it imported as if we thought this land a land of magicians, that sent forth spirits of the air into all parts, to bring them news and intelligence of other countries.' It was answered by us all, in all possible humbleness, but yet with a countenance taking knowledge that we knew that he spake it but merrily, 'That we were apt enough to think there was somewhat supernatural in this island; but yet rather as angelical than magical. But to let his lordship know truly what it was that made us tender and doubtful to ask this question, it was not any such conceit, but because we remembered he had given a touch in his former speech, that this land had laws of secrecy touching strangers.' To this he said; 'You remember it aright; and therefore in that I shall say to you I must reserve some particulars, which it is not lawful for me to reveal; but there will be enough left to give you satisfaction.

'You shall understand (that which perhaps you will scare think credible) that about three thousand years ago or somewhat more, the navigation of the world, (specially for remote voyages,) was greater than at this day. Do not think with yourselves that I know not how much it is increased with you within these six-score years; I know it well: and yet I say greater then than now; whether it was, that the example of the ark, that saved the remnant of men from the universal deluge, gave men confidence to adventure upon the waters; or what it was; but such is the truth. So had the Carthaginians, their colony, which is yet further west. Toward the east, the shipping of Egypt and of Palestina was likewise great. China also, and the great Atlantis (that you call America), which have now but junks and canoes, abounded then in tall ships. This island (as appeareth by faithful registers of those times) had then fifteen hundred strong ships, of great content. Of all this there is with you sparing memory, or none; but we have large knowledge thereof.

'At that time, this land was known and frequented by the ships and vessels of all the nations before named. And (as it cometh to pass) they had many times men of other countries, that were no sailors, that came with them; as Persians, Chaldeans, Arabians; so as almost all nations of might and fame resorted hither; of whom we have some strips and little tribes with us at this day. And for our own ships, they went sundry voyages, as well as to your Straits, which you call the Pillars of Hercules, as to other parts in the Atlantic an Mediterrane Seas; as to Paguin (which is the same with Cambaline and Quinzy, upon the Oriental Seas, as far as to the borders of the East Tartary.

'At the same time, and at an age after, or more, the inhabitants of the great Atlantis did flourish. For thought the narration and description which is made by a great man with you, that the descendants of Neptune planted there; and of the magnificent temple, palace, city, and hill; and manifold streams of goodly navigable rivers, (which, as so many chains, environed the same site and temple); and the several degrees of ascent whereby men did climb up to the same, as if it had been a scala coeli; be all poetical and fabulous: yet so much is true, that the said country of Atlantis, is well that of Peru, then called Coya, as that of Mexico, then named Tyrambel, were might and proud kingdoms in arms, shipping, and riches: so mighty, as at one time (or at least within the space of ten years)(they both made two great expeditions; they of Tryambel through the Atlantic to the Mediterrane Sea; and they of Coya through the South Sea upon this our island. And for the former of these, which was in to Europe, the same author amongst you (as it seemeth) had some relation from the Egyptian priest whom he citeth. For assuredly such a thing there was. But whether it were the ancient Athenians that had the glory of the repulse and resistance of those forces, I can say nothing: but certain it is, there never came back either ship or man from that voyage. Neither hand the other voyage of those of Coya upon us had better fortune, if they had not met with enemies of greater clemency. For the king of this island (by name Altabin) a wise man and a great warrior, knowing well both his own strength and that of this enemies, handled the matter so, as he cut off their land-forces from their ships; and entoiled both their navy and their camp with a greater power than theirs, both by sea and land; and compelled them to render themselves without striking stroke: and after they were at his mercy, contenting himself only with their oath that they should no more bear arms against him, dismissed them all in safety. But the Divine Revenge overtook not long after those proud enterprises. For within less than the space of one hundred years, the great Atlantis was utterly lost and destroyed: not by a great earthquake, as your man saith, (for that whole tract is little subject to earthquakes,) but by a particular deluge or inundation; those countries having at this day, far greater rivers and far higher mountains to pour down waters, than any part of the old world. But it is true that the same inundation was not deep; not past forty foot, in most places, from the ground: so that although it destroyed man and beast generally, yet some few wild inhabitants of the wood escaped. Birds also were saved by flying to the high trees and woods. For as men, although they had building in many places higher than the depth of the water, yet that inundation, thought it were shallow, had a long continuance; whereby they of the vale that were not drowned, perished for want of food and other things necessary. So as marvel you not at the thin population of America, nor at the rudeness and ignorance of the people; for you must account your inhabitants of America as a young people; for that there was so much time between the universal flood and their particular inundation. For the poor remnant of human seed which remained in their mountains peopled the country again slowly, by little and little; and being simple and savage people, (not like Noah and his sons, which was the chief family of the earth,) they were not able to leave letters, arts, and civility to their posterity; and having likewise in their mountainous habitations been used (in respect of the extreme cold of those regions) to clothe themselves with the skins of tigers, bears, and great hairy goats, that they have in those parts; when after they came down into the valley, and found the intolerable heats which are there, and knew no means of lighter apparel, they were forced to begin the custom of going naked, which continueth at this day. Only they take great pride and delight in the feathers of birds, Dan this also they took from those their ancestors of the mountains, who were invited unto it by the infinite flights of birds that came up to the high grounds, while the waters stood below. So you see, by this main accident of time, we lost our traffic with the Americans, with whom of all others, in regard they lay nearest to us, we had most commerce. As for the other parts of the world, it is most manifest that in the ages following (whether it were in respect of wars, or by a natural revolution of time,) navigation did every where greatly decay; and specially far voyages (the rather by the use of galleys, and such vessels as could hardly brook the ocean,) were altogether left and omitted. So then, that part of the intercourse which could be from other nations to sail to us, you see how it hath long since ceased; except it were by some rare accident, as this of yours. But now of the cessation of that other part of intercourse, which might be by our sailing to other nations, I must yield you some other cause. For I cannot say (if I shall say truly,) but our shipping, for number, strength, mariners, pilots, and all things that appertain to navigation, is as great as ever: and therefore why we should sit at home, I shall now give you an account by itself: and it will draw nearer to give you satisfaction to your principal question.

'There reigned in this island, about nineteen hundred years ago, a King, whose memory of all others we most adore; not superstitiously, but as a divine instrument, though a mortal man; his name was Solamona; and we esteem him as the lawgiver of our nation. This king had a large hear, inscrutable for good; and was wholly bent to make his kingdom and people happy. He therefore, taking into consideration how sufficient and substantive this land was to maintain itself without any aid at all of the foreigner; being five thousand six hundred miles in circuit, and of rare fertility of soil in the greatest part thereof; and finding also the shipping of this country might be plentifully set on work, both by fishing and by transportations from port to port, and likewise by sailing into some small islands that are not far from us, and are under the crown and laws of this state; and recalling into his memory the happy and flourishing estate wherein this land then was, so as it might be a thousand ways altered to the worse, but scare any one way to the better; thought nothing wanted to his noble and heroical intentions, but only (as far as human foresight might reach) to give perpetuity to that which was in his time so happily established. Therefore amongst his other fundamental laws of this kingdom, he did ordain the interdicts and prohibitions which we have touching entrance of strangers; which at that time (though it was after the calamity of America) was frequent; doubting novelties, and commixture of manners. It is true, the like law against the admission of strangers without licence is an ancient law in the kingdom of China, and yet continued in use. But there it is a poor thing; and hath made them a curious, ignorant, fearful, foolish nation. But our lawgiver made his law of another temper. For first, he hath preserved all points of humanity, in taking order and making provision for the relief of strangers distressed; whereof you have tasted.' At which speech (as reason was) we all rose up, and bowed ourselves. He went on. 'That king also, still desiring to join humanity and policy together; and thinking it against humanity to detain strangers here against their wills, and against policy that they should return and discover their knowledge of this estate, he took this course: he did ordain that of the strangers that should be permitted to land, as many (at all times) might depart as would; but as many as would stay should have very good conditions and means to live from the state. Wherein he saw so far, that now in so many ages since the prohibition, we have memory not of one ship that ever returned; and but of thirteen persons only, at several times, that chose to return in our bottoms. What those few that returned may have reported abroad I know not. But you must think, whatsoever they have said could be taken where they came but for a dream. Now for our travelling from hence into parts abroad, our Lawgiver thought fit altogether to restrain it. So is it not in China. For the Chineses sail where they will or can; which sheweth that their law of keeping our strangers is a law of pusillanimity and fear. But this restraint of ours hath one only which is admirable; preserving the good which cometh by communicating with strangers, and avoiding the hurt; and I will now open it to you. And here I shall seem a little to digress, but you will by and by find it pertinent. Ye shall understand (my dear friends) that amongst the excellent acts of that king, one above all hath the pre-eminence. It was the erection and institution of an Order or Society which we call Salomon's House; the noblest foundation (as we think) that ever was upon the earth; and the lanthorn of this kingdom. It is dedicated to the study of the Works and Creatures of God. Some think it beareth the founder's name a little corrupted, as if it should be Solamona's House. But the records write it as it is spoken. So as I take it to be denominate of the King of the Hebrews, which is famous with you, and no stranger to us. For we have some parts of his works which with you are lost; namely; that

Natural History which he wrote, of all plants, from the cedar of
Libanus to the moss that groweth out of the wall, and of all things that
have life and motion. This maketh me think that our king, finding
himself to symbolize in many things with that king of the Hebrews
(which have lived may years before him), honoured him with the title
of this foundation. And I am the rather induced to be of this opinion,
for that I find in ancient records this Order or Society is sometimes
called Salomon's House and sometimes the College of the Six Days'
Works; whereby I am satisfied that our excellent king had learned
from the Hebrews that God had created the world and all that therein is
within six days; and therefore he instituting that House for the finding
out of the true nature of all things, (whereby God might have the more
glory in the workmanship of them, and men the more fruit in the use of
them,) did give it also that second name. But now to come to our
present purpose. When the king had forbidden to all his people
navigation into any part that was not under his crown, he made
nevertheless this ordinance; That every twelve years there should be
set forth out of this kingdom two ships, appointed to several voyages;
That in either of these ships there should be a mission of three of the
Fellows or Brethren of Salomon's House; whose errand it was only to
give us knowledge of the affairs and state of those countries to which
they were designed, and especially of the sciences, arts, manufactures,
and inventions of all the world; and withal to bring unto us books,
instruments, and patterns in every kind; that the ships, after they had
landed the brethren, should return; and that the brethren should stay
abroad till the new mission. these ships are not otherwise fraught,
than with store of victuals, and good quantity of treasure to remain
with the brethren, for the buying of such things and rewarding of such
persons as they think fit. Now for me to tell you how the vulgar sort
of mariners are contained from being discovered at land; and how they
that must be put on shore for any time, colour themselves under the
names of other nations; and to what places these voyages have been
designed; and what places of rendez-vous are appointed for the new
missions; and the like circumstances of the practique; I may not do it:
neither is it much to your desire. But thus you see we maintain a trade,
not for gold, silver, or jewels; nor for silks; nor for spices; nor any
other commodity of matter; but only for God's first creature, which

was Light: to have light (I say) of the growth of all parts of the world.' And when he had said this, he was silent; and so were we all. For indeed we were all astonished to hear so strange things so probably told. And he, perceiving that we were willing to say somewhat but had it not ready, in great courtesy took us off, and descended to ask us questions of our voyage and fortunes; and in the end concluded, that we might do well to think with ourselves what time of stay we would demand of the state; and bade us not to scant ourselves; for he would procure such time as we desired. Whereupon we all rose up, and presented ourselves to kiss the skirt of his tippet; but he would not suffer us; and so took his leave. But when it came once amongst our people that the state used to offer conditions to strangers that would stay, we had work enough to get any of our men to look to our ship, and to keep them fro going presently to the governor to crave conditions. But with much ado we refrained them, till we might agree what course to take.

We took ourselves now for free men, seeing there was no danger of our utter perdition; and lived most joyfully, going abroad and seeing what was to be seen in the city and places adjacent within our tedder; and obtaining acquaintance with many of the city, not of the meanest quality; at whose hands we found such humanity, and such a freedom and desire to take strangers as it were into their bosom, as was enough to make us forget all that was dear to us in our own countries: and continually we met with many things right worthy of observation and relation; as indeed, if there be a mirror in the world worthy to hold men's eyes, it is that country. One day there were two of our company bidden to a Feast of the Family, as they call it. A most natural, pious, and reverend custom it is, shewing that nation to be compounded of all goodness. This is the manner of it. It is granted to any man that shall live to see thirty persons descended of his body alive together, and all above three years old, to make this feast; which is done at the cost of the state. The Father of the Family, whom they call the Tirsan, two days before the feast, taketh to him three of such friends as he liketh to choose; and is assisted also by the governor of the city or place where the feast is celebrated; and all the persons of the family, of both sexes, are summoned to attend him. These two days the Tirsan sitteth in consultation concerning the good estate of the family. There, if there be any discord or suits between any of the family, they are compounded and appeased. There, if any of the family be distressed or decayed, order is taken for their relief and competent means to live. There, if any be subject to vice, or take ill courses, they are reproved and censured. So likewise direction is given touching marriages, and the courses of life which any of them should take, with divers other the like orders and advices. The governor assisteth, to the end to put in execution by his public authority the decrees and orders of the Tirsan, if they should be disobeyed; though that seldom needeth; such reverence and obedience they give to the order of nature. The Tirsan doth also then ever choose one man from amongst his sons, to live in house with him: who is called ever after the Son of the Vine. The reason will hereafter appear. On the feast-day, the Father or Tirsan cometh forth after divine service into a large room where the feast is celebrated; which room hath an half-pace, is a chair placed for him, with a table and carpet before it. Over the chair is a state, made round or oval, and it is of ivy; an ivy somewhat whiter than ours, like the leaf of a silver asp, but more shining; for it is green all winter. And the state is curiously wrought with silver and silk of divers colours, broiding or binding in the ivy; and is ever of the work of some of the daughters of the family; and veiled over at the top with a fine net of silk and silver. But the substance of it is true ivy; whereof, after it is taken down, the friends of the family are desirous to have some leaf or sprig to keep. The Tirsan cometh forth with all his generation or lineage, the males before him, and the females following him; and if there be a mother from whose body the whole lineage is descended, there is a traverse placed in a loft above on the right hand of the chair, with a privy door, and a carved window of glass, leaded with gold and blue; where she sitteth, but is not seen. When the Tirsan is come forth, he sitteth down in the chair; and all the lineage place themselves against the wall, both at his back and upon the return of the half-pace, in order o of their years without difference of sex; and stand upon their feet. When he is set; the room being always full of company, but well kept and without disorder; after some pause there cometh in from the lower end of the room a Taratan (which is as much as an herald) and on either side of him two young lads; whereof one carrieth a scroll of their shining yellow parchment; and the other a cluster of grapes of gold, with a long foot or stalk. The herald and children are clothed with mantles of sea-water green satin; but the herald's mantle is streamed with gold, and hath a train. Then the herald with three curtesies, or rather inclinations, cometh up as far as the half-pace; and there first taketh into his hand the scroll. This scroll is the King's Charter, containing fit of revenew, and many privileges, exemptions, and points of honour, granted to the Father of the Family; and is ever styled and directed, To such an one our well-beloved friend and creditor: which is a title proper only to this case. For they say the king is debtor to no man, but for propagation of his subjects. The seal set to the king's charter is the king's image, imbossed or moulded in gold; and though such charters be expedited of course, and as of right, yet they are varied by discretion, according to the number and dignity of the family. This charter the herald readeth aloud; and while and while it is read, the father or Tirsan standeth up, supported by two of his sons, such as he chooseth. then the herald mounteth the half-pace, and delivereth the charter into his hand: and with that there is an acclamation by all that are present in their language, which is thus much: Happy are the people of Bensalem. Then the herald taketh into his hand from the other child the cluster of grapes, which is of gold, both the salk and the grapes. But the grapes are daintily enamelled; and if the males of the family be the greater number, the grapes are enaamelled purpoel, with a little sun set on the top; if the females, then they are enamelled into a greenish yellow, with a crescent on the top. The grapes are in number as many as there are descendants of the family. This golden cluster the herald delivereth also to the Tirsan; who presently delivereth it over to that son that he had formerly chosen to be in house with him: who beareth it before his father as an ensign of honour when he goeth in public, ever after; and is thereupon called the Son of the Vine. After this ceremony ended, the father or Tirsan retireth; and after some time cometh forth again to dinner, where he sitteth alone under the state, as before; and none of his descendants sit with him, of what degree or dignity soever, except he hap to be of Salomon's House. He is served only by his own children, such as are male; who perform unto him all service of the table upon the knee; and the women only stand about him, leaning against the wall. The room below the half-pace hath tables on the sides for the guests that are bidden; who are served with great and comely order; and towards the end of dinner (which in the greatest feasts with them lasteth never above an hour and an half) there is an hymn sung, varied according to the invention of him that composeth it, (for they have excellest poesy,) but the subject of it is (always the praises of Adam and Noah and Abraham; whereof the former two peopled the world, and the last was the Father of the Faithful: concluding ever with a thanksgiving for the nativity of our Saviour, in whose birth the births of allare only blessed. Dinner being done, the Tirsan retireth again; and having withdrawn himself alone into a place where he maketh some private prayers, he cometh forth the third time, to give the blessing; with all his descendants, who stand about him as at the first. Then he calleth them forth by one and by one, by name, as he pleaseth, though seldom the order of age be inverted. The person that is called (the table being before removed) knelleth down before the chair, and the father layet his hand upon his head, or her head, and giveth the blessing in these words: 'Son of Bensalem, (or Daughter of Bensalem,) thy father saith it; the man by whom thou hast breath and life speaketh the word; The blessing of the everlasting Father, the Prince of Peace, and the Holy Dove be upon thee, and make the days of thy pilgrimage good and many.' This he saith to ever of them; and that done, if there be any of his sons of eminent merit and virtue, (so they be not above two,) he calleth for them again; and saith, laying his arm over their shoulders, they standing; 'Sons, it is well ye are bron, give God the praise, and persevere to the end.' ánd withal delivereth to either of them a jewel, made in the figure of an ear of wheat, which they ever after wear in the front of their turban or hat. This done, they fall to music and dances, and other recreations, after their manner, for the rest of the day. This is the full order of that feast.

By that ime six or seven days were spent, I was fallen into strait acquaintance with a merchant of that city, whose name was Joabin.

He was a Jew, and circumcised: for they have som few stirps of Jews yet remaining among them, whom they leave to their own religion. Which they may the better do, because they are of a far differing disposition from the Jews in other parts. For whereas they hate the name of Christ, and have a secret inbred rancour against the people amongst whom they live: these (contraiwise) give unto our Saviour many high attributes, and love the nation of Bensalem extremely. Surely this man of whom I speak would ever acknowledge that Christ was born of a Virgin, and the he was more than a man; and he woudl tell how Gow made him ruler of the Seraphims which guard his throne; and they call him also the Milken Way, and the Eliah of the Messiah; and many other high names; which though they be inferior to his divine Majesty, yet they are far from the language of other Jews. And for the country of Bensalem, this man would make no end of commending it: being desirous, by tradition among the Jews there, to have it believed that the people thereof were of the generations of Abraham, by another son, whom they call Nachoran; and that Moses by a secret cabala ordained the laws of Bensalem which they now use; and that when the Messiah should come, and sit in his throne at Hierusalem, the king of Bensalem should sit at his feet, whereas other kings should keep a great distance. But yet setting aside these Jewish dreams, the man was a wise man, and learned, and of great policy, and excellently seen in the laws and customs of that nation. Amongst other discourses, one day I told him I was much affected with the relation I had from some of the company, of their custom in holding the Feast of the Family; for that (methought) I had never heard of a solemnity wherein nature did so much preside. And because the propagation of families proceedeth from the nuptial copulation, I desired to know of him what laws and customs they had concerning marriage; and whether they kept marriage well; and whether they were tied to one wife? For that were population is so much affected, and such as with them it seemed to be, there is commonly permission of plurality of wives. This this he said, 'You have reason for to commend that excellent instituition of the Feast of the Family. And indeed we have experience, that those families that are partakers of the blessing of that feast do flourish and prosper ever after in an extraordinary manner. But hear me now, and I will tell you what I know. You shall understand that there is not under the heavens so chase a nation as this of Bensalem; nor so free from all pollution or foulness. It is the virgin of the world. I remember I have read in one of your European books, of an holy hermit amongst you that desired to see the Spirit of Fornication; and there appeared to him a little foul ugly Aethiop. But if he had desired to see the Spirit of Chastity of Bensalem, it would have appeared to him in the likeness of a fair beautiful Cherubin. For there is nothing amonst mortal men more fair and admirable, than the chaste minds of this people. Know therefore, that with them are no stews, no dissolute houses, no courtesans, nor any thing of that kind. Nay they wonder (with detestation) at you in Éurope which permit such things. They say ye have put marriage out of office: for marriage is ordained a remedy for unlawful concupiscence; and nature concupiscence seemeth as a spur to marriage. But when men have at hand a remedy more agreeable to their corrupt will, marriage is almost expulsed. And therefore there are with you seen infinite men that marry not, but chuse rather a libertine and impure single life, than to be yoked in marriage; and many that do marry, marry late, when the prime and strength of their years is past. And when they do marry, what is marriage to them but a very bargain; wherein is sought alliance, or portion, or reputation, with some desire (almost indifferent) of issue; and not the faithful nuptial union of man and wife, that was first instituted. Niether is it possible that those that have cast away so basely so much of their strength, should greatly esteem children, (being of the same matter,) as chaste men do. So likewise during marriage, is the case much amended, as it ought to be if those things were tolerated only for necessity? No, but they remain still as a very affront to marriage. the haunting of those dissolute places, or resort to the courtesans, are no more punished in married men than in batchelors. And the depraved custom of change, and the delight in meretricious embracements, (where sin is turned into art,) maketh marriage a dull thing, and a kind of imposition or tax. They hear you defend these things, as done to avoid greater evils; as advourtries, deflowering of virgins, unnatural lust, and the like. But they say this is a preposterous wisdom; and they call it Lot's offer, who to save his guests from abusing, offered his daughters: nay they say farther that there is little gained in this; for that the same vices and appetites do still remain and abound; unlawful lust being like a furnace, that if you stop the flames altogether, it will quench; but if you give it any vent, it will rage. As for masculine love, they have no touch of it; and yet there are not so faithful and inviolate friendships in the world again as are there; and to speak generally, (as I said before,) I have not read of any such chastity in any people as theirs. And their usual saying is, "That whosoever is unchase cannot reverence himself;" and they say, "That the reverence of a man's self is, next religion, the chiefest bridle of all vices." ' And when he had said this, the good Jew paused a little; whereupon I, far more willing to hear him speak on than to speak myself, yet thinking it decent that upon his pause of speech I should not be altogether silent, said only this: 'That I would say to him, as the widow of Sarepta said to Elias; that he was come to bring to memory our sins; and that I confess the righteousness of Bensalem was greater than the righteousness of Europe.' At which speech he bowed his head, and went on in this manner: 'They have also many wise and excellent laws touching marriage. They allow no polygamy. They have ordained that noe do intermarry or contract, until a month be passed from their first interview. Marriage without consent of parents they do not make void, but they mulct it in the inheritors: for the children of such marriages are not admitted to inherit above a third part of their parents' inheritance. I have read in a book of one of your men, of a Feigned Commonwelath, where the married copule are permitted, before they contract, to see one another naked. this they dislike; for they think it a scorn to give a refusal after so familiar knowledge: but because of many hidden defects in men and women's bodies, they have a more civil way; for they have near ever town a couple of pools, (which they call Adam and Eve's pools,) where it is permitted to one of the friends of the man, and another of the friends of the woman, to see them severally bathe naked.'

And as we were thus in conference, there came one that seemed to be a messenger, in a rich huke, that spake with the Jew: whereupon he turned to me and said; 'You will pardon me, for I am commanded away in haste.' The next morning he came to me agian, joyful as it seemed, and said, 'There is word come to the governor of the city, that one of the Fathers of Salomon's House will be here this day seven-night: we have seen none of them this dozen years. His coming is in state; but the cause of his coming is secret. I will provide you and your fellows of a good standing to see his entry.' I thanked him, and told him, I was most glad of the news.' the day being come, he made his entry. He was a man of middle stature and age, comly of person, and had an aspect as if he pitied men. He was clothed in a robe of fine black cloth, with wide sleeves and a cape. His under garment was of excellent white linen down to the foot, girt with a girdle of the same; and a sindon or tippet of the same about his neck. He had gloves that were curious, and set with stone; and shoes of peach-coloured velvet. His neck was bare to the shoulders. His hat was like a helmet, or Spanish Montera; and his locks curled down it decently: they were of colour brown. His beard was cut round, and of the same colour with his har, somewhat lighter. He was carried in a rich chariot without wheels, litter-wise; with two horses at either end, richly trapped in blue velvet embroidered; and two footmen on each side in the like attire. The chariot was all of cedar, gilt, and adorned with crystal; save that the fore-end had pannels of sapphires, set in borders of gold, and the hinder-end the like of emeralds of the Peru colour. there was also a sun of gold, radiant, upon the top, in the midst; and on the top before, a small cherub of gold, with wings displayed. The chariot was covered with cloth of gold tissued upon blue. He had before him fifty attendants, young men all, in white sattin loose coats to the mid-leg; and stockings of white silk; and shoes of blue velvet; and hats of blue velvet; with fine plumes of divers colours, set round like hat-bands. Next before the chariot went two men, bare-headed, in lenen garments down to the foot, girt, and shoes of blue velvet; who carried the one a crosier, the other a pastoral staff like a sheep-hook; neither of them of metal, but the crosier of blam-wood, the pastoral staff of cedar. Horsemen he had none, neither before nor behind his chariot: as it seemeth, to avoid all tumult and trouble. Behind his chariot went all the officers and principals of the Comapnies of the City. He sat alone, upon chshions of a kind of excellent plush, blue; and under his foot curious carpets of silk of divers colours, like the Persian, but far finer. He held up his bare hand as he went, as blessing the people, but in silence. The street was wonderfully well kept: so that there was never any army had their men stand in better battle-array, than the people stood. The windows likewise were not crowded, but every one stood in them as if they had been placed. When the shew was past, the Jew said to me: 'I shall not be able to attend you as I would, in regard of some charge the city hath laid upon me, for the entertaining of this great person.' three days after, the Jew came to me again, and said; Ye are happy men; for the Father of Salomon's House taketh knowledge of your being here, and commanded me to tell you that he will admit all your company to his presence, and have private conference with one of you that ye shall choose: and for this hath appointed the next day after to-morrow. And because he meaneth to give you his blessing, he hath appointed it in the forenoon.' We came at our day and hour, and I was chosen by my fellows for the private access. We found him in a fair chamber, richly hanged, and carpeted under foot, without any degrees to the state. He was set upon a low throne richly adorned, and a rich cloth of state over his head, of blue satin embroidered. He was alone, save that he had two pages of honour, on either hand one, finely attired in whiche. His under-garments were the like that he saw him wear in the chariot; but instead of his gown, he had on him a mantle with a cape, of the same fine black, fastened about him. When we came in, as we were taught, we bowed low at our first entrance; and when we were come near his chair, he stood up, holding forth his hand ungloved, and in posture of blessing; and we every one of us stooped down, and kissed the hem of his tippet. that done, the rest departed, and I remained. Then he warned the pages forth of the room, and caused me to sit down beside him, and spake to me thus in the Spanish tongue:

'GOD bless thee, my son: *I will give thee the greatest jewel I have. For I will impart unto thee, for the love of God and men, a relation of the true state of Salomon's House. Son, to make you know the true state of Salomon's House, I will keep this order. First, I will set forth unto you the end of our foundation.   Secondly, the preparations and instruments we have for our works. Thirdly, the several employments nad functions whereto our fellows are assigned. And fourthly, the ordinances and rites which we observe.

'The end of our Foundation is the knowledge of Causes, and secret motions of things; and the enlarging of the bounds of Human Empire, to the effecting of all things possible.

'The Preparations and Instrtuments are these. We have large and deep caves of several depths: the deepest are sunk six hundred fathom; and some of them are digged and made under great hills and mountains: so that if you reckon together the depth of the hill and the depth of the cave, they are (some of them) above three miles deep. For we find that th edepth of a hill, and the depth of a cave, they are (some of them) above three miles deep. For we find that the depth of a hill, and the depth of a cave from the flat, is the same thing; both remote alike from the sun and heaven's beams, and from the open air. These caves we call the Lower Region. And we use them for all coagulations, indurations, refrigerations, and conservatons of bodies. We use them likewise for hte imitation of naural mines; and the producing also of new artificial metals, by compositions and materials which we use, and lay there for many years. We use them also sometimes, (which may seem strange,) for curing of some diseases, and for the prolongation of life in some hermits that choose to live there, well accommodated of all things necessary; and indeed live very long; by whom also we learn many things.

'We have burials in several earths, where we put divers cements, as the Chineses do their porcellain. But we have them in greater variety, and some of them more fine. We have also great variety of composts, and soils, for the making of the earth fruitful.

'We have high towers; the highest about half a mile in heigh; and some of them likewise set upon high mountains, so that the vantage of the hill with the tower is inthe highest of them three miles at least. And these places we call the Upper Region: accounting the air between the high places and the low, as a Middle Region. We use these towers, according to their several heights and situations, for insolation, refrigeration, conservation; and for the view of divers meteors; as winds, rain, snow, hail; and some of the fiery meteors also. And upon them, in some palces, are dwellings of hermits, whom we visit sometimes, and instruct what to observe.

'We have great lakes both salt and fresh, whereof we have use for the fish and fowl. We use them also for burials of some natural bodies: for we find a difference in things buried in earth or in air below the earth, and things buried in water. We have also pools, of which some do strain fresh water out of salt; and others by art do turn freshwater into salt. We have also some rocks in the midst of the sea, and some bays upon the shore, for some works wherein is required the air and vapour of the sea. We have likewise violent streams and cataracts, which serveus for many motions: and likewise engines for multiplying and enforcing of winds, to set also on going divers motions.

'We have also a number of artificial wells and fountains, made in imitation of the natural sources and baths; as tincted upon vitriol, sulphur, steel, brass, lead, nitre, and other minerals. And again we have little wells for infusionsn of many things, where the waters take the virtue quicker and better than than in vessels or basons. And amongst them we have a water which we call Water of Paradise, being, by that we do to it, made very sovereign for health, and prolongation of life.

'We have also great and spacious houses, where we imitate and demonstrate meteors; as snow, hail, rain, some artificial rains of bodies and not of water, thunders, lightnings; also generations of bodies in air; as frogs, flies, and divers others.

'We have also certain chambers, which we call Chambers of Health, where we qualify the air as we think good and proper for the cure of divers diseases, and preservation of health.

491

'We have also fair and large baths, of several mixtures, for the cure of diseases, and the restoring of man's body from arefaction: and others for the confirming of it in strength of sinews, vital parts, and the very juice and substance of the body.

'We have also large and various orchards and gardens, wherein we do not so much respect beauty, as variety of ground and soil, proper for divers trees and herbs: and some very spacious, where trees and berries are set whereof we make divers kinds of drinks, besides thte vineyards. In these we practise likewise all conclusions of grafting and inoculating, as well of wild-trees as fruit-trees, which produceth many effects. And we make (by art) in the same orchards and gardens, trees and flowers to come earlier or later than their seasons; and to come up and bear more speedily than by their natural course they do. We make them also by art greater much than their nature; and their fruit greater and sweeter and of differing taste, smell, colour, and figure, from their nature. And many of them we so order, as they become of medicinal use.

'We have also means to make divers plants rise by mixtures of earths without seeds; and likewise to make divers new plants, differing from the vulgar; and to make one tree or plant turn into another.

'We have also parks and inclosures of all sorts of beasts and birds, which we use not only for view or rareness, but likewise for dissections and trials; that thereby we may take light what may be wrought upon the body of man. wherein we find many strange effects; as continuing life in them, though divers parts, which you account vital, be perished and taken forth; resuscitating of some that seem dead in appearance; and the like. We try also all poisons and other medicines upon them, as well of chirurgery as physic. By art likewise, we make them greater or taller than their kind is; and contrariwise dwarf them, and stay their growth: we make them more fruitful and bearing than their kind is; and contrariwise barren and not generative. Also we make them differ in colour, shape, activity, many ways. We find means to make commixtures and copulations of different kinds;

which have produced many new kings, and them not barren, as the general opinion is. We make a number of kinds of serpents, worms, flies, fishes, of putrefaction; whereof some are advances (in effect) to be perfect creatures, like beasts or birds; and have sexes, and do propagate. Neither do we this by chance, but we know beforehand of what matter and commixture what kind of those creatures will arise.

'We have also particular pools, where we make trials upon fishes, as we have said before of beasts and birds.

'We have also places for breed and generation of those kinds of worms and flies which are of special use; such as are with you your silk-worms and bees.

I will not hold you long with recounting of our brew-houses, bakehouses, and kitchens, where are made divers drinks, breads, and meats, rare and of special effects. Wines we have of grapes; and drinks of other juice of fruits, of grains, and of roots: and of mixtures with honey, sugar, manna, and fruits dried and decocted. Also of the tears or woundings of trees, and of the pulp of canes. And these drinks are of several ages, some to the age or last of forty years. We have drinks also brewed with several herbs, and roots, and spices; yea with several fleshes, and white meats; whereof some of the drinks are such, as they are in effect meat and drink both: so that divers, especially in age, do desire to live with them, with little or no meat or bread. And above all, we strive to have drinks of extreme thin parts, to insinuate into the body, and yet without all biting, sharpness, or fretting; insomuch as some of them put upon the back of your hand will, with a little stay, pass through to the palm, and yuet taste mild to the mouth. We have also waters which we ripen in that fashion, as they become nourishing; so that they are indeed excellent drink; and many will use no other. Breads we have of several grains, roots, and kernels: yea and some of flesh and fishg dried; with divers kinds of leavenings and seasonings: so that some do exremely move appetites; some do nourish so, as divers do live of them, without any other meat; who live very long. So for meats, we have some of them so beaten and made tender and mortified, yet without all corrupting, as a weak heat of the stomach will turn them into good chyulus (chyme), as well as a strong heat would meat otherwise prepared. WE have some meats also and breads and drinks, which taken by men enable them to fast long after; and some other, that used make the very flesh of men's bodies sensibly more hard and tough, and their strength far greater than otherwise it woudl be.

'We have dispensatories, or shops of medicines. wherein you may easily think, if we have such variety of plants and living creatures more than you have in Europe, (for we know what you have,) the simples, drugs, and ingredients of medicines, must likewise be in so much the greater variety. We have them likewise of divers ages, and long fermentations. And for their preparations, we have not only all manner of exquisite distillations and separations, and especially by genetle heats and percolations through divers strainers, yea and substances; but also exact forms of composition, whereby they incorporate almost, as they were natural simples.,

'We have also divers mechanical arts, which you have not; and stuffs made by them; as papers, linen, silks, tissues; dainty works of feathers of wonderful lustre; excellent dyes, and many others; and shops likewise, as well for such as are not brought into vulgar use amongst us as for those that are. For you must know that of the things before recited, many of them are grown into use thorughout the kingdom; but yet if they did flow from our invention, we have of them also for patterns and principals.

'We have also furnaces of great diversities, and that keep great diversity of heats; fierce and quick; strong and constant; soft and mild; blown, quiet; dry, moist; and the like. But above all, we have heats in imitation of the sun's and heavenly bodies' heats, that pass divers inequalities and (as it were) orbs, progresses, and returns, whereby we produce admirable efects. Besides, we have heats of dungs, and of bellies and maws of living creatures, and of their bloods and bodies; and of hays and herbs laid up moist; of lime unquenched; and such like. Instruments also which generate heat only by motion. And farther, places for strong insolations; and again, places under the earth, which by nature or art yield heat. These divers heats we use, as the nature of the operation which we intend requireth.

'We have also perspective-houses, where we make demonstrations of all lights nad radiations; and of all colours; and out of things uncoloured and transparent, we can represent unto you all several colours; not in rain-bows, as it is in gems and prisms, but of themselves single. We represent also all multiplications of light, which we carry to great distance, and make so sharp as to discern small points and lines; also all colorations nof light: all delusions and deceits of the sight, in figures, magnitudes, motions, colours: all demonstrations of shadows. We find also divers means, yet unknown to you, of producing of light originally from divers bodies. We procure means of seeing objects afar off; as in the heaven and remote places; and represent things near as afar off, and things afar off as neara; making feigned distances. We have also helps for the sight, far above spectacles and glasses in use. We have also glasses and means to see small and minute bodies perfectly and distinctly; as the shapes and colours of small flies nad worms, grains and flaws in gems, which cannot otherwise be seen; obversations in urine and blood, not otherwise to be seen. We make artificial rainbows, haloes, and circules about light. [I bet Harriot was fascinated by this meeting]. We represent also all manner of reflexions, refractions, and multiplications of visual beams of objects.

'We have also precious stones of all kinds, many of them of great beauty, and to you unknown; crystals likewise; and glasses of divers kinds; and amongst them some of metals vitrificated, and other materials besides those fo which you make glass. Also a number of fossils, and imperfect minerals, which you have not. Likewise loadstones of prodigious virtue; and other rare stones, both natural and artificial.

'We have also sound-houses, where we practise and demonstrate all sounds, and their generation. We have harmonies which you have not, of quarter-sounds, and lesser slides of sounds. Divers instruments of music likewise to you unknown, some sweeter than any you have; together iwth bells and rings that are dainty and sweet. We represent small sounds as great and deep; likewise great sounds extenuate and sharp; we make divers tremblings and warblings of sounds, which in their original are entire. We represent and imitate all articulate sounds and letters, and the voices and notes of beasts and birds. WE have certain helps which set to the ear do further the hearing greatly. We have also divers strange and artificial echoes, reflecting the voice many times, and as it were tossing it: and some that give back the voice louder than it came; some shriller, and some deeper; yea, some rendering the voice differing in the letters or articulate sound from that they receive. We have also means to convey sounds in trunks and pipes, in strange lines and distances.

'We have also perfume-houses; wherewith we join also practices of taste. We multiply smells, which may seem strange. We imitate smells, making all smells to breathe out of other mixtures than those that give them.   We make divers imitations of taste likewise, so that they will deceive any man's taste. And in this house we contain also a confiture-house; where we make all sweet-meats, dry and moist, and divers pleasant wines, milks, broths, and sallets, far in greater variety than you have.

'We have also engine-houses, where are prepared engines and instruments for all sorts of motions. There we imitate and practise to make swifter motions than any you have, either out of your muskets or any engine that you have; and to make them and multiply them more easily, and with small force, by wheels and other means: and to make them stronger, and more violent than yours are; exceeding your greatest cannosn and basilisks. We represent also ordnance and instruments of war, and engines of all kinds: and likewise new mixtures and compositions of gun-powder, wildfires buring in water, and unquenchable. Also fire-works of all variety both for pleasure and use. We imitate also flights of birds; we have some degrees of flying in the air; we have ships and boats for going under water, and brooking of seas; also swimming-girdles and supporters. Wé have divers curious clocks and like motions of return, and some perpetual motions. We imitate also motions of living creatures, by images of men, beasts, birds, fishes, and serpents. We have also a great number of other various motions, strange for equiality, fineness, and subtilty.

'We have also a mathematical house, where are represented all instruments, as well of geometry as astronomy, exquisitely made.

'We have also houses of deceits of the senses; where we represent all manner of feats and juggling, false apparitions, impostures, and illusions; and their fallacies. Ánd surely you will easily believe that we that have so many things truly natural which induce admiration, could in a world of particulars deceive the senses, if we would disguise those things and labour to make them seem more miraculous. But we do hate all impostures and lies: insomuch as we have severely forbidden it to all our fellows, under pain of ignominy and fines, that they do not show any natural work or thing, adorned or swelling; but only pure as it is, and wihtout all affectation of strangeness.

'These are (my son) the riches of [123] Salomon's House.

---

[123] See Essays - Sir Francis Bacon : and refer to The Advancement of Learning" and compare with his History of the World:

and The Life of the Valiant & Learned Sir Walter Raleigh, Knight with his Tryal at Winchester printed 1677 by J.D. for Benjamin Shirley, and Richard Tonson, under the Dial of St. Dunstans Church in Fleet Street, and under Grays-Inn Gate next Grays-In Lane: where mention is made of judicious Essays: "Authors are perplext under what Topick to place him, whether of Stateman, Seaman, Souldier, Chymist, or Chronologer; for in all these he did excel. He could make every thing he read or heard his own, and his own he could easily improve to the greatest Advantage. He seem'd to be born to that only which he went about, for Dexterous was he in all his Undertakings, in Court, in Camp, by Sea, by Land, with Sword, with Pen. Witness in the last,

The literary works of Sir Walter Raleigh:

'For the several employments and offices of our fellows; we have twelve that sail into foreign countries, under the names of other nations, (for our own we conceal;) who bring us the books, and abstracts, and patterns of experiments of all other parts. These we call Merchants of Light.

'We have three that collect the experiments which are in all books. These we call Depredators.

'We have three that collect the experiments of all mechanical arats; and also foliberal sciences; and also of practices which are not brought into arts. These we call Mystery-men.

'We have three that try new experiments, such as themselves think good. These we call Pioneers or Miners.

'We have three that draw the experiments of the former four into titles and tables, to give the better light for the drqawing of observations and axioms out of them. These we call Compilers.

'We have three that bend themselves, looking into the experiments of their fellows, and cast about how to draw out of them things of use and practice for man's life, and knowledge as well for works as for plain demonstration of causes, means of natural divinations, and the easy and clear discovery of the virtues and parts of bodies. These we call Dowry-men or Benefactors.

History of the World
History of Guiana
His Remains.
Judicious and *Select Essays (PRO - KB8/58) and Observations on the first Invention of Shipping, the Misery of Invasive War, the Navy and Royal Sea-Service, with his Apologie for his Sea-Voyage to Guiana.
Wars with Forreign Princes dangerous to our Common-wealth; or Reasons for Forreign Wars answered.
An excellent manuscript of the present State of Spain, with a most Accurate Account of his Catholique Majesties Power, and Riches; with the Names and Worth of the most considerable Persons in that Kingdom - Finis."

'Then after divers meetings and consults of our whole number, to consider of the former labours and collections, we have three that take care, out of them, to direct new experiments, of a higher light, more penetrating into nature than the former. These we call Lamps.

'We have three others that do execute the experiments so directed, and report them. These we call Inoculators.

'Lastly, we have three that raise the former discoveries by experiments into greater observations, axionms and aphorisms. These we call Interpreters of Nature.

'We have also, as you must think, novices and apprentics, that the succession fo the former employed men do not fail; besides a great number of servants and attendants, men and women. And this we do also: we have consultations, which of the inventions and experiences which we have discovered shall be published, and which not: and take all an oath of secrecy, for the concealing of those which we think fit to keep secret: though some of those we do reveal sometimes to the state, and some not.

'For our ordinances and rites: we have two very long and fair galleries: one of these we place pattersn sna dsamples of all manner of the more rare and excellent inventions: in the other we place the statua's of all principal inventors. There we have the statua of your Columbus, that discovered the West Indies: also the inventor of ships: your monk that was the inventor of ordnance and of gunpowder: the inventor of music: the inventor of letters: the inventor of printing: the inventor of observations of astronomy: the inventor of works in metal: the inventor of glass: the inventor of silk of the worm: the inventor of wine: the inventor of corn and bread: the inventor of sugars: and all these by more certain tradition than you have. Then have we divers inventors of our own, of excellent works; which since you have not seen, it were too long to make descriptoins fo them; and besides, in the right understanding of those descriptions you might easily err. For upon every invention of value, we erect a statua to the inventor, and give him a liberal and honourable reward. These statua's are some of brass; some of marble and touch-stone; some of cedar and other special woods gilt and adorned: some of iron, some of silver; some of gold.

'We have certain hymns and services, which we say daily, of laud and thanks to God for his marvellous works: and forms of prayers, imporing his aid and blessing for the illumination of our labours, and the turning of them into good and holy uses.

'Lastly we have circuits or visits of divers principal cities of the kingdom; where, as it cometh to pass, we do publish such new profitable inventions as we think good. And we do also declare natural divinations of diseases, plagues, swarms of hurtful creatures, scarcity, tempests, earthquakes, great inundations, comets, temperature of the year, and divers other things; and we give counsel thereupon what the people shall do for the prevention and remedy of them.'

And whe he had said this, he stood up; and I, as I had bene taught, kneeled down; and he laid his right hand upon my head, and said: 'God bless thee, my son, and God bless this relation which I have made. I give thee leave to pulish it for the good of other nations; for we here are in God's bosom, a land unknown.' And so he left me; having assigned a value of about two thousand ducats, for a bounty to me and my fellows. For they give great largesses where they come upon all occasions.

[THE REST WAS NOT PERFECTED]

Sir Francis Bacon

Sir Francis Bacon – chronological Table

1561 [124]22 January: Born at York House in the Strand,

1573 April :Enters Trinity College Cambridge

1576 June Admitted to Gray's Inn to study law and went to Paris with the Ambassador, Sir Amyas Paulet.

1579 22 February : Death of his father Nicholas Bacon

1582 27 June Admitted Utter Barrister at Gray's House

1584 23 November: MP for Melcombe

1586 MP for Taunton

1586 He played a prominent part in the proceedings and urged the Execution of Mary Queen of Scots, an act for which he later apologised to her son, King James I of England.

1589 MP for Liverpool

1591 Befriended by Robert Devereux, the Second Earl of Essex. Essex gave him gifts, such as a house in Twickenham.

1592 Wrote: A Conference with Pleasure - published 1870

1593 MP for Middlesex

1594 Gesta Grayorum, a device presented at Gray's Inn

1595/6 Formularies and Elegancies compiled (published 1859, 1883)

1597 MP for Southampton

1597 Published: Essays, Colours of Good and Evil, Meditationes Sacrae

---

[124] p.119 Essay XXXIX of Custom and Education: Sir Francis Bacon's Essays

Queen Elizabeth I was born on the 7th September 1533. Her accession to the Throne of England took place on the 2nd April 1559.

"I remember in the beginning of Queen Elizabeth's (I) time of England, an Irish rebel condemned put up a petition to the deputy, that he might be hanged in a with and not in an halter, because it had been so used with former rebels".

1601   Bacon Repaid the kindness of The Earl of Essex (otherwise known as the Earl of March), and was appointed as a Commisioner to investigate the charges against him and to examine the participants of the Essex Rebellion. Essex was executed on Ash Wednesday 1601 after spending a fortnight in the Devereux Tower. Queen Elizabeth I waited for Essex to send the ring she had previously given him (and she had told him that if ever he was in danger, he should send her the ring): This ring he sent to Lady Nottingham and she withheld it from the Queen, but confessed upon her deathbed and Queen Elizabeth replied: 'May God forgive you for I never shall'

1603   24 March Queen Elizabeth dies: Having been unable to sleep for 20 days   from the 1st March.

1603   23 July, Knighted by King James I

1604   Apology in certain imputations concerning the late Earl of Essex
[125]

1605 The Advancement of Learning:

1606   10 May, Married Alice Barnham

1613   26 October: Attorney-General

1616   9 June: Privy Councillor

1617   Lord Keeper

1618   Went to the Lords

1618   Lord Chancellor

1618   Lord Verulum

1620   October : Novum Organum

1621   27 January: Created Viscount St. Albans

1621   30 January: Meeting of Parliament

1622   History of Henry Vii

1621   3rd May: Sentenced by the House of Lords for corruption: Sir Edward   Coke, Lord Coke [1552 - 1634] the famous English lawyer, assisted in the impeachment of Bacon. See his famous Law

---

[125]*Strange,the Earl of Derby, (poisoned 1593), [Raleigh, Harriot and Marlowe accused of atheism and stabbed by Ingram Frizer on the 30th May 1593, at the home of Mistress Eleanor Bull for the sum of 12d, Frizer pardoned in self defence; two witnesses being present : Robert Poley and Nicholas Skeres: for their participation in scientific studies in 1593] with the Wizard Earl arrested in 1605 with the Wizard Earl of Syon, Henry Percy being implicated in the Gunpowder Plot] : See my notes on Gunpowder Plot theory

Reports [Reports and Institutes] in at least I - XI Volumes.

1626 [9 April]: Died at Highgate having caught a chill on his way home in the snow, and urging his carriage be stopped, he desired to perform an experiment to discover the antiseptic properties of snow. Sir Francis Bacon had never married and had no children at the time of his death.

Bacon died of the chill this experiment brought upon him. As death carried him off he left debts behind him to the tune of £22,000.   See his Essay 'Of Expense XXVIII: "And 'Of Riches p.87 "Riches are for spending, and for honour and good actions. But ordinary expense ought to be limited by a man's estate.' - [Sir Walter Raleigh].

His Literary Achievements
Essays
[126]The Advancement of Learning
New Atlantis
Cogitata et Visa [Thoughts and Conclusions] published 1653
Valerius Terminus of the Interpretation of Nature Published 1734
De Interpretatione Naturae Proaemium [Preface to 'of the Interpretation of Nature': published 1653
Temporis Partus Maximus
De Augmentis Scientiarum (forming part of Instauratio Magna - a great reconstruction of Science)
Novum Organum (a fragment of Instauratio Magna)
King Henry vii ([127]King Henry viii) - 1621

---

[126]Plato gave only an augury in his 'Republic'

"And Love doth hold my hand and makes me write... to XLV: Of lovers' ruin some thrice tragedy, I am not I, pity the tale of me."

A Conference with Pleasure

Bacon undertook the History of Henry VII as a solace in his reverse of fortune and made use of this history by composing a work beginning with the houses of York and Lancaster having referred to [128]Polydore Vergil's history of England in Latin consisting of twenty-seven books. Bacon also consulted another Latin writer Bernard Andre for some few points on history says the Rev. J. Rawson Lumby, B.D. and then turned to work in the form of three chronicles of Hall, Grafton and Stow. He drew on Sir Thomas More's History of the Life and Death of King Edward V and of the usurpation of Richard III.

---

[127] John Speed (1552-1629) says The Rev. J. Rawson Lumby, B.D. was one of the most industrious writers of this period on the subjects of antiquities and history, and his compilations, derived in great part from the collections in the libraries of Sir Robert Cotton, and the contributions of Sir Henry Spelman and other antiquaries, are of considerable value. Speed was originally a tailor and so had not great advantages from education, but yet his 'History of Great Britaine' was long the best in existence. He wrote also the 'Theatre of the Empire of Great Britain,' and a work on the Genealogies of Holy Scripture under the title of 'A cloud of witnesses.'

[128] Polydore Vergil (d.1555) was an Italian ecclesiastic, born at urbino. He was sent over to England for the collection of Peter's Pence, and while in England was preferred to the Archdeaconry of Wells. His History of England in Latin consists of twenty-sevenbooks and was begun by him in the latter years of Henry VII, and finished in the following reign.

"I am of the same politics,
 as Shakespeare, Bacon, and every sane man."
Tennyson.
A Fragment of an Essay - Of Fame
by Sir Francis Bacon

"The poets made Fame a monster. They describe her in part finely and elegantly; and in part gravely and sententiously. They say, look how many feathers she hath, so many eyes she hath underneath; so many tongues; so many voices; she pricks up so many ears.

This is a flourish: there follow excellent parables; as that she gathereth strength in going; that she that she goeth upon the ground, and yet hideth her head in the clouds; that in the day time she sitteth in a watch tower, and flieth most by night; that she mingleth things done with things not done; and that she is a terror to great cities. But that which passeth all the rest is: they do recount that the Earth, mother of the Giants, that made war against Jupiter and were by him destroyed, thereupon, in an anger, brought forth Fame: for certain it is, that rebels, figures by the Giants, and seditious fames and libels, are but brothers and sisters, masculine and feminine. But now, if a man can tame this monster, and bring her to feed at the hand, and govern her, and with her fly other ravening fowl and kill them, it is somewhat worth. But we are infected with the style of the poets. To speak now in a sad and serious manner: there is not, in all the politics, a place less handled, and more worthy to be handled, that this of fame. We will therefore speak of these points: what are false fames, and what are true fames, and how they may be best discerned; how fames may be sown and raised, how they may be spread and multiplied, and how they may be checked and laid dead; and other things concerning the nature of fame. Fame is of that force, as there is scarcely any great action wherein it hath not a great part; especially in the war. Mucianus undid Vitellius by a fame that he scattered, that Vitellius had in purpose to remove the legions of Syria into Germany, and the legions of Germany into Syria: whereupon the legions of Syria were infinitely inflamed. Julius Caeser took Pompey unprovided, and laid asleep his industry and preparations, by a fame that he cunningly gave out, how Caesar's on soldiers loved him not, and, being wearied with the wars and laden with the spoils of Gaul, would forsake him as soon as he came into Italy. Livia settled all things for the succession of her son Tiberius, by continual giving out that her husband Augustus was upon recovery and amendment. And of the Great Turk from the janizaries and men of war, to save the sacking of Constantinople and other towns, as their manner is. Themistocles made Xerxes ,king of Persia, post apace out of Graecia, by giving out that the Grecians had a purpose to break his bridge of ships which he had made athwart Hellespont. There be a thousand such like examples; and the more they are, the less they need to be repeated; because a man meeteth with them every where. Therefore let all wise governors have as great a watch and care over fames, as they have of the actions and designs themselves."

The rest was not finished.

<u>1621   3rd May:</u>
Sir Francis Bacon was sentenced by the House of Lords for corruption: Sir Edward Coke, Lord Coke [1552 - 1634] the famous English lawyer, assisted in the impeachment of Bacon. See his famous Law Reports [Reports and Institutes] in at least I - XI Volumes.

A CompleteTable of William Shakespeare's Plays
And the Dates they were written and revised
Not in Year order

Compiled by Dr. G.B. Harrison (William Clowes and Sons Limited
London and Beccles: MCMXXXIV

	Written	Revised	Publised
Two Gentlemen of Verona			1623
The Comedy of Errors	1594	1597	1623
Love's Labour's Lost	1593	1597	1598
All's Well That Ends Well	1603		1623
A Midsummer Nights Dream	1594		1600
The Taming of the Shrew	1593		1623
The Merchant of Venice	1596		1605
Much Ado about Nothing	1598		1600
Henry IV	1597		1598
King	1599		1600
King Henry VI (I)	1592		1623
King Henry VI (II)	1592		1623
King Henry VI (III)	1592	1594	1623
Richard III	1593		1597*
Henry VIII	1613		1623
Romeo & Juliet	1595	1597	1599
Hamlet			
[compare with Kyd's Er Hamlet			
	1603	1604	1623
1593(1591(when writing with Marlowe)			
Cymbeline	1610		1623
Othello	1604		1622
King Lear	1605	1606	1608
Macbeth	1606		1623
Timon of Athens	1607		1623

Triolus and Cressida	1600	1603	1609
Pericles	1576	1607	1609
Corlialanus	1607		1623
Julius Caeser	1599		1623**
Anthony and Cleopatra		1607	1623***
The Merry Wives of Windsor	1599(?)		1602
+Twelfth Night or ['or what you will']	1581	1602	1623
As You Like It	1590	1599	1623
Measure for Measure	1578	1604	1623
A Winter's Tale	1588	1611	1623
The Tempest	1611	1613	1623****
King John	1591	1596	1623
The Tragedy of King John	1595	1597	1598*****

Venus and Adonis	1593*	
The Rape of Lucrece	[129]1594*	
The Sonnets	******	
Compare with Sidney's Sonnets		1609

[Sidney's widow married The Earl of Essex (otherwise known as the Earl of March) and was present at the Battle of Zutphen with Sidney and Sir Francis Walsingham, who daughter was married to Sir Philip Sidney.}

+ The Twelfth Night, or what you will...

"[As from Arthur B. Allen: 'One of the Middle Temple Students, John Manningham, kept a diary in which he noted on February 2nd 1601,: !At our feast we had a play called Twelfth Knight or what you will" but he makes no mention of its author - William Shakespeare. In all probability it was the first performance of that Play].

---

[129] In the Scottish Court no weltering be, I am not I pity the life of me.

HIC JACET: SIR WALTER RALEIGH

An Index to the Characters in Shakespeare's Plays

Tennyson: 'I am of the same Politics as Shakespeare, Bacon and every sane man."

Compiled by Dr. G.B. Harrison (William Clowes and Sons Limited London and Beccles: MCMXXXIV

[130]Aaron   Titus Andronicus

Abbot of Westminster   [131]King Richard II

---

[130] Dr G.B. Harrison says: "Titus Andronicus was first printed in 1594, and reprinted in 1600 and again in 1611. there is a record of its first performance at the Rose Theatre on January 24th 1594, in the account book of Philip Henslowe, when it brought him in £3.8s., which indicates a full house. Subsequent performances on January 28th and February 6th were worth 40s. There is a contemporary drawing illustrating the episode of "Tamora pleading for her sons going to execution," which shows the very mixed costuming used on the Elizabethan stage. Titus Andronicus himself is dressed in a Roman breastplate; he wears a cloak draped over one shoulder, and a pair of theatrical buskins; he is crowned with a laurel wreath. His two guards wear Elizabethan costumes. Tamora wears a very full, loose, embroidered costume which belongs to no period. Her hair is flowing and is surmounted by a crown. The sons and Aaron the Mor wear garments which are hybrid between the Roman square-necked breastplate and the fashion of Henry VIII's Court... ...

"To order well the state
that like events may ne'er it ruinate.

Critics, careful of Shakespeare's reputation, have striven to find another author for parts at least of this play; but Francis Meres, in 1598, and the editors of the First Folio include it in Shakespeare's work. It seems to have been popular, and audiences who liked to sup full well of horros were amply satisfied. The simple explanation seems to be that Shakespeare in his early days, seeing the popularity of the horrors in the Spanish Tragedy (Thomas Kyd), endeavoured to give the public what it wanted.

For Thomas Kyd, Marlowe and The Earl of Essex all played a part in Raleigh's School of Night. The Earl of Essex was a writer of wordes too.

---

[131] On the 9th Deceber 1595, at a supper for Cobham, Robert Devereux the Second Earl of

HIC JACET: SIR WALTER RALEIGH

Abergavenny, Lord   King Henry VIII

Essex, with Lady Hoby and his sister: Essex jokes to Cobham about Richard II, written by Christopher Marlowe in possession of Earl of Pembrokes Company [Marlowe wrote for them after 1590]. Lord Cobham died in March 1597 and the 2nd Lord Hunsdon succeeded as Chamberlain. Lady Mary Hoby and Lady Scrope his sisters. Sir Thomas Hoby was a Diplomat and Linguish. Edward Hoby married Lord Hunsdon's daughter Mary 1582.

King Henry VIII (G.B. Harrison) This play was the last to be performed at the Globe Theatre and during its performance the Globe Theatre was set afire. "Was first published in First Folio in 1623. (Written about 1613) telling the story of the fall of Buckingham. Buckingham says just before his fall:

This holy* fox,   (*Raleigh's nickname)

Or wolf, or both (for he is equal ravenous

As he is *subtle; and as prone to mischief   (*a Ben Johnson character and

As able to peform it: his mind and place   Ben Johnson tutor to Wat

Infecting one another, yea, reciprocally   Raleigh in France in 1613)

Only to show his pomp as well in France

As here at home, suggests the king our master

To this last costly treaty, the interview

That swalloed'd so much treasure, and like a glass

Did break i' the rinsing.

Wat Raleigh's tutors were Harriot, Kemys and Raleigh himself; then Oxford, and after Prince Henry's death a year in France with Ben Johnson. Wat Raleigh and Prince Henry were the same age.

Abhorson	Measure for Measure
Abram	Romeo and Juliet
[133] Achilles	Triolus and Cressida
Adam	As You Like It
[134] Adrian	The Tempest
Adriana	The Comedy of Errors
Aegeon	The Comedy of Errors
Aemilia	The Comedy of Erros
Aemilius	Titus Andronicus
[135] Aemilius Lepidus	Julius Caeser

A letter from Sir Henry Wotton on July 2nd 1613:

"Now, to let matters of state sleep, I will enterain you at the present with what hath happed this week at the Bank's side. The King's Players had a new play, called *'All is True'* representing some principl pieces of the reign of Henry the 8th, which was set forth with many extraordinary circumstances of pomp and majesty, even to the matting of the stage, the Kings of the Order with their Georges and Garter, the Guards with their embroidered coats, and the like: sufficient in truth within a while to make greatness very familiar, if not ridiculous. Now, King Henry, making a masque at the Cardinal Wolsey's house, and certain cannons being shot off at his entry, some of the paper, or other stuff, wherewith one of them was stopped, did light on the thatch, where being thought at first but an idle smoke, and their eyes more attentive to the show, it kindled inwardly, and ran round like a train, consuming within less than an hour the the whole house to the very ground. This was the fatal period of that virtuous fabric; wherein yet nothing did perish, but wood and straw, and a few forsaken cloaks; only one man had his breeches set on fire, that would perhaps have broiled him if he had not by the aid of a provident wit put it out with boottle-ale".

[133] the Second Earl of Essex Robert Devereux was compared to Achilles
[134] The Tempest was acted at court on November 1st, 1611. And acted for the Wedding festivities of Princess Elizabeth with Elector Palatine in February 1613. Published in 1623. "We are such stuff as dreams are made on and our little life is rounded with a sleep." A play about Sea voyages
[135] "['Sir Walter Raleigh classes Julius Caeser and Coriolanus with 2 Henry VI as plays in which 'the common people are made ludicrous and foolish'].

Julius Caeser was written in 1599 and a record appears in the diary of Platter a German that he saw the play on the 21st September of that year. The story is taken from Plutarch's lives of Caeser, Brutus andn Antonius. The First Folio is dated 1623. Not much of a time span there.

HIC JACET: SIR WALTER RALEIGH

Aeneas	Triolus and Cressida
Agamemnon	Triolus and cressida
Agrippa	Antony and Cleopatra
Agrippa, Menenius	Coriolanus
[136] Ague-Cheek, Sir Andrew	Twelfth Knight
Ajax	Triolus and Cressida
Alarbus	Titus Andronicus
[137] Albany, Duke of	King Lear

---

[136] *The Twelfth Night, or what you will...*

"[As from Arthur B. Allen: 'One of the Middle Temple Students, John Manningham, kept a diary in which he noted on February 2nd 1601: At our feast we had a play called Twelfth Knight or what you will" but he makes no mention of its author - William Shakespeare. In all probability it was the first performance of that Play].

Sir Walter Raleigh on the other hand, was the Twe*lfth* Knight, because he was knighted on 12th Night at the Feast of the Epiphany on the 12th January 1585: at Hampton Court, and there he was honoured for his bravery at the Battles of Montconteur and Jarnac; for his former bravery in Ireland under the Leadership of Lord Grey in 1581 and Queen Elizabeth I awarded and rewarded him with 40,000 acres in Ireland and Lismore Castle: where he penned such lines as 'the face that launched a thousand ships' and thereafer Walter Ralegh introduced Edumund Spenser to Court and the Queen she cried: 'Ralegh! when will you cease to be a beggar': and he replied : 'When your Majesty ceases to be a Patron!'

[137] I believe the identity of King Lear to be King John 1199 - 1216. He was known as John of Lackland. Quoting from Britain's Kings and Queens by Sir George Bellew, KCB, KCVO: "Born at Oxford, Crowned at Westminster 27 May 1199 and Buried at Worcester. King Richard's next brother, Geoffrey, left a son, Arthur, and a daughter, Eleanor, but they were passed over in favour of John, King Henry II's youngest son. There have been attempts to whitewash the characters of some of our less admired sovereigns, but John, it seems, would require more than whitewash: he does not seem to have had a single redeeming feature. He was, we are told, a tall figure of a man, with a corpulence and face which reflected his profilgate and indulgent life. He lost most of his French possessions; he broke his father's heart by his unfaithfulness; he rebelled against his brother; he quarrelled with the Pope, causing the country to be laid under an interdict, which meant that the churches were closed and the consolations of religion, which were perhaps the only consolations which the poor had, were denied; he tried to have his nephew Arthur blinded, and was probably responsible for his murder; and though he divorced his first wife, Isabel of Cloucester, great grand-daughter of Henry I, on the grounds of consanguinity, he was careful to retain her inheritance. the list of King John's malefactions and stupidities is endless, yet one good thing emerged from his reign. In 1215 the barons forced him to seal the Magna Carta, which, though in fact

Alcibiades	Timon of Athens
Alencon, Duke of	King Henry VI, Part I
Alexander	Triolus and Cressida
Alexander Iden	King Henry VI, Prt 2
Alexas	Antony & Cleopatra
Alice	King Henry V
Alonso	The Tempest
Amiens	As You Like It
Andronicus, Marcus	Titus Andronicus
Andronicus Titus	Titus Andronicus
[138]Angelo (a goldsmith)	The Comedy of Errors
Angelo (deputy of Duke of Vienna)	Measure for Measure
Angus	Macbeth
Anne Bullen	Henry VIII
Anne, Lady	King Richard III
Antenor	Triolus and Cressida
Antigonus	A Winter's Tale
Antiochus	Pericles
Antiochus, daughter of	Pericles
Antipholus of Ephesus	The Comedy of Errors
Antipholus of Syracuse	The Comedy of Errors
Antonio (The Merchant of Venice)	The Merchant of Venice
Antonio (usurping Duke of Milan)	The Tempest

---

framed to limit the prerogative of the Crown and and extend the power of the barons, has since become the foundation stone of an Englishman's liberty. The bad king, who, as all the world knows, lost his treasure which was to him "everything in the world which he valued next to his own life" whilst fording a river near the Wash, died (possibly of poison) in Newark Castle. He left a widow, his second wife Isabella, the daughter of Aymer, Count of Angouleme, and the mother of his five children. After her husband's death she married the Count of Lusignan, and later took the veil.

[138] The Comedy of Érrors the goldsmith's wife: (Compare to the play Sir Thomas More Bard: Whether I please, thou art my prize and I pleade purchase of you. : Doll - Compell me ye dogges face thou thinkst thou hast the goldsmithes wife in hand, whom thou enticedst from her husband with all his plate, and when thou turndst her home to him again, madste him (like an asse) for for his wifes boorde.

Antonio (a sea Captain)	Twelfth Knight
Antonio (brother of Leonato)	Much Ado About Nothing
Antonio (father of Proteus)	Two Gentlemen of Verona
Antony, Mark	Antony and Cleopatra
Apemantus	Timon of Athens
Apothecary, An	Romeo and Juliet
[139] Archbishop of Canterbury (Cranmer)	King Henry VIII
Archbishop Canterbury (Cardinal Bouchier)	King Richard III
Archbishop of Canterbury	King Henry V
Archbishop of York (Scroop)	King Henry IV, Parts 1 and 2
Archbishop of York (Thomas Rotherham	King Richard III
Achduke of Austria	King John
Archibald	King Henry IV, Parts 1 and 2
Archidamus	A Winter's Tale
Ariel	The Tempest
Armado, Don Adriano De,	Love's Labour's Lost
Arragon, Prince of	The Merchant of Venice
[140] Artemidorus	Julius Caeser

---

[139] Compare to the play Sir Thomas More written in about 1592-3 by at least three dramatist, E Tyllney, Anthony Munday and Thomas Kyd and Dekker: Three pages later appended by Shakespeare and now in British Museum. E. tyllney wrote in the wrote in the margin of text of Sir Thomas More: Fol.3a. "Leave out ye insurrection wholy & ye cause ther off & begin with Sr Tho: Moore att ye mayors sessions wt a reportt afterwards off his good servic don being hrive off London uppon a mutiny agaynst ye Lubards only by A short reportt & not otherwise at your own perrilles. E Tyllney." (with commentaries by J. W. Wilson and A.W. Pollard 1923).

And then compare with Ben Johnson's style in Three Comedies - the Alchemist.

Anthony Munday dramatist wrote John a Kent John a Cumber dated Decembris 1596 a fragmentary inscription, a play then in the possession of Lord Mostyn. John a Kent, Sir Thomas More and the preliminaries of Heaven of the Mind dated 22 December 1602 in Additionanl MS. 33384 at the British Museum.

Arthur	King John
Arviragus	Cymbeline
Audrey	As You Like It.
Aufidius, Tullus	Corliolanus
Aumerle, Duke of	King Richard II
Autolycus	A Winter's Tale
Auvergne, Countess of	King Henry VI, Part I
Bagot	King Richard II
Balthasar (Servant of Rome)	Romeo and Juliet
Balthazar (a merchant)	The Comedy of Errors
Balthazar (Servant to Portia)	The Merchant of Venice
Balthazar (Servant to Don Pedro)	Much Ado About Nothing
Banished Duke	As you Like It
Banquo	Macbeth
Baptista	Taming of the Shrew
Badolph (Soldier in King's Army)	King Henry IV, Part 2
Bardolph (follower of Falstaff)	The Merry Wives of Windsor
Bardolph Lord	King Kenry IV, Part 2
Barnadine	Measure for Measure
Bassanio	The Merchant of Venice
Bassett	King Henry VI, Part I
Bassianus	Titus Andronicus

---

[140]
Raleigh was an expert on Roman history as can be seen from this History of the World part I written for Prince Henry (see also Bacon's Essays [xx of Counsel - *in counsel isi stability*] where the wisdom of Solomon is mentioned *Plenu rimarum sum:* one futile person, that maketh it his glory to tell, will do more hurt than many, that know it their duty to conceal. Solomon is also mentioned in New Atlantis). Whoever did write Essays also wrote the Advancement of Learning and New Atlantis. The problem with New Atlantis (attributed to Sir Francis Bacon, being that Bacon did not sail to or from Peru). Raleigh burned the second volume of History of the World before the eyes of his publisher Mr Raymond Burr, before he was beheaded on the 29th October 1618 and he said to Mr Burr "It shall undo no more since this ungrateful world is unworthy of it" Bacon goes on to say in Essay IX *"we see, likewise, the scripture calleth envy an evil eye;* and the astrologers call the evil influences of the stars *evil aspects:* which words lead us back to Julius Caeser and King Lear. For envy is a gadding passion, and walketh the streets, and doth not keep home: *Non est curiosus, quin iden sit malevolus.*

Bastard of Orleans	King Henry VI, Part I
Bates	King Henry V
Beatrice	King Henry V
Beau, Le	As you Like It
Beaufort, Cardinal	King Henry VI, Part 2
Beaufort, Henry	King Henry VI, Part 1
Beaufort, John	King Henry VI, Part 1
Beaufort, Thomas	King Henry VI, Part 1
Bedford, Duke of (brother of King Henry V)	King Henry V
Bedford, Duke of (Regent of France)	King Henry VI, Part 1
Belarius	Cymbeline
[141]Belch, Sir Toby	Twelfth Knight
Benedick	Much Ado About Nothing
Berkley, Earl	King Richard II
Bernado	Hamlet
Bertram	All's Well that Ends Well
[142]Bianca (mistress of Cassio)	Othello

---

[141] Compare with Ben Johnson's Three Comedies.

[142] This is classified as the greatest of William Shakespeare's plays. In Act 1 sc. 3 "The Anthropophagi, and men whose heads do grow beneath their shoulders. These things to hear would Desdemona seriously incline."

and Raleigh says on page 70 in his Discoverie of the Large Rich and Bewtiful Empyre of Guaina 1596:

Next unto Arui there are two rivers Atoica and Caora, and on that braunch which is called Caora are a nation of people, whose heades appeare not above their shoulders, which though it may be thought a meere fable, yet for mine owne part I am resolved it is true, because every child in the provinces of Arromaia and Canuri affirme the same: they are called Ewaipanoma: they are reported to have their eyes in their shoulders, and their mouths in the middle of their

Bianca (sister of Katharina)	Taming of the Shrew
Bigot, Robert	King John
Biondello	Taming of the Shrew
Biron	Love's Labour's Lost
Bishop of Carlisle	King Richard II
Bishop of Ely	King Henry V
Bishop of Ely (John Morton	King Richard II
[143]Bishop of Lincoln	King Henry VIII
Bishop of Winchester (Gardiner)	King Henry VIII
Blanch	King Henry VIII
Blount, Sir James	King Richard III
Blunt, Sir Walter	King Henry IV, Parts 1 and 2
Bolingbroke (a conjouror)	King Henry VI, part 2
Bolinbroke, Henry (afterwards King Henry IV)	King Richard II
Bona	King Henry VI, part 2
Borachio	Much Ado About Nothing
[144]Bottom	A Midsummer Nights Dream
Bouchier, Cardinal	King Richard III
Boult	Pericles
Bourbon, Duke of	King Henry V
Boyet	Love's Labour's Lost

---

breasts, & that a long traine of hairre groweth backward betwen their shoulders. the sonne of Topiaware, which I brought with mee into England tolde mee that they are the most mightie men of all the land, and use bowes, arrowes, and clubs thrice as bigge as any of Guiance, or of the Orenoquepoini, and that one of the Iwarawakeri tooke a prisoner of them the year before our arrivall there, and brought him into the borders of Arromaia his fathers Countrey:

[143] Bishop of Lincoln King Henry VIII (and in Ill May Day Scene Sir Thomas More scene IV A Street in St. Martin's le Grand: 'Then gallant bloods you whoes fre sowles doo skorne to beare the inforsed wrongs of alians ad rage to ressolutione fier the howses of theis audatious strangers: this is Saint Martins and yonder dwells Mutas a welthy Piccarde at the Greene Gate de Barde Peter van Hollocke Adrian Martine with many more outlandishe fugetius shall theis enjoy mpriveledge then wee in our owne cuntry lets become their slaives since justis kepes not them in greater awe wele be ourselves rough ministers at lawe."

[144] The course of true love never did run smooth. But either it was different in Blood.

[145]Brantio	Othello
Brakenbury, Sir Robert	King Richard III
Brandon	King Henry VIII
Briarius the 100 handed man	William Shakespeare
Brutus, Junius	Coriolanus
Brutus, Marcus	Julius Caeser
Buckingham, Duke of	King Richard III
Buckingham, Duke of	King Henry VI, Part 2
Buckingham, Duke of	King Henry VIII
Bullcalf	King Henry IV, part 2
Bullen, Anne	King Henry VIII
Burgundy, Duke of	King Henry V
Burgundy, Duke of	King Henry VI, Part 1
Burgundy, Duke of	King Lear
Bushy	King Richard II
Butts, Dr	King Henry VIII
[146]Cade, Jack	King Henry VI, Part 2

---

[145] Othello: Act I Scene I: "In complement extern'tis not long after but I will wear my heart upon my sleeve. (Sir Philip Sidney sonnets "XXX ... 'If in the Scotch Court be no weltring yet: These questions busy wits to me do frame; I, cumbred with good manners, answer do, But know not how. For still I think of you'. And so Sidney continued to ponder how he may continue to write his Sonnets for dear Queen Mary of Scots the prisoner of vicious malice and hatred of the Roman religeon and yet still remain annonymous to the Court: "And Love doth hold my hand and makes me write... to XLV: Of lovers' ruin some thrice tragedy, I am not I, pity the tale of me." - (For daws to peck at: I am not what I am". Act I sc. see - Raleigh "In my Travellers History" - The Anthropopagi and men whose heads do grow beneath their shoulders.

[146] Dekker as an apprentice Dramatist was allowed to try his hand in it. "This found its way on to the Stationers Register in March 1594 as *the first part of the Contention.* I may note that I am quite content to be no more (and no less) certain of Shakespeare's authorship of our three pages than of his authorship of the Jack Cade scenes." Dekker wrote for the Admirals Men in and after January 1598.

Cadwal	Cymbeline
Caesar Octavius	Antony and Cleopatra
Caius, Dr.	The Merry Wives of Windsor
Caius, Lucius	Cymbeline
Caius, Marcius Coriolanus	Coriolanus
Calchas	Triolus and Cressida
Caliban	The Tempest
Calphurnia	Julius Caeser
Cambnridge, Earl of	King Henry V
Camilloi	A Winter's Tale
Campeius, Cardinal	King Henry VIII
Canidius	Antony and Cleopatra
Canterbury, Archbishop of (Cardinal (Bouchier)	King Richard III
Canterbury, Archbishop of	King Henry V
Canterbury, Archbishop of (Cranmer)	King Henry VIII
Caphis	Timon of Athens
Capucius	King Henry VIII
Capulet	Romeo and Juliet
Capulet, Lady	Romeo and Juliet
Cardinal Beaufort	King Henry VI, Part 2
Cardinal Bouchier	King Richard III
Cardinal Campeius	King Henry VIII
Cardinal Pandulph	King John
Cardinal Wolsey	King Henry VIII
Carlisle, Bishop of	King Richard II
Casca	Julius Caesar
Cassandra	Triolus and Cressida

Dekker also had connections with Shakespeare's company before this in January 1599 and he was arrested for debt at their suit, and ransomed by his new employers. "It may be worth noting that in his first entry of his name Henslowe spells it 'Dickers' and in thet second entry 'Dicker'. Now a "Thomas Dycker, a Gent' had a daughter Dorcas christened at St. Giles' Cripplegate, on 27 October 1594 (DNB). There is no proof that this was our Thomas Dekker but it seems likely.

For further mention of Jack Cade see also Sir Walter Raleigh's Trial 17th November 1603.

[147]Cassio — Othello

Cassius — Julius Caeser

Catesby, Sir William — King Richard III

Cathness — Macbeth

Cato, Young — Julius Caesar

Celia — As You Like It

Ceres — The Tempest

Cerimon — Pericles

Charles (a wrestler) — As You Like It

Charles (the Dauphin) — King Henry VI, Part I

Charles VI (King of France) — King Henry V

Charmian — Antony and Cleopatra

Chatillon — King John

Chiron — Titus Andronicus

Christopherus Sly — Taming of the Shrew

Christopherus Ursick — King Richard III

Cicero — Julius Caeser

Cinna (a poet) — Julius Caeser

Cinna (a conspirator) — Julius Caeser

Clarence, Duke of — King Richard III

Clarence Thomas (Duke of) — King Henry IV, Part 2

Claudio (a young gentleman) — Measure for Measure

Claudio young Florentine Lord) — Much Ado About Nothing

Claudius (King of Denmark) — Hamlet

Claudius (servant to Brutus) — Julius Caeser

Cleomenes — A Winter's Tale

Cleon — Pericles

Cleopartra — Antony and Cleopatra

Clifford, Lord — King Henry VI, Parts 2 and 3

Clifford, Young — King Henry VI, Part 2

Clitus — Julius Caeser

---

[147] Beware the Green Eyed Monster

Cloten	Cymbeline
Clown (Servant to Mistress	Measure for Measure
[148]Clown (Servant to Olivia)	Twelfth Knight
[149]Cobweb	A Midsummer Night's Dream
Coleville, Sir John	King Henry IV, Part 2
Cominius	Coriolanus
Conrade	Much Ado About Nothing
[150]Constable of France, The	King Henry V
Constance	King John
Cordelia	King Lear
Corin	As You Like It
Coriolanus	Coriolanus
Cornelius (a Courtier)	Hamlet
Cornelius (a physician)	Cymbeline
Cornwall, Duke of	King Lear

---

[148] Compare with Ben Johnson's Three Comedies: Volpone, Bartholomews Fair and The Alchemist

[149] Compare Ben Johnson's Volpone

[150] Compare with Christopher Marlowe's Massacre of Paris (a play about St. Bartholomew's Massacre and the Duke of Guise). Christopher Marlowe was stabbed through the eye on the 30th May 1593 and died instantly at the home of Mistress Bull who at that time ran an Eating House where Marlowe had been invited to dine with Ingram Frizer, the servant of Thomas Walsingham. Ingram Frizer his murderer, was pardoned after the Inquest. The two witnesses, Robert Poley and Richard Skeres were witnesses to the murder and were earlier spies for Sir Francis Walsingham in the Babington Plot - a Plot to free Mary Queen of Scots.

There is a connection between the arrest of Thomas Kyd, who wrote the Spanish Tragedy (a forerunner to Hamlet) and the murder of Marlowe. Kyd and Marlowe used to share a writing chamber. The play Sir Thomas More to which Shakespeare tried to append three pages bears wording from the riots taking place at this time (1593) and Thomas Kyd was one of the first to be arrested after being suspected of being involved in the plot to drive out Strangers from the City of London and the ryhme put up on the Dutch churchyard are words from the play Sir Thomas More. It is quite clear that Shakespeare did not write Sir Thomas More and sections of the play are written in a neat Italian hand (Kyd used to translate from English into Italian and also wrote in a Scrivener's hand, since he had been apprenticed to his father Francis Kyd who was a member of the Company of Scriveners in 1557.

costard	Love's Labour's Lost
Count of Rousillon	All's Well that Ends Well
Countess of Auvergne	King Henry VI, Part I
Countess of Rousillon	All's Well that Ends Well
Court	King Henry V
Cranmer	King Henry VIII
Cressida	Triolus and Cressida
Cromwell	King Henry VIII
Curan	King Lear
Curio	Twelfth Knight
Curtis	Taming of the Shrew
Cymbeline	Cymbeline
[151]Dame Quickly	King Henry IV, Parts 1 and 2
[152]Dardanius	Julius Caeser
[153]Daughter of Antiochus	Pericles
Dauphin, the	King John
Davy	King Henry IV, Part 2
Decius Brutus	Julius Caesar
Diphobus	Triolus and Cressida
Demitrius (friend of Anthony)	Antony and Cleopatra
Demetrius (in love with Hermione)	A Midsummer Nights Dream

---

[151] Compare with Ben Johnson's style

[152] Compare with Raleigh's speeches in his Trial at Wincester 17th November 1603 and his literary style in New Atlantis. And his final words to the Dean "Caeser will raise me up I trust"

[153] George Chapman Dramatist was the expert on Greek history and translated the 7 books of the Illiads of Homer. See Shakespeare's Pericles Troilus and Cressida, and Timon of Athens. George Chapman was murdered in 1594 and was one of Raleigh's friends.

Demetrius (son to Tamora)	Titus Andronicus
Dennis	As you Like It
Denny, Sir Anthony	King Henry VIII
Dercetas	Anthony and Cleopatra
Desdemona	Othello
Diana (daughter to Widow)	All's Well that Ends Well
Diana	Pericles
Dick	King Henry VI, Part 2
Diomedes (a Grecian commander)	Triolus and Cressida
Diomedes (attendant on Cleopatra)	Antony and Cleopatra
Dion	A Winter's Tale
Dionyza	Pericles
Doctor Butts	King Henry VIII
Doctor Caius	The Merry Wives of Windsor
Dogberry	Much Ado About Nothing
Dolabella	Anthony and Cleopatra
Doll Tearsheet	King Henry IV, Part 2
Domitius Enobarbus	Antony and Cleopatra
Don Adriano de Armado	Love's Labour's Lost
Donalbain	Macbeth
Don John	Much Ado About Nothing
Don Pedro	Much Ado About Nothing
Dorcas	A Winter's Tale
Dorset, Marquis of	King Richard III
Douglas, Earl of	King Henry IV, Part I
Dromio of Ephesus	The Comedy of Errors
Dromio of Syracuse	The Comedy of Errorss
[154] Duchess of Gloster	King Richard II
Duchess of York	King Richard II
Duchess of York (mother if King Edward IV)	King Richard III
Duke of Albany	King Lear
[155] Duke of Alencon	King Henry VI, Part I

---

[154] Duchess of Gloster King Richard II whilst the Duke of Gloster appears in King Lear so they must have separated from some reason only known to Shakespeare.

Duke of Aumerle	King Richard III
Duke of Bedford (brother of King Henry V)	King Henry V
Duke of Bedford (Regent of France)	King Henry VI, Part I
Duke of Bourbon	King Henry V
Duke of Buckingham	King Richard III
Duke of Buckingham	King Henry VI, Part 2
Duke of Buckingham	King Henry VIII
Duke of Burgundy	King Lear
Duke of Burgundy	King Henry V
Duke of Burgundy	King Henry VI, Part I
Duke of Clarence	King Richard III
Duke of Clarence, Thomas	King Henry IV, Part 2
Duke of Cornwall	King Lear
Duke of Exeter (uncle to King Henry V)	King Henry V
Duke of Exeter	King Henry VI, Part 3
Duke of Florence	All's Well that Ends Well
Duke of Gloster (afterwards King Richard III)	King Richard III
Duke of Gloster (uncle and Protector	King Henry VI, Parts 1 and 2

---

[155] Le duc de Alencon is the "Frog Prince" who was engaged to Queen Elizabeth I in at the time of St Bartholomew's Massacre.   I cannot understand how he found himself in the wrong period of history and went back into the days of King Henry VI. Le Duc d'Alencon, Catherine d'Medici's youngest son, was almost twenty years younger than Elizabeth. Although Elizabeth wanted to put her Court into mourning in the wake of St Bartholomew's Massacre, this would have meant that she would have had to cease negotiations for she was keen to have her 'Frog Prince' visit her in England and the Queen had been receiving letters from Alencon regularly. Plans had to be put off yet again, as Elizabeth received news that Alencon had been imprisoned in France for conspiring with the Huguenots and that his brother, the Duke of Anjou had been elected King of Poland, in preference to Ivan the Terrible.He eventually marries the daughter of the King of Spain. Le Duc d'Alencon then inherited the title of the Duke of Anjou, and began courting the daughter of Philip of Spain, forgetting about the marriage negotiations between himself and Queen Elizabeth I of England and the Queen of England wept once more at her plight, and a broken love affair brought about by her Advisers.

to King Henry VI)	
Duke of Lancaster	King Richard II
Duke of Milan	Two Gentlemen of Verona
duke of Norfolk	King Richard II
Duke of Norfolk	King Henry VI, Part 3
Duke of Norfolk	King Henry VIII
Duke of Orelans	King Henry V
Duke of Somerset	King Henry VI, Parts 2 and 3
Duke Suffolk	King of Henry VI, Part 2
Duke of Suffolk	King Henry VIII
Duke of Surrey	King Richard II
Duke of Venice	The Merchant of Venice
Duke of Venice	Othello
Duke of York (cousin to the King)	King Henry V
Duke of York (uncle to King Richard II)	King Richard II
Duke of York (son of King Edward IV)	King Richard II
Dull	Love's Labour's Lost
Dumain	Love's Labour's Lost
Duncan	Macbeth
Earl Berkley	King Richard II
Earl of Cambridge	King Henry V
Earl of Douglas	King Henry IV, Part I
Earl of Essex	King John
Earl of Gloucester	King Lear
Earl of Kent	King Lear
Earl of March (Edmund Mortimer)	King Henry IV, Part I
Earl of March (afterwards King	King Henry VI, Part 3 Edward IV)
Earl of Northumberland	King Richard II
Earl of Northumberland (Henry Percy)	King Henry IV, Parts 1 and 2
Earl Northumberland	King Henry VI, Part 3
Earl of Oxford	King Henry VI, Part 3
Earl of Oxford	King Henry Richard III
Earl of Pembroke (William Mareshall)	King John
Earl of Pembroke	King Henry VI, Part 3

Earl of Rutland	King Henry VI, Part 3
Earl of Salisbury (William Longsword)	King John
Earl of Salisbury	King Richard II
Earl of Salisbury	King Henry VI, Parts 1, 2
Earl of Suffolk	King Henry VI Part i
Earl of Surrey (son of Duke of Norfolk)	King Richard II
Earl of Surrey	King Henry VIII
Earl of Warwick	King Henry V
Earl of Warwick	King Henry VI, Parts 1, 2, 3
Earl of Westmoreland (friend of King Henry IV)	King Henry VI, Parts 1, 2
Earl of Westmoreland	King Henry V
Earl of Westmoreland	King Henry IV, Parts 1, 2
Earl of Worcester	King Henry IV, Parts 1, 2
Earl Rivers	King Richard III
Edgar	King Lear
Edmund (Earl of Rutland)	King Henry VI, Part 3
Edmund (bastard son of Gloster)	King Lear
Edmund Mortimer (Earl of March)	King Henry IV, Part 1
Edmund Mortimer (Earl of March)	King Henry VI, Part 1
Edmund of Langley	King Richard II
Edward (son of a Plantagenet)	King Henry VI, Part 2
Edward, (Earl of March)	King Henry VI, Part 3
Edward, Prince of Wales	King Henry VI, Part 3
Edward, Prince of Wales	King Richard III
Edward IV, King	King Richard III
Egeus	A Midsummer Night's Dream
Eglamour	Two Gentlemen of Verona
Elbow	Measure for Measure
Eleanor	King Henry VI, Part 2
Elinor	King John
Elizabeth	King Richard III
Ely, Bishop of (John Morton)	King Richard III
Ely, Bishop of	King Henry V

Emilia (wife of Iago)	Othello
Emilia (a lady)	A Winter's Tale
Enobarbus, Domitius	Antony and Cleopatra
Eros	Antony and Cleopatra
Erpingham, Sir Thomas	King Henry V
Escalus (a lord of Vienna)	Measure for Measure
Escalus (Prince of Verona)	Romeo and Juliet
Escanes (lord of Tyre)	Pericles
Essex, Earl of	King John
Euphronius	Antony and Cleopatra
Evans, Sir Hugh	The Merry Wives of Windsor
Exeter, Duke of (uncle to King Henry V)	King Henry V
Exeter, Duke of	King Henry VI, Part 3
Exiled Duke	As You Like It
Fabian	Twelfth Night
Falstaff, Sir John	King Henry IV, Parts 1, 2
Falstaff, Sir John	The Merry Wives of Windsor
Fang	King Henry IV Part 2
Fastolfe, Sir John	King Henry VI, Part 1
Faulconbridge, Lady	King John
Faulconbridge, Philip	King John
Faulconbridge, Robert	King John
Feeble	King Henry IV, Part 2
Fenton	The Merry Wives of Windsor
[156]Ferdinand (King of Navarre)	Love's Labours Lost
Ferdinand (son of King of Naples)	The Tempest
Fitz-Peter Geoffrey	King John
Fitzwater, Lord	King Richard III
Flaminius	Timon of Athens
Flavius (a Roman tirbune)	Julius Caeser
Flavius (steward to Timon)	Timon of Athens
Fleance	Macbeth

---

[156] Compare with Christopher Marlowe's Massacre at Paris

Florence, Duke of	All's Well that Ends Well
Forence, Widow of	All's Well that Ends Well
Forizel	A Winter's Tale
Fluellen	King Henry V
Flute	A Midsummer Night's Dream
Ford, Mrs	The Merry Wives of Windsor
Fored, Mrs	The Merry Wives of Windsor
Fortinbras	Hamlet
France (the Constable of)	King Henry V
France, King of	All's Well that Ends Well
France, King of	King Lear
France, Princess of	Love's Labour's Lost
Fancisca	Measure for Measure
Francisco (a soldier)	Hamlet
Francisco (a lord of Naples)	The Tempest
Frederick	As You Like It
Friar John	Romeo and Juliet
Friar Laurence	Romeo and Juliet
Froth	Measure for Measure
Gadshill	King Henry IV, Part 1
Gallus	Anthony and Cleopatra
Gardiner (Bishop of Winchester)	King Henry VIII
Gargrave, Sir Thomas	King Henry VI, Part 1
Geffrey Fitz-Peter	King John
George (follower of Cade)	King Henry VI, Part 2
George (Duke of Clarence)	King Henry VI, Part 3
George (Duke of Clarence)	King Richard III
Gertrude	Hamlet
Ghost of Hamlet's Father	Hamlet
Glansdale, Sir William	King Henry VI, Part 1
Glendower, Owen	King Henry IV, Part 1
Gloster,Duchess of	King Richard II
Gloster, Duke of (brother of King Henry V)	King Henry V

Gloster, Duke of (uncle and protector to King Henry VI)	King Henry VI, part 1
Glocester, Duke of (afterwards King Richard III)	King Richard II
Gloster, Earl of	King Lear
Gloster, Prince Humphrey of	King Henry IV, part 2
Gobbo, Launcelot	The Merchant of Venice
Gobbo, Old	The Merchant of Venice
Goneril	King Lear
Gonzalo	The Tempest
Gower	Pericles
Gower	King Henry IV, Part 2
Gower (officer in King's army)	King Henry V
Gandpre	King Henry V
Gratiano (brother of Brabantio)	Othello
Gatiano (friend of Antonio and Bassanio)	The Merchant of Venice
Green	King Richard II
Gregory	Romeo and Juliet
Gremio	Taming of the Shrew
Grey, Lady	King Richard II
Gregory	Taming of the shrew
Grey, Lady	King Henry VI, Part 3
Grey, Lord	King Richard III
Grey, Lord Thomas	King Henry V
Griffith	King Henry VIII
Grumio	Taming of the Shrew
Guiderius	Cymbeline
Guildenstern	Hamlet
Guildford, Sir Henry	King Henry VIII
Gurney, James	King John
Hamlet	Hamlet
Harcourt	King Henry IV, Part 2
Hastings, Lord (enemy of the King)	King Henry IV, Part 2
Hstings, Lord	King Henry VI, Part 3
Hastings, Lord	King Richard III
Hecate	Macbeth

Hector	Triolus and Cressida
Helen (woman to Imogen)	Cymbeline
Helen (wife of Menelaus)	Triolus and Cressida
Helena (a gentlewoman)	All's Well that Ends Well
Helena (in love with Demetrius)	A Midsummer-Night's Dream
Helenus	Triolus and Cressida
Helicanus	Pericles
Henry	King Richard III
Henry Bolingbroke (afterwards King Henry IV)	King Richard II
Henry (Earl of Richmond)	King Henry VI, part 3
Henry (Earl of Richmond, afterwards King Henry VII)	King Richard III
Henry Percy	King Richard II
Henry Percy	King Henry IV, Parts 1, 2
Henry Percy (Hotspur)	King Henry IV, Parts, 1, 2
Henry, Prince	King John
Henry (Prince of Wales)	King Henry IV, Parts 1, 2
Henry IV, King	King Henry IV, Parts 1, 2
Henry V, King	King Henry V
Henry VI, King	King Henry VI, parts, 1, 2 and 3
Henry, VIII, King	King Henry VIII
Herbert, Sir Walter	King Richard III
Hermia	A Midsummer-Night's Dream
Hermione	A Winter's Tale
Hero	Much Ado About Nothing
Hippolyta	A Midsummer-Night's Dream
Holofernes	Love's Labour's Lost
Horatio	Hamlet
Horner, Thomas	King Henry VI, Part 2
Hortensio	Taming of the Shrew
Hensius	Timon of Athens
Hostess	Taming of the Shrew
Hostess Quickly	King Henry IV Parts 1, 2
Hubert De Burgh	King John

Hume	King Henry VI, Part 2
Humphrey, (Duke of Gloster)	King Henry VI, Part 2
Humphrey, Prince, of Gloster	King Henry IV, Part 2
Iachimo	Cymbeline
Iago	Othello
Iden, Alexander	King Henry VI, Part 2
Imogen	Cymbeline
Iras	Antony and Cleopatra
Iris	The Tempest
Isabel	King Henry V
Isabella	Measure for Measure
Jack Cade	King Henry VI, Part 2
James Gurney	King John
Jamy	King Henry V
Jaquenetta	Love's Labour's Lost
Jaques (son of Sir Rowland de Bois)	As You Like It
Jaques (a lord attendant an exiled Duke)	As You Like It
Jessica	The Merchant of Venice
Joan La Pucelle	King Henry VI, Part 1
John	King Henry VI, Part 2
John, Don	Much Ado about Nothing
John, Friar	Romeo and Juliet
John of Gaunt	King Richard II
John, Prince of Lancaster	King Henry IV, Parts 1, 2
John Talbot	King Henry VI, Part 1
Jourdain, Margery	King Henry VI, Part 2
Julia	Two Gentlemen of Verona
Juliet	Measure for Measure
Juliet (daughter of Capulet)	Romeo and Juliet
Julius Caesar	Julius Caeser
Junius Brutus	Coriolanus
Juno	The Tempest
Justice Shallow	King Henry IV, Part 2
Katharina	Taming of the Shrew
Katharine (a lady attending on Princess of France)	Love's Labour's Lost

Katharine, Queen	King Henry VIII
Kent, Earl of	King Lear
King Edward IV	King Richard III
King Henry IV	King Henry IV Parts 1, 2
King Henry V	King Henry V
King Henry VI	King Henry VI, Parts 1, 2
and 3	
King Henry VIII	King Henry VIII
King John	King John
King of France	All's Well that Ends Well
King of France	King Lear
King Richard II	King Richard II
King Richard III	King Richard III
Lady Anne	King Richard III
Lady Capulet	Romeo and Juliet
Lady Faulconbridge	King John
Lady Grey	King Henry VI, part 3
Lady Macbeth	Macbeth
Lady Macduff	Macbeth
Lady Montague	Romeo and Juliet
Lady Mortimer	King Henry IV, Part 1
Lady Northumberland	King Henry IV, Part 2
Lady Percy	King Henry IV, Part 1
Laertes	Hamlet
Lafeu	All's Well that Ends Well
Lancaster, Duke of	King Richard II
Lancaster, Prince John of	King Henry IV, Parts 1, 2
Launce	Two Gentlemen of Verona
Launcelot Gobbo	The Merchant of Venice
Laurence, Friar	Romeo and Juliet
Lavinia	Titus Andronica
Lear	King Lear
Le Beau	As You Like It

Lenox	Macbeth
Leonardo	The Merchant of Venice
Leonatus, Posthumus	Cymbeline
Leonine	Pericles
Leontes	A Winter's Tale
Lepidus, M. Aemilius	Antony and Cleopatra
Ligarius	Julius Caeser
Lincoln, Bishop of	King Henry VIII
Lion	A Midsummer-Night's Dream
Lodovico	Othello
Longaville	Love's Labour's Lost
Longsword, William	King John
Lord, A	Taming of the Shrew
Lord Abergavenny	King Henry VIII
Lord Bardolph	King Henry IV, Part 2
Lord Chief Justice	King Henry IV, Part 2
Lord Clifford	King Henry VI, Parts 2, 3
Lord Fitzwater	King Richard II
Lord Grey	King Richard III
Lord Hastings	King Richard III
Lord Hastings (enemy of the King)	King Henry IV, Part 2
Lord Hastings	King Henry VI, Part 3
Lord Lovel	King Richard III
Lord Marshal, The	King Richard II
Lord Mowbray	King Henry IV, Part 2
Lord Rivers	King Henry VI, Part 3
Lord Ross	King Richard II
Lord Sands	King Henry VIII
Lord Say	King Henry VI, Part 3
Lord Scales	King Henry VI, Part 2
Lord Scroop	King Henry V
Lord Stafford	King Henry VI, Part 3
Lord Stanley	King Richard III
Lord Talbot	King Henry VI, Part 1
Lord Willoughby	King Richard II

Lorenzo	The Merchant of Venice
Louis, the Dauphin	King John
Louis, the Dauphin	King Henry V
Louis XI	King Henry VI, Part 3
Lovel, Lord	King Richard III
Lovel, Sir Thomas	King Henry VIII
Luce	The Comedy of Errors
Lucentio	Taming of the Shrew
Lucetta	Two Gentlemen of Verona
Luciana	The Comedy of Errors
Lucilius (friend of Brutus and Cassius)	Julius Caeser
Lucilius (servant to Timon)	Timon of Athens
Lucio	Measure for Measure
Lucius (a Lord)	Timon of Athens
Lucius (a servant)	Timon of Athens
Lucius (servant to Brutus)	Julius Caeser
Lucius (son of titus)	Titus Andronicus
Lucius, Young	Titus Andronicus
Lucullus	Timon of Athens
Lucy, Sir William	King Henry VI, Part 1
Lychorida	Pericles
Lysander	A Midsummer-Night's Dream
Lysimachus	Pericles
Macbeth	Macbeth
Machbeth, Lady	Macbeth
Macduff	Macbeth
Macduff, Lady	Macbeth
Macmorris	King Henry V
Malcolm	Macbeth
Malvolio	Twelfth Night
Mamillius	A Winter's Tale
Marcellus	Hamlet
March, Earl of (Edmund Mortimer)	King Henry IV, Part I
March, Earl of (afterwards King Edward IV)	King Henry VI, part 3

Marcus Andronicus	Titus Andronicu
Marcus Antonius	Julius Caeser
Marcus Brutus	Julius Caeser
Mardian	Antony and Cleopatra
Mareshall, William	King John
Mararelon	Triolus and Cressida
Margaret (attendant on Hero)	Much Ado About Nothing
Margaret (widow of King Henry VI)	King Richard III
Margaret, Queen	King Henry VI, Part 3
Margery Jourdain	King Henry VI, Part 2
Maria (lady attending Princess of France)	Love's Labour's Lost
Mariana (neighbour to Widow of Florence)	All's Well that Ends Well
Mariana (the bethrothed of Angelo)	Measure for Measure
Marina	Pericles
Mark Antony	Antony and Cleopatra
Marquis of Dorset	King Richard II
Marquis of Montague	King Henry VI, Part 3
Marshal, The Lord	King Richard II
Martext, Sir Oliver	As You Like It
Martius	Titus Andronicus
Marullus	Julius Caeser
Macaenas	Antony and Cleopatra
Melun	King John
Menas	Antony and Cleopatra
Menecrates	Antony and Cleopatra
Menenius Agrippa	Coriolanus
Menteth	Macbeth
Mercade	Love's Labour's Lost
Mercutio	Romeo and Juliet
Messala	Julius Caeser
Metellus Cimber	Julius Caeser
Metellus Cimber	King Henry VI, Part 2
Michael	King Henry IV Parts 1, 2
Michael, Sir	King Henry IV, Parts 1, 2

Milan, Duke of	Two Gentlemen of Verona
Miranda	The Tempest
Mistress Overdone	Measure for Measure
Mr Ford	The Merry Wives of Windsor
Mr Page	The Merry Wives of Windsor
Mrs Anne Page	The Merry Wives of Windsor
Mrs. Page	The Merry Wives of Windsor
Mrs Quickly (a tavern hostess)	King Henry IV, Parts 1, 2
Mrs Quickly (a hostess; wife of Pistol)	King Henry V
Mrs.Quickly (servant to Dr. Cauis)	The Merry Wives of Windsor
Montague	Romeo and Juliet
Montague, Lady	Romeo and Juliet
Montague, Marquis of	King Henry VI, Part 3
Montano	Othello
Montgomery, Sir John	King Henry VI, Part 3
Montjoy	King Henry V
Moonshine	A Midsummer-Nights Dream
Mopsa	A Winter's Tale
Morgan	Cymbeline
Morocco, Prince	The Merchant of Venice
Mortimer, Edmund (Earl of March)	King Henry IV, Part i
Mortimer, Edmund (Earl of March)	King Henry VI, Part 1
Mortimer, Lady	King Henry IV, Part 1
Mortimer, Sir Hugh	King Henry VI, Part 3
Mortimer, Sir John	King Henry I, Part 2
Morton	King Henry IV, Part 2
Morton, John	King Richard III
Moth (a fairy)	A Midsummer-Night's Dream
Moth (Page to Armado)	Love's Labour's Lost
Mouldy	King Henry IV, Part 2
Mowbray	King Richard II
Mowbray, Lord	King Henry IV< Part 2
Mustard-Seed	A Midsummer-Night's Dream
Mutius	Titus Andronicus
Nathaniel, Sir	Love's Labour's Lost

Nerissa	The Merchant of Venice
Nestor	Troilus and Cressida
Norfolk, Duke of (Thomas Mowbray)	King Richard II
Norfolk, Duke of	King Richard III
Norfolk, Duke of	King Henry VI, Part 3
Norfolk, Duke of	King Henry VIII
Northumberland, Earl of	King II
Northumberland, Earl of (Henry Percy)	King Henry IV Parts 1, 2
Northumberland, Earl of	King Henry VI, Part 3
Northumberland, Lady	King Henry IV< Part 2
Nurse to Juliet	Romeo and Juliet
Nym	King Henry V
Nym	The Merry Wives of Windsor
Oberon	A Midsummer-Night's Dream
Octavia	Anthony and Cleopatra
Octavius Caesar (a Roman triumvir)	Julius Caeser
Octavius Caesar (a Roman triumvir)	Anthony and Cleopatra
Old Gobbo	Merchant of Venice
Oliver	As You Like It
Ophelia	Hamlet
Orlando	As you Like It
Orleans, Duke of	King Henry V
Orsino	Twelfth Night
Osric	Hamlet
Oswald	King Lear
Othello	Othello
Overdone, Mistress	Measure for Measure
Owen Glendower	King Henry IV, Part i
Oxford, Earl of	King Henry VI, Part 3
Oxford, Earl of	King Richard III
Page, Mr.	The Merry Wives of Windsor
Page, Mrs.	The Merry Wives of Windsor
Page, Mrs. Anne	The Merry Wives of Windsor
Page, William	The Merry Wives of Windsor
Pandarus	Triolus and Cressida
Pandulph, Cardinal	King John
Panthino	Two Gentleman of Verona

Paris (son of Priam)	Troilus and Cressida
Paris (a young nobleman)	Romeo and Juliet
Parolles	All's Well that Ends Well
Patience	King Henry VIII
Patroclus	Triolus and Cressida
Paulina	A Winter's Tale
Peas-Blossom	A Midsummer's Night's Dream
Pedant	Taming of the Shrew
Pedro, Don	Much Ado About Nothing
Pembroke, Earl of	King Henry VI, Part 3
Pembroke, Earl of (William Mareshall)	King John
Percy, Henry	King Henry IV, Parts 1, 2
Percy, Henry	King Richard 2
Percy, Henry (Hotspur)	King Henry IV, Parts 1,2
Percy, Lady	King Henry IV, Parts 1, 2
Percy, Thomas	King Henry IV, part 1, 2
Perdita	A Winter's Tale
Pericles	Pericles
Peter (a friar)	Measure for Measure
Peter (Horner's man)	Kingn Henry VI, Part 2
Peter (servant to Juliet's nurse)	Romeo and Juliet
Peter of Pomfret	King John
Peto	King Henry IV, Parts 1, 2
Petruchio	Taming of the Shrew
Phebe	As You Like It
Philario	Cymbeline
Philemon	Pericles
Philip	King John
Philipo Faulconbridge	King John
Philo	Anthony and Cleopatra
Philostrate	A Midsummer-Night's Dream
Phrynia	Timon of Athens
Pierce, Sir, of Exton	King Richard II
Pinch	The Comedy of Errors

Pindarus	Julius Caeser
Pisanio	Cymbeline
Pistol (follower of Sir John Falstaff)	The Merry Wives of Windsor
Pistol (follower of Sir John Falstaff)	King Henry IV Part 2
Pistol (soldier in King's army)	King Henry V
Plantagenet, Richard	King Henry VI, Parts 1, 2, 3
Poins	King Henry IV, Parts 1, 2
Polixenes	A Winter's Tale
Poloius	Hamlet
Polydore	Cymbeline
Popeius Sextus	Anthony and Cleopatra
Popilius Lena	Julius Caeser
Portia (a rich heiress)	The Merchant of Venice
Portia (wife of Brutus)	Julius Caeser
Posthumus, Leonatus	Cymbeline
Priam	Triolus and Cressida
Prince Henry	King John
Prince Humphrey of Glocester	King Henry IV, Part 2
Prince John of Lancaster	King Henry IV, Parts 1, 2
Prince of Arragon	The Merchant of Venice
Prince of Morocco	The Merchant of Venice
Prince of Wales	King Richard III
Prince of Wales, Henry,	King Henry IV, Part 2
Princess of France	Love's Labour's Lost
Proculeius	Antony and Cleopatra
Prospero	The Tempest
Proteus	Two Gentlemen of Verona
Provost	Measure for Measure
Publius (a Roman Senator)	Julius Caeser
Publius (son of Marcus Andronicus	Titus Andronicus
Pucelle, Joan La	King Henry VI, Part 1
Puck	A Midsummer-Night's Dream
Pyramus	A Midsummer-Night's Dream
Queen (wife of Cymbeline)	Cymbeline
Queen Elizabeth	King Richard III
Queen Katharine	King Henry VIII
Queen Margaret	King Henry VI, Part 3

Queen to King Richard II	King Richard II
Quickly, Mrs. (a tavern hostess)	King Henry IV, Parts 1, 2
Quickly, Mrs. (servant to Dr. Cauius)	The Merry Wives of Windsor
Quince	A Midsummer Night's Dream
Quintus	Titus Andronicus
Rambures	King Henry
Ratcliff, Sir Richard	King Richard III
Regan	King Lear
Reignier	King Henry VI, Part 1
Reynaldo	Hamlet
Richard	King Henry VI, Parts 2, 3
Richard, Duke of Gloster	King Richard III
Richard, Duke of York	King Richard III
Richard Plantagenet	King Henry VI, Parts 1, 2 3
Richard II, King	King Richard II
Richard III, King	King Richard III
Richmond, Earl of	King Richard III
Rivers, Earl	King Richard III
Rivers, Lord	King Henry VI, Part 3
Robert Bigot	King John
Robert Faulconbridge	King John
Robin	The Merry Wives of Windsor
Robin Goodfellow (Puck)	A Midsummer-Night's Dream
Roderigo	Othello
Rogero	A Winter's Tale
Romeo	Romeo and Juliet
Rosalind	As You Like It
Rosaline	Love's Labour's Lost
Rosencrantz	Hamlet
Ross, Lord	King Richard II
Rosse	Macbeth
Rotheram, Thomas	King Richard III
Rousillon, Count of	All's Well that Ends Well
Rousillon, Countess of	All's Well that Ends Well
Rugby	The Merry Wives of Windsor

Rumour	King Henry IV, Part 2
Rutland, Earl of	King Henry VI, Part 3
Salarino	The Merchant of Venice
Saleirio	The Merchant of Venice
Salisbury, Earl of (William Longsword) King John	
Salisbury, Earl of	King Henry V
Salisbury, Earl of	King Henry VI, Parts 2,1
Salisbury, Earl of	King Richard II
Sampson	Romeo and Juliet
Sands, Lord	King Henry VIII
Saturninus	Titus Andronicus
Say, Lord	King Henry VI, Part 2
Scales, Lord	King Henry VI, Part 2
Scarus	Anthony and Cleopatra
Scroop	King Henry IV, Parts 1, 2
Scroop, Lord	King Henry V
Scroop, Sir Stephen	King Richard II
Sebastian (brother of King of Naples)	The Tempest
Sebastian (brother of Viola)	Twelfth Night
Seleucus	Antony and Cleopatra
Sempronius	Timon of Athens
Sextus Pompeius	Antony and Cleopatra
Seyton	Macbeth
Shadow	King Henry IV, Part 2
Shakespeare with 100 hands	Briarius the mythological giant
Shallow (a country justice)	King Henry IV, Part 2
Shallow (a country justice	The Merry Wives of Windsor
Shylock	The Merchant of Venice
Sicinius Velutus	Coriolanus
Silence	King Henry IV, Part 2
Silius	Anthony and Cleopatra
Silvia	Two Gentlemen of Verona
Silvius	As You Like It
Simonides	Pericles
Simpcox	King Henry VI, Part 2
Simple	The Merry Wives of Windsor

HIC JACET: SIR WALTER RALEIGH

Sir Andrew Ague-Cheek	Twelfth Night
Sir Anthony Denny	King Henry VIII
sir Henry Guildford	King Henry VIII
Sir Hugh Evans	The Merry Wives of Windsor
Sir Hugh Mortimer	King Henry VI, Part 3
Sir Humphrey Stafford	King Henry VI, Part 2
Sir James Blount	King Richard III
Sir James Tyrrel	King Richard III
Sir John Coleville	King Henry IV, Part 2
Sir John Falstaff	King Henry IV, Parts 1, 2
Sir John Falstaff	The Merry Wives of Windsor
Sir John Fastolfe	King Henry VI, Part 1
Sir John Montgomery	King Henry VI, Part 3
Sir John Mortimer	King Henry VI, Part 3
Sir John Somerville	King Henry VI, Part 3
Sir John Stanley	King Henry VI, Part 2
Sir Michael	King Henry IV, Part 1
Sir Nathaniel	Love's Labour's Lost
sir Nicholas Vaux	King Henry VIII
Sir Oliver Martext	As you Like It
Sir Pierce of Exton	King Richard II
sir Richard Ratcliff	King Richard III
Sir Richard Vernon	King Henry IV, Part 1
Sir Robert Brakenbury	King Richard III
Sir Stephen Scroop	King Richard III
Sir Thomas Erpingham	King Henry V
Sir Thomas Gargrave	King Henry VI, Part 1
Sir Robert Brakenbury	King Richard III
sir Stephen Scroop	King Richard II
Sir Thomas Erpingham	King Henry V
Sir Thomas Gargrave	King Henry VI, Part 1
Sir Thomas Grey	King Henry V
Sir Thomas Lovell	King Henry V
Sir tomas Vaughan	King Richard III
sir Toby Belch	Twelfth Night

Sir Walter Blunt	King Henry IV, Parts 1, 2
sir Walter Herbert	King Richard III
Sir William Ctesby	King Richard III
Sir William Glansdale	King Henry VI, Part 1
Sir William Lucy	King Henry VI, Part 1
Sir William Stanley	King Henry VI, Part 3
Siward	Macbeth
Siward, Young	Macbeth
Slender	The Merry Wives of Windsor
Smith (the Weaver)	King Henry VI, Part 2
Snare	King Henry IV, Part 2
Snout	A Midsummer Night's Dream
Snug	A Midsummer Night's Dream
Solanio	The Merchant of Venice
Solinus	The Comedy of Errors
Somerset, Duke of	King Henry VI, Parts 2, 3
Somerville, Sir John	King Henry VI, Part 3
Southwell	King Henry VI, Part 2
Speed	Two Gentlemen of Verona
Stafford, Lord	King Henry VI, Part 3
Stafford, Sir Humphrey	King Henry VI, Part 2
Stanley, Lord	King Richard III
Stanley, Sir John	King Henry VI, Part 2
Stanley, Sir William	King Henry VI, Part 3
Starveling	A Midsummer-Night's Dream
Stephano (a drunker butler)	The Tempest
Stephano (servant to Portia)	The Merchant of Venice
Strato	Julius Caeser
Suffolk, Duke of	King Henry VI, Part 2
Suffolk, Duke of	King Henry VIII
Suffolk, Earl of	King Henry VI, Part 1
Surrey, Duke of	King Richard II
Surrey, Earl of (son of Duke of Norfolk)	King Richard III
Surrey, Earl of	King Henry VIII
Talbot John	King Henry VI, Part 1
Talbot, Lord	King Henry VI, Part 1

Tamora	Titus Andronicus
Taurus	Antony and Cleopatra
Tearsheet, Doll	King Henry IV, Part 2
Thaisa	Pericles
Thaliard	Pericles
Thersites	Triolus and Cressida
Theseus	A Midsummer-Night's Dream
Thisbe	A Midsummer-Night's Dream
Thomas	Measure for Measure
Thomas, Duke of Clarence	King Henry IV, Part 2
Thomas Horner	King Henry VI, Part 2
Thurio	Two Gentlemen of Verona
Thyreus	Antony and Cleopatra
Timandra	Timon of Athens
Time	A Winter's Tale
Timon	Timon of Athens
Titania	A Midsummer-Night's Dream
Titinius	Julius Caesar
Titus Andronicus	Titus Andronicus
Titus lartius	Coriolanus
Touchstone	As You Like It
Tranio	Taming of the Shrew
Travers	King Henry IV, Part 2
Trebonius	Julius Caesar
Trinculo	The Tempest
Troilus	Troilus and Cressida
Tubal	The Merchant of Venice
Tullus Aufidius	Coriolanus
Tybalt	Romeo and Juliet
Tyrrel, Sir James	King Richard III
Ulysses	Triolus and Cressida
Ursula	Much Ado About Nothing
Uswick, Christopherus	King Richard III
Valentine (a gentleman of Verona)	Two Gentlemen of Verona
Valentine (attendant on the Duke of	

545

William Mareshall (Earl of Pembroke)	King John
William Page	The Merry Wives of Windsor
Williams	King Henry V
Willoughby, Lord	King Richard II
Winchester, Bishop of (Gardiner)	King Henry VIII
Witches, Three	Macbeth
Wolsey, Cardinal	King Henry VIII
Woodville	King Henry VI, Part 1
Worcester, Earl of	King Henry IV, Parts 1, 2
York, Archbishop of (Scroop)	King Henry IV Parts 1, 2
York, Archbishop of (Thomas Rotheram)	King Richard III
York, Duchess of	King Richard II
York, Duchess of (mother of King Edward IV)	King Richard III
York, Duke of (cousin to the King)	King Henry V
York, Duke of (uncle to King Richard II)	King Richard II
York, duke of (son of King Edward IV)	King Richard III
Young Cato	Julius Caesar
Young Clifford	King Henry VI, Part 2
Young Lucius	Titus Andronicus
Young Marcius	Coriolanus
Young Siward	Macbeth

Shedding some light surrounding the mysteries of Elizabethan literature and the Plays/Last Will and Testament of William Shakespeare (Overseer of his Will)/and the Burdett-Coutts Connection to the first folios of William Shakespeare's Plays and the Raleigh-Throckmorton Gunpowder Plot (1605) Theory

By Barbara O'Sullivan

The Shakespeare-Quiney-Bushell-Greville-Winter-Arden-Sheldon-Russell-Catesby-Tresham Connection

Hoby was connected to the II Earl of Essex who was the Queen's cousin/and through marriage to Sir Philip Sidney's widow, Penelope Devereux)

Raleigh was connected through marriage into the Throckmorton family, to Bess Throckmorton (Queen Elizabeth I maid of Honour) and to the conspirators of the Gunpowder Plot and Arden/Shakespeare/Bushell/Quiney = who became, between them the purchasers of Shakespeare's first folios (Burdett-Coutts) and the overseer of Shakespeare's Will.

Greville, Sheldon, and Catesby were also second cousins, through their grandmothers, the three sisters Willington.

"Hoby was bluer-blooded and married to the Queen's cousin. He translated a Spanish book on the theory and practice of war, reported to Elizabeth on Armada preparations in 1588, and sailed on the Cadiz expedition in 1598, [with Raleigh and the II Earl of Essex]. In 1607 Hoby acquired the monopoly of wool-buying in Warwickshire and Staffordshire. He also wrote some anti-papist pamphlets, including one called 'A Countersnarl for Ishmael Rabshacheh a Cecropidan Lycaonite'. The Hoby Tombs at Bisham are of striking beauty, particularly the obelisk with the Hunsdon swans.' – The Life and Times of William Shakespeare.

Lord Burleigh – William Cecil = Robert Cecil = Nicholas Bacon's daughter married Sir Thomas Hoby. Thomas Hoby's son Edward Hoby married Lord Hunsdon's daughter (1582)

Sir Anthony Cooke – King's Governor or Guardian = Cecil = (Lord Burghley) = Robert Cecil = Lord Salisbury = Nicholas Bacon = Francis Bacon = Thomas Hoby (diplomat and linguist) = Edward Hoby (m. Lord Hunsdon's daughter)

Francis Bacon

Thomas Kyd's possible Patron:

The Earl of Sussex Players
Henry Radcliffe, 4th Earl of Sussex – knighted by Henry FitzAlan 19th Earl of Arundal
Born April 10/December 14 (1530) d. 19th January 1593
He was married to

4th Earl of Sussex died 19th January 1593
Christopher Marlowe was murdered on 30th May, 1593.
Kyd was arrested 18 May 1593
Robert Greene Dramatist died of starvation in 1592
Dekker was arrested for debt in 1598 by the Shakespeare Company, but almost certainly wrote some part of King Henry VI.
Lord Strange, the Earl of Derby died 1594
Sir Edward Bushell servant with Heminges and Phillips (and probably Shakespeare) to Ferdinando Stanley, Lord Strange, Earl of Derby. Gentleman usher to the Earl of Essex. Lieutenant of infantry in Ireland. Knighted 1604, Equerry to James I and Charles I.
The Earl of Pembroke, Henry Herbert died the same year as Sir Philip Sidney (1586)
Sir Philip Sidney (1554-1586)

His widow married the Robert Devereux, 2nd Earl of Essex

Kyd wrote letters to Bridget, 5th Countess of Sussex

Bridget married Henry Radcliffe,s son, 5th Earl of Sussex
Her maiden name was Bridget Morrison

5th Earl of Derby, Lord Ferdinando Strange (b.1559) d. 1594
the Patron of Lord Strange's Men who were renamed Derby's Men
It is believed that Shakespeare was involved with this Troupe both as
an actor and dramatist

Lord Derby died the same year as the troupe produced the plays Titus
Andronicus and the Trilogy:
Henry VI Part I, Henry VI, Part 2 and Henry VI, Part 3

Christopher Marlowe wrote Edward II for the Earl of Pembroke
Players in 1591
Which is referred to in a letter written to Robert Devereux, 2nd Earl of
Essex (died 1601)

A rival troupe "The Lord Chamberlain's Men" were formed in 1594.
Lord Hunsdon (Hoby married Hunsdon's daughter) – Hunsdon was
cousin of Queen Elizabeth I, ("Hunsdon's Men"), Henry Carey see
Marlowe's Inquest, [Queen Elizabeth's cousin through his mother
Mary Boleyn, Anne Boleyn's sister] reorganized the Company and it
became linked with William Shakespeare. [See dark lady Sonnetts -
XXXIII - XLIII].

(Lord Salisbury Robert Cecil) = (Nicholas and Francis Bacon) – Sir
Thomas Hoby and Edward Hoby= and Lord Hunsdon's daughter
connected

Edward Sheldon's son, William, purchased the first folio of
Shakespeare's plays (Burdett Coutts copy) now in Folger Library
Throckmorton = ~Winter = Berkeley = Hussey = Ingleby = Bourne =
Arden (kinsman of Shakespeare's mother, Mary Arden) = Sheldon of

HIC JACET: SIR WALTER RALEIGH

Beoley = Catesby of Lapsworth, Stratford on Avon and Milcote –
Sheriff of Warwickshire (1577) owned Shottery Meadow, and intimate
with Sir Edward Greville) = Tresham = Robert Winter, Thomas
Winter, John Winter, John Grant (Gunpowder Plot), Sheldon, John
Russell (brother of Thomas Russell, overseer of William
Shakespeare's Will); = Robert Catesby (Gunpowder Plot), Francis
Tresham (Gunpowder Plot 1605) – Guido Fawkes (who was Guido?)

Sir Walter Raleigh married Elizabeth Throckmorton and her brother
Arthur Throckmorton was racked for implication in the Babbington
Plot – A plot which involved sending coded letters to and from Mary
Queen of Scots (a staunch Catholic and mother of King James I who
was taken away from her as a baby, and never allowed to see her and
brought up as a Protestant); in an effort to free her, which was
unsuccessful. This indicates to me that the Throckmorton family were
Catholics. Sir Walter Raleigh was connected through marriage to the
Gunpowder Plot conspirators, and also to the owner of the First Folio
of Shakespeare's plays and to the overseer of Shakespeare's Will
(John Russell).

The Winter brothers who were descendants of the
Throckmorton/Hussey/Arden family, were therefore Raleigh's
relatives through marriage. The Winter brothers (possibly the sons of
those Winter brothers executed in the Gunpowder Plot), accompanied
Raleigh on his second voyage to Guiana in 1617.

Kett or Cade – Robin Hood – words spoken at Raleigh's trial – The
Black Prince of Bordeaux and King John or Richard?

King Richard II play
The Bisham Tombs/Hoby

Sir Philip Sidney (1554-1586) married Frances Walsingham in 1583
Sir Philip Sidney's widow married Robert Devereux in 1590

The Earl of Leicester was Shakespeare's Patron

Earl of Pembroke (Henry Herbert(?) died the same year as Sir Philip Sidney and Christopher Marlowe wrote the play Edward II for the Earl of Pembroke Players. (1591) (see letter to Earl of Essex (d.1601) which refers read at a supper attended by the Earl of Essex, Lord Cobham (Raleigh's enemy), and Lady Hoby. Lady Hoby was married to the Earl of Essex brother, Walter Devereux, and then married Thomas Sidney, brother of Sir Philip Sidney. (Hoby Tombs at Bischam).

Robert Greene Dramatist died in 1592 of starvation (Groatsworth of Wit, and Henry Greene's scraps etc.)

Lord Strange – Earl of Derby (Ferdinando Stanley) – died 1594 (possibly poisoned).

Kyd and Marlowe engaged to write for the Earl of Sussex players in 1591 – (King Henry plays?)

Son of Thomas Radcliffe, Fourth Earl of Sussex, (Governor of Ireland 1553-1557) Viscount Fitzwalter) died 1593 the same year as the murder of Marlowe and the arrest and imprisonment of Thomas Kyd.

And then Kyd writes to Bridget Countess of Sussex whilst in prison in 1593.

Thomas Kyd registers the play King Henry VI at Stationers Hall, Stationers Register 1594.

Dekker wrote some part of the play Sir Thomas More but was arrested for debt by the Shakespeare company (Walsingham's Men) in 159 – Dekker was attached to The Admirals Men.

The Earl of Pembroke's Players acted Edward II.

The Earl of Southampton married Elizabeth Vernon.

Mortimer is referred to in the play Sir Thomas More. Roger Mortimer (1330)

"To the memory of my Beloved, the Author, Mr William Shakespeare" by Ben Johnson

written by Ben Johnson - 1572 to 6 August 1637 - (65)

"To draw no envy, Shakespeare, on thy name,
Am I thus ample to thy book and fame;
While I confess thy writings to be such,
As neither Man nor Muse can praise too much.
'Tis true, and all men's suffrage. But these ways
Were not the paths I meant unto thy praise:
For silliest ignorance on these may light,
Which, when it sounds at best, but echoes right:
Or blind affection, which doth ne'er advance
The truth, but grope, and urgeth all by chance;
Or crafty malice might pretend this praise
And think it ruin where it seemed to raise.
These are, as some infamous bawd or whore
Should praise a matron: what could hurt her more?
But thou are proof against them and, indeed,
Above the ill fortune of them, or need.
I therefore will begin: Soul of the Age!
The applause, delight, the wonder of our stage!
My SHAKESPEARE, RISE! I will not ledge thee by
Chaucer, or Spenser, or bid Beaumont lie
A little further, to make thee a room:
Thou art a monument without a tomb,
Thou art alive still while thy book doth live,
And we have wits to read, and praise to give.
That I not mix thee so, my brain excuses,
I mean with great but disproportioned Muses;
For if I thought my judgment were of years,
I should commit thee surely with thy peers,
And tell how far thou dist our Lyly outshine,
Or sporting Kyd, or Marlowe's mighty line.
And thou hadst small Latin and Less Greek,

HIC JACET: SIR WALTER RALEIGH

From thence to honour thee I would not seek
For names, but call forth thund'ring Aeschylus,
Euripides, and Sophocles to us;
Pacuvius, Accius, him of Cordova 's death,
To live again, to hear thy buskin tread,
And shake a stage; or when thy socks were on,
Leave thee alone for a comparison
Of all that insolent Greece or haughty Rome
Sent forth, or since did from their ashes come.
Triumph my Britain, thou haste one to show,
To whom all scenes of Europe homage owe.
He was not of an age, but for all time!
And all the Muses still were in their prime,
When like Apollo, he came forth to warm
Our ears, or like a Mercury to charm!
Nature herself was proud of his designs,
And joyned to wear the dressing of his lines,
Which were so richly spun, and woven so fit,
As, since, she will vouchsafe no other wit.
The merry Greek, tart Aristophanes,
Neat Terence, witty Plautus, now not please;
But antiquated and deserted lie,
As they were not of nature's family.
Yet gentle Shakespeare, must enjoy a part.
For though the poet's matter nature be,
His art doth give the fashion; and that he
Who casts to write a living line, must sweat
(such as thine are) and strike the second heat
Upon the Muses's anvil, turn the same,
And himself with it, that he thinks to frame,
Or for the laurel he may gain to scorn;
For a good poet's made, as well as born.
And such wert thou! Look how thy father's face
Lives in his issue, even so the race
Of Shakespeare's mind and manners brightly shines

In his well turned and true filed lines,
In each of which he seems to shake a lance,
As brandished at the eyes of ignorance.
Sweet Swan of Avon![157]   What a sight it were
To see thee in our waters yet appear,
And make those flights upon the banks of Thames,
That you did take Eliza and our James!
But stay, I see thee in the hemisphere
Advanced, and made a constellation there!
Shine forth, thou Star of Poets, and with rage
Or influence chide or cheer the drooping stage,
Which, since thy flight from hence, hath mourned like night,
And despairs day, but for thy volume's light."

Ben Johnson (1573 to 1637)

FINIS,

---

[157] reference to Chapman's "Great Swan's Quill when he completed Christopher Marlowe's Hero and Leander after his murder by Ingram Frizer, (where Marlowe was stabbed in the eye at the home of Mistress Eleanor Bull in Deptford on the 30th May 1593. [J.L. Hotson : 1925]

The Curator of Manuscripts at The British Library Department of Manuscripts

William Shakespeare (1564-1616) and more particularly, the play entitled Sir Thomas More (Harley MS 7368) which will be displayed in a glass Shakespeare case in the late Spring or early Summer of 1988 with the following label:

'The Booke of Sir Thomas More' about 1593-1595 : Harley 7368 f.9.
Shakespeare the artist

This document is generally accepted as the only literary manuscript to survive from the pen of the greatest English playwrigt. The playhouse copy, or 'Booke', of which it forms part is a collaborative revision of an earlier drama tracing the career andn downfall of Henry VIII's staunchly Catholic lord chancellor. It is copied mostly in the hand of Anthony Munday, with additions and revisions made by five other dramatists, including Dekker, Chettle and perhaps Heywood. Another hand, commonly labelled 'hand D' wrotet the insurrection or 'Ill May Day' scene that runs to three pages, the first of which is shown here. The nature of the revisions proves it to be an authorial rather than merely a scribal addition, and its attribution to Shakespeare is based mainly on features of treatment, style, imagery and spelling that can all be parallelled in his known work. The evidence of handwriting, however, which depends on comparison with the six surviving signatures, is rather more ambiguous. [161]

This incomplete transcript, written as early as 1593 or as late as 1601, was submitted for a licence to Edmund Tillney, Master of the Revels, who noted down cuts required to be made in politically sensitive material before performance. These specifically mention the May Day scene of which he wrote 'Leaue out ye insurrection wholy & ye cause thereoff & begin wt Sr Tho: Moore att ye mayors sessions wt a reportt afterwareds off his good service don being Shrive off London vppon a mutiny agaynst ye Lumbards. Only by a shortt reportt & nott otherwise att your own perilles. El Tyllney'. [102]

The Inns of Courts and the opening of the Royal Exchange
23 January 1571

The opening of the London Bourse took place on the 23rd January 1571 and was opened by Queen Elizabeth I. It was a central house like the Bourse in Antwerp and had been a long awaited event in London. The thousands of London merchants could meet to transact their official business there. The planning of the London Bourse had been conducted by Thomas Gresham and he had spoken of his plan on the 9th February 1566 at the house of Alderman Rivers, where Sir William Garrard, Sir William Cheaton and Thomas Rowe had been present. Thomas Gresham had promised the London Merchants that within its first month of opening the London Bourse would be prsented to the City and Mercers Company. After the official opening by Queen Elizabeth the London Bourse was renamed the Royal Exchange opposite the Bank of England.

Money in Elizabethan Times

'When Queen Elizabeth I came to the Throne she removed all bad coinage from her Realm by having all debased coins marked with a greyhound, a portcullis, a lion, a harp, rose or fleur-de-lys.

In the second year of her reign Elizabeth deemed that one pound in weight of gold be 23 carats, 3 1/2 grains fine should be coined into thirty six pounds by tale,

making twenty-four soverigns at 30s a piece.

Or 48 ryals at 15s a piece
Or 72 angels at 10s a piece
Or 144 half angels at 5s a piece

A pound weight of crown gold of 22 carats fine and 2 carats allay was coined into 33 pounds by tale, making 33 Sovereigns at 20s each

or 66 half sovereigns at 10s a piece
or 132 Crowns at 5s a piece
or 264 Half Crowns.

A pound weight of silver of 11 ounces 2 pennyweight fine and 18 penny weight allay was coined into three pounds by tale. The coins were half-shillings, groats, quarter shillings, half-groats, three-halfpenny pieces, pence and farthings.

In the 43rd year of her reign the pound weight of gold made 73 Angels, at 10s each, or 146 half-Angels and ten shillings in a tale.

But the pound weight of gold of 22 carats and 2 carats allay made 33 Sovereigns and a half at 20 Shillings each.

or 67 half-sovereigns
or 134 Crowns

or 268 half-crowns making thirty three pounds ten shillings in a tale.

A pound weight of old standard silver was made into three pounds two shillings by tale, that is into Crowns, half-Crowns, shillings, sixpences, twopences, pence, and half-pence.

Elizabeth's gold coins were Sovereigns, half-sovereigns or ryals, nobles, double nobles, angels, half-angels, pieces of an angel and a half, three angels, Crowns and half-Crowns.

Her silver coins were Crowns, half-Crowns, Shillings, Sixpennies, Groats, Threepences, Twopences, Pennies, Penny half pence, Half-pence, and Farthings.

Elizabeth also coined Irish shillings called Harpers because each coin bore the arms of Ireland upon it. Ie. The Three Harps.

No brass or copper coins were coined in England before the reign of James I. Some of the Shilling bore the design of a Dove or a Drke upon it, which tradition tells us was in memory of Sir Francis Drake's voyage round the World. [See the Money Book by Arthur Groom (Rockcliff) for more information].

Raleigh was a discoverer and a privateer, daring to sail into Spanish waters and waylay the fleets of ships belonging to King Philip of Spain which were filled with silver from his portuguese mines. Raleigh had fought at the Battle of Cadiz in 1596 and had fired the "St Philip" in revenge for the death of his cousin Sir Richard Grenville in 1591 at the Battle of the Azores, where he died on board that great ship as a Spanish prisoner. Raleigh had sworn to be avenged for the "Revenge". Raleigh had sustained a great injury to his right leg during that terrible Battle and had from that day forward, walked with the aid of a stick to hold him upright because his leg had been maimed.

Sir Walter had been the favourite Knight of Queen Elizabeth and lived at her Court for ten years before she banished him for daring to seduce and marry Bess Throckmorton the Queen's own Maid of Honour.

In January 1592 the Queen had given him Sherborne Castle

The marriage had taken place in November 1591 at a little parish church in Lillington, Dorset] without the Queen's knowledge and Bess had been five months with child. Their child, a boy, whom they named Damerei Raleigh had been born to them on the 29th March 1592, but died shortly after his arrival into this World and was buried in Dorset. The Earl of Essex (otherwise known as the Earl of March), had stood as Godfather to the child and when the Queen learned of this news through a court letter writer named Wooton she read his letter:

"S.W.R., as it seemeth, hath been too inward with one of Her Majesty's Maids; I fear to say who, but if you should guess at E.T. you may not be far wrong. The matter hath only now been apparent to all eyes, and the lady hath been sent away, but nobody believes it can end there. S.W.R. hath escaped from London for a time; he will be speedily sent for and brought back, where what awaiteth him nobody knoweth, save by conjecture. All think the Tower will be his dwelling, like a hermit poor in pensive place, where he may spend his endless days in doubt. It is affirmed that they are married; but the Queen is most fiercely incesed, and, as the bruit goes, threateneth the most bitter punishment to both the offenders. S.W.R will lose, it is thought, all his places and preferments at Court, with the Queen's favour; such will be the end of his speedy rising, and now he must fall as low as he was high, at the which many will rejoice. I can write no more at this time, and do not care to send this, only you will hear it from others. All is alarm and confusion at this discovery of the discoverer, and not indeed of a new continent, but of a new incontinent'.

Raleigh, who had set out on a privateering expedition on the 6th May 1592 as an Admiral, was ordered back to Court, having been previously told by the Queen that he must relinquish his position to Frobisher. Frobisher overtook him on the 7th May and Raleigh held on until Cape Finistere.

Immediately he returned to the court, he and Bess Throckmorton his new wife were carried off to the Tower of London on the 7th August 1592 and held in the Brick Tower.

Secretary Burleigh's son Cecil was sent to quell the riot and calm the looters but he could do little except send for Raleigh who was brought to the scene accompanied by his Tower Keeper, and as Cecil observed the reaction of his sailors who cried out for him. Cecil wrote a letter to the Queen's Privy Councillor, recording and relaying what he had seen:

"I assure you Sir, his poor servants, to the number of 140 godly men, and all the mariners came to him with such shouts of joy as I never heard a man more troubled to quiet them in my life. But his heart is broken for he is very extreme pensive, longer than he is busied, in which he can toil terribly. The meeting between him and Sir John Gilbert [Raleigh's half brother Sir Humphrey Gilbert] was with tears on Sir John's part. Whensoever he is saluted with congratulations for liberty, he doth answer: "No, I am still the Queen of England's poor captive".

Sir Walter was released in September 1592 to quell the rebellious sailors who were looting the East Indian Carrack, the "Madre de Dios", a treasure ship which Raleigh's expedition had captured. She was a 'floating castle' with 800 inhabitants'. Among the great cargo were pepper, cloves, and cinnamon, cochineal, mace, nugmegs and musk. The pepper among the loot was worth £102,000. There were chests of precious stones, pearls, amber and ebony; satins, tapestries and silks. It took ten English ships to carry the cargo from Dartmouth to London. The sailors in the West Country went mad and started looting the ship when they heard that Raleigh was held in the Tower. One sailor alone was found to have in his possession 'a chain of orient pearls, two chains of gold, four great pearls of the bigness of a fair pea, four forks of crystal and four spoons of crystal set with gold and stones, and two cords of musk, and rushing to meet them were 2000 merchants. In one deal with a merchant, 1,800 diamonds and 300 rubies were purchased for £130.'

Raleigh wrote a letter to Burleigh and said 'in particular how Her Majesty might be profited by the Carrack, according to the offer I made. My promise was not to buy my bondage but my liberty, and I hope, of Her Majesty's favour. Fourscore thousand pounds is more than ever a man presented Her Majesty as yet. If God have sent it for my ransom, I hope Her Majesty will accept it'. The Queen in the end claimed half the treasure and Raleigh was rewarded with nothing more than his Freedom.

Bess was still held captive until the end of 1592 after which they moved to Sherborne Castle in Dorset.

Their second son, Wat Raleigh was born in late October and on the 1st November, 1593 he was baptised at a little church in the Hamlet of Lillington.

Robert Devereux, being the Second Earl of Essex, the Queen's cousin once removed, became the new favourite at Court, introduced by the Earl of Leicester and Lettice Knollys his mother.

Elizabethan Clothing

The rich Lords wore:

Velvet suits trimmed with silver and jewellery
Silk hats worn indoors and out
Padded doublets buttoned down the front and attached to breeches by
tags and laces, known as points.

The doublets were slashed to show a second colour underneath and
this was a fashion during the reign of Henry VIII. The armhole of the
doublet was hidden with rolls of material known as tabs, and also
known as pickadils. Later by epaulettes.

Breeches were worn with stockings (sometimes sewn to them and
known as wholehose).

Ruffs were worn at the neck and wrists (sometimes in layers)

Towards the end of the century leg of mutton sleeves were worn
instead of tight fitting sleeves.

Over the doublet gentlemen wore a cloak, often faced with gold or
silver lace or embroidered with pearls.

Rich ladies wore:

Ruffs: Up to the second year of Elizabeth's reign ruffs were made from
a material known as holland. The queen then demanded that ruffs be
made of lawn and cambric which had to be starched and stiffened.

Dutch women were sent for to starch and stiffen the russ for Elizabeth
(who could find no one to carry out this work) and a Mistress
Dingham Vander Plasse, a Flemish woman arrived at her Court. She
had come to London in 1564 and her skill earned her a reputation
when she set up as a Professor in the art of ruff making and starching

ruffs. She taught others the method for the sum of four to five pounds.
She another charged 20 shillings if they also wished to learn how to
make the starch itself.

The starch was made from wheat flour, bran and roots, according to
the grain required, but it was also coloured white, red, blue or purple.

In addition to the starch which was not enough by itself to create the
desired effect, they used:

"A certain device made of wires, crested or the purpose and whipped
all over either with gold, thread, silver, or silk in ringlets called an
under-propper". Upon these devices were erected the "stately arches
of pride", the starched ruff row upon row, until we come finally to "the
master-devil ruff, rich beyond measure in gold, silver, or silk lace and
which sparkled all over with suns, moons, stars and other devices."

Chemises and petticoats, laced bodices and hooped or padded skirts.

Gowns and cloaks and scented gloves
Stomachers
Sleeves
Farthingales, ruffs and feathers.

The Spanish Farthingale was held out by cane hoops and remained in
fashion until 1580s and was then replaced by the French Farthingale
which had a roll of material at the waist to push out the skirt to right
angles to fall vertically to the instep. The French farthingale was eithe
rthe shape of a circle, an oval or a semi-circle and held out the skirt at
thte back only.

Bodices were used to press in the waist with pieces of metal or wood
sewn into bodice.

Hips were padded.

Silk stockings
Court shoes
Low cut jewelled slippers for indoor wear
High cork soles or overshoes with cloth upper for outdoor wear.

Women slept naked or in a night smock
Men and women wore kerchiefs round their heads or wore nightcaps and medical authorities suggest they should have holes in the top of the caps.

Wigs were clustered with jewels and pearls
Scents and pomanders were used more liberally than soap by men and women.

Soap was imported from Spain and Italy the products of Castile and Venice and was also made in Bristol. It cost 4d a pound.

Baths were rarely taken except for medicinal purposes.

One scent invented by Henry VIII contained rose water, muck ambergris and civet. Nutmegs, aloes and storax were used in other scents.

Queen Elizabeth was particularly fond of marjoram. The ingredients were placed in pomanders and attached to a sash at the end of a girdle.

HIC JACET: SIR WALTER RALEIGH

Cosmetics for Elizabethan Women

Beauty was considered to be a white skin, fair hair, high smooth forehead, thin eyebrows, red lips and small feet.

Women bleached their hair by sitting in the sun protected by a mask held in position by a button in the teeth.

White powder made of ground alabaster or a dangerous preparation of white lead mixed with vinegar or with borax and sulphur
Lotions and ointtments containing lemon juice

Milk of Almonds

White wine, egg white, oil of tartar, honey, beeswax, rose petals, herbs, asses milk and ground jawbones of hogs.

Hair was dyed

Lips painted red with cochineal, white of hard boiled egg, green figs, alum and gum arabic; or madder, red ochre or my red crystalline mercuric sulphide.

Cheeks were glazed with eggwhite
Lines representing thin veins were painted on the bosoms
(Unmarried women lefts breasts largely exposed)

Kohl was used to outline eyes and belladonna to enlarge pupils.

Treatment for spots and freckles: Birch tree sap was found innocuous sand effective. Ground brimstone, oil of turpentine and soliman, formed froms sublimate of mercury, eventually led to a skin as ravaged and white as lead as it left it mummified.

Care of Elizabethan Teeth with a Recipe devised by Sir Hugh Platt

The teeth were cleaned by rubbing with a mixture of powdered pumice stone, brick and coral, which took off the stain and enamel, or by rinsing with solutions of honey and burned salt, or sugar and honey.

Sir Hugh Platt said: "do not clean teeth with Aqua fortis, otherwise within a few dressings they would probably be forced to borrow a rank

Platt advocated: Take a quart of honey, as much vinegar, half so much wine, and boil them together and wash the teeth therewith now and then."

Physicians and tooth drawers recommended wood for toothpicks, but silver and gold implements were commonly used as being more suited

Silk Stockings

The silk stockings were introduced in England at about the time of Edward VI. At the same time as the flat cap and Sir Thomas Gresham presented a pair of silk stockings to the young King.

The first pair of silk stockings made in England were manufactured during the reign of Elizbaeth I as were worsted stockings. William Rider apprentice to Thomas Burdet saw a pair of worsted stockings in the house of an Italian merchant. This pair had been brought into the country from Mantua. Rider borrowed the stockings and took them home to examine them. He made a similar pair which he presented to the Earl of Pembroke. This led to the invention of the stocking frame.

The stocking frame was invented by William Lee, a gentleman and a scholar. Lee was deeply in love with a woman who spent her time knitting stockings. The lady rejected his proposals of marriage and he invented the stocking frame to teach her a lesson and to put her ouf of business or entice her into marriage. He practised his new invention at Calverton a little village near Nottingham. All the stocking manufacturers were against him and his life was made a misery. Lee moved from Calverton to Rouen and made a great fortune until Henry IV of France was murdered and then he lost his business and all his money and died of a broken heart in Paris.

Alphabetical List of Elizabethans
(not exhaustive or complete)

Alleyn, Edward, Actor Retired 1597 until 1600 - [158]See Henslowe's
Diaries 1602 Aubrey, John[159]

Babington, Sir Anthony,[160]

Baines, Nicholas - A Servant of The Earl of Essex) - Witness at the murder of

Christopherus Marlowe - Dramatist and friend of Sir Walter Raleigh

Bacon, Sir Francis[161]

Baines, Richard[162]

Bacon, Sir Nicholas, Lord Keeper of the Common Seal, d. 22 February 1579

[Brother in law of William Cecil]

Burbage

Bull, Mistress Eleanor[163]

Cecil, Robert, son of Lord Burleigh

Chettle, Harry, Dramatist

---

[158] September 1602 Pays £6.18s "properties for the play "Mortymore". [source Holinshead chronicles]

[159] Recorded facts in his notebooks of gossip regarding William Shakespeare from William Beeston who was the son of oen of Shakespeare's fellow-actors.

[160] The Babington Plot - A plot to free Mary Queen of Scots from her imprisonment - A French brewer passed Mary's coded letters to Sir Francis Walsingham's Agent and Walsingham persecuted Sir Anthony Babington, who was a former Page of Lord Shrewsbury.

[161] See Chronological list of Achievements

[162] A Spy for Sir Francis Walsingham in the Babington Plot and a witness to the murder of Christopher Marlowe in 1593.

[163] Christopher Marlowe was murdered at her Eating House in Deptford on Wednesday 30th May, 1593 at 10 o'clock.

Curry, William, witness at the Inquest of Christopherus Marlowe

Coke, Sir Edward, Lord Chief Justice of Common Pleas, (Attorney General) - married Burghley's grandaughter (Lady Hatton)

Cook, Prudence, Servant to Francis Kyd d. 2 September 1563 buried St Mary Woolnorth

Day, John, Dramatist

Danby, William - Gentleman (Coroner of the House of Queen Elizabeth I,[164]

Dekker, Thomas - Dramatist

Derby, The Earl of, died 16 April 1594 (Raleigh's friend)

Draper, Nicholas, Gentleman, witness at the Inquest of Christopherus Marlowe

Dudley, Robert - Earl of Leicester [

Edward II, b. 1307, d. 1327 [Caernarvon Castle 23 February]; Deposed 1327.

Buried at Gloucester; murdered at Berkeley Castle[165]. Compare to King Lear for historical content

Greene, Robert - Dramatist - died Autumn 1592: [Harry Vi played at Rose Theater][166]

Guise, Henri le Duc[167], Uncle of Mary Queen of Scots, murdered Chateau de Blois 1588 - [Leader of the Catholics] - See Mary queen of Scots Trial 1587

Randall, Woolstan, Gentleman, witness at the Inquest of Christopher Marlowe

Robert Greene [See his Memoires]

Hatton, Sir Christopherus, Privy Councillor 1593[168]

---

[164] Views the body of Christopher Marlowe at Deptford Strand in the County of Kent "per Willemum Danby Friday 1st June, 1593 - Patent Rolls Chancery 35.

[165] Compare his history to that of King Lear for historical content.

[166] Wrote 2 brief autobiographies as he lay dying in 1592.

[167] Recaptured Calais on 8th January 1558 : Lost to France for 211 years

[168] One of his servants executed in the Babington Plot [A plot to free Mary Queen of Scots]

Heminge

Henslowe [Author of Diaries [from 1591 to 1602] [169] [Sept. 1602] [170],
[171]

Hunsdon, Lord Henry, Queen Elizabeth I's cousin - and Court Chamberlain

Kyd, Francis - Dramatist b.   d.

Kyd [172], Thomas son of Francis Kyd b.   d. [173] [174],

Munday, Anthony - Dramatist : [Lord Admiral's Men - 1597]

Marlowe [175], Christopherus - Dramatist [176][177] Pembroke, The Earl of -

Dramatic Company 1590 [acted the play Edward II, [178] on the 30th January 1593 [179].

Newgate Prison - built 1218, enlarged and improved by the Lord Mayor of

---

[169] Records to lost plays March 1588/89 £6.00 to Dramatists Chettle and Porter for a play called "The Spencers"

[170] Pays £6.18s "properties for the play 'Mortymore'

[171] Henslowe's diary records Spanish Tragedie 1592

[172] Arrested 18 May 1593, taken to Newgate Prison and tortured. Keeper of Newgate William Deyos: Keeper Puckering

[173] Thomas Kyd wrote to Lady Sussex in May/June 1593, whilst imprisoned at Newgate. Kyd buried 15 August 1594 (aged 36 - at St. Mary Woolnorth)

[174] Kyd in service to Henry, fourth Earl of Sussex in 1587 to 1588
Kyd - Dramatic work - Cornelia registered on 26 January 1594

[175] Christopher Marlowe wrote for the Earl of Sussex Players in 1591

[176] Educated at Corpus Christi College, Cambridge [from December 1580 to 1587] absent Feb-July 1587 - the year of Mary Queen of Scot's Trial: [Compare with Sonnets: {Dark Eyed Lady :   }

[177] Marlowe's Play the Massacre at Paris, mentions the uncle of Mary Queen of Scots, (Henri duc of Guise - Leader of the Catholics) and the poisoned gloves. St Bartholomew's Massacre took place in Paris on August 24, 1572. The Babington Plot Henri duc of Guise passes coded letters to Mary Queen of Scots in August 1586.

[178] [written by Christopher Marlowe at the end of 1591 or beginning 1592] - King Edward II was born in 1307 at Caernarvon Castle 23 February. He was depoised in 1327 and murdered at Berkeley Castle. He is buried at Gloucester.

[179] William Jones registerered this Play 1 month after Marlowe's death on 6th July, 1593

London, Richard Whittington in 1423, thereafter no improvements made.

Leicester, Lady - the mother of The Earl of Essex (otherwise known as the Earl of March)

Lord Strange, Players - See Ferdinando Stanley[180]

Perrott, Lady (sister of The II Earl of Essex – Robert Devereux)

Penelope Rich[181]

E. Tilney [Tyllney]

Radcliffe, Robert[182]

Shakespeare, John - Constable of the Court of Leat - 1568 Baillif]

Shakespeare, William[183] - Dramatist [entered London as an actor 1585-1587]

Sidney[184] Sir Philip b. 1554, d. 1586 Arnham[185] : Sir Philip Sidney present at St Bartholomews Massacre Paris (24.8.1572).

Sussex, Countess, Bridget - (see Radcliffe, Robert)

Sussex, Henry Fourth Earl[186]

---

[180] Produced Harry Vi at Rose Theatre, 1592: 10,000 people went to see it in first 6 months of its appearance. Well known Dramatist, Robert Greene, died in that year.

[181] See Raleigh's poem "To his Mistress... He that is rich in words must needs discover, that he is poor in that which makes a lover."

[182] married Bridget Countess of Sussex in 1592 (when she was aged 16)

[183] born April 23 1564, Baptised Stratford upon Avon. 26 April Parish Church, d. [   ] 1592 - third and eldest son of Mary Arden and John Shakespeare who held municipal offices of Stratford upon Avon

[184] A child poet who became a master of Sonnets and wrote 108 Sonnets and eleven songs of Astrophel and Stella, metrical versions of Psalms. (Grosart 1877)

[185] Sir Philip Sidney, Poet, died at Arnham 1586, his widow Frances Walsingham, daughter of Sir Francis Walsingham (Spymaster of the Catholics), married the Second Earl of Essex, the Queen's cousin - Queen Elizabeth I was furious. The II Earl of Essex brother, Walter Devereux, was married to Lady Hoby,

[186] Thomas Kyd and Christopher Marlowe engaged to write for the Sussex Players in 1591. Marlowe wrote the play Edward II for the Earl of Pembroke Players, which is referred to at a supper attended by the Lady Scrope and the Robert Devereux,. Second Earl of Essex. The Earl of Essex' ancestry dated back to Edward II. Lady Hoby was once married to Thomas

Essex, Robert Devereux - Nobleman - Second Earl : in Stratford 1587
Poley, Robert - second witness to the murder of Christopherus
Marlowe 1593
Queen, Mary of Scots,
Skeres, Nicholas - Murderer of Christopherus Marlowe 1593 [Folio
Throckmorton, Elizabeth[187]
Throckmorton, Francis
Throckmorton, Arthur - Raleigh's brother in law (catholic), Courtier -
trailed by Sir Francis Walsingham in [   ] and taken into custody
from a lodging house by the Docks near Tower, racked twice for his
part in the Babington Plot.
Walsingham, Sir Francis[188]
Warwick, Lady - friend of Lady Perrott
Worcester, Earl of - His Company of Players
Whitgift, Archbishop - 1593 - Privy Councillor

Henry Duc de Guise

Was assasinated noble of the House of Lorraine and uncle of Mary Queen of
Scots, he was murdered at Chateau de Blois in 1588. Mary Queen of Scots
mother was Mary of Guise.

Sidney, the brother of Sir Philip Sidney.

[187] The wife of Sir Walter Raleigh - m. November, 1591

[188] Famous for his system of counter-espionage against the Roman Catholics: Queen Elizabeth
nicknamed him her "Spy". He was William Cecil's Son-in-law and Sir Philip Sidney's Father
in law.

HIC JACET: SIR WALTER RALEIGH

Queen Elizabeth I born Greenwich Palace 7th September 1533. Anne Boleyn beheaded 1536). Dated May 24th   1603.

Sir Francis Drake Born Tavistock Devonshire, 1545. Died aboard ship 1596. In 1585 Frobisher was his Vice Admiral. Sir Francis Russell the Earl of Bedford was his Godfather. Sir Walter Raleigh was his cousin through his father's first wife. Dake served as Vice Admiral at the Armada in 1588 under Lord Howard:

Throckmorton Family

Arthur Throckmorton Raleigh's brother in law - A courtier
Sir Nicholas Throckmorton Queen Elizabeth's ámbassador at Paris
Francis Throckmorton involved in Babington Plot (racked twice on orders of Sir Francis Walsingham).

Christopher Marlowe: Born Canterbury February 6th 1564. Murdered: At the age of 29 years, on 30 May 1593. Son of John Marlowe of the Shoemakers Guild. Educated at King's School Canterbury (quarterly stipend of £1) from 1580-81. Then to Cambridge University and then a scholarship on Archbishop Matthew Parker's foundation at Corpus Christi (Benedictine College), Batchelors Degree 1583-4.
Commenced studying for Master of Arts in 1587. Going up to London he attached himself to the Lord Admiral's Company, for which he composed the greater part of his plays. Enjoyed the friendship of Mr Thomas Walsingham, Sir Thomas Walsingham his son, and Sir Walter Raleigh.

Edward de Vere - 1550-1654 :17th Earl of Oxford. Brought up in Cecil's household and married Anne Cecil.

The Earl of Leicester Died 1568 leaving a widow of 24. Leicester was suspected of poisoning Lord Sheffield. Lady Sheffield bore Leicester a son, Robert Dudley. Leicester also had an affair with Francis Howard, Lady Douglas, Sheffield's sister). Leicester was jealous of Christopher Hatton who was Queen Elizabeth I's 'skipping sheep' his nickname since Hatton was a talented dancer.

Lord Robert Dudley

Lord Robert Dudley was Master of the Horse and died in 1588. Dudley was one of the Queen's favourites.

HIC JACET: SIR WALTER RALEIGH

William Pickering

Another of the Queen's favourites, he was friendly with Henry Howard, the Earl of Surrey. He was stopped by the Earl of Arundel and Lord Steward from entering Privy Council.

Ben Johnson Born 1572 and Educated at Westminster, paid for by an unknown Patron. William Camden was the Headmaster. He was a soldier in the Low Countries and then an actor for a time. From 1597 he wrote plays for Henslowe: "Hot anger soon cold" and "Richard Crookback", and "Every Man in his Humour ". Died 6th August 1637. He was a close friend of Sir Walter Raleigh and teacher to Wat Raleigh in Paris in the year1613/1614.

Sir Edward Coke - Lord Chief Justice of the Common Pleas; (Attorney General) Married Burleigh's grand daughter Lady Hatton.

Sir William Cecil (Lord Burleigh) Secretary of State up to 1572 appointed Lord High Treasurer. He was 38 years old at Elizabeth's accession. Educated at Stamford School and then St John's Cambridge. He was influenced by Cheke, Ascham and Thomas. He had served Edward VI but not Mary Tudor. His employment with Queen Elizabeth I lasted 38 years. His brother in law was Nicholas Bacon, Lord Keeper in 1558. He was overseer of Elizabeth's Estates.

Lord Clinton Lord High Admiral: Minister of Defence. An expert on Military Affairs. Clinton married Bessie Blount (one of Henry VIII's mistresses) and then married Lady Elizabeth Fitzgerald, "the Fair Geraldine of Surrey's" Sonnets.

The Earl of Arundel - The Lord Steward - Henry Fitzalan.

Sir Thomas Parry - Treasurer of the Royal Household.

Kate Ashley - Mistress of the Maids of Honour

Roger Ashcham - Queen's Latin Secretary

Harry Carey – Lord Hunsdon – Lord Chamberlain 1585, cousin of Queen Elizabeth I. Lord Hunsdon was present at the Inquest into the murder of Christopher Marlowe. The Earl of Essex servant was present at Marlowe's murder and I believe that this caused a rift which was never healed, between Sir Walter Raleigh and The Second Earl of Essex.

Hunsdon's Men – Chamberlain's Men and Lady Hoby

HIC JACET: SIR WALTER RALEIGH

List of books other books available by Barbara O'Sullivan, Author

Available to order at all good bookshops or through www.lulu.com, or Amazon.com, or Amazon.co.uk and other on-line bookshops.

Title	ISBN	Publisher
Monica O'Sullivan's Traditional British Cookery Book	97809559912-33	Caesar Publishing
The Chiswick Villain – 1834 (Based on True Crimes of Moll Raby and James Ashley) A Novel	9780955991219	Caesar Publishing
The Ancient Mirror Sonnets and Poems	978095576186	Caesar Publishing
Twelve Elizabethan Tales – Short Stories	9780955976131	Caesar Publishing
The Sailor King's People – A Novel	9780955976193	Caesar Publishing
The King's Quinto: The Life and Times of Sir Walter Raleigh (1552-1618) – Hardback	9780955976179	Caesar Publishing
The King's Quinto: The Life and Times of Sir Walter Raleigh (1552-1618) – Paperback – 204 pages	9780955976117	Caesar Publishing
Hic Jacet: Sir Walter Raleigh 1552-1618– Paperback – 580 pagesAlso available	9780955991202	Caesar Publishing

in Hardback		
Tales of Woe – Short Stories	9780955976148	Caesar Publishing
More Tales of Woe – Short Stories	9780955976155	Caesar Publishing
The Innocent Master Harrison (The Murder of Doctor Andrew Clenche) – 1596 (True Crime)	9780955976100	Caesar Publishing
Various Amazon Shorts (e-books) available at Amazon.com		
Various Mobipocket e-books available at Amazon.com		

Barbara O'Sullivan

Barbara O'Sullivan

1587901R0

Printed in Great Britain
by Amazon.co.uk, Ltd.,
Marston Gate.